Meaning, Narrativity, and the Real

Jan M. Broekman

Meaning, Narrativity, and the Real

The Semiotics of Law in Legal Education IV

Springer

Jan M. Broekman
Penn State Law
University Park
PA, USA

ISBN 978-3-319-28174-2 ISBN 978-3-319-28175-9 (eBook)
DOI 10.1007/978-3-319-28175-9

Library of Congress Control Number: 2016931855

Printed on acid-free paper

This Springer imprint is published by SpringerNature
The registered company is Springer International Publishing AG Switzerland.

Preface

Writing is vanity, unless it's for the friend. Including the friend one doesn't know yet.

The Invisible Committee: *To Our Friends*, MIT Press, October 2014.

The second volume of this series on Legal Semiotics in the context of Legal Education suggested in 2013, that *Lawyers* are *Making Meaning*. Do they? And if that is indeed the case, do they create Meaning on the basis of their professional skills and needs only, or do they create Meaning(s) thanks to a broader and deeper insight into the philosophical dimensions of the Meaning concept? The first possibility seems to be the case in general, and the second may therefore be in need of specific and more explicit attention. Not that there has never been previous consideration of meaning in sciences, law and legal discourse or in philosophy. On the contrary, the beginnings of the twentieth century provided far-reaching studies on the concept, which were also specifically different from the vested views of the seventeenth and eighteenth century characterizing the Anglo-Saxon dimensions of Occidental philosophy. Most heavily profiled was the interest in *significs* in London, Amsterdam and other European centers and universities, focusing on the theoretical dimensions of *meaning* and *sign*.

Victoria Lady Welby's 1903 publication *What Is Meaning?: Studies in the Development of Significance* as well as her 1911 *Significs and Language* were powerful signs of a renewed interest in and the development of new views on meaning. A particular interest for law and legal discourse unfolded in those same days and was honored by the official appointment of the Dutch lawyer, legal scholar, poet and politician Jacob Israel de Haan as an academic lecturer at the University of Amsterdam, as one reads in his 1916 Inaugural Lecture entitled "Wezen en taak der rechtskundige significa" [The Essence and Task of Legal Significs]. *Significs* was already, even as this lecture was being delivered, on the edge of a name change that would broaden the field: a change towards the current globally accepted concept of *semiotics*. It was particularly the US philosopher Charles Sanders Peirce in his often-intense philosophical correspondence with Lady Welby, who objected to the limitations of *significs* and pleaded for the wider philosophical term *semiotics*. For lawyers acting as meaning-makers, this extension is important and a valuable chance to reconsider meaning as a matter of signs in law and language *tout court*.

A first and most important component pertaining to the background of this book lies in *the close ties of the meaning concept with language and linguistic articulation*. They are certainly a rich motivation to reach out into the deeper philosophical dimensions of meaning in a semiotic context. That is of interest for the law student in Civil as well as Common Law. Human behavior clearly depends on rules and such behavior appears also in law most often as a rule-following activity, but that is never without a wider linguistic basis of conduct. There is no meaning without language, one should conclude, or at least not beyond the scope of linguistic articulation. Legal meaning-making is, as all meaning, a matter of partitioning and narrativity. The meaning of a red traffic light and the human conduct caused by this light in traffic (therein called a sign) is narrated during introductions to the law, in which that meaning is presented as a fact—not as a fable, a fiction or a peculiar form of articulation. But are meanings facts, or are they just presented as facts, and what do facts and meanings mean in those different contexts? *Semiotics* has offered a framework for answering that question, although that framework is not fully in touch with the necessary philosophical perspectives at issue.

A second characteristic of this book is found in *re-viewing the bounds between semiotics and philosophy*. The study of law leads to the necessary implementation of studies of legal semiotics because of the great variety of *signs* in legal discourse. A further argument is that semiotics understands law as a *process* (and not as a thing) within which *signs* play a dominant role. This leads to a reconsideration of how lawyers think and act, because this always results from legally determined preconditions or prescripts; the latter will illustrate the wide range of meaning in law. The foundations of this urgency to consider the semiotics of law in legal studies were laid in the study of meaning. The famous 1923 publication of C.K. Ogden and I.A. Richards *The Meaning of Meaning* prepared for new views on language and discourse, so that signs, language and meaning could be regarded in their close, yet openness-creating relationships.

A third characteristic of this book should be stressed from its very beginning on: each philosophical step unfolding in view of meaning leads to an address to the law student and recapitulates the issues treated in each chapter in order to explain for a law student the legal-semiotic implications. They form in that regard a special path to an all-too-often neglected dimension of today's legal education in both families, in Civil and in Common Law.

The book is divided into two parts: the first is on philosophical and linguistic issues related to meaning; the second explores its emphasis on partitions and partitioning, including the relations between attitude, meaning and levels of language.

The first chapter unfolds the importance of *silence* in cosmic dimensions. The concept of silence leads to a particular appreciation of *articulation*—the perhaps widest form of creation. Since linguistic articulation plays a major role in human knowledge and meaning, language is in this book a foundational theme. Special attention is given to Klages' logocentrism, to Wittgenstein's attention to silence and in that framework to meaning viewed in relation to cosmic and creational forms of meaning. An address to the law student concludes this chapter while it introduces semiotic considerations of law and legal discourse.

The second chapter is in particular dedicated to the concept of attitude and attitude change, without which meaning cannot exist. *Attitude* is the English translation of the German: *Einstellung*, a cornerstone in Edmund Husserl's phenomenology. The origins and uses of that concept are investigated, as well as its pivotal role in philosophical considerations of meaning. They excel in what Husserl presented as *Einstellungsänderung*, translated as *attitude change*. It is by means of changing attitudes that meaning comes to the fore. With that dynamic dimension, partitioning and plurality become important. All those themes are covered in an imaginary Skype conversation between Edmund Husserl and Charles Sanders Peirce. A step from that Skype conversation into the address to the law student completes the focus on these themes.

The third chapter brings the reader straightforwardly to an important presupposition in twentieth century philosophy, psychology and linguistics. Later in the book, it will be explained how exactly this presupposition guides modern brain research. The slogan "the word is basic unit of language" represents a key notion founding linguistic articulation as well as the philosophy of language. It fortified a "more geometrico" thought formation, limited and fixated the concept of meaning, and functioned in exposés of Searle and Frege, of linguists like Shaumyan and Kristeva, and philosophers like Benjamin and Rosenzweig. They are all confronted with the relatively simple presupposition that "a word is a basic unit"—a popular slogan in their time. Its meaning is mirrored in what is called the "particle story" and the "master–master discourse". Law's position in view of the semiotic consequences is precisely the theme of the third chapter's address to the law student.

The fourth chapter focuses on particles and partitioning: a coherent theme that includes most of the meaning-making aspects in science, art and philosophy. The overarching idea is that everything can be partitioned into elementary parts: in other (epistemological) words, in everything a particle story is in effect. This thesis and its consequences are illustrated by means of an analysis of a well-known poem of Paul Celan (1920–1970), by an analysis of variations of quantum physics (Heisenberg, Einstein, Hawking, Bohm) including modern thoughts on waves and particles, and on a deeper-reaching view on Cubist painting and in particular Paul Cezanne's specific brushstrokes. The essentials of those exemplary analyses are reviewed in a fourth address to the law student, with insights into the particle theory in law and a lawyer's discursive activity.

The fifth chapter is based on the preceding exposés and focuses on various theories of *holism*, in particular the idea of *wholeness* in the philosophy of David Bohm. His *holism* is analyzed in the light of particle thinking, and the consequences of that holism for quantum views in physics are discussed. That leads to another than traditional view on meaning: meaning is not a one-to-one term to be used in our understanding, but rather a *process,* and in that process from situation to situation, a specific *constellation*. The final address to the law student in this book leads from there to an overview of law and the manifest absence of theory in law. New and conclusive views on meaning in law are offered here.

The final, sixth chapter offers an in-depth philosophical consideration of meaning without historically or systematically showing a cause, a primordial understanding or anything else that can be fixated as an origin. Meaning appears rather as an articulation evolving from cosmic silence towards linguistic expressivity. Brain evolutions making such an articulation possible (in particular the human neocortex) and their basic philosophy of language are presented. This is completed with a further interpretation of the Torah's Creation narration and the Paradise story that follows. Both show the deep impact of the phenomenon of mirroring: instead of reference to a (cosmic or universal) reality, they appear to be narrative forces that govern human articulation. In that light the Great Partition is also a cause, but by no means a causal explanation for meaning. The book's purpose is a confrontation with this creative ambiguity.

Ambiguity in our articulations may be discovered when the process of meaning is analyzed—that ambiguity is completely absent if one can experience the support and friendship of friends. Hence the quotation originating in the most recent publication of the Invisible Committee that "writing is a vanity unless it's for a friend". Writing is, however, never solely *for* a friend; writing needs also to be *supported* by friends. The subject-object relationship, cherished by so many philosophers in so many ages, is to be discredited when writing is at issue. If one theme of this book can be found in the observation of Peirce and others that "a word/sign alone is not a word/sign", then that theme has been a deeply anchored experience of the author of this book. If any friend confirmed and put into practice what is understood as the "unity of mind and body"—one of the key themes of the book in the frame of meaning—then there are two such friends to be mentioned in this Preface. Dr. Philip T. Grier, Carlisle USA, must receive deep respect and warm gratitude for corrections, suggestions and discussions of this text. The book would not have been written without these treasures he communicated so promptly and elegantly. Dr. Frank Cauwenbergs, orthopedic surgeon in Brussels, Belgium, confirmed the unity of mind and body by bringing his support and medical skills into practice, without which the physical act of writing this book and reflecting on its problems could not have been performed. To mention those friends is not solely an act of gratitude but also a confirmation of this book's thesis, which honors multiplicity and acknowledges that no human being is ever able to be thinking and to be active on his own. The Series *The Semiotics of Law in Legal Education*, this fourth volume included, has been greatly supported by the Springer Editors Diana Nijenhuijzen and Neil Olivier; we render our thanks to both.

State College, PA, USA Jan M. Broekman

Contents

Part I
Philosophy and Language

Chapter 1
Silence

1 Silence, Cosmic and Cultural

> Our view of man will remain superficial so long as we fail … to find, beneath the chatter of words, the primordial silence, and so long as we do not describe the action which breaks the silence. The spoken word is a gesture, and its meaning the world"
>
> (M. Merleau Ponty: *Phénoménologie de la Perception, 1945*)

Pick a "Post-it" note, write 'Y' on it and fix it somewhere. So, wherever it sticks, 'Y' is its meaning. Is this one of the basic issues, if not *the* basic feature of any theory of meaning? We generally agree that such theories draw our attention to problems of reference, sign and assigning, qualification, interpretation and many others duly discussed in philosophical handbooks and encyclopedias. But we keep silent about the implicit theory of meaning pertaining to our "Post-it" act—yet silence is a key concept of philosophy.

1.1 Peirce, His Porch and Its Silence

When asked about his favored concept in philosophy, the US philosopher Charles Sanders Peirce would suggest with a smile of various remembrances: "Think silence". A fascinating suggestion: the theme is not at the centre of interest for Occidental philosophers—those who focus on the issue are often said to be under the influence of Oriental thought. But a question remains: "when the focus is on meaning, what about *silence*?" Indeed, meaning seems not always and everywhere to be present and actual: meaning grows, changes and always displays a complex process character. Silence could be an important source of meaning. Is that so? Is

J.M. Broekman, *Meaning, Narrativity, and the Real*,
DOI 10.1007/978-3-319-28175-9_1

that idea not too rashly concluded? Consider that meaning seems rather to be based on a certain mastership of articulation, on bringing words to their exact place, and not on silence.

Peirce knew that tension—hence his smile. On the porch of *Arisbe*, his mansion in the Northeast of Pennsylvania, he strongly felt himself to be in pure nature. Until a train whistle breaches the silence and makes him realize that he is fully encapsulated in human culture. Was that a particular sign? The breach he experienced and reflected upon is given much attention when his writings and worldviews are being discussed. Philosophical and even cosmological dimensions seemed relevant for the concept of meaning and meaning formation; discussions concerning the philosophical articulation of his experience grew global. The expression 'silence' has apparently more signification than one would expect—Peirce's thoughts and experiences form a unique starting-point because of his gift for intertwining everyday experience and philosophical reflection in such a powerful manner.

A train whistle in Pennsylvania is indeed the starting point. William A. Pencak described in his remarkable 1985 essay "Charles S. Peirce and Arisbe" how it "must have occurred frequently at Arisbe, as a train whistle would be audible four and one-half miles away in the stillness of the Pike County wilderness. Since Peirce was an insomniac in his last years who fell asleep writing in his chair he must have been wakened and disturbed and felt it keenly." Peirce even mentioned to Lady Welby an imagined balloon ride; that air trip shows in essence a disturbed calmness and stillness—an idea strongly focusing the experience of a breach.[1]

1.2 The Breach of Silence

Peirce gave equivalent articulations, such as 'shock', 'surprise' or 'brutality' a comparable function. All reinforce the urge to reflect upon a 'breach', and in particular a 'breach of silence'. What does that mean? The breach is a sign: a sign of Firstness—an idea Peirce parallels with Kant's 'manifold of sense' and considers predominant in feeling, will and thought. *Firstness unleashes an energy that articulates reality when the breach occurs.* This is what Peirce had in mind when he reluctantly introduced the triad of Firstness, Secondness and Thirdness as key concepts of philosophy on their way to articulating reality. There is indeed a connotation of *beginning* and *unfolding* related to Firstness, which has caused a worldwide interest in the subject, since it suggests that here is a beginning of philosophical articulation *tout court.* But Firstness also belongs to a larger and more complex triad: there is no Firstness as a 'pure beginning', because if that were the case, Firstness would not be a sign. *Firstness is rather an* episode *and a* sign *of a process of division within an infinite totality.*

[1] William A Pencak: "Charles S. Peirce and Arisbe" in: *Proceedings of the annual meetings of the Semiotics Society of America,* 1985, id.: William A. Pencak: *History, Signing In. Essays in History and Semiotics.* P. Lang, New York etc. 1993, p. 39 ff.

That is essential for the much-debated expression "breach of silence". Peirce has seldom brought 'the breach' as such to the fore, but 'the breach' has always been at the center of Firstness—'the breach' is rather its hidden meaning than its clear articulation. Focusing on the Peircean concept is thus relevant for any understanding of *meaning*. This particular concept might have profiled Peirce's position in occidental philosophy. It leads us to (a) the breach itself, (b) the quality of the silence in which the breach occurs, and (c) a new look at meaning.

1.3 Meaning and the Breach of Silence

The meaning of a 'breach' of silence and the meaning of 'Firstness' are intimately related. Firstness has remained the most challenging Peircean concept up to now, and is generally presented as the result of a breach. That intertwining of meanings reaches beyond an incidental experience or everyday occurrence. We are confronted with a layered structure of meaning(s): the 'breach of silence' is determined to be characterized as "Firstness", and 'Firstness' as 'breach of silence'—but the latter only *after* the breach took place. Two occurrences are experienced as possessing each other's meaning. One should read Peirce's articulations of his train-whistle experience on the porch in the light of this double-meaning play, as he writes the fragment his editors entitled "Shock and the Sense of Change" (1905), one of the literary *and* philosophical forms of his famous porch-experience showing multiplicity and diversity in articulation.[2]

"A whistling locomotive passes at high speed close beside me. As it passes the note of the whistle is suddenly lowered from a well-understood cause. I perceive the whistle, if you will. I have, at any rate, a sensation of it. But I cannot be said to have a sensation of the change of note. I have a sensation of the lower note. But the cognition of the change is of a more intellectual kind. That I experience rather than perceive. It is [the] special field of experience to acquaint us with events, with changes of perception. Now that which particularly characterizes sudden changes of perception is a shock. A shock is a volitional phenomenon. The long whistle of the approaching locomotive, however disagreeable it may be, has set up in me a certain inertia, so that the sudden lowering of the note meets with a certain resistance. That must be the fact; because if there were no such resistance there could be no shock when the change of note occurs. Now this shock is quite unmistakable. It is more

[2] Peirce offers a more encompassing philosophical context, saying: "We perceive objects brought before us; but that which we especially experience—the kind of thing to which the word "experience" is more particularly applied—is an event. We cannot accurately be said to perceive events; for this requires what Kant called the "synthesis of apprehension," not however, by any means, making the needful discriminations. See: Ch.S. Peirce: *The Collected Works*, (Hartshorne and Weiss, Eds), Cambridge, Harvard UP, Vol. I, Book 3: *Phenomenology*, par 336. See in parallel: Harvard Lecture 2 April 1903: *"On Phenomenology"*. CP V, par 46: "The sense of shock is as much a sense of resisting as of being acted upon. (…) so it is when anything strikes the senses".

particularly to changes and contrasts of perception that we apply the word 'experience'."

However, despite being generally accepted, an identification of Firstness and Origin seems problematic.[3] The broadest understanding of Firstness, emerging from a breach, was in Peirce's 1903 Harvard lecture, where Firstness was described most famously as "that rare faculty, the faculty of seeing what stares one in the face, just as it presents itself, unreplaced by any interpretation, unsophisticated by any allowance for this or for that supposed modifying circumstance". Yet, this is offered to us as a phenomenological look at *Beginning* and a starting point for every possible philosophical *Articulation* of reality "simply to open our mental eyes and look well at the phenomenon …".[4] Is that an approximation of the "breach of silence", intertwined with perception, sensation, cognition, experience, shock or change? The question is not only skeptical in its reference to multiple layers of meaning, but also to one observation, which remained beyond Peirce's attention. *If a "breach of silence" is the origin of Firstness* (and the latter the Beginning of any process of articulating reality) *then there is a primordial and more encompassing silence in which the breach of silence can take place at all.* In contrast to traditional philosophical considerations, we should thus accept different types of 'silence', which leave the simple idea of 'silence as non-speaking' far behind.[5]

1.4 The Quality of Silence

The quality of silence as referred to in the 'breach of silence' seems an issue of great interest. The characterization of that quality has cosmological implications beyond doubt and will be important for our understanding of meaning. All that will be a leading motive throughout this book in various phases. If Firstness emerges from the breach, and is at the same time *the* Beginning of the articulation of reality, then it is remarkably parallel to Edmund Husserl's suggestion, that this emerging articulation is a matter of "Einstellungsänderung" (attitude change). To begin, we underline that *change* and *breach* must take place *in* a 'something', which Peirce characterized as 'silence' and Husserl as 'attitude' (a concept that Peirce also used to characterize Firstness). What is this "*in*"?

When we focus on *silence* and the meaning of Firstness, we must conclude that there are indeed different types of silence to consider. If not, there could never be a break, a shock, a change or even a sensation, feeling or perception, Peirce concludes correctly from his "porch-experience". Does it suffice to notice that the 'breach of

[3] Phenomenological evidence of this identification (in contrast to these pages) is still basic in: Jan M. Broekman: "Firstness and Phenomenology" in: *Prospects of Legal Semiotics,* Anne Wagner & Jan M. Broekman (Eds), Springer 2010, p. 54 ff.

[4] The Peirce Edition Project: *The essential Peirce. Selected Philosophical Writings,* Vol. 2. Indiana UP 1998, p. 147.

[5] See Broekman: "Firstness and Phenomenology", Op. Cit., p. 54 ff: "2.4. Rupture".

silence' must take place *in* silence, so that there is a silence *before*—and a silence *after* the breach? Most probably not, because already the consideration that a 'silence after—' may not be identical to the 'silence before—' makes it clear that a more differentiated analysis and characterization is necessary. So the following characterization by means of distinct phases seems a plausible hypothesis. We distinguish:

A. A *cosmic silence*
B. A silence to be characterized as an *articulatory setting*
C. A silence *in the process of articulation,* and
D. A silence *articulated.*

In the course of this book, we refer to each of the four phases as A, B, C, and D, respectively. A primary and very short commentary on this distinction includes, that A (the cosmic silence) precedes *any* articulation[6]; the way Peirce speaks of a feeling of 'naturalness' or Husserl of a 'naïve-natural attitude' indicates that precedent character. It does not suggest any causality that has this cosmic order in its grip. So there is no possibility to circumscribe this type of silence in any way and with any words. It thus includes the fact that there is in A no meaning existent or possible for articulation, expression or even experience.[7]

[6]This leads to the insight that *articulation* engenders in the realm of silence. From the Torah's *Paradise* to Plato's *Cave* we think in images about cosmos and consciousness. But there are others who think in breaches of silence rather than images. Does the "Big Bang" belong to the latter? There must exist "silence" *before* a "breach of silence" can take place. Those two types of silence are, however, not necessary equal. A "cosmic silence" prevails, in which a "breach" may exceptionally lead to articulation. Not *all*-cosmic silence should be conceived as ready for articulation! Does the "Big Bang" breach the cosmic silence like the train whistle the notion of nature? Can that be? Is that correct? If the dimensions of the cosmic silence concern all universes, it could also be that the "Bang" did not breach *all* silence, and did not lead to articulation other than in *limited* cosmic regions. In that case, we conclude that the Big Bang is a metaphor stemming from just that special region of cosmic silence fit for articulation. There is no guarantee that other regions of cosmic silence also do, so that an immense uncertainty about the foundations of the metaphor opens up. Is the concept Big Bang perhaps a misplaced metaphor, focusing only on a type of silence that can be articulated, and not *all*-cosmic silence? What relevance has this insight for modern physics? Must we understand physics as a theory formation on the basis of images or as an articulation force on the basis of breaches (as the Big Bang) in cosmic silence? Most probably: the Big Bang did not definitely annihilate cosmic silence *in toto*.

[7]The first lines of the Torah try to escape this impossibility of circumscribing through the use of words like "bewilderment and void, with darkness over the surface of the deep", and identify any articulation of A by "an Act of God Whose Beginning is just a matter of Expounding". A "cosmic silence" prevails, in which a "breach" may exceptionally lead to articulation. But not *all* the entire cosmic silence should be conceived as ready for articulation. Cosmic silence seems in this light a process with breaches and zones of silence that allow articulation.

The latter is present in B, C and D—although each time in a different manner. The three together could nevertheless be characterized as the domain of meaning. B (the articulatory setting in cosmic silence) is mainly mentioned as an indication of a possible difference in quality of silence. If there is first a total indifference (in A), a second (B) must be a sphere in which articulation could eventually emerge. That possibility must exist in (A) if a 'reality' is ever to be articulated as 'existing'. However, the quality of B focuses entirely on C (silence in the process of being articulated—whereby 'silence' is no longer understood in terms of A but rather in terms of B). The articulation process of reality has changed A (the cosmic silence) into a silence in which a form of consciousness emerges in parallel with the transition of A. It is clear, that B and C together form the basis for D (silence articulated) in which linguistic patterns dominate and the concept of (human) language can be maintained. This pattern of A, B, C and D forms the background of Peirce's Firstness, which is, as a breach in A, determined as the development trough B and C towards D and its (linguistics) articulation.

1.5 New Focus on Meaning

Focus on Meaning shows how the path from 'no meaning' towards 'meaning' originates in an inarticulate sphere we characterized as A. In his 1903 lecture on "Phenomenology" Peirce called this path of meaning-making (leading to Firstness) the acquiring of a *faculty*—which is not in the first place a psychological feature but rather a phenomenological one, making out "what are the elements of appearance that present themselves to us …".[8] That faculty is a matter of articulation and presupposes language within a diversity of means of expression. A more encompassing view on meaning thus results from a more sophisticated consideration of 'silence'. We have only suggested some outlines of the latter, and will continue their differentiation in the course of our explorations.

It is, however, already possible to propound that an unimaginable and inexpressive cosmological order exists, which must be circumscribed as *having (or: representing) no meaning.* It is even impossible to state that the mentioned cosmic silence can be considered as a phenomenological, philosophical or scientific fact. Yet it appears that meaning emerges where B can be presupposed, and C as well as D

A 'Cosmic silence' is not without differentiation, change, force or process-character. The moment Hashem God gave the Torah, Zornberg concludes, silence was absolute, "there was no echo, the silence was there to create awareness that there is nothing aside from Him". The Torah "was given when the process of decreation, the decomposition of the world, has reached its completion. In the silence of a time before the Creation, before individuation and separation, none of the 'stipulations', the found constructions of previous worlds, exist. The question of meaning erodes all the facades of reality." See A. G. Zornberg: *The Beginning of Desire,* Doubleday NY 1995, p. 31. Meanings reach from Firstness and related first signs of consciousness towards philosophy and physics as their most sophisticated forms of consciousness.

[8] Peirce, see note 4.

comes into articulation—as preconditions for the articulation of reality. That emergence contains the roots of meaning. This observation pertains to the basic insight that meaning, as involved in D, emerges from a plurality of socio-cultural processes, but that B and C additionally make room for all sorts of individual meaning-making initiatives and actions. These become fixated in D—a sphere in which meanings seem codified. The Peircean as well as the Husserlean way of outlining Firstness or attitude change confirms this tendency towards fixation of meaning in the context of social and cultural articulations (we often call these 'narratives').[9]

It is difficult to properly understand the role of (human) consciousness and the development of the human mind/brain in this indeterminable context. The issue is that neither consciousness nor mind are separated from the outlined developments and thus from the limits of the emergence of meaning. *Any focus on meaning* in the context of cosmic silence and breach makes us conclude that meaning begins its path to full articulation from the first traces of potentials in B on, emerges clearly in C, and is refined to the point of fixation in D, where we encounter language and all its forms of fixation. Peirce's "breach of silence" seems in this light a process that dominates what we called "silence in the process of articulation" (C). Any linguistic behavior expressing itself with "Post-it" notes, in the way we initially mentioned, appears as an almost final stage of the process of intertwining patterns of emergence—cosmological as well as paleontological and evolutionarily biological—a cosmic silence comprising the developments of humans. Meaning is not a simple concept; it is never fixated but always a process; its use is via but never completely identical with linguistic patterns. Our explorations in this book will therefore mainly focus on meaning in the phases C and D.

2 Silence and the Sign Pool

Any philosophical approach to meaning has to take into consideration how this concept concerns two of the four distinguished spheres of silence, namely those which follow *after* the evolving of a silence as a setting prepared for possible articulation, which is *after* (B). It implies that meaning comes into existence only after a 'breach' or 'change', which differs from Peirce's insight, because the breach brings preparedness but not yet fulfillment and action. And the breach cannot be articulated in any way *before* an unfolding of the type of cosmic silence that has the potential (not necessarily the actualization) for articulation. So the question is, whether Peirce's fiercely defended Firstness really covers anything that has to do with what he identified as 'nature/natural' or which Husserl identified as 'naïve-natural'. Does modern physics answer the question? In any case, it is one of the most profound issues of a philosophy of meaning. To choose the expression 'sign pool' for our most frequently explored terms 'daily life' or 'everyday life' is a

[9] See Christopher Booker: *The Seven Basic Plots—Why We Tell Stories*. Continuum Press, London/New York 2004. P. 215.

particular exercise in maintaining meaning. The component 'sign' is derived from the fact that Peirce explained how "everything can be(come) a sign" and the component "pool" reminds us that water and air belong to our environment in ways that are equivalent to earth and the firm ground we stand on. Water has its global importance in reality as well as symbolically and its equivalence to silence is a surprising theme in the Torah and related narrations concerning the Creation.

Do we swim—do all of us? Did we swim in the sign pool when we came home safely after hours of driving in dense traffic, and do we then swim again? Do we swim when we read and appear to understand a book? Will we swim when we love, explain a viewpoint, or pluck stars from heaven? Yes, we do. The swimming sustains us more than words can articulate. Consider swim-expressions such as speech, conversation, language performance, and the like. We swim. Being is swimming, in the pool—and the pool is more than water: it is community, togetherness, social patterns and cultural life.

2.1 Life and Signs

Living is pooling, 'watch the water' its slogan. We are *immersed* in the many and variable signs around us. Social manners, ethical guidelines, grammatical correctness, knowledge in general, focus on pooling and the pool's content are *signs that profile*. The endless variety of signs challenges *and* encourages us to construct what we call *reality*. People do like the pool: they applaud the metaphor. All appreciate the idea that the sign pool is our significant home, our construct of silences articulated in all possible and probable variations. That certainty is important, and is in parallel with the many pleasures we associate with the swimming and its pool. Those pleasures seem endless: when Peirce considered how "the universe was perfused with signs", he did not guess that our cosmologists would highlight the fact that the universe itself is a sign in the midst of universes, which we will never perceive because they will never encounter a human consciousness. What cannot be imagined reaches beyond itself by means of scientific statements of a cosmological nature. Each pool is within a pool, like each text has its surface- and its deep structure: that feeling of relativity makes us swim. We should consider that the pool is deeper than we perceive during our swimming, as we do when we read a text. Dimensions reach beyond boundaries that mark our world as different from an external world, which is evidently more encompassing than our knowledge and imagination can teach us.

The sign-pool is not only filled with events, facts, linguistic entities, but also with opinions, memes, and related intertwining expressions. Some present themselves as 'meaning', others suggest a future or possible understanding when they appear to refer to layers of biological or social insight and knowledge. Its contextual features are omnipresent the moment we enter the pool, meaning exists for us even before our birth. Do not forget: neurons format memes; geological timetables stage our ethical viewpoints—we never create them out of nothing.

Peirce wrote 1908 to Lady Welby, that 'language is only the extreme form of expression'—we notice that when we swim, read or experience the plurality of expression beyond everyday language otherwise. Peirce wanted to share with Lady Welby the experience that life itself is expression resp. articulation. That expressivity reaches much wider than whatever native language we speak.

Law is a particular dimension of pooling; we fight for keeping it so—the rule of law is more than a simple rule; it is rather a social icon, which we want to extend institutionally as well as politically. Feeling safe is the most appreciated temperature of the waters we daily swim; the pool delivers those feelings and lays foundations for our behaviors and expectations pertaining to the behavior of others. That is the powerful charm of legal semiotics: how do signs in the pool set us free and protect us at the same time? Roberta Kevelson's book title: "Law as a System of Signs" became a guideline in itself: the pool is a safety system! System? Is the pool a system? Or not? The pool in life and law: differences between them are included in our focus on pooling. Is that focus realistic, or just an idea to revive a social dream, a heritage of Hobbes, a galaxy-wheeling dream, a vision with unknown dimensions and power in real life?

2.2 *Pool and Everyday*

The question is disquieting. Do we need dreams to become ourselves? Do we not cherish them in daily life—and is life (and law within life) not a dream? What else makes us live? If we do live, don't we live by the grace of the pool, the pond of signs that secures our course of life because we swim? Following, or at least considering the signs all around us leads to real life dimensions, so why would impressions about the pool not be realistic, and a legitimate theme in philosophical considerations? Even such ideas disquiet. They are a breach with the naturalness of our swimming. They are as if we do no longer swim, but just look: overlook the pool to estimate its dimensions, its value, its function and meaning. Any breach shows its attitude: separation, interrogation, second thoughts, destruction of evidence, all this needs a life sustained by such a frame of mind.

The two expressions: "pool" and "everyday life-[world]" are almost equivalent. Their differences are based on their profiles and determining topics. This could surprise: are those key issues, which directly shape our lives, exchangeable articulations? Husserl was indeed very surprised, and that inspired him to emphasize the importance of his concept "Lebenswelt" (everyday-life world). His basic motivation could be ours. In the mid-1930s of the twentieth century, he claims, our sciences lost their meaning and sense for our daily lives. The distance between science and life became so overwhelmingly that our staggering profits derived from their techniques and fields of application do not make any sense other than a 'blind' profit.[10]

[10] Edmund Husserl: *Die Krisis der Europäischen Wissenschaften und die Transzendentale Phänomenologie,* M. Nijhoff, Den Haag 1954, Husserliana Bd. VI, p. 105 ff. [The Crisis of European Sciences and Transcendental Philosophy], 1970 [1936/54, Carr, D., transl.].

Had Husserl been able to have a discussion with Peirce, he would have told him that the idea that "everything can be(come) a sign" is basic for an attitude, which creates the abyss between the sense of science and life. Peirce would then have been surprised to hear his colleague indicate how individuals (and Occidental society in its totality) understand and practice whatever sign may occur in an alienating and instrumental manner. That qualifies any in-depth contemplation about meaning and sign as *useless*. It is important to consider how this creates a specific and dangerous *silence* about the essentials of life. Such a silence is the subject of a philosophy of culture which determines: what is still in the process of articulation (C) and what can already be qualified as articulated in languages as well as in other building blocks of our everyday world (D).

2.3 Life—World

To call this life-world (Lebenswelt): the 'sign pool', underlines that perspective. It also colors the context in which individuals and their cultural patterns merge, amalgamate and pull together. There is no need to underline how relevant this characterization is for law and legal discourse. The two focus on managing what occurs in the phase in which silence (as non-cosmic silence) is articulated (D) and fixated in words and other linguistic components as well in socially accepted habits with a comparable fixation effect. If (legal as well as physical) sciences no longer contribute to meaning and sense in everyday life (Lebenswelt), then a moral and legal justification of sciences and scientifically produced ideas and products seems threatened. Tensions between scientific specializations and their outcomes in social life on the one hand and the truth-value of the inherent thought patterns of sciences on the other form an important feature of modern life—of life as a sign pool. Apart from immediate practicability, has science a meaning in life? Perhaps our IT-supported fictions in film, literature and music fill the meaning gap, but they do so outside of the ways ethics and meaning once played a role in the sciences. The truth and the factual are even no longer perceived as components in tension within the sign pool also called 'life'.

The expression 'pool' thus contributes not only to a sign-inspired analysis of meaning, but also to a deeper understanding of the fundamental multiplicity inherent in meaning—even during the deepest crises of society. The fact that the sign-pool is *not* a pool filled with signs/water remains problematic. Peirce taught us that nothing *is* a sign but everything *can become* a sign. All relations with signs are a matter of *becoming* rather than of *being*. It also implies that an existing sign is *becoming*, is in process. The sign-pool is, like life itself, a pool in becoming, which is a complicated experience. Two major gaps in past studies on meaning are related within the context of the sign-pool: the recognition of meaning with *particle* character, and the functions of those particles in a *force field,* as Lewin's social psychology inspired us to conclude. Both are related to language, so that meaning depends entirely on a particular layer of linguistic expressiveness involved in a particle-bound attitude. That insight throws an important light on a feature of everyday language, which is only *one* of the layers of language. That layer seems often to be our native tongue, our natural language, because here we swim in the self-conviction that we are deciphering the signs of everyday life. Is the pool not filled with materials and objects to please, protect, guide and support us in life? But an articulation of meaning in the life-world or the sign pool is only possible *after* meaning making *has been made* possible. The sign pool shows a constitutive passivity in so far as it functions in preparing for sign functions and meanings to become effective. The latter are not simple building blocks, which are 'naturally' available for life's unfolding. The creation of meaning is not just a coalescence of sense- or signification-particles. When we swim we experience the suggestion that the pool is endless and beyond measure. When we look over the pool, we experience the restrictions of meaning in our words. Is the pool a token for the restrictive character of our speech-acts?

Meanings emerge with life experienced as a pool or world. They are never implanted into our lives as if they were elements stemming from an outside reality—studies of human paleontology and evolutionary life prove this while using their calendars comprising millions of years. The dynamics of silence as a cosmic power unfold continuously when we recall in meaningful ways how our life-world is characterized as a sign pool.

3 Logocentric Silence

Can one avoid complications by putting *the word* in the center of all possible and necessary articulations and focus on it as we do every day? Does a philosophical approach to meaning lose some of its most bewildering implications when *the word* is claimed to be the major concept? Logocentrism claims in general that "word" and/or "speech-act" are epistemologically superior. All aspects and all secrets of our presence in the world are sustained by and fundamentally linked with *logocentric* metaphysics. It is an observation, which includes the idea that our presence in the world is necessarily mediated by word or principle. Klages (1872–1956) called this view "logocentrism", and showed its inner dynamics in discussing the tensions between "Geist" (spirit) and "Seele" (soul), in other words: between our spiritual principles and the realities of our daily life. This will lead us in a next chapter to focus on theories pertaining to "the word" as the main carrier of meaning. But we emphasize here already that such a word-directed approach creates *a veiled silence* in all articulation processes but one: that of the word, which inhibits a deeper insight into meaning. One should not forget, that this *cosmology of the separate*, this *dominance of partitioning* is typical for Occidental metaphysics, as already Plato unveiled. That cosmology is based on the principle of identity and of non-contradiction—both principles are foundational for Western philosophy. As a result, philosophy demanding presence, constancy and coherence becomes a power of silence, because any contradiction, disorder or marginality is banned, and wholeness is not necessarily the result of such a ban. This can be read in the Celan poem we analyze in Chap. 4.

Such a silence reminds us, that the general idea of a "cosmic silence" should help us understand how all articulations occur in a *later* stage after an initial unfolding of cosmic reality. Articulations (in terms of the first pages of this book) are fully developed in phases C and D, with the restriction that there is an already active borderline between B and C. The latter is the phase in which our construct of silences can lead to silences articulated, or to "reality". Phase A is in its entirety, like the majority of segments of phase B, "not fit for articulation" and are also designated as "silence". It interests, however, that the phases B, C and D lose the character of "silence" that phase A will never lose: the *cosmic character* that even modern physics is not able to definitively explain or articulate. As a result, we can state the phases B, C and D are sequentially influenced by social and cultural features, and thus carry meanings of the concept "silence" which differ from phase A. It follows that a *logocentric* approach to meaning is not a theme of physics, but a discussion point within cultural studies, linguistics, semiotics and philosophy. "What does 'Logos' mean" we ask, "and what does it mean in general when the 'Word' is at the absolute center of each linguistic articulation?" That is the essential question here.

Let us not forget how socio-cultural studies only conceive cosmic silence as an occurrence at the borderlines between the regions B and C. The character of cosmic silence remains within our conceptual thought-formation. The borderline is in itself an epistemological issue and also not a subject of physics or cosmological theories. It will therefore perhaps be seen as a beginning of 'Reality to be' under the epistemological consideration that reality is understood as "silence articulated" whereby cosmic silence remains the Great Unknown and Unknowable. From here it may be clear how Peirce's Firstness might for him be (within the regions C and D) a 'feeling', perhaps a 'contrast to what is not' or a purely "situational fact leading to reflection" (the train whistle).

3.1 Mind and Meaning

The meaning of something implies an involvement of that "something" in a particular process. One tends to interpret "to mean" as entering a type of sign pool understood as a field that is "expressivity-based on the word". But this is a limitation of meaning, sustained by a focus on the word as the basic unit of language and linguistic articulation. It certainly fits with an understanding of meaning to become in itself *literal*—a tendency in modern sciences as well as law, social ethics and modern philosophy. This thread inherent in the reduction to "the literal *only*" may throw new light on interpretation and hermeneutics (both are never an issue of words or texts alone), which are related to signs or a sign. Are signs indeed the 'point zero' of language and meaning?

One of the cosmic riddles coming very near to socio-cultural and philosophical reflection is, that despite the definite incomprehensibility of cosmic silence (A), a desire reigns for silence to be effective at the borderlines of B and certainly in C. That desire unfolds via meaning in fields of an increasing power of articulation. The desire for silence expresses itself most powerfully in linguistic articulations, for instance in declaring an occasional articulation to be "indisputable", or self-evident, or final and fixated, or even as purely natural.

This dynamic will be reinforced where meaning (philosophically embedded in logics and metaphysics) seems founded in a perception and a science of reality as suggested in the theories of Newton. In those theories on reality (a) material objects exist individually and (b) can be at precisely determinable locations and (c) follow definite trajectories. Despite the predominance of our modern global interest in the plurality of languages, symbols, signs, particles and processes, this ensemble of long-lived Newtonian views seems difficult to change. The close links between meaning and its metaphysical or ontological foundations is older than our interest in signs. 'Meaning' as a concept was in the history of occidental thinking subordinated to the sign.

The classical *Vocabulaire Technique et Critique de la Philosophie,* authored by André Lalande and published in Paris during many years since 1902, did not even mention 'meaning' when it pointed to the parallels among the French 'signification' and the German 'Bedeutung' as well as the Italian 'Significazione' and the English 'signification'. The dictionary reveals its ontological and metaphysical foundations in stressing that "signification is necessary for human reason … and any reflective thought-formation of humans. And reason is of utmost importance for signification". The sign dominates because signification is what a sign represents, for instance the sense of a word or a phrase.

3.2 Mauthner

Fritz Mauthner (who was close to the "Amsterdamse Signifische Kring"[11] and in his approach to language even more critical than Lady Welby) describes in his "Wörterbuch der Philosophie", 1914, how words carry a sense and find meaning on the basis of a number of metaphysical presuppositions. Even logical and abstract concepts relate to human language—Mauthner's differentiation between word and meaning are therefore parallel to speech and thought. But word and meaning cannot be separated in a living language: *meaning is the soul of the word*, he formulates. Moreover, meaning differs along time and cultural space, so that *the* "meaning of …" does not exist. In contrast to Lalande, special mention of English theory of meaning comes to the fore in Mauthner's dictionary. When unfolding his critical approach to language, he gives that approach the name 'significs'. In a more general sense he distinguishes the prevailing daily uses of language (Peirce would speak about 'habits') from the individual's use, which relates to the particularities of a speaker or writer.

[11] W. Schmitz, *De Hollandse Significa*, Assen/Maastricht 1990 p. 110 f.

Mauthner mentions also a third type of language presentation, which he calls the 'value-meaning' [Wertbedeutung]—a term that indicates the specific value one gives to a particularly cherished expression or word. The Dutch legal significian Jacob Israel de Haan spoke of "waardevolle woorden" [valuable words] to indicate the same.[12] We experience the enormous importance of the concept of meaning: a loss of meaning through a loss of its inherent dynamics is also the end of language and of human communication. A lack of reliability of meaning is a lack of language's primary function: communication and transference of knowledge grounded in such relationships, Mauthner writes. Hence his critical view that language is not able to provide us any objective basis for communication and knowledge, neither in everyday issues nor in scientific, and certainly not in philosophical, questions.

How does this relate to logocentrism? One of the dominant points of interest is that meaning is always the meaning of a some-*thing. Meaning as the "meaning of…" depends on the "of…"* and this dependency could very well be the reason for the difficulties encountered in unfolding a scientific or linguistic emancipation of the concept. To say that meaning is always "the meaning of…" presupposes a foundational relationship between meaning and reality, which can lead easily to the logocentric position. We articulate meaning as if we succeed in saying by means of that articulation how things really are. In that speaking we consider it *natural* to (a) distinguish between meaning and reality, and moreover (b) to relate the two by means of *reference*. The *Stanford Encyclopedia of Philosophy* treats semantic theories as a major chapter of a theory of meaning for that reason.

The twentieth century shows how a *logocentric* attitude cannot get rid of its implicit *teleologic* character. A 'transcendental signified' (Derrida) seems to be the final authority for all meaning and for every semiotic- or deconstructionist theory because all meaning making has to serve a well-determined *telos*, which carries a diversity of names in occidental culture. Even such principles like *expressibility, reference* or *speech-activity* are unable to free themselves from this legacy. Those philosophical thoughts culminate in a *solo* position of 'the word'. Notice how sign relations and meaning questions are always observed via the semiotic relation par excellence: the signifier-signified relation—a relation between two words articulated by two words. Only in that well-determined guise should the full presence of a consciousness unfold. What a human consciousness wants to achieve must relate to some 'origin', to a 'first' or a 'source', and hence the general fascination of Peirce's Firstness. What is signified refers always to its signifier—without that reference there exists no meaning, Firstness teaches us. A signifier only creating and sustaining one exclusive meaning, is therefore an authoritarian signifier.

Is any meaning possible beyond or different from this signifier-signified relation? This naïve question touches on an additional philosophical observation: questions on meaning are dualistically formatted and expressed in binary phrases. Expressions like "signifier-signified", "expression-content" or "sensible-intelligible" are only reflections of the dictionary as it pertains to meaning, reflections of its binary wordings.

---

[12] See Schmitz, Op. Cit, p. 161. (see also this book: Chaps. 2 and 3).

So one asks: *is there meaning beyond binary thinking?* Can a semiotic discipline unfold without being chained by dualisms? To find meaning, one should perhaps reach out into that unknown region beyond dualisms, where one does not need to conclude how things are different from others, how it should be B and not A, or how P should not be replaced by Q. Read the young Lady Welby, read Husserl, Frege, Barthes, Eco, Derrida: a final recourse to understanding meaning leads to the sign as the most fruitfully concentrated *dual* feature on which semiotics can stand. The Peircean triadic conception of semiotics is different, because his difference is not embedded in a cosmos with a dual character, as his evolutionary logic or his principle of Firstness explains. Is Peirce's understanding of a sign the end of all possible semiotics, or the opposite: a new beginning of semiotics?

That is a vital question for the concept of meaning. The fate of meaning is not only confined to literature and hermeneutics but reaches also, and most remarkably, from semiotics to quantum mechanics, from language and literature to mathematics and conversely.[13] It is clear in the midst of those approaches: meaning is not a thing or a something. One rather discovers that meaning is a multifaceted concept that represents presence, presentation and even reference. This insight positions meaning in the center of semiotics, which perhaps changes basic structures and important philosophical ideas on reference.

No wonder that after a full century, meaning has not yet accomplished its emancipation, given the fact that meaning remains in the main linked to sounds, signs, sentences, or texts as the major component of semiotics. *Adding speech to this list cannot lead to a more prolific semiotic understanding of meaning as long as speaking and speech are understood as 'the use of words'*. Any alternative puts the *logocentric* attitude in perspective and unfolds a new understanding of speech because of its connection with the 'speech potential'. This connection opens new ways of understanding meaning and suggests a renewal of semiotics as a multi-discipline.

3.3 Klages' Logocentrism

Those thoughts seem encapsulated in a predominantly Anglo-Saxon philosophy and linguistics, in particular the overall emphasis on the word as language's primary particle. If we change perspective and focus on German instead of English philosophy, our patterns of understanding meaning also change. *German* philosophers who contributed most to an unfolding and foundational research into the concept of meaning in the first decades of the twentieth century are Frege, Klages and Husserl. *Naturphilosophie*, *Vitalismus* and *Lebensphilosophie* met in Ludwig Klages with an

[13] John K. Sheriff: *The Fate of Meaning. Charles Peirce, Structuralism, and Literature.* Princeton UP 1989, and—Id.—: *Charles Peirce's Guess at the Riddle*, Indiana UP 1994. The history from Husserl's 'Ausdruck', [expression] and Peirce's sign, to Derrida's criticism of the logocentric attitude as well as the series of categories such as signifier-signified, expression-content, sensibility-intelligibility shows the strength of this metaphysical commitment.

important *biocentric* metaphysics, which has remained largely unnoticed in Anglo-Saxon philosophy.

Klages studied the connections between *meaning* and *logocentrism*—a term not originated by Derrida[14]—with a *vitalist* attitude. He emphasizes that an "error arises when we confuse real connections with merely conceptual relationships in representational forms, on which all remaining forms and cases equally depend, is the gradual, ceaseless disempowerment of the name that is promoted by the *logocentric* school of thought, during its 3500 year quest to consummate the destruction of thought. *Logocentric* thought always pronounces its verdict in favor of the alleged reality of the concept or of the fact".[15] The concept is precisely *the solo position of the word* when we should understand language, articulation and expressivity. But that is only one aspect of the issue.

Klages' multivolume work "*Der Geist als Widersacher der Seele*" [The Spirit as Adversary of the Soul] shows how an "Ausdruck" [Expression] can evaporate in a "Wort" [Word] because of the power of fixation of the latter. The vitality and life-quality of an "Ausdruck" is implied in Klages' thoughts as well as in the thoughts of Frege and Husserl. He places an emphasis on 'soul'/'everyday life': activity, liveliness, and change. That position is in contrast to the word and its fixation, which causes silence while determining meaning. So, one should ask, is the logocentric view an improvement or an impoverishment for a theory of meaning?

3.4 Logocentrism and the Word

It seems that a connection between *word* and *meaning* articulated in the English language is more a matter of intellectual, rational, conceptual profiling than in the German language.[16] The latter does not in the first place focus on the term *Wort*

---

[14] Derrida mentions how Peirce aimed at "the de-construction of the transcendental signified", whereas he himself identified logocentrism and the metaphysics of presence as the exigent, powerful, systematic, and irrepressible desire for such a signified". In: *Of Grammatology*, Trl G.C. Spivak, Johns Hopkins UP 1976, p. 49.

[15] Klages adds: "In order to be able to preserve its faith in the reality of things, "naturalism" bases itself upon an unconscious (or conscious!) acceptance of the unification of name and concept through the agency of the thing. In order to maintain its faith in the reality of concepts, "idealism" unconsciously (or consciously!) insists on the unification of name and thing through the agency of the concept . . . "See: *Cosmogonic Reflections. By Ludwig Klages.* See: Joe Pryce, at: *Internet Archive*, May 14, 2001.

[16] Husserl's ideas on meaning have been concentrated in his 1908 lectures, which were close to the *Logische Untersuchungen*, in particular to vol. II., 1913. He focuses on *Wortlautbewußtsein* and *Bedeutungsbewußtsein*, viewing the sound (Laut) as the medium for understanding what we call the 'speech potential'. A contemporary translation of "*Wortlautbewußtsein*" would be '*Speech/word potential*'. But the epistemological complication is clear. Husserl could propagate a "regional" ontology and the translation is based on an *inter*regional ontology. His recourse to sound is replaced by quantum notions and frames of quantum knowledge: the position of the particle, the mutual relation between wave and particle, the epistemological input of David Bohm's

[*word*] but rather on the term *Ausdruck* [Expression] with its emotive and life-stream bond with *meaning*, and that is a *vitalistic* attitude. Klages cautions us to realize that we tend to attribute not enough importance to those life-components because our feelings must almost always be rational and conscious. When he underlines, as an example, how reality is composed of images [*Bilder*] and not of rational elements or feelings, he follows German traditions. While studying meaning, he emphasizes that we should understand the "reality of images" [*Wirklichkeit der Bilder*] in approximately the same manner as Husserl stresses. Husserl wrote a year before Peirce's death in 1914 about *ontology* being *an eidetic science.*[17] "Klages almost seems to have found the very words with which to speak that which has hitherto been considered to be beyond the powers of speech", Nobel Prize author Hermann Hesse wrote. Can the reality of images, apart from our daily maintenance of meanings, be encountered at the borderlines of the sayable?[18]

3.5 Speech and the Utterance of Words

We say in the context of our everyday language: "speech brings words to life by means of our speaking". Is that correct? Or does that answer represent only a number of unchecked presuppositions, which show that we never thought about conceiving speech as an independent concept, and that we want to remain within the boundaries of *logocentrism*? We pretend to know what speech is and what its vital acts embrace, and we hope to make life more colorful and important through them. Is, one argues, the possibility to enter speech not always available? Indeed, *to enter speech by means of the utterance of words* seems self-evident. Yet this remains only a bewildering possibility, a perhaps uneasy access to unknown regions of existence.

theory about the reality of the particle. And, in Husserl there is always a *Bewußtsein* in function, whereas in an *inter*regional ontology there are *forces* to detect, at a distance from a (human) consciousness.

[17] E. Husserl: *Ideen zu einer reinen Phänomenologie und phänomenologischen Philosophie.* [Ideas Pertaining to a Pure Phenomenology and to a Phenomenological Philosophy—First Book: General Introduction to a Pure Phenomenology], 1982 [1913. Kersten, F., transl] The Hague, M. Nijhoff, §9.

[18] If Klages has a place in the German approach to meaning, Edmund Husserl certainly also has. A first glance at, in particular, the second volume of his "*Logische Untersuchungen*", [Logical Investigations] 1913 makes clear how the founder of phenomenology brings the concepts of "Ausdruck" and "Bedeutung" [Expression and Meaning] together and this togetherness seems linked with the Sign from the very beginning. By means of reflection on the concept of meaning the second volume reads as a study on language. Husserl gave a lecture in 1910/1911 in Göttingen on "Logik als Theorie der Erkenntnis" [Logic as Theory of Knowledge] But when studying the *Logische Untersuchungen*, one is impressed by the fact that *we should qualify this book today as a study on language, language consciousness and the engenderment of speech* and from here, based on observations pertaining to language, also as a study on knowledge/meaning. All is unfolded with a focus on word-speech coherence; neither of the two is in phenomenology perceived as an independent issue in its own right.

It can boil down to the question whether speech articulates and/or orders particles of language to unfold human communication. What implication does the use linguistic elements have? [19]

Yet, we focus on them once we enter the life of speech. We feel the many shortcomings of our spoken words. Expressiveness seems reduced, shortened, shrinking when we articulate. We all know that, and we know it all. Hence our ardent interest in interpretation, translation, repetition, shift, multitasking amidst words and languages. And we all know more than one language, although we are not always aware of the wealth that wonderful package called 'speech' contains. What is speech in itself, beyond the use of components belonging to our linguistic culture all around? And reading, what has reading to do with speech? We read a novel to figure out a meaning from life, to find its motives, ideas, purposes, thought patterns—to become guided, educated by them. Images of the mind are part and parcel of that sort of education. The story we read in the text before our eyes is full of experiences and events going to be transformed into images in our mind. "I once read …"; "I was on the edge of saying … and found a bewildering quantity of images in front of my spiritual eye".

We read words by deciphering their images in the mind. Do they contain prescriptions for behavior? Is everyday reality taking its flight into more abstract, more general, more spatially valid regions beyond the boundaries of languages and other means of expression? What do we have in mind when we are confronted with them, what do they tell us, to what category of knowledge do they belong—these are all questions with one particular focus: how word and speech relate. We feel emotions around the speaking and reading we engaged in; Husserl's concentration on a consciousness should be remembered when meaning comes to the fore. Is mimesis assuming our power of self-determination while we speak? Indeed, meaning is a crucial concept for all the background pages of life—not only (and mostly not at all) for everyday sentences because we live not while considering them at a critical distance. We live *thanks to* them, but not *with* them. So: what have words to do with speech in a logocentric perspective?

[19] Our thesis is, that any theory of meaning which does not take the coherence of word and speech as a major issue in the process of meaning making, will fail. Traditional theories of meaning focus on the word, or even on the verb as word, and do not critically consider the slogan of the 'word as a basic linguistic unit' as important in the creation of meaning. It is of interest, however, that various philosophers, also in the twentieth century, had a vague notion of the reduction of meaning when focusing on the single word and its determinative role: Peirce in his triads, Husserl in his logics and theory of meaning, are excellent examples. A decisive focus on a shift—in Husserl's terms: an attitude change—from a particular regional ontology (trusted by traditional philosophy) to another (such as quantum theory) comes to the fore. This is not a game of words: a change of ontology always determines our articulation of being, as vested in one or another field of science. Quantum mechanics has explored a field that was neglected by philosophical epistemology: speech being the dynamic of each word without which a word cannot function in language and its realm of meaning. Attention to this force may also put logocentrism in perspective. Is the force of *logos* limited to the utterance of a word, and does this limitation challenge us to consider the word as the basic unit of language?

3.6 Speech and Words

Speech is there *before* the word, before articulation and its fixations, before writing and its reading. So, does speech coordinate or even inhabit consciousness before it comes to a speech utterance, as if it were a coming out, a division, a separation, or a birth occurring to that very same consciousness? Perhaps it all occurs first vaguely, rather un-consciously, as a potential, and only later as an articulation. This shows how absurd it is to suggest, what seems normal in a logocentric view: "Speech is *using* words"—and no more than that!

Reference to a word in its quality of '*language particle*' appears to be the foundation for the *logocentric* tendency in occidental culture and as a consequence also for any unfolding of semiotics. Remember Klages: meaning will be killed in the word because of its power of fixation. Not only meaning, but also semiotics as a philosophical and scientific discipline, fades away if it is not successful in restoring its dynamic character. An emancipation of meaning seems closely linked with that restoration, perhaps the greatest challenge in the silence we mentioned.

But how one makes the first steps outside a predominant *logocentric* approach and whether one can assess the consequences of that step, remains a difficult issue. The search for an inspiring parallel is on such occasions most common in scientific as well as in philosophical discourses. The parallel in our context should focus on *particles* evolving in social as well as physical space-time. This focus implies, as Hawking made clear, a switch *from* a field of knowledge "in which material objects have an individual existence, can be located at definite locations, follow a definite path" *to* one in which "an object's position, path, and even its past and future are not precisely determined".[20] That is indeed a step, which connects two different worlds: the Newtonian on one side and the quantum theoretical on the other. The implied challenge is that speech must be regarded along the lines of *both* theories, and both with equal weight. First we will discuss Newtonian views: later we must look at speech as conceived from the viewpoint of quantum mechanics and as influenced by thought patterns that put the particle concept in a central position. The existence of both types of speech is an argument in theories of meaning!

Yet 'meaning' remains in both types, even in their clearest pronunciation, 'meaning of…', just as Peirce clarified 'signs' as 'signs of…'. This was for him the beginning of further research into the characteristics and ontological status of a sign, and those insights are also fruitful for meaning embedded in expressivity. "A word", Peirce wrote after having read Lady Welby's study on meaning, "has meaning for us in so far as we are able to make use of it in communicating our knowledge to others and in getting at the knowledge that these others seek to communicate to us. *That is the lowest grade of meaning.*"[21] So other grades have to follow! Let us not forget how expression, meaning and sign are in an equal position in so far as Searle's 'what can be said' implies 'what can be said in language', therefore: 'what

[20] Stephen Hawking: *The Grand Design.* New York 2010, p. 67.

[21] Peirce, *CP* 8. 176. (Italics are mine JMB).

can be said *in words*'. The latter leads us to define the speech act as 'the basic unit of communication'—not unlike words, which are generally understood as the basic unit of language.

3.7 Consciousness and Meaning

It seems important for any consideration pertaining to communication via utterances of words, that meaning appears as a specific mental state of humans. Meaning is in the framework of that state often understood as an event, which in its turn is understood as a process in the central nervous system of vertebrates. That formulation is deeply related with the life-qualities of vertebrates, of humans in particular, and reads like Klages' characterization of the 'Seele' [Soul]. Exactly this complex pattern of relations makes levels of meaning dependent on whether individual or social meanings are at stake. They also condition philosophical problems, for instance those inherent in the mind-brain relationship, or our understanding of a consciousness. Klages understood the latter as *the main power* of expression, or (often in another sense) consciousness as expressing *a point of origin* of expressiveness. Both culminate in a *logocentric* thought pattern of word articulation (a form of 'use') conceived as the activity of a human consciousness. The word was viewed as the particle, which made language and linguistic uses ultimately possible.

3.8 Derrida, Metaphysics

The connection between human consciousness and the engenderment of meaning is one of Jacques Derrida's major themes. The latter mentioned Peirce more than once, in particular in his *Grammatology*: "Peirce considers the indefiniteness of reference as the criterion that allows us to recognize that we are indeed dealing with a system of signs. *What broaches the movement of signification is what makes its interruption impossible. The thing itself is a sign.*" This quotation highlights the importance Derrida gives to the 'what is—' question (in relation to Husserl's multiple levels of ontology), whereby the dynamics of signification could be a key concept. Where are the dynamics in meaning? Not in solving the riddle of 'what is a sign or designated issue' but rather in the absoluteness of the necessity to move on, Derrida would say. Is the impossibility of interruption or the absolute need to go on signifying truly an issue of dynamics in meaning making? An absence of choice and a denying of multiplicity reign when interruption becomes impossible. That absence remains based on dualisms. What profiles signification is, that there is no choice apart from choice, so there is no nothing beyond the nothing of negation.

For that reason Peirce emphasized his cosmologic views, which cause for instance his appeal to Tyche as well as his wish to walk the path to heterogeneity. All these are steps towards a metaphysical viewpoint. Thinking a sign implies thinking a First, a source, in other words: *one* pole of a duality without knowing whether duality is the last and final form for meaning. A theory of signs is part of a cosmology and of a view on the world, and matter as the outcome of an ongoing articulation of reality. To understandthis is to understand a specific all-embracing dynamics, with signs of an essence. Therefore one reads Derrida: "The difference between Husserl's and Peirce's phenomenologies is fundamental since it concerns the concept of the sign and of the manifestation of presence, the relationships between the re-presentation and the originary presentation of the thing itself (truth) (…) The self-identity of the signified conceals itself unceasingly and is always on the move. The property of the *representamen* is to be itself and an other to be produced as a structure of reference, to be separated from it. The *property* of the *representamen* is not to be *proper*, that is to say absolutely *proximate* to itself. The represented is always already a *representamen*. (…) From the moment that there is meaning, there is nothing but signs."[22] Does meaning indeed seal the flow called signification, in order to become itself—in other words: does the signification process need the silence created by the veil of dualism? Is a dynamics beyond duality unknown in the emergence of meaning?

Derrida's Grammatology represents perhaps his deepest thought on language and meaning. It shows how *the word* is epistemologically superior in our knowledge and the many ways in which we know. Any type of logocentric metaphysics seems indispensable in this pattern of thought. Yet it implies *reductive* features: the existence of an original, irreducible object representing the logos must always be presupposed. Focus on that particular 'object' is in essence a reduction of meaning.

Our presence in the world is necessarily mediated through an articulation of silence, as indicated in the first section of this chapter on "Silence". Its ideal representation is the logos—but that understanding and representation is founded on reductions from type A silence towards its accomplishment in type D, the type D being specified as the complete fixation through precisely defined meanings. The latter is in the light of this view indeed a realm of fixation and of reduction. That realm unfolds on the basis of B, the type of silence that begins to be prepared for eventual articulation.

Here one can understand how the logocentric view and its metaphysical principles show that *all meaning is founded upon reduction*. This reductive process, loaded with meaning as it is, reaches from the borderlines of B (the susceptibility for articulation) to the ultimate limits of D (fixated meanings in artificial and formal languages). This is indeed to be read in Derrida: *writing functions as speech*, which allows an absolute concept of logos and metaphysics. His particular contribution to logocentrism is, however, not how he walks the path to metaphysics, but the insight that the chain of signification becomes a 'trace of presence-absence'. One should notice, that such considerations *mainly* play in C, in the field of the sayable—which is also the main region of meaning's unfolding.

[22] J. Derrida: *De la Grammatologie.* Paris 1967. [Of Grammatology. Trl G.C. Spivak, The Johns Hopkins University Press 1997, p. 49 f.].

One asks, whether any *Logos* ever includes considerations of meaning. Does the *Logos* support a relativity of articulation? Such issues pertain to *transitions* that give life to meaning when emerging from the outskirts of B and begin to unfold in C, and are often taken back when the reductive forces in D appear too strong. So it appears that any consideration of 'the word' and its position in articulation fields will not pertain to the word as such, but to the multiple meanings of a word and significations as a field that has silence as its origin. This could lead to ordering life's multiplicity by means of referring to metaphysics as a primordial manner of articulation.

Logocentrism shows that this reference relates most intimately to every meaning concept, and cannot unveil how that same act of reference is ultimately reductive. *Is meaning condemned to meaninglessness because meaning is always reductive?* That question is our underlying motive in the next two paragraphs, which underline the fact that meaning's major considerations focus on Silence of type C, whereas those of type D ultimately lead to meaning in its task of delivering, workable fixations—the risk of meaninglessness included. Meaning is never a product, but always product *and* producer at the same time, within one context. This dynamic coherence appears to be in the light of meaning as originating in a non-expressible cosmic silence, a supreme form of intertwining. Silence and culture belong together, whereby the first depends (if it ever depends) on the second for being articulated. That is an experience of a socio-cultural approach, which unfolds beyond physics. On the basis of this motive, attention is first given to the German poet and philosopher Hugo von Hofmannsthal and in particular to his famous *Lord Chandos* letter. The same motivation will inspire us when we reconsider the philosopher Ludwig Wittgenstein's words on 'silence' at the conclusion of his *Tractatus.*

4 The Chandos Letter

A 1902 essay of the German-Austrian poet, Nobel Prize Winner and philosopher Hugo von Hofmannsthal reads as a strong and particular sign in the context of Occidental culture of those years. Both do deliberately focus on *silence* as a meaningful component of human *speech.* It is extremely important to keep in mind that the meaning of this *silence* does not cover any component of the meaning of "cosmic silence" (indicated earlier as "A") but meaning as articulated particularly in region C of silence *tout court.* One reads Hugo von Hofmannsthal's famous 1902 "Ein Brief" (in the Anglo-Saxon world quoted as "The Lord Chandos Letter") which he conceived in the days when he transited from poetry to drama and became librettist for the composer Richard Strauss.[23] That move served a Wagnerian ideal—the conception of a "Gesamtkunstwerk": *a total work of art, a fusion of poetry, drama and music in which spirit and worldliness would unify meaning and thus*

[23] *Rotenberg*, Joel (Ed.). "The Lord Chandos Letter and Other Writings. Introduction by *Banville*, John". In: *The New York Review of Books*, 2005, NY, pp. xii, 117.

withstand the ages. It concerned feelings and insights about *silence* as it can or cannot be articulated. Here—and we underline the importance of this parallel—one has to unveil what Peirce expressed indirectly (perhaps even beyond his intention) in his "train whistle" experience: questions about a breach of silence, or of a mistrust of articulation are only possible within what we called *silence tout court*. That type of silence does not contain phase A silence alone; the Chandos letter especially involves phase C with a view as to the qualities of D, whereas it reflects on the powers and possibilities of B. This is the position of the letter in the terminology used to characterize *meaning* as an evolving and utterly dynamic concept.

A sentence of Hippocrates is quoted in the letter in Latin by Francis Bacon: "Qui gravi morbo correpti dolores non sentient, iis mens aegrotat", which was not translated by von Hofmannsthal into German, and which reads in its English translation: "One who is suffering from a severe illness yet feels no pain is sick in mind". The line, most probably written around 400 BC on the Greek island Kos, should describe the precarious self after the loss of evidence with which a mind relates to the outer world, its culture, i.e. its silence in a process of articulation (B). If that loss is real but not felt, what uncertainty relations reign between a speaker and the meaning of his words, and what can then be said in a truthful and reliable manner?

4.1 The Meaning of the Chandos Letter

"I would fain give you an answer such as you deserve, fain reveal myself to you entirely, but I do not know how to set about it", writes the author of the letter. Its centerpiece is thus a severe illness and that illness is the letter's metaphor for a loss, which remains without name because its proper cause remains generally unnoticed. But it has a sickness of mind as its consequence—the Chandos letter expresses that consequence, and thus broadens the scope of the problem in Western culture at the beginning of the twentieth century.

Von Hofmannsthal may not have been aware of how his introduction of a *medical* metaphor (the line on a severe illness yet feeling no pain and therefore being sick in mind) entails what the Ancient Greek called *semeiotics*: the study of signs and the making of meaning. His quotation from the Hippocratic corpus would have had no rhetorical or argumentative power if those words were not understood and presented as a *sign*. Galen of Pergamon developed his medical theories approximately two centuries later upon such Hippocratic insights (so that he received the qualification "father of modern medicine") while coupling even more strictly the semiotic dimensions with the medical ones by suggesting that *a physician must read an illness as a text*. The reading of the physician furthers his medical diagnosis and determines the therapy at hand. Emphasis on that reading is, however, accompanied by several bewildering insights. We mention three.

First, there is always uncertainty and a lack of clarity about the facts of morbidity in medical discourse, as the Chandos letter clearly shows in its literary turns and twists. Facts in medicine are generally not understood at the level of signs, because *signs in medicine* are in essence perceived as *deciphered symptoms*. That difference shows clearly how the Chandos letter problematizes the transition of a meaning (the meaning of *sign*: the heart of the issue at stake) from silence in phase C to silence in phase D. Does *silence* in the letter already pertain to a fixation of meaning, as is most often the case in phase D? But symptoms deserve only such status insofar as they can be deciphered—so: what does this mean? The circular observation shows that not any physical component, but the conceptualization of knowledge forms the great barrier in medicine. Bachelard called this insight "the epistemological obstacle par excellence."[24] As a consequence, a medical practitioner experiences how he loses his institutionally secured ability to conduct a discourse on matters of morality or philosophy as well as on life and death. He is in that regard in the same position as Lord Chandos, the author of the letter. The epistemological obstacle causes a situation of the mind in which one has lost, as the text suggests, 'the ability to think or speak of anything coherently and to express insights gained moments before' as C is meant to become D. The Hippocratic quotation seems to describe perfectly what happens when we are urged to understand a sign or symptom. *The illness referred to in the letter is that we are chained to a process of self-explanation without reliable reference to a scientific and/or cultural discourse.* That is important, because these discourses are conceptual systems altogether.[25] In other words: the Von Hofmannsthal letter pertains to deeply engraved semiotic issues (among them the problems of meaning and reference), which touch the metaphysical base of life and thought.

Second, the illness mentioned in the quotation is not an individual fate and cannot serve as an excuse for remaining silent and inactive in discourse. To put illness as a sign in the forefront is still at issue in modern medicine, although the consideration "sign of what?" has become hardly answerable in medicine's modernity because of its loss of discursive reference (a consequence of specialization in medicine). It appears very clear that any natural, everyday-language for articulating that consideration is missing, and nothing can break that silence. Problems inherent in this silence are the major subject of the letter and not a single kaleidoscopic composite can mirror the breach of reference appropriately. The breach shows how a Self lacks its voice as well as its language, and written words represent an elusive alienation. With the loss of a fixated meaning of signs, norms can no longer be formulated, nor can they function as a social beacon. The disjunction between *signifier* and *signified* opened a vertiginous prospect where the limits of language and linguistic articulation are at stake.

[24] Bachelard, G: *La formation de l'esprit scientifique*, 1938. [The Formation of the Scientific Mind. (Transl.: M. McAllester Jones) Boston, 2002].

[25] This observation does not only challenge a human consciousness in terms of Western traditions, but also the cultural embedding of scientific and philosophical observations in its totality with its globalizing conclusions in social- and other sciences, see *Ethan Watters*: "We Aren't the World" at http://www.psmag.com/magazines/pacific-standard-cover-story/joe-henrich-weird-ultimatum-game-shaking-up-psychology-economics-53135/ and: J. Henrich, St., Heine, J. & Norenzyan, A: "The Weirdest People on the World" at http://www2.psych.ubc.ca/~henrich/pdfs/Weird_People_BBS_final02.pdf.

That same disjunction is covered in law and legal discourse by *authority*, because the latter is inherent in the performance of a legal speech act. Lawyers create an exceptional situation when they speak: the disjunction, which Von Hofmannsthal's letter describes, is neglected (or compensated) by the spoken word *as soon as it is a spoken* legal *word*. Lawyers do not like to speak about law in a natural and everyday, non-legal language because the inherent authority of legal language is missing as soon as they change the character of their discourse. In other words: the meaning of a sign in legal discourse is not unfolding through, but created by, the speaker. A question whether the 'world-we-*articulate*' is the 'world-that-*is*' is for them without interest because of this character of a legal speech act and its inherent performance. Semiotic considerations of legal language address the main issue of the Chandos letter, one could say, because the legal practitioner is mostly unaware that he reads his own handwriting when he reads the signs of/in the legal case.

Third, there are not only semiotic complexities in the letter, as linked with the introduction of the medical metaphor, but there were at the turn of the century also complexities of a wider scope, which pertain to *the general condition of Western culture and the understanding of a Self.* At stake is the loss of power to "express (...) lightness and jest, which only great men, convinced of the perilousness of life yet not discouraged by it, can master". It may be startling to consider the challenge to read the condition of mind and of culture *as a text*! That call implies a quest for meaning—which is evident for us in retrospect, but was not evident for poets, philosophers or scientists in the year of the Chandos letter. The call was heard, and the conditions of an inner Self were challenged only at the beginning of a fascinating process: '*the emancipation of the concept of meaning*'. The letter reports on how a failure of language robbed the author of self-confidence and creativity. 'Meaning' would for us be one of the central categories to analyze and reinforce, but it is of interest that the complaint, the letter and the philosophical context of the time in which this document was conceived, did not refer to the concept of meaning as a received concept in science and philosophy.

Although Chandos feels time and again as if he is on the brink of recovery and thoughts begin to form in his mind anew, he ultimately only understands himself as a broken man, who is left mourning the abilities he lost. Neither academic nor everyday discourse, nor the reciting of classical works, for instance, those of Cicero or Seneca, brings him back to those lost treasures. Silence reigns in the letter as if it were a spillover from an omnipresent "cosmic silence". Only if the crisis of language and a deep mistrust of the word are acknowledged, might newly engendered thoughts and means of expression arise. The cultural climate of the days of the Chandos letter is therefore captured in these two phrases: the '*emancipation of meaning as a concept*' and '*the mistrust of the word*'. They are sometimes independent and more often intertwined—an issue for research and contemplation in itself—the basis for a new understanding of discourses in terms of semiotic concepts.[26] Is *silence* as brought to the fore in Von Hofmannsthal's letter a sign for twentieth century Western culture? That seems to be the case, and an in-depth

[26] In particular *legal* discourse.

semiotic understanding delivers the only appropriate reading—notwithstanding its perhaps trivial façade.

4.2 The Emancipation of Meaning

An *emancipation of meaning as a philosophical concept*, one could conclude, required several decades, and the question whether it has finally taken place during the beginning of the twenty-first century cannot be definitively answered. Has a semiotic understanding of *silence* been a sign loud enough during those first decades in which new physics, new sciences and new social insights appeared to blossom, which were overruling traditional meanings and washing the importance of silence away? We focus on the transitional writings of Lady Welby-Gregory (1837–1912). She published in broadly respected academic journals during the last days of the nineteenth century, such as *Mind* and *The Monist*. Her first philosophical book publication was the 1903 *What is Meaning? Studies in the Development of Significance*. Her approach to meaning was in terms of *significs*, a neologism that came surprisingly close to the term *semiotics* as conceived in the philosophy of Peirce. The term "theory of meaning" was developed later in the twentieth century as distinguished from a theory of naming (Plato, Locke and others) and figured in a great number of philosophical disputes over the last half-century. Unfortunately, that term has also been used to mean a great number of different things. A first sort of theory of meaning is a *semantic* theory, assigning semantic contents to expressions of a language. These differ according to whether they assign propositions as the meanings of sentences and, if they do, what view they take of the nature of these propositions. A second type of theory states the facts in virtue of their semantically determined expressions and thus comes near to Peircean semiotics.

The general process of *emancipation of meaning* dates from Lady Welby's first book until the publication of C.K. Ogden and I.A. Richards' *The Meaning of Meaning*, 1923.[27] These authors published their text because, as they stated in their introduction, "the moment seems to have arrived when an effort to draw attention to Meanings may meet with support." One sort of support came from the psychologists of those days, another from the manifestly inadequate forms of speech creeping into High Courts and political debates in the English Parliament. The dates from 1903 to 1923 are those of the suggested emancipation process pertaining to the concept of meaning. Petrilli quotes the Ogden specialist Terrence Gordon, who suggested that "The Meaning of Meaning" was a firm recognition of Welby's significs, not simply

[27] The complexity of many implications of this view inspired *Ogden* apparently more than Richards. *Sebeok* published a letter with a postscript from *Richards* in which the latter criticizes *Hardwick*'s reconstruction in his edition of the *Peirce-Welby* letters. The tenor of *Richards*' criticism is, that "*Ramsey*, as a Winchester Schoolboy, used to review the toughest things…", indicating that *Ramsey*'s role in promoting thoughts of *Peirce, Welby, Wittgenstein* and others was largely overestimated in *Hardwick*'s edition. See: Thomas A. *Sebeok*: *Semiotics in the United States*, Indiana UP 1991, p. 137.

a matter of affinities but of a closure by means of the exploration of a new dimension of meaning now embedded in significs. An almost final emancipation of the concept in Ogden and Richard's book opened up what today is understood as a sign-theory, leading to the elaboration of a technical definition of context that underpins the entire book. Petrilli concludes that today's sign-theory may be considered as a further development of significs/semiotics. She mentions that Ogden and Richards were not alone in stimulating this development, but were accompanied by Peirce, Vailati, Bakhtin and others.[28]

Lady Welby published her second book in 1911: *Significs and Language: The Articulate Form of Our Expressive and Interpretive Resources,* and contributed in the same year to the famous edition of the *Encyclopedia Britannica* (still available on its website). One finds there very traditional descriptions like: "SYMBOL (Gr., a sign), the term given to a visible object representing to the mind the semblance of something which is not shown but realized by association with it". And one encounters Lady Welby with her text on SIGNIFICS: "The term "Significs" may be defined as the science of meaning or the study of significance, provided sufficient recognition is given to its practical aspect as a method of mind, one which is involved in all forms of mental activity, including that of logic." It is striking how the traditional explanation of *symbol* follows after this refreshingly new entry on *sign/significs* in this 1911 edition.

5 Tractatus, Meaning, Silence

"Silent/silence" was the last word of Ludwig Wittgenstein's 1922 "Tractatus Logico-Philosophicus". One could say in hindsight, that exactly this word made his text famous. What sense does it have, and what meaning should it convey to the reader who has just finished a layered philosophical text at some distance from comparable traditional philosophical books and essays? Was "silence"—think of Lord Chandos' peculiar circumstances—the conclusion we expected to read? Does it represent the meaning of the essay?

5.1 Meaning

Any elaborate answer will ultimately pertain to *meaning*. This has hitherto not been considered in the standard literature about the Tractatus. The text *shows* rather than *argues* how meaning, although often individually active, stems from extremely general and non-individualistic sources and regions. Some of them form a background

---

[28] For an analysis of several of these articles from 1891 on, see *Hardwick,* Charles S.: *Semiotic and Significs: Correspondence between Charles S. Peirce and Victoria Lady Welby.* (Assistance of James Cook) Indiana UP 1977, p. xx ff.

in logics, mathematics and other articulations at the borderlines of natural and artificial languages. But in general, meanings seem to have originated in indefinable and often mysterious spheres. That route can (with the help of insights and terminologies explained in the paragraphs above) be described as *a path from cosmic silence to super-individualistic articulation,* fixation and application. That path is ours. It is ours as individuals and ours as a society and its cultural embedding.[29] *Wittgenstein's Tractatus is written as a sign.* It wants to be the sign of the unknown and unknowable character of elements assembling the road to meaning.

5.2 Bertrand Russell

Bertrand Russell's drafts of an "Introduction" to Ludwig Wittgenstein's "Tractatus" do not, however, fully honor these insights. Wittgenstein did not agree with either the German draft or the English final version. Russell begins the ultimately published text, underlining how the essay honors "Symbolism".[30] The concept relates to more than one philosophical question. If one thing symbolizes another, we are led to ask, "what relation must one fact (such as a sentence) have to another in order to be *capable* of being a symbol for that other?". Moreover, *accurate* Symbolism is defined as "Symbolism in which a sentence 'means' something quite definite." The two remarks focus indeed on the central issue: one remark pertains correctly to *meaning.* Closely related, however, we meet another on "the sentence" or "the word" as the basic unit of language. This latter formulation was already shortly criticized in the above lines will be deeper criticized in following chapters. As a consequence, Russell describes the "perhaps most fundamental thesis of Mr. Wittgenstein's theory" as follows: "Given the syntax of a language, the meaning of a sentence is determinate as soon as the meaning of the component words is known. In order that a certain sentence should assert a certain fact there must, however the language may be constructed, be something in common between the structure of the sentence and the structure of the fact". This description of the Tractatus' essence leads to what was formulated in the very beginning: "Starting from the principles of Symbolism and the relations which are necessary between words and things in every language, it applies the results of this inquiry to various departments of traditional philosophy, showing in each case how traditional philosophy and traditional solutions arise out of ignorance of the principles of Symbolism and out of misuse of language". To fulfill this task, Russell adds, the Tractatus passes "successively to

[29] It is not ours without protest, resistance and attempts to liberating insights. See: Comité Invisible: *L'insurrection qui Vient*, Paris 2007, in particular p. 81 ff.

[30] The misunderstandings because of this terminology are important in hindsight and might elucidate what was unarticulated in Wittgensttein's mind. The concept of "Symbolism" was used and perceived differently from today, and in fashion as the 1923 Ogden & Richards publication showed in their subtitle: C.K. Ogden and I.A. Richards: *The Meaning of Meaning. A study of the Influence of Language upon Thought and of the Science of Symbolism*, London 1923.

Theory of Knowledge, Principles of Physics, Ethics, and finally the Mystical (das Mystische)."[31]

One can guess that Russell's use of the expression "symbol" and "symbolism" was in Wittgenstein's mind not a representation of his continuous confrontation with the unknowable, hence it formed a misunderstanding of the semiotic (i.e. meaning-related) impetus of his text. It is in hindsight indeed strange when the reader is invited by Russell to notice that a part of the "Tractatus ... deals with Symbolism", which leads to a concern "with the conditions which would have to be fulfilled by a logically perfect language". Wittgenstein may well have thought that Russell should better have read and applied the Welby article on "Significs" in the Encyclopedia Britannica 1911 as a basis for understanding the "Tractatus".[32] What about Russell's insight in this text?

5.3 Vienna

Any focus on the *Tractatus Logico-Philosophicus* shows how *the sign* and *sign functions* are a central issue in all respects. They do not, however, reach conclusions about semiotic perspectives in that text nor in any context of the book. Reading Wittgenstein gives rise to the feeling that Peircean insights about sign and sign functions had appeared hitherto only in a pre-semiotic form. An example would be the insight that a sentence functions as the context for a word, and the latter has a sign function only in that context. Peirce claimed that a sign alone is not a sign. Now consider that notwithstanding its high philosophical value, Wittgenstein's *Tractatus*

[31] Bertrand Russell: *Introduction* in: Ludwig Wittgenstein: *Tractatus Logico-Philosophicus*, Routledge & Kegan Paul, London 1958[7th Ed.], p. 7.

[32] Russell must have read the *Encyclopedia Britannica 1911* edition which presents: SYMBOL, the term given to a visible object representing to the mind the semblance of something which is not shown but realized by association with it. This is conveyed by the ideas usually associated with the symbol; thus the palm branch is the symbol of victory and the anchor of hope. Much of early Christian symbolism owes its origin to pagan sources, the interpretations of the symbols having a different meaning".

The same source had no philosophically reliable commentary for sign, only in its connection with sign-board, saying "SIGN—Board, strictly a board placed or hung before any building to designate its character. The French *enseigne* indicates its essential connection with what is known in English as a flag, and in France banners not infrequently took the place of signboards in the middle ages. Sign-boards, however, are best known in the shape of painted or carved advertisements for shops, inns, &c., they are in fact one of various emblematic methods used from time immemorial for publicly calling attention to the place to which they refer. The ancient Egyptians and Greeks are known to have used signs, and many Roman examples are preserved, among them the widely-recognized bush to indicate a tavern, from which is derived the proverb "Good wine needs no bush." In some cases, such as the bush, or the three balls of pawnbrokers, certain signs became identified with certain trades, but apart from these the emblems employed by traders—evolving often into trade-marks—may in great part be grouped according to their various origins." The same edition contained, however, Lady Welby's text on significs. The philosophical and psychological distance between the two is extremely important.

does, as we already mentioned, function as a *sign* for the origins and first recognitions of ideas that unfold only later in philosophy. Among these ideas is semiotics, so that a study of Wittgenstein's *Tractatus* pertains to its sign-function within culture and history, with an emphasis on semiotics, the Peircean study of signs. What sign, what cultural value is involved here? Above all: how could the *meaning* of that famous book change when such questions are raised?

An influential issue is Viennese culture around the turn of the century. At least three books might help to deepen our understanding of the cultural ties to Wittgenstein's *Tractatus*. The three include essential themes such as meaning, language, logic, thought formation, representation, imaging and consciousness.[33] They are, however, not specific to Viennese culture, which gives us reason to defend a wider context of understanding with an emphasis on semiotic themes. The latter direct our attention to Lady Welby's Amsterdam connections and in particular to the Amsterdam Signific Circle.[34] Wittgenstein's rather adventurous and difficult organization of the trip to The Netherlands had several dimensions, which are partly described in Von Wright's Introduction to the text he discovered in Vienna and published as the *Prototractatus*, and partly in Russell's autobiography.

Von Wright reports in his introduction to the *Prototractatus* how Wittgenstein left Cambridge, moved to Norway and sold his furniture and other things. That money "was evidently used to finance Wittgenstein's visit to Holland and meeting with Russell in December 1919", v. Wright writes. 'Holland', meant: The Hague, the Netherlands, where the meeting indeed took place in mid-December. Russell writes "(…) where we spent a week arguing his book line by line (…)".[35] The trip was already planned in August of the same year, when he suggested in a letter from the post-war prison camp to meet Russell in a politically neutral place: Switzerland or Holland. It seems unclear what type of copy of the Tractatus Wittgenstein had with him when he was in Holland. But it is certain that the episode was in the midst of the year-long difficulties in having the essay published—a period that already had begun with the summer 1918 refusal by the Vienna publishers Jahoda & Siegel. It is important to emphasize that Russell had been reading Wittgenstein (and most probably discussing with him, apart from his own *Principles of Mathematics*) with a well-acquired knowledge of Peirce's theory—as outlined in a Peirce letter from

[33] Allan Janik & Stephen Toulmin: *Wittgenstein's Vienna*, New York 1971; Carl E. Schorske: *Fin-de-Siècle Vienna,* New York 1981; Eric R. Kandel: *The Age of Insight,* New York 2012. See also: L. Wittgenstein: *Prototractatus*, Cornell UP 1971 and -Id.-: *Tractatus Logico-Philosophicus,* London 1922; –Id.-: *Vermischte Bemerkungen* Frankfurt/M. 1977, *Culture and Value,* Chicago UP 1980.

[34] See Jan M. Broekman & Larry Catá Backer: *Signs in Law—A Source Book*, Springer 2015, Part II, p. 27–89.

[35] See B. Russell: *The Autobiography of Bertrand Russell.* London 1948, Vol. II, p. 100: "The furniture and books which he had had in Cambridge were stored there, and he expressed a willingness to sell them to me. (…) They were in fact worth far more than he supposed, and it was the best bargain I ever made. This transaction made it possible for Wittgenstein to come to The Hague (…)". A report about the content of the week's talks with Wittgenstein is completely absent in the autobiography, apart from a suggestion: "arguing his book line by line".

October 12, 1904. As we know from Charles Hardwick, who edited the Peirce-Welby letters, Lady Welby had, copied that letter and sent it to Russell. Peirce had already written a review of Lady Welby's "*What is Meaning?*" (1903) and Russell's *The Principles of Mathematics (1903)* for *The Nation* in 1903.[36] Susan Petrilli broadens the strong connections between Peirce, Welby and the Amsterdam Signific Circle on the one hand and Wittgenstein's text on the other when writing:

"Wittgenstein distinguished between 'names' and 'propositions,' analyzing the relation among 'names' or 'simple signs' used in the proposition, where the object or meaning is of the conventional order. Welby also spoke of simple signs, of 'bare signs.' In Wittgenstein's view, the rule or code that relates the sign to the object of reference is conventional, that is, arbitrary, and therefore cannot be discovered simply by guessing".[37] Similarly to Wittgenstein's analysis in the *Tractatus,* Petrilli suggests, "(…) Welby's language analysis is not limited to describing phenomena of signification, language and thought, but rather aims to account for their generation.[38] (…) Meaning may be defined as a class of verbal and nonverbal sign materials that reciprocally defer to each other. Each term is either an interpretant sign or an interpreted sign of the other, depending on signifying context, in semiotic processes where the interpretant sign replaces the interpreted sign, which it somehow develops. Identity of the sign can only be defined in continuous deferral and shift

[36] Ch. Hardwick (Ed.): *Semiotics and Significs. The Correspondence between Charles S. Peirce and Victoria Lady Welby,* Indiana UP 1977, p. xxx: "Russell's opinion was mixed. He was not much impressed by Peirce's division between Firstness, Secondness and Thirdness. […] Russell went on to comment "… I hold it quite essential to have a method of expressing relations, and I have always thought very highly of Dr. Peirce for having introduced such a method." Hardwick adds importantly: "But if Russell and Cook Wilson are not overtly impressed by Peirce's letter, Peirce did acquire a disciple in C.K. Ogden, who, while a student at Cambridge, was a protégé of Lady Welby." His later work with I.A. Richards: *The Meaning of Meaning* forms for Hardwick "the first serious consideration of Peirce's work in semiotic". It is not difficult to also register close connections with Wittgenstein's Tractatus: the manuscript was discussed in The Hague with a Russell who was much more informed about and engaged in significs/semiotics than we normally consider.

[37] Petrilli remarks here: "Arbitrariness is a category proposed by Ferdinand Saussure [1857–1913] in *Cours de linguistique generale*, 1916. He characterizes the relation between *signifiant* and *signifié* in individual words, or in individual nonverbal signs that so form 'conventional,' social codes, with this word".

[38] Petrilli considers: "The work of scholars like Welby and the others so far mentioned, contribute to illustrating the more complex levels of signifying, expressive and communicative processes, without reducing them to the mere status of information transmission and message exchange. Each of these authors calls our attention to the importance for signifying processes of iconism, otherness, and relations among signs beyond systemic restrictions. This orientation also helps evidence the dialectical-dialogic nature of interpretivetranslative processes in the relation between the categories of 'unity' and 'distinction,' as Welby argues, between the 'centripetal forces' and 'centrifugal forces' operating in language, as Bakhtin puts it (1975), and, therefore, between the power of centralization and decentralization, between monologism and polylogism, monolingualism and plurilingualism, respectively oriented by the logic of identity or the logic of otherness. Thanks to such dialectics, knowledge and truth are never given once and for all, but, on the contrary, are open to investigation and subject to modification in the continuous work of adapting to and generating new contexts and communicative practices, beginning from everyday life.

processes: to be this sign here, a sign must always be interpreted and become other thanks to the interpretant sign that translates and develops its meaning".[39]

Several remarks are due in relation to this rich and insightful quotation. First, there is *the cultural and philosophical context.* It is not only Wittgenstein's manuscript that waits to see the light of day and find its public. Around 1919, the year of Wittgenstein's meeting with Russell in The Hague, The Netherlands, there existed a bewildering number of insights that waited to become public and enter the philosophical debate. Some of them are mentioned in the Petrilli quotation above, and what was known in those days under the name "significs" is perhaps one of the most promising motives. Wittgenstein's meeting with Russell focused on the question of whether to publish the manuscript; but seeing Russell and talking to him included many issues beneath the surface of difficulties pertaining to that prospect. Overseeing the latter is a prominent subject of the books on Wittgenstein, Vienna and the turn of the century. The most elaborate proof of this constellation is in Janik & Toulmin's book, in particular in the pages that mention Russell and were written by Toulmin, who studied under Wittgenstein in 1941 and 1946–1947 at Cambridge. Toulmin's thesis that Wittgenstein was not understood in Cambridge and that Russell's attempt to write an appropriate introduction to the Tractatus failed in Wittgenstein's eyes because he was "a Viennese genius who exercised his talents and personality on philosophy among other things, and just happened to be living and working in England", seems too narrow.[40] Its exclusive focus on Vienna, or on Vienna as a symbol of alienation from Anglo-Saxon traditions, does not pay due respect to the variety of European centers wrestling with the new cultural and philosophical insights at hand.

5.4 Peirce and Russell on Meaning

That context leads us to Peirce again, who wrote a positive review of Welby's "What is Meaning" and Russell's "The Principles of Mathematics" in The Nation.[41] Russell had knowledge of that review, which led to an intensive correspondence between Welby and Peirce, edited by Charles S. Hardwick—texts which play a dominant role in Peirce studies and semiotic analyses. Prior to that publication, a daughter of Lady Welby, Mrs. Henry Cust, published a book in 1931 on her mother's correspondence. The Introduction to that book by L.P. Jacks, clarifies what the striving for recognition of the concept of meaning implied in the Russell—Wittgenstein context.[42] It reads: "All science, all cosmology, all metaphysics, all theology, all art even—yes, art most of all—are attempts to compel the universe to declare 'what it

[39] Susan Petrilli: *Signifying and Understanding.* De Gruyter Mouton, The Hague 2009, p. 541 f.

[40] Janik & Toulmin, Op.Cit., p. 22.

[41] Peirce: C. P. 8, 171.

[42] Mrs. H. Cust: *Other Dimensions. A Selection from the Later Correspondence of Victoria Lady Welby*. Introduction: L.P Jacks, Jonathan Cape, London 1931. See pp 12 and 13.

means'. In that question lies the generating source of intellectual and spiritual activity, the driving power of all that may be summed up under the name of philosophy. The impulse that prompts philosophy, and sustains it through the ages, is thus identically the same as that which prompts and sustains the question 'what do you mean?' addressed to the speaker of an obscure sentence or the writer of an obscure book".

The proximity of the idea "to read the illness as a text" (remember the Chandos letter) to the insight that "the universe may be compared to a spoken sentence imperfectly heard" bridges millennia, and still fascinates. "The only legitimate ultimate why is the question Why do we ask why, why do we want to know why? Why should life be a riddle and why do we want to 'solve' it?"—Lady Welby wrote.

There are clearly two different though related issues at stake: on the one hand the necessity to think of language as a composite of words, and on the other to overcome or even be inspired by a growing mistrust of the word as the sole carrier of meaning. The two are, of course, closely related. But their distinction relates to a further differentiation between *significs* and *semiotics*, whereas that same distinction leads *en plus* to the power of significs and semiotics in law and legal discourse, whereby sign and meaning acquire new articulations. Studies of meaning as initiated by Lady Welby focused on the word as the main constitutive element of language beginning with her early articles and the 1903 edition of her book on that subject. She analyzed different kinds of sense within the broader concept of meaning through in-depth studies of three particular words: sense, meaning and significance. Relations between them and their neighboring concepts such as ethics, aesthetics, pragmatics, norms and (social) values would result in the understanding of more levels of human language and consciousness. That was the task of *significs* she saw ahead of her, while keeping traditional ideas about language alive.

Peirce envisaged a broader science of semiotic that embraced all sorts of signs (there is not one single type of sign!), which include icons, symbols, indices etc., as well as—on the same level of analysis and observation—the relations of signs with objects and interpretants. This is important, because the semiotic project is not an issue of the word alone, as Peirce continuously stresses. Word-language is the most prominent in our daily language explorations but in that same context we refer to other languages, which we are less aware of and master less strictly; body language is a good example here. So this is one of the important differences between *significs* and *semiotics*.

More differences between them become very clear: significs concentrates on words/components being reliable in a natural language, whereas semiotics is aware of the need to go beyond any mistrust of word-language. Peirce's correspondence with Lady Welby reveals that awareness. Wittgenstein did not aim to contribute to significs or semiotics, but he was thinking of all of this. His notes written between 1929 and 1948 and published in 1967 by Anscombe and Von Wright with the title "Zettel" clearly show fragments of a developing theory of signs.

So Welby, so Wittgenstein. In her path-breaking studies on Lady Welby's works, Petrilli highlights how the latter "underlines the need to critique language, to highlight the signifying power of words and expressions, and to better define their meanings in light of the context of discourse which they somehow include—the terms 'person', 'self', 'life', 'religion' are signaled as examples.[43] Reference to the larger context is necessary for the purpose of minimizing the negative effects of misunderstanding and improving the work of conceptualization". Such observations are perfectly in line with the approaches and attitudes of several other *signific* movements and circles, among them the Amsterdam *Signific Circle* which both Russell and Wittgenstein had knowledge of. Members of the Amsterdam *Circle* refer on the one hand to the wealth of possibilities when critically analyzing the word as a major component of language, and on the other to a deep mistrust about the meaning a word appears to have and to transmit. The two approaches are fruitful in so far as they fit in to a genuine insight into the decline of the Occident (*Spengler*) as well as the meaning of *Wittgenstein*'s last sentence in his *Tractatus*: "7. Wovon man nicht sprechen kann, darüber muß man schweigen"/"Whereof one cannot speak, thereof one must be silent" (Ogden). "What we cannot speak about we must pass over in silence" (Pears/McGuiness).

5.5 *The Tractatus' Silence*

The contrast between Russell's understanding of the Tractatus and Wittgenstein's most probable intentions might bring us back to the last word of the essay. What is the meaning of the disputed concept of 'silence'? Russell did not pay attention to the engenderment of that final word; his approach focused on the "newness" of the text as a philosophy of language and its symbolic functions. The position of Russell has been outlined so that we can now draw some conclusions pertaining to the term "silence".

1. We already suggested in the opening sentences of this paragraph how *a path from cosmic silence to super-individualistic articulation* and application was in the background of Wittgenstein's multifaceted observations. It would have been unfitting for Russell to conclude that Wittgenstein's Tractatus is written as a sign—a sign of the existence of many unknown and unknowable elements that built the road to meaning. Meaning and silence intertwine here, and that intertwining characterizes the construction of the entire text—including the treacherous mathematical order of its fragments.[44] The latter does *not* conceal the look-around attitude of the author!
2. Russell was completely, but Wittgenstein only partly and hesitatingly, accepting of the idea of language being founded on "the word as the basic unit of language",

[43] Susan Petrilli,. *Signifying and Understanding. Reading the Works of Victoria Welby and the Signific Movement.* De Gruyter/Mouton, Berlin 2009, p. 139–141,747.

[44] It is interesting that the numbers in the *Prototractatus* (Prototractatus: An early version of Tractatus logico-philosophicus, Hardcover—1971 B. F. McGuinness (Editor) are not always correctly maintained. See: Jinho Kang: "On the Composition of the Prototractatus" in *The Philosophical Quarterly*, Vol. 55, 2005, p. 1–20.

and therefore words being "eminent particles of linguistic articulation". This atomistic philosophy can be supported while maintaining the concept of symbol but *not* the idea of meaning as context-dependent, or of Peirce's insight that "a sign on its own is not a sign".[45] Can one, in this light, treat the concept of meaning "as a word"? Wittgenstein tried, and gave up.[46] Russell did not notice.

3. Russell's remark on the "content" and "thematic order" of the Tractatus text, as we already quoted: "successively to Theory of Knowledge, Principles of Physics, Ethics, and finally the Mystical (das Mystische)" is a serious misunderstanding. That so-called order is not an order of coherent themes, propositions, subjects and philosophical insights, but the indication of fields where the author had been looking around in while philosophizing, challenging and evaluating his own and others' views, considering "Whereof one cannot speak …"
4. The Tractatus is in essence a collection of fragments, attempts, stages of *possible* thoughts without definable result and without fixated functions or conclusions, which belong to traditionally anchored philosophical schemes. What Russell does not focus on in his discussion with Wittgenstein in The Hague, or propose to address in his Introduction, is the *process character* of the text—as suggested in the title "Tractatus". The process brings Wittgenstein to consider a transcendence of *silence as non-speaking* in an internal turn, which has not been articulated. This turn provides the essential depth of meaning in the last sentence. If one can or cannot speak, then this articulation will fail when we speak *about* or *to, from* or *for* and thus fail to speak *in* —which is the place where one honors the process of meaning and being. *Silence and Tractatus*: in the midst of zone or phase C[47] the author focuses on the borderlines of silence and articulation (B) and warns us about the dangers of fixation and a standstill of vital processes when articulation was finalized in phase D.[48] "While looking around", the Tractatus concludes, "look back at silence":—this is the essence of the text.

6 Legal Semiotics (1): Silence and 'Saying for Law'

Why focus on semiotics in law, and not on legal liability, personhood, justice, legal correctness or logic in the first place? Those issues would be more relevant, it seems. Everyone entering the law's discourse might encounter them, whereas no one will

---

[45] Ch. S. Peirce: *Letter to Lady Welby, 23 December 1908*: "I define a Sign as anything which is so determined by something else, called its Object, and so determines an effect upon a person, which effect I call its Interpretant, that the latter is thereby mediately determined by the former".

[46] See Wittgenstein's much debated idea quoted everywhere as "meaning in use", and the fate of that slogan in pragmatism, positivism and other philosophical discourses.

[47] Exemplary is the discussion with Russell and his introductory text.

[48] We distinguished and explained on page 7 those phases: (A) A *cosmic silence*; (B) A silence to be characterized as an *articulatory setting*; (C) A silence *in the process of articulation,* and (D) A silence *articulated.*

be urged to begin with considerations on meaning in a semiotic context. Yet, one has to keep in mind that legal practitioners have no other instrument to unfold in their profession than *language*, broadly formulated: *linguistic articulations*. They not only 'use' language to perform their tasks, but they are also determined by the limits of languages. It is always possible that they change the natural character of their words, for instance by means of professionalizing their expressions, but they have to keep the reference to the natural language that happens to be the context of their activity. It means in essence that they are bound by *meanings articulated in linguistic concepts*. Lawyers can give names to occurrences, even without our (laymen's, citizens') understanding—but those names are founded in a "say for law" of a judge, with emphasis on the *saying*. In other words: there is no unsayable law, nor any mystic source for the application of laws or for legislation. The conclusion fascinates: *law is exclusively tied to linguistic articulation.* Is that a stable bridge towards the study of a theory of sign and meaning, called semiotics?

6.1 Semiotics

A lawyer pleading before a Court to be allowed and being able to 'say for law' touches in this pleading on the most important fragments of social life. She was in a position to ask a group of functionaries for permission to qualify the issue(s) at hand in a particular manner: the legal manner. At the same time she asked to work from now on with the words 'said for law' in all structures of representation she encounters. Those structures reach from her client in particular to society in general. That position, including the meanings involved and the signs it is being allowed to bear, is deeply social by its nature. No wonder that legal semiotics should be(come) a pillar of legal education.

The example of the lawyer asking the Court 'to say for law' includes a particular social structure, which we generally call 'institutional'. Those features do *not* relate to the particular language in the first place, but to the social structure we qualify as 'legal'. As law students or as lawyers we have to recognize that we belong to that institution. It says *firstly*, that the lawyer asking the Court is and should be *a lawyer like all others.* There is no exception to that rule, and the language in effect before the Court has in that regard only one type of speaker. *Secondly*, the meaning of 'saying/being said for law' is *not* in the hands of the lawyer or of judges speaking, but generally in the hands of *others*—possibly also non-lawyers (members of a Jury, for instance). This complex structure indicates how legal signs often refer to a diversity of social meanings and interpretations of meaning. Lawyers speak as if they utter a natural language but their application of that language suggests at least a parallel realm of meaning: law as an institution. This immanent parallel between natural language and artificial language—initiated in the latter—has been explored by philosophers of language in the twentieth century, such as Russell and Wittgenstein, as well as specialists in research on meaning such as Lady Welby (1903), De Haan (1916), Ogden & Richards (1923) or Ch. Morris (1946). Their philosophy of language was in many regards also a philosophy of law and legal discourse. Those philosophical approaches concerned the foundational dimensions of a lawyer's activity, with priority given to their specific management of meaning—which includes legal semiotics.

6.2 Mistrust

The case of the mistrusted word may bewilder anyone who enters whatever form of legal education. The possibility in itself, and each reality which does not immediately dismiss such mistrust, is at least challenging. It is fascinating to enter the field of the study of (legal) signs in law, or 'legal semiotics' from this angle. Most certainly, it has more weight in law and legal discourse than in any other type of linguistic articulation. Consider what a lawyer can advise his client or how a judge can formulate his final judgment, when he or she mistrusts the word used to express an opinion because it does not guarantee its power of reference, or provide any certainty about the precise fitting and meaning of the utterance? One should not underestimate the power of *semiotics* (the study of signs) in its attempt to understand the problematic social consequences of such mistrust, which was so culturally *en vogue* at the beginning of the twentieth century.

But mistrust is not the only component to be encountered in legal semiotics, as the three preceding volumes have shown.[49] Understanding human discourse (of which legal discourse is an outstanding example) is always confronted with arbitrariness and uncertainty in the determination of meaning. First, there is a link between concept and context—the meaning of one word can differ importantly if used in context *'a'* or in context *'b'*. That uncertainty is repeated continuously, as the difference between a word-directed and a world-directed approach shows. Both: the world of words (as in logocentrism) and the world of the 'real worlds' (as in Klages' "soul") should be analyzed according to the nature of signs. What strikes one first, is that signs urge us to analyze relations rather than 'things'. But a dimension of severe mistrust comes again to the fore when both types of signs are characterized as 'arbitrary'. Are they also arbitrary as *legal* signs? Indeed, meanings depend on social conventions and habits rather than on stable fixations of connections between sign/word and object/thing, as the social and legal structure of a Court proves.

It is important for law and legal discourse that a mistrust of the word is seldom admitted to enter surface levels of legal talk and texts.[50] One observes rather the

[49] See: Jan M. Broekman & Francis J. Mootz III (Eds): *The Semiotics of Law in Legal Education.* Springer 2011; Jan M. Broekman & Larry Catá Backer: *Lawyers Making Meaning. The Semiotics of Law in Legal Education II.* Springer 2013; Jan M. Broekman & Larry Catá Backer: *Signs in Law—A Source Book. The Semiotics of Law in Legal Education III.* Springer 2015.

[50] *Kristeva,* Julia. *Semeiotikè. Recherches pour une sémanalyse.* Paris 1969, p. 278 f. *Greimas,* Algirdas J. & *Rastier,* François:"The Interaction of Semiotic Constraints" in: *Yale French Studies,*

inverse: at the surface levels words are studied and fixated, and must *avoid* a confrontation with other meanings, those other-than-spoken or written at the surface of daily life, or accepted as belonging to a professional discourse! Those tactics of avoidance are a determinative part of law and legal discourse, and the struggle to implement them was always a feature of an unfolding education in law.

6.3 Legal Education

To study law is never a solitary activity; it requires training and skill formation in complex social behaviors. To study law is a specific form of socialization at various levels. It differs importantly from classical ex-cathedra education and prioritizes focusing on meaning in each mixture of information, discussion and decision-making in the field. It is in this light a remarkable fact that readers of books on law are not accustomed to consulting even a few pages on legal education.

Yet, the forms of legal education touch the heart of the matter: such an education should and could duplicate the intentions of law and legal discourse. What else is law striving for than equilibrated information about social norms and values, meanings and attitudes, for short: the dynamics of life in society? Law students discuss, create and check opinions, write and read, listen and decide. All these properties have the appropriation and execution of language and linguistic articulation as their main theme. Structures determining speech-acts and texts bearing the qualification "law" or "legal" are the law student's field!

6.4 Surface- and Deep Structure

Word and meaning travel from depth to surface and back into deep levels of language, and again from deep layers of linguistics articulation to levels of manifestation. We all know those dynamics from our everyday-life experiences, but it is difficult to understand and accept that law and legal discourse form no exception in that regard. The Dutch legal scholar J. I. De Haan stressed that a word never has the same meaning for two different individuals: "This is even true for a speaker and a hearer in the same conversation, not even when they live in 'the same shades of will'. And, what is more, a word has not continuously the same meaning in the hands of the same user. A word never carries exactly the same meaning twice. The expression "the" meaning of a word is incorrect and misleading. That is also the case with the claim that the word "has" a meaning. A word "has" no meaning or meanings; it "is" united with an infinite number of meanings by something that

Vol. 41, 1968. *Greimas* A.J: *Sémantique Structurale* (1966) [Engl. Tr.: Structural Semantics: An Attempt at a Method, 1983].

cannot be perceived (…) Thinking cannot split or unite the continuous and the discrete, but it can only separate and unite them *at the same time*."[51]

No linguist ever expressed the concept of 'the word' in a purer sense than the Dutch mathematician and philosopher G. Mannoury, who stated: "The word is reciprocal and thus equal; it is relation and thus difference. It is the act of the speaker and the act of the hearer to separate what is inseparable and to fixate what is not lasting. The word is indefensible definiteness".[52] It is most remarkable how these words remained unnoticed. The more we reflect upon words, the more we become aware of their importance for general, and in particular legal, discourse.

The "law-language" theme remains one of the primary interests of lawyers and legal theoreticians until today. The trajectory of legal semiotics leads from the *mistrust of the word* towards an insight into the *dynamics of meaning* based on a functional understanding of expressiveness in time and space, between the surface of language and its deep-reaching levels of engenderment.[53]

6.5 Sign and Norm

The situation in which one encounters three components of legal discourse: (a) the problem of inadequate expression, (b) the need to understand the flexibility of language, and (c) the central position of meaning, is more complex and reaches further than any traditional philosophy of law has suggested. To understand law "as a system of signs" (*Kevelson*'s slogan) means that we should understand the engenderment of law and legal discourse the way we understand the engenderment of a sign, so eloquently described by Peirce. The "as" in this *Kevelson* phrase does not only mean: "like", or "as identical as possible", but also: "the same manner in which". One concludes: the "as" can be understood as indicating the dynamics of the meaning-making process in law and of law.[54] Understanding those dynamics is perhaps a final step in the emancipation of the concept of meaning, which unfolds when grasping the context and engenderment of a sign. As a consequence, there are two inspiring steps to be discovered:

- The *first* consists in perceiving the interdependence of all components of discourse. Not one element of language we use or produce is ever beyond interdependency with others: a word alone is not a word; just as a sign alone is not a sign. That includes also an approach to "sign, meaning, and norm". Any

[51] J.I. de Haan: "Essence and Task of Legal Significs" in Jan M. Broekman & Larry Catá Backer: *Signs in Law—A Source Book.* Springer 2015 p. 55 f.

[52] Gerrit Mannoury: "Significs and Philosophy" (1922) in: Broekman & Catá Backer: *Signs in Law*, Op. Cit., p. 41 f.

[53] It is fascinating how this mistrust seems a theme of the exchange of ideas among Peirce and Lady Welby during their years of correspondence from 1898 to 1912 (see Hardwick, note v).

[54] Roberta Kevelson. *The Law as a System of Signs*. Plenum Press, London/New York 1988; Jan M Broekman. & Larry Catà Backer: *Lawyers Making Meaning*. Op. Cit., p. 195 f.

meaning-making process is therefore an issue of context and of transparency: only thanks to existing meanings can other meanings brought into existence.
- The *second* consists in keeping an eye on the dynamics between the surface- and the deep structure of discourse. A word spoken or written is always temporarily located at the surface of a communicative activity; it can at any moment disappear or be made to disappear into the layers of engenderment whence it came. How is a norm characterized in this theoretical framework, how a sign, and what about meaning here?

6.6 Meaning and the Third

Sign and meaning are entangled in mutual relationships, which are in their turn at home in triadic patterns of relation. Norms can only fulfill their social role as an outcome of those triadic relations. That indicates the dubious character of understanding 'Law as Command'—a widely accepted analytical theory about law's origin. Norms surface thanks to a third. A third is an always present and functional interpretant under the condition that sign and meaning are at stake.

Peirce confirms that this interpretant should not exclusively focus on being immersed in a cultural pessimism or a reigning mistrust of the word when one speaks. Russell made a thoughtful remark on the patterning of the interpretant, when he wrote in November 1905 to Lady Welby: "… any triadic relation f (x, y, z) may be reducible to the assertion between y and z of a relation which is a function of x. But this only gives equivalence; philosophically the meaning is changed, though not the truth or falsehood. …"

Indeed, only triadic relations give signs a meaning and sense. If that is correct and inspiring (beyond traditional analytical philosophy of law and language—which it seems to be) then the "interpretant" does not interpret anything, but functions in such a way that a sign can exist and be perceived to be functioning in the surface of language and discourse. In other words: *the third is not a referent: the third only makes reference possible.*

Where semioticians took the non-sign as referent for the sign, they understood the third as something autonomous and fixed as if it concerned an object in physical sciences. An overcoming of mistrust in relations is, however, by no means the result of any fixation. When considering sign, meaning and norm in their intimate relationships it appears that semiotics will fail to combat cultural pessimism so long as it considers that pessimism as a (cultural) object. It shows also how the characterization of the non-sign in relation to the engenderment of the sign is a semiotic issue par excellence. Peirce meant to suggest that the meaning of a sign is "a final cause": meaning does not create the sign, but meaning brings the sign to the surface in order to have it function linguistically and discursively there. Any exclusive focus on the functioning of the sign (as in analytical philosophy) diminishes the necessary consideration of that surface structure of the sign (as in semiotics). There is no other *telos* of the sign than its being/functioning-in-the-surface—which never endures over the ages.

These considerations and their focus on the semiotic understanding of sign, meaning and norm are not new. They can be read and meditated as written in Wittgenstein's *Philosophical Investigations*. Perhaps they appear here in a new light—clearer, and/or differently colored. His § 583 reads: "But you talk as if I weren't really expecting, hoping, *now*—as I thought I was. As if what were happening *now* had no deep significance.—What does it mean to say: "What is happening now has significance" or "has deep significance"? What is a *deep* feeling? Could someone have a feeling of ardent love or hope for the space of one second—*no matter what* preceded or followed that second?—What is happening now has significance—in these surroundings. The surroundings give it its importance. And the word "hope" refers to a phenomenon of human life. (A smiling mouth *smiles* only in a human face.)" The exploration of language in meaning, including political and economic forces, directs meaning's emancipation. Meaning in the sign pool of life and law colors the specific position and forms the ultimate goal for each participant in legal education.

References

Bachelard, G. 1938. *La formation de l'esprit scientifique* [The Formation of the Scientific Mind. Trans. M. McAllester Jones. Boston, 2002].

Bohm, David. 1980. *Wholeness and the implicate order*. London: Routledge & Kegan Paul.

Booker, Christopher. 2004. *The seven basic plots—Why we tell stories*. London/New York: Continuum Press.

Broekman, Jan M. 2010. Firstness and phenomenology. In *Prospects of legal semiotics*, ed. Wagner Anne and Jan M. Broekman. Dordrecht, Heidelberg, London, New York: Springer.

Broekman, Jan M., and Larry Catá Backer. 2013. *Lawyers making meaning. The semiotics of law in legal education II*. Dordrecht, Heidelberg, London, New York: Springer.

Broekman, Jan M., and Larry Catá Backer. 2015. *Signs in law—A source book, the semiotics of law in legal education III*. Dordrecht, Heidelberg, London, New York: Springer.

Broekman, Jan M., and Francis J. Mootz III (eds.). 2011. *The semiotics of law in legal education*. Dordrecht, Heidelberg, London, New York: Springer.

Cust, Mrs Henry. 1931. *Other dimensions. A selection from the later correspondence of Victoria Lady Welby*. Introduction: L.P Jacks. London: Jonathan Cape.

de Haan, J.I. 1916. The essence and task of legal significs. In *Signs in law—A source book*, ed. Jan M. Broekman and Larry Catá Backer. Springer.

Derrida, Jacques. 1976. *Of Grammatology* (Trans. G.C. Spivak). Baltimore: Johns Hopkins University Press.

Greimas, Algirdas J. 1970. *Du Sens. Essais Sémiotiques*. Paris: Seuil.

Greimas, Algirdas J. 1976. *Sémiotique et sciences sociales*. Paris: Seuil [The Social Sciences: A Semiotic View. Trans. P. Perron and F.H. Collins. Minnesota University Press 1980].

Greimas, Algirdas J., and François Rastier. 1968. The interaction of semiotic constraints. *Yale French Studies* 41: 86–105.

Hardwick, Charles S. (ed.). 1977. *Semiotic and significs: The correspondence between Charles S. Peirce and Victoria Lady Welby* (Assistance of James Cook). Bloomington: Indiana University Press.

Hawking, Stephen, and L. Mlodinow. 2010. *The grand design*. New York: Bantam Books.
Husserl, Edmund. 1913. *Logische Untersuchungen. Prolegomena zur reinen Logik* [Logical investigations. Prolegomena for a pure logic], 1900, 2nd ed. Halle: Max Niemeyer.
Husserl, Edmund. 1954. *Die Krisis der Europäischen Wissenschaften und die Transzendentale Phänomenologie*. Den Haag: M. Nijhoff; Husserliana Bd. VI. 1970 [The Crisis of European Sciences and Transcendental Philosophy. Trans. D. Carr].
Husserl, Edmund. 1982. *Ideen zu einer reinen Phänomenologie und phänomenologischen Philosophie.* [Ideas Pertaining to a Pure Phenomenology and to a Phenomenological Philosophy—First Book: General Introduction to a Pure Phenomenology, 1913. Trans. F. Kersten]. The Hague: M. Nijhoff.
Janik, Allan, and Stephen Toulmin. 1971. *Wittgenstein's Vienna*. New York: Simon & Schuster.
Kevelson, Roberta. 1988. *The law as a system of signs*. Plenum Press, New York & London.
Kristeva, Julia. 1969. *Semeiotikè Recherches pour une sémanalyse*. Paris: Seuil.
Lalande, André. 1951. *Vocabulaire technique et critique de la philosophie*, 6th ed. Paris: Presses Universitaires de France.
Mannoury, Gerrit. 1922. Significs and philosophy. In *Signs in law—A source book*, ed. Jan M. Broekman and Larry Catá Backer. Springer.
Mauthner, Fritz. 1914. *Wörterbuch der Philosophie*, 2 vols. München/Leipzig: Georg Müller Verlag.
Peirce, Ch. S. 1958. *The collected papers of Charles Sanders Pierce*, ed. Charles Hartshorne and Paul Weiss, vol. I–VI, 1931–1935; ed. Arthur W. Burks, vol. VII–VIII. Cambridge, MA: Harvard University Press.
Peirce Edition Project. 1998. *The essential Peirce. Selected philosophical writings,* 2 vols. Bloomington: Indiana University Press.
Pencak, William A. 1985. Charles S. Peirce and Arisbe. In *Proceedings of the annual meetings of the Semiotics Society of America.*
Pencak, William A. 1993. *History signing in. Essays in history and semiotics*. New York: P. Lang.
Petrilli, Susan. 2009. *Signifying and understanding. Reading the works of Victoria Welby and the Signific Movement*. The Hague: De Gruyter Mouton.
Rotenberg, Joel. (ed.). 2005. The Lord Chandos letter and other writings. Introduction by John Banville. In: *The New York review of books*. New York: Basic Books.
Russell, Bertrand. 1958. Introduction. In *Tractatus Logico-Philosophicus*, 7th ed, ed. Ludwig Wittgenstein. London: Routledge & Kegan Paul.
Russell, Bertrand. 1967. *The autobiography of Bertrand Russell*, 3 vols. London: G. Allen.
Schmitz, W. 1990. *De Hollandse Significa*. Assen/Maastricht: Van Gorcum.
Sebeok, Thomas A. 1991. *Semiotics in the United States*. Bloomington: Indiana University Press.
Sheriff, John K. 1994. *Charles Peirce's guess at the riddle*. Bloomington: Indiana University Press.
Welby, Victoria Lady. 1911. *Significs and language*. London: Macmillan and Co.
Wittgenstein, Ludwig. 1922. *Tractatus Logico-Philosophicus*. London: Routledge & Kegan Paul.
Wittgenstein, Ludwig. 1971. *Prototractatus*. Ithaca: Cornell University Press.
Zornberg, A.G. 1995. *The beginning of desire*. New York: Doubleday.

Chapter 2
Attitude

1 Meaning and Attitude

Meaning, we underlined more than once, is not a thing, not a fixed categorization, not a sticker used in daily life for laying down the qualifications of our appreciation. The classical question "what is meaning" (Lady Welby), "what is the meaning of meaning" (Ogden & Richards), or "meaning as normative discourse" (Morris) should not lead us to fixated ontological statements or analytical observations about such entities, but to *attitudes* and their multiple contexts in life. Meaning engages in dynamics, development, engendering, process and multiplicity as well as in layers of linguistic and other forms of expression. A major issue in any theory of meaning is encapsulated in the observation that there is no meaning possible without dynamic expressivity and its language.

What does that mean? Is expression so closely linked to language that anything that cannot be expressed in language is deemed impossible? Searle suggested this when introducing his "principle of expressibility". Any such limitation would influence the relations between language and expression and therefore determine the process of meaning making. Or should we consider the opposite and imagine that our thinking is only constituted by means of available linguistic expressions? That would in its turn impose harsh limits to meaning making.

Both positions are vehemently debated in modern philosophy; neither of them solves the riddle of meaning. The closeness of expression and language, in classical linguistics often articulated as ties between sound and meaning, does apparently not tolerate any fixated issues, determinations, positions or other rock-solid, stabilized concepts. *Meaning is process*, and any destruction of its fluidity, dynamics and multiplicity destroys its bearing. The concept of 'attitude' should overcome a fixation of the meaning process in its entirety—does it?

The first type of thought formation concerning 'attitude' that philosophers encounter and often encapsulate in their own approach, is a *psychology-bound* type of thinking. It is correct to mention that philosophy and psychology are intertwined

J.M. Broekman, *Meaning, Narrativity, and the Real*,
DOI 10.1007/978-3-319-28175-9_2

in most aspects of understanding the concept 'attitude'. The grip of psychologists on the concept varies according to society's needs, and forms of pragmatic understanding to master social situations by means of understanding and managing attitudes are researched. All this creates a vital interest in understanding philosophically the process of meaning and in particular of meaning *making*. That is a conclusion from any overview of social psychology or other branches of psychology linked to attitude and attitude-change: concepts that are important in philosophy.

2 Attitude in Psychology and Philosophy

A recent Wikipedia lemma explaining "Psychological Attitude" has 38 pages and refers in addition to multiple adjoining uses of the concept. In particular "attitude change" relates to modern structural insights into the human psyche and into psychological treatments, such as the famous/infamous "cognitive dissonance theory" or the "techniques of information processing", which appeal to mastering origins, effects and changes of individual- and eventually group attitudes. Competing fields are, for instance, business ethics or argumentation policies predicting and organizing human behavior *tout court*. All find common ground in attempts to order and to categorize attitudes as types of (mostly individual) behavior. The latter attempt is an important philosophical issue, which includes an empiricist and above all utilitarian approach.

2.1 *Readiness to Act*

The writings of Jung and also Katz are outstanding examples of attitude studies in psychology.[1] C. G. Jung was impressed by the wealth of attitudes that characterizes a human being; he understood an attitude as "*the readiness of the psyche to act or react in a certain way*". Philosophers would have interrogated him once he makes that description operational, because a limited structure of knowledge and activity forms the framework for attitude and attitude-related action in the case of Jung's definition. "Readiness" or "preparedness" refers to a specifically structured social field or (in larger perspective) a specific ideal-type (Max Weber's expression[2]). The major actor in this pattern of readiness is named by Jung "the human psyche"—a concept naively selected without considering any philosophical implication of that concept functioning in a central position. The duality of "action and reaction" adds

[1] C.G.Jung: *Psychologische Typen*, Zürich 1921 [Engl. Ed: *Psychological Types*, London 1971]; Daniel Katz: "The functional approach to the study of attitudes", in: *Public Opinion Quarterly*, 1960.

[2] See Peter Ghosh: *Max Weber and "The Protestant Ethic"*, Oxford 2014, and: Duncan Kelly; "Not a Donkey" in: *Times Literary Supplement*, Feb. 13, 2015, p. 3f.

to philosophical hesitations to understand "attitude" thusly. They multiply once one considers the descriptions of an attitude's content. Those reach from "conscious and unconscious" towards "extraversion and introversion" or "rational and irrational" (whereby thinking and sensing, feeling and intuition are differentiated) and from "individual and social" towards "inter-attitudinal structures", which are values and ideologies adhered to and activated by the human psyche. In 1960 Daniel Katz added parallel types, such as "utilitarian, knowledge-directed, ego-defensive and value-expressive" types of attitude. All those characteristics lead in social psychology to issues of compliance, identification and/or internalization as a psyche's attitude. One should not confine these attitude categories to psychology alone—they also play a role in approaching a philosophy of language.

2.2 Views in Context

Attitudes are often understood as forces driving a philosophical view within a linguistic environment. That context is often (not unlike Jung's presupposed 'society' as included in the possibility to act and to react) a pattern of dominant thoughts and thought patterns, which could change through attitude-related means.[3] Definitions are then steering forces to articulate reality; identities are markers in that process and classifying verbs contribute to make certain ways of understanding problems seem 'natural'. All are operative at the borderlines between philosophy and information technology, linguistics and hermeneutics. They also border on a philosophy of language, which functions as the background of such considerations. "In practice seemingly useful but in philosophical reflection requiring deeper consideration" is the description of the attitude-concept positioned in a modern philosophy of language. One sentence from the 618 documents on "Attitude" in the *Stanford Encyclopedia of Philosophy* makes this clear. Under the heading of "Fictional Discourse" the *Encyclopedia* writes: "utterances of sentences of a discourse are best seen not as efforts to say what is literally true, but as a useful fiction of some sort".[4]

That *Encyclopedia* sentence does not only inform but also challenges philosophical considerations, such as: (a) a *preference* is expressed in these words; (b) "are best seen" clearly expresses a component of a *more general* attitude; (c) the suggestion "to say what is literally true" is *philosophically problematic* and (d) the words "as a useful fiction of some sort" express *the limits of utilitarianism* in understanding the concept of meaning. What seems influenced by a philosophical viewpoint called 'utilitarianism' appears near to the thought patterns of a psychology focusing on 'attitude'. Those are the hard facts on attitude being entangled in psychological options. They are altogether philosophically problematic, as Peirce, Husserl and others around the turn of the century made clear.

[3] See a most recent version of this issue in: Martin Staude: *Meaning in Communication, Cognition, and Reality*, Imprint Academic 2013, p. 231 ff: "Communicative vs. psychic activation".

[4] http://plato.stanford.edu/search/searcher.py?page=2&query=Attitude; Page 2.

3 Husserl on Logic, 1896 and 1908

At the turn of the century the "attitude"—concept played an important role in philosophical debates. Their unfolding mainly took place in British and German philosophy of those days. A clearly visible link with 'meaning' contributed to the emancipation of the concept.[5] But, remarkably enough it did, not immediately direct attention to language and articulation as a dominant form of life, but rather to logic and the purity of that science as a foundation of all knowledge.

3.1 Psychologism

That concern about an origin also had a keyword: the German notion of "*Psychologismus*" was translated into the English term "*Psychologism*". And, above all, it had two outstanding authors as representatives: Frege and Husserl—the first in line with Russell, Wittgenstein and British philosophy, the other as founder of a transcendental phenomenology. Keeping the concept of "attitude" at a distance from psychological uses and interpretations seemed a first requirement for both. Husserl's 1896 lectures in Halle, Germany,[6] contained a critical view on *psychologism* at all levels of a theory of knowledge. That critical position remains linked with Logic, Epistemology and a Theory of Science. The *Preface* of the *Prolegomena* emphasized: "What should have been easy to grasp and clear to perceive in the representations of a traditional or a revised logic: the rational essence of the deductive sciences with their formal unity and symbolic methodology, appeared to be dark and problematic in a confrontation with the reality of the deductive sciences. The more I penetrated analytically, the more I became aware that the logic of our days could not even touch the actual sciences, although it, that logic, should clarify and ground those sciences."[7]

The implications of that in-depth study were not appreciated in all British philosophy, as Fritz Heinemann (Oxford, UK) made clear in 1959.[8] The *Prolegomena* showed in Heinemann's view a manifest neglect of the work of Frege and his

---

[5] Jan M. Broekman: "The Emancipation of Meaning: Sign, Meaning, Norm" in: *Positivität, Normativität und Institutionalität des Rechts. Festschrift für Werner Krawietz zum 80. Geburtstag.* (Aarnio c.s., Eds), Duncker & Humblot, Berlin 2013, p. 375 ff.

[6] They lead to the First Volume of the famous *Logische Untersuchungen* [Logical Investigations] published from 1900 on and called *Prolegomena zur Reinen Logik* [Prolegomena to a Pure Logic].

[7] Edmund Husserl: *Logische Untersuchungen. Prolegomena zur reinen Logik,* [Logical Investigations. Prolegomena for a Pure Logic] 2nd Ed., Halle 1913. p. V.

[8] F. Heinemann: "Schicksal und Aufgabe der Philosophie im Zwanzigsten Jahrhundert" [Fate and Task of Philosophy in the 20th Century] in: *Die Philosophie im XX. Jahrhundert* [Philosophy in the XX. Century], Stuttgart 1959 (1963 2nd Ed.), p. 270, He did so while deepening the abyss between German and British philosophy: "phenomenology as such, in the form Husserl designed and defined, has failed … but thanks to its lack of clarity, it was fruitful and offered new perspectives in Europe." See also p. 280f.

attempt to ground arithmetic in logics (as did Russell and Whitehead while attacking *psychologism*). He also criticizes Husserl for accepting Frege's idea of a pure logic in contrast to any psychologist's pursuance of logics, without even mentioning Frege's name; he likewise criticized Husserl for discussing the idea of "purity" itself as a major feature of logic. The latter remark represents the center of Husserl's ideas on 'attitude' and 'meaning' as laid down in the text of his 1908 lectures in Göttingen entitled *Vorlesungen über Bedeutungslehre,* published only in 1987.[9] That text is not given much attention in research on meaning and was completely unknown when Heinemann wrote his critical lines.

To understand the issue is in the first place to understand the distance from any *psychologism*. In his *Preface* Husserl writes in a positive sense about the results of a psychological analysis of questions pertaining to the origin of mathematical representations or the design of practical methods linked to the uses of the mathematics. However, any transference from psychological to logical components must bring a lack of clarity and continuity. That creates a solid doubt about the question whether the objectivity of science and logic can concur with a psychological foundation of the latter, and it challenges Husserl to consider the issue after he wrote his *Philosophy of Arithmetic* in 1891, so heavily criticized by Frege three years later.

Husserl strives for what he calls a 'pure' logic and a 'pure' theory of knowledge. That purity became criticized because of its radical character—a critique, which is understandable in two ways. One is the absolutism and the other the newness of the designed orientation. A background is in the Lalande *Dictionary of Philosophy*, 1950 edition, which characterizes *psychologism* as "the pretention of psychology to absorb philosophy, or at least be its foundation".[10] Wundt is quoted for having stated in 1910 that the word 'Psychologismus' only indicates that logical knowledge is in essence psychological, so that the term 'logicism' indicates that *the whole of philosophy should finally become a psychology.*[11] A battle of words has seldom resulted in such a vehement battle of culture.

3.2 *Attitude and Phenomenology: 1908*

All this remains important for phenomenology and its practice of "attitude". It contains the insight that meaning cannot be understood on the basis of partitioning between meaning-creating acts (which are always in flow and time-bound), and meanings as self-identical, timeless, fixated and ideal entities. Meaning manifests itself in specific creative acts. That is the dominant suggestion in the 1908 lectures.

---

[9] Edmund Husserl: *Vorlesungen über Bedeutungslehre, Sommersemester 1908*. (U. Panzer, Ed.) [Lectures on Theory of Meaning, Summer Semester 1908] Husserliana Bd. XXVI, M. Nijhoff, Dordrecht 1987.

[10] André Lalande: *Vocabulaire technique et critique de la philosophie*, 6th Ed. Paris 1951, p. 856.

[11] See remarks on Wundt in the lemma "*Psychology*" by R.S.Peters & C.A.Mack in: Paul Edwards (Ed.): *The Encyclopedia of Philosophy*, Vol. 7, New York 1967, p. 26.

But with that thought, emphasis on the *act* still dominates. A more differentiated view on the *object* without which meaning cannot exist is still lacking because there has always to be 'a something' to which meaning is ascribed. What challenges logic and science, knowledge and life, is the abyss between act and object. Here unfolds the essence of Husserl's methodological concern embedded in the question of how one could appreciate that differentiation without transforming it into a rock-solid (and thus meaningless) fixation? With that question, the function of 'attitude' comes to the fore, but at the greatest possible distance from any *psychologism. The exploration of the concept 'attitude' (German: 'Einstellung') in Husserl's work has its origin in the battle around the position of psychologism in logic.*

4 Attitude as a Philosophical Concept

Whatever Heinemann could have criticized in the views on Logic of Husserl v. Frege, he should have admitted that the latter was rather insensitive as far as attitudes directing a philosophical investigation were concerned.[12] However, the *attitude of a philosopher regarding worldviews and thought patterns* cannot be left beyond attention. Husserl, when he reconsidered his texts of the *Logische Untersuchungen* for a second edition, concluded that appreciating the theoretical status of logic and knowledge does not lead automatically to psychologisms or logicisms. The 1908 lectures on *Meaning* in Göttingen were an important step. While performing those philosophical meditations, Husserl is more than once (and often deeply) confronted with his anti-psychologistic approach, which refers to a distinction that has perhaps not been considered thoroughly enough. His *Prolegomena* are thus necessarily focusing (a) on meaning created by acts, which are generally volatile flows of experiences, and (b) on meaning as a fixated, in itself identical timeless entity. Is that his *'embarras du choix'*?

The 1908 lectures deliver an interpretation of that distinction: Meaning is what individualizes itself in components of acts: a process experienced as meaning making. But this formulation shows that the theory of meaning implicated in the *Logische Untersuchungen* relies too heavily on 'experience'—with 'act' as its keyword. This is a well-known viewpoint for Husserl, who wanted to explore a 'pure' phenomenology. Purity was a sign of Husserl's vision on logic and science, despite Heinemann's qualification that this embraces an intolerable absolutism/radicalism.

[12] See F. Stjernfeldt: *Natural Propositions. The Actuality of Peirce's Doctrine of Dicisigns.* Docent Press, Boston 2014, p. 16: "A well-worn myth in the history of philosophy tells us that it was Frege's scathing review of Husserl's first book *Philosophie der Arithmetik* (1890) which prompted Husserl to a volte-face". See Chapter 2.2, pp. 16–24.

4.1 Phansic and Ontic

As soon as the phenomenological reduction emerges as an important component of phenomenology, the emphasis on the *act* in meaning making appears too one-sidedly *noetical*, emphasizing the "concept", "idea", "intelligence" or "understanding" (the νοεῖν being: "to intend", "to perceive", "to see", "to understand").[13] Husserl's conclusion is that one should envisage *two* concepts of meaning: (a) one related to the *act*, called "phansic" and (b) one emphasizing the *being*, and called "ontic", or later: the *object* side of meaning. It should not be necessary to add, that the two are always understood in their process character. The two are, in other words, intertwin*ing* and never only and forever intertwin*ed*! They exist each in their own right and with their own quality and there is no reason or method to melt them together by thinking them as dual or dialectical, or just as aspects of one and the same higher-leveled concept. It means, that they are dependent upon each other *because each is the result of a particular level of thought formation, the product of a specific attitude*. This understanding has an immense importance for our twentieth century philosophy, and in particular for a theory of meaning after Lady Welby or Ogden & Richards. Husserl reminds us in 1908: "… every existential presupposition pertaining to a real world and the scientific research of the phenomena of knowledge as occurrences of reality … is a mixture of a clarification of the essence of that world and natural explanations (via natural sciences and psychology)".[14]

The basic error of *Psychologismus* is, once more, to apply *all* occurrences to human experiences and to pretend that this type of explanation suffices for reality *tout court*. A different trajectory, a change in the ways we think correlations between act and object, for short: 'a correlative concept' is needed. But that concept must be based on a specific understanding of an attitude as far as meaning is concerned. That idea seems very near to the philosophy of Charles Sanders Peirce who stated that such a 'correlative concept' is defined by the fact that it treats linguistic expressions as truly meaningful signs. A differentiation between "the expression itself" and "what the expression expresses as: 'meaning'" should be respected like the differentiation between "act" and "object", and envisage verbal consciousness.[15]

That formulation builds a bridge between the 1908 *Vorlesungen* and the 1923/24 *Erste Philosophie* [*First Philosophy*] as well as the 1926 *Vorlesung über Urteil und Bedeutung* [*Lecture on Judgment and Meaning*]. The necessity of a change of view

[13] An appropriate interpretation of *immanence* occurs only at a phenomenological level, so that the idea of a "transcendental immanence" emerges here. For the specialist we add: *intentional sense-images* can unfold that phenomenological way *in* immanence.

[14] E. Husserl: *Vorlesungen über Bedeutungslehre, Sommersemester 1908*. (U. Panzer, Ed.) [Lectures on Theory of Meaning, Summer Semester 1908] Op. Cit., p. 5.

[15] See F. Stjernfelt: *Diagrammatology. An Investigation on the Borderlines of Phenomenology, Ontology, and Semiotics*. Springer 2007, p. 144: "The missed encounter between the two seems to have a background in both of them misunderstanding the other's account of logic. Peirce emphatically saw logic as an ideal, normative science—Husserl likewise saw it as an ideal science, but emphatically not as a normative science".

arises with those formulations and first considerations. The particular change in the understanding of *attitude* is of central importance for the theory of meaning on Husserl's path to a transcendental phenomenology. His concerns with Logic and Theory of Knowledge focus correlatively more and more on Meaning.[16] It follows that the tension between primary (linguistic) experience and thematic meaning, shared by linguists like Shaumyan, was also Husserl's concern. One is astonished to realize that all this was presented already in 1908. Of central importance is the experience that "with the change of the way our consciousness explores, which we call different ways of meaning, goes a change of the constitutive object-sphere hand in hand."[17] Not only the way of thinking but also what we observe and experience in those distinct ways is important. A different way of perceiving correlates always with a reality that results from our thoughts. Husserl calls that perception a 'categorial object(ivity)' expressed in linguistic acts and articulations. The latter differs therefore from object(ivity) as such. The lectures paid exceptional attention and gave extraordinary weight to what only can be translated into English as "attitude".

4.2 *Einstellung*

There are in the German text of the *Vorlesungen* various expressions in use before they become finally anchored in the word "*Einstellung*" [attitude]. They are in general words embedded in everyday language, such as "Blickstellung" [positioning of view] or "Nominalisierung" [naming/categorizing], together with "Haltung" [posture/style], "ability to experience'" and "evidence position", "Stellungnahme" [positioning] and even "Aussage" [statement]. A major essay on Kant from 1924 mentions those different concepts and systematizes their function more elaborately.[18] Husserl introduces here one of the most enduring views of his transcendental

[16]The Editor of the 1908 *Vorlesungen*, Ursula Panzer, refers in her Introduction of the *Lectures* to the intellectual climate in Göttingen and München, which focused in those days on the manifold problems of Meaning. She also refers to a PhD publication on that subject: F.G.Schmücker: *Die Phänomenologie als Methode der Wesenserkenntnis unter besonderer Berücksichtigung der Auffassung der Münchner-Göttinger Phänomenologenschule*, [Phenomenology as a Method to Acquire Knowledge about Essence in the Particular Views of the School of Phenomenologists in Munich and Gottingen] München 1956.

[17]Husserl, *Vorlesung 1908*, p. 38.

[18]E. Husserl: *Erste Pilosophie—Erster Teil: Kritische Ideengeschichte*. M. Nijhoff, Den Haag 1956, R. Boehm (Ed.), pp. 236, 244 f, 247/248. It is remarkable how Husserl's considerations in view of an insight in the subject-structures emerging from factual towards transcendental experiences, was inspired by Kant's view on the "Ich-Spaltung" [the partition of the I] and his description of identity and difference in the human Ego as explained in the *Kritik der Reinen Vernunft*, [*Critique of pure Reason*], B 492. Kant suggested what Husserl followed: to contemplate the discord of the Ego/Reason with itself. (*Kr.d.r.V.*, A VI) For a deeper insight in the relations between Husserl and Kant, see Jan M. Broekman: *Phänomenologie und Egologie,* Den Haag, M. Nijhoff, Series *Phaenomenologica* Bd 12, 1963, Ch. 3 & 5.

phenomenology: the difference of positions expressed in a "natürliche Einstellung" [a natural attitude] and a "nicht-natürliche Einstellung" [a non-natural attitude].[19]

With those two concepts, Husserl places us indeed before a great partition. His "*Erste Philosophie" 1923/24*, [*First Philosophy*] should therefore be recognized far beyond a transcendental phenomenology. It should rather be understood as a twentieth century consideration of the *Platonic*- or on an equal footing, the *Genesis*-narration/discourse in occidental culture. It is striking that a link between (a) human knowledge and (b) a modern theory of knowledge and (c) meaning is embedded in the difference between a natural- and a non-natural attitude. As if occidental philosophy is the story of those two attitudes and their consequences, retold in many languages and in many cultural contexts. Indeed, "the great partition" has to be retold and its narratives given the opportunity to clarify the existential concept of meaning.

5 The Intellectual Climate of "Einstellung" [Attitude]

A host of general philosophical issues is connected with the expression "Einstellung" [attitude]. The majority of them are certainly not linked with psychology as a field of human sciences, or with epistemology as a general theory of knowledge. One of the aspects closely connected with the uses and intentions of the concept stems from the general intellectual climate in which Husserl brought the expression to the fore.

A particular feature of Husserl's phenomenology, generally called "the phenomenological reduction", challenges every philosophical work in progress. It suggests a subject's direct access to an essence, and is thus an approach which appears to work out as an ontological issue in its own right.[20] That idea will remain important during the entire history of phenomenology and should therefore be intensified in contemporary philosophy. We do not discuss whether his renewal of method (in itself near to Plato's *thaumazein*) was successful. We rather focus on how *any* phenomenological and philosophical approach includes a particular act, which Husserl calls 'Einstellungsänderung'. Any attitude change challenges us to reconsider 'meaning', in particular because 'meaning' and 'attitude' are closely tied concepts.

[19] A hitherto unwritten study on Edmund Husserl and Martin Buber would not be limited to comparisons between principles of phenomenology and dialogue. The concepts of 'Einstellung' and 'Haltung', both translated as 'attitude', are of greater philosophical importance. Buber begins his famous 1923 "Ich and Du" [I and Thou] with the statement that the world of any human being is characterized by a discordant or even a contradictory *attitude* because of the foundational words (or rather the word-pairs 'I-Thou' and 'I-It') that can be spoken: "Die Welt ist dem Menschen zwiefältig nach seiner zwiefältigen Haltung". *Attitude* is the key concept here, like in Husserl's phenomenology.

[20] "Ontology" recent: Bruno Latour: *An Inquiry into Modes of Existence,* Harvard UP 2013.

5.1 *Von Schiller, 'Dichtung' and Philosophy*

The intellectual impetus to highlight Einstellung/attitude as a cornerstone of a philosophical methodology is fascinating. Husserl was already in his younger years, during his "Gymnasium" education stimulated to read Friedrich von Schiller's essay: "Über naïve und sentimentalische Dichtung".[21] The word "Dichtung" referred in that essay not solely to poetics but rather to the general concept called "literature"—and that underlined its importance for Occidental culture in those days. This differentiation has indeed influenced European aesthetics and literature for more than two centuries. The text presented by Von Schiller imposed the idea that different types of literature will be created *strictly under the influence of genuinely different attitudes (Einstellungen).* That is not a random philosophical remark but an issue that touches all creative writing and can be understood as an instrument to understand worldviews as well as philosophical and scientific approaches. Hence the various expressions at home in everyday language, which Husserl mentioned before he arrived in his philosophy at a focus on 'Einstellungen'. It means that differing philosophical views must all be understood on the basis of various 'Einstellungen' as their major component—but it also means that philosophy is not alone here. Literature too should be experienced with the author's 'Einstellung' as its decisive and constitutive moment.

5.2 *Naïve and Sentimental*

Von Schiller's distinction between naïve and sentimental literature is thus at issue in questions of literature, aesthetics as well as in philosophy. One could even say that Schiller's approach is unique in so far as he generates a genuine philosophical analysis of poetic and literary features in cultural context. The latter seem important in view of the need to better understand the profile of modernity. The Nobel Prize Winner Orhan Pamuk recently confirmed this view. A novel is a literary genre in which the distinction is clearly effective. Spontaneity in writing a novel or composing a poem as if it were a completely natural act is opposed to any 'reflective' sensibility. "Being a novelist", Pamuk concludes not unlike Szondi, "is the art of being both naïve and reflective at the same time".[22] The two attitudes determine not only literature but also the complete expressivity of mankind. 'Sentimental' is the

[21] Edmund Husserl's daughter Mrs. Elisabeth F.C. Rosenberg-Husserl mentioned this biographical topic in a conversation with this author in Göttingen (Germany) in 1958. See F. von Schiller: "Über naïve und sentimentalische Dichtung". Its essays were separately published in *DIE HOREN* 1795 & 1796. They formed a completed essay published in 1800 in the same German Journal established by F. Schiller. The Journal was named after three Greek Goddesses: Eunomia, Dike and Irene—now issuing its 253rd volume.

[22] Orhan Pamuk: *The Naïve and the Sentimental Novelist*, Harvard UP, 2010, p. 13; Peter Szondi: "Das Naïve ist das Sentimentalische. Zur Begriffsdialektik in Schillers Abhandlung" [The Naïve

catchword for accessing that process, since it refers to the thoughtful but troubled poet/writer who has lost his childlike character and naiveté. A state of mind trenched in natural simplicity caught up in its emotions and thoughts should desperately try to master them. For that naive mind, the meaning of reality has just to be portrayed, represented, brought up in his articulations. In that realm of meaning, philosophy should unfold. How?

The sentimental attitude is from the very beginning conflated with doubts, uneasiness, and insecurity about words that should grasp reality and meaning—a source of mistrust, as was discussed in the Chandos letter. Pamuk writes: "…he is exceedingly aware of the poem he writes, the methods and techniques he uses, and the artifice involved in his endeavor…the sentimental-reflective poet questions everything he perceives, even his very senses. And he is concerned about educative, ethical, and intellectual principles when he casts his perceptions into verse. "Von Schiller, positioning himself against Goethe as a more intellectual and less naïve poet, emphasizes that the latter seems unable to include his own situation in the total framework of his perception and experience. He writes: "Nature provided the naive poet (or writer) the favor to always work as an undivided, in every moment independent and complete totality in which humanity can really be represented. The sentimental poet received the power and the strong urge to restore that unity, which was annihilated through the powers of abstraction, which belong to the sentimental, and in doing so to restore the completeness of humanity itself as empowered by itself. As a result, she can transform herself from a situation of limitation towards limitlessness. The common task of both literary styles is to provide humanity its own genuine and complete expressiveness—without that purpose, none of them could justify the name poet or writer.… I named the naïve poetry/literature *a favor of nature*, to underline that reflection takes no part in this. I meant the *real* nature: one should carefully distinguish from the *true* nature, which is the *subject* of naïve poetry/literature. Real nature exists everywhere, but true nature is seldom found; the latter results from an inner necessity of being."[23]

One should not underestimate the general influence of the Von Schiller essay in European literature. For instance Reiss ventures the thesis that Von Schiller deeply felt how a human mind in the waning of the eighteenth century could be inadequate in the face of life. "It could neither do justice to it nor could it command sufficient weight to counteract life's demands. To create art, the product of the mind, was therefore a second-rate activity in comparison with any whole-hearted committal to life (whatever that may mean)".[24] Reiss reminds us that Thomas Mann's 1910 essay *Geist und Kunst [Mind and Art]* was meant to be a counterpart to Von Schiller's classic essay. Mann stressed, some four decades later, with an eye on Von Schiller, Nietzsche and Klages, that it was wrong to praise life at the expense of mind. Indeed,

is the Sentimental. On the Conceptual Dialectics of Schillers Essay] in: *Lektüren und Lektionen.* [Readings and Lectures] in: *Schriften II [Writings II],* Suhrkamp 1978, p. 59f.

[23] F. von Schiller: *Sämtliche Werke* [Complete Works] Cotta, Stuttgart 1879, Vol. XII, p. 148 f.

[24] Hans Reiss: *The Writer's Task from Nietzsche to Brecht*, McMillan, London 1978, p.100f.

'at the expense of mind', literature or philosophy cannot flourish—Husserl experienced this as well as Peirce.[25]

5.3 Highlighting "Einstellung"

In our general treatment of the *Einstellung*, there is no special emphasis on this issue. This is also lacking in what is called "the phenomenological technique" in phenomenological literature. Yet, this should be the case. Insight into the intellectual climate concerning phenomenology and its method, which embraces the concept 'Einstellung/attitude' most prominently, engenders some important conclusions.

(a) The expression, which later became essential in the entirety of a transcendental phenomenology, belonged already for a long time to Husserl's dictionary. His Gymnasium education included a reading and discussion of the abovementioned Schiller essay.
(b) The Von Schiller text from 1800 was also important for philosophy and its critique of culture at the turn of the twentieth century. This highlights, how the 'Gegenwart" [the 'now', the 'momentary'] is always a *stage* of a culture, so that the question is whether philosophy or art can really contribute to the critical situation of each 'Gegenwart'. Nietzsche as well as Thomas Mann emphasized that art seldom helps create the *ideal*, which humans cherish about their *actual* culture. As Kant observed in earlier times, individuals dissociate from themselves when experiencing their belonging to humanity.
(c) Husserl's use of the concept 'Einstellung/attitude' was not strange or alienating, innovative or revolutionary, super-specialized or just belonging to the vocabulary of a new branch of occidental philosophy. It was at home in his own education as well as in the climate of the twentieth century's industrial revolution, the latter delineating the concept of modernity. His new age was, like Von Schiller's, determined by "Les Querelles des Anciens et des Modernes".
(d) The word 'Einstellung' received a specific signification within phenomenological research on meaning since his *Logische Untersuchingen* and the 1908 *Vorlesungen über Bedeutungslehre,* and became for the first time a key issue in

[25] On Peirce and Schiller, see: Jeffrey Bernouw: "Aesthetic for Schiller and Peirce, A Neglected Origin of Pragmatism" in: *Journal of the History of Ideas* Vol. 49, No 4. 1988, pp. 607–632 UPenn Press. Bernouw states: it is reasonable to conclude that the influence of Schiller was active at the end as well as at the inception of Peirce's philosophical development, spanning more than 50 years of his life. In his correspondence with Lady Welby in 1908 he refers her to Schiller's Aesthetic Letters, "the first book of philosophy I ever read," saying "it made so much impression upon me as to have thoroughly soaked my notion of 'play,' to this day." Firstness includes the intuition/invention of being confronted with an Einstellungsänderung. That is a *novum* in English philosophy, neglected in the UK and the US. There is new light on the importance of a comparison between Husserl and Peirce: their proximity is here, (in the confrontation with the First, or the naive-natural), and it is a confrontation that seems overwhelming.

the course of the development of his '*Kritische Ideengeschichte' [Critical History of Ideas]*, known as the *1923/24 Erste Philosophie.*[26]

6 Attitude as a Phenomenological Issue

It appears that a diversity of Einstellungen/attitudes determines an even larger diversity of meanings. Husserl's philosophy is a matter of intertwining Attitude and Meaning, one could say. To achieve meaning, one needs attitude. In the light of our preceding paragraph and its short description of the intellectual climate in which Einstellung/attitude came to the fore, it appears that this insight "*to attain meaning determinations, one needs changes of attitude*" is a key to understanding the links between phenomenology and meaning.

The concept Einstellung/attitude was brought into the open by Husserl in the second Annex to his *Erste Philosophie* in an essay entitled: *Kants Kopernikanische Umdrehung und der Sinn einer solchen Kopernikanischen Wendung überhaupt*, [*The Copernican Turn and the Sense of such a Copernican Turn in general*] dated February–May 1924.

6.1 Kant and Subjectivity

The text shows a deep affinity with the Kantian project and its importance for phenomenology. Central are the conditions under which a communicative subject can acquire an appropriate insight into the ontological conditions of a real world. The Copernican turn is an example of the way philosophy should deal with that purpose. Any knowledge of an existence-for-a-'myself/me' is also a mundane knowledge; all processes of knowledge are in essence subjective in the sense that they are anchored in the manifold relationships of parts of the 'I', as Kant discovered and Husserl named *Ich-Spaltung* [*the Splitting of the I*].

Contemplations of that form of subjectivity lead to a surprising conclusion: Einstellung/attitude *is inspired in full by Kant, in particular by his Copernican turn and its understanding of the 'I/''Self'*. That conclusion has two accompanying insights. (1) Kant's thoughts move *de facto* within the framework of a phenomenological attitude. Husserl states clearly: the Copernican turn is a sign for "attitude change". And: (2) the most essential determination of any philosophical approach is whether philosophy takes place in a "naïve attitude" or in an attitude of "radical self-determination". The latter challenges Husserl to conceive new ways of knowing in transcending the Kantian project. This is why the Copernican turn became a new philosophical method with the phenomenological reduction as its example.

[26] Edmund Husserl: *Erste Philosophie (1923/24)* Erster Teil: *Kritische Ideengeschichte.* R. Boehm (Ed.), Op. Cit.

A methodological self-reflection upon the natural way of thought formation and the possible turns towards other, non-naïve and non-natural ways is needed. They lead ultimately to a transcendental philosophy. *Husserl understands attitude change as a new type of philosophical theory*, and writes: "We humans are subjects who experience the world, know, evaluate and treat it; and at the same time we are an object of that world and thus objects of our experiencing, evaluating and acting. … As theorists we understand and grasp the universe; as humans we belong to it."[27]

6.2 Attitude Change as Philosophical Theory

Immediately after those lines comes the issue of Einstellung: "All this will be performed in the natural attitude; it is the form in which the total natural-practical evolvement of a human life takes place. It was from millennium to millennium the only form until philosophy and science delivered unique motivations for a change." *The 'natural' attitude changes*—that is the *basso continuo* of all considerations about the project of a transcendental-phenomenological philosophy in the course of his lifetime. Indeed, the insight pertaining to the foundational function of attitudes and their changeability plays a determinative role all around.

The necessary change in attitude finds its foundation in experience and perception: "In a natural attitude, in the fundamental attitude of an evolving life without reflection, we perceive the thing/object and not the perception; the unity and not the multiplicity of the subjective within which it constitutes itself as a specific unity."[28] As a consequence, it is of greatest importance "to envisage the fundamental difference between a natural and a transcendental reflection", and that difference constitutes in the first place a differentiation between attitudes as if it were the 'bending back to itself' of a consciousness.

6.3 Self-Reflection

The clearest example for such a movement is according to Husserl the phenomenon of 'self-reflection'. The latter is a bending back to a self and a partition between various moments of the "I"—experience. This confirms a search for identity in self-doubling, a self-experience in which all parts of the self appear equivalently as parts of the world. All possible modifications of the "I" are modifications of the Self. They are thus phenomena, which Husserl deduces from Kantian insights into the Ego and calls *Ich—Spaltung* [The splitting of the "I"]. One has to acknowledge that no consciousness or knowledge would be possible without this split.[29] Husserl's

---

[27] E. Husserl: *Erste Philosophie*—Op. Cit., 1956, p. 236, 239.

[28] Op. Cit.: p. 260.

[29] Op. Cit.,: p. 262.

description of the Kantian Ego as (a) a process and (b) a split (a discord with itself) is unique in the history of twentieth century philosophy. The concept of a 'Split Ego' as encountered in the work of Kant forms the basis for his theory of attitude and attitude change—all correlations with linguistic expressiveness and ontology included.[30] They advance the insight that "the 'I' is originally not engendered in experience … but in life (the I is what it is not *for* the I but it is the *I itself*)".[31]

The splitting of the Ego (as diagnosed by Kant) and *the general importance of this Ego-partition* (as explored by Husserl) *form the origins of 'Einstellung/attitude'*: It is therefore not Husserl's transcendental phenomenology in general, which provides us an appropriate insight into the origins and importance of attitude. However, the phenomenological context clarifies more than any Kantian philosophy the fact that *linguistic* (in the form of a philosophy of language) and *ontological* (in the form of a cosmology based on modern physics) issues connect with 'attitude' and 'meaning'. It was already mentioned that the word 'Einstellung' received a specific signification on meaning after Husserl's *Logische Untersuchingen* and the 1908 *Vorlesungen über Bedeutungslehre.* It became for the first time a key issue in the course of the development of his *'Kritische Ideengeschichte' [Critical History of Ideas],* known as the *1923/24 Erste Philosophie.*

6.4 Ego Implications

The Kantian insights into the *Ego* form a historically and systematically unique access to 'Einstellung'. This central thesis is accompanied by three important implications:

First, the role of "attitude—language—ontology" remains widely neglected in the reception of Husserl's transcendental phenomenology. *Second,* the close ties between Ego-structure (Kant) and subject-analysis (Husserl) is a philosophical issue in its own right.[32] *Third,* neglecting the two foregoing implications brings the danger of not considering the concept of *meaning* in its appropriate context.

The Einstellung/attitude as a philosophical issue is not even mentioned in phenomenological discussions including publications, colloquia and related events, although—to formulate the same in a positive sense—some phenomenologists came near to recognizing it. For instance E. Levinas once said in a 1957 Royaumont Colloquium: "The phenomenologists … agree among themselves to approach questions in a certain way, rather than adhere to a certain number of fixed propositions".

---

[30] See: I. Kant: *Kritik der reinen Vernunft [Critique of Pure Reason],* B 58, B 156, B 153. See also the structure of Kantian concepts such as: 'Selbstaffektion' [Self-affection] or 'Achtung' [respect].

[31] See the many and rich explanations on the "I" in: *Ideen zu einer reinen Phänomenologie und phänomenologischen* Phillosophie [Ideas on a pure Phenomenology and a phenomenological Philosophy], Op. Cit., pp. 236–281.

[32] Any misunderstanding or misjudgment of that relation leads to philosophical inaccuracies, as was the case with the German "Psychologismus".

The same is true for presenting phenomenology as a specific method. The method should in the first place be an open method, applicable in many philosophical regions. A phenomenological reduction makes one for instance perceive that which lies behind a naïve vision on things as a field of radical experience. Approach, method or reduction are not enough to characterize what is needed, nor is a further concern about Husserl's slogan "Zu den Sachen". He limits his reasoning to that issue and does not discover that it is a slogan for attitude-change: "the phenomenological description searches for the meaning of the finitude in the finitude itself." That characterizes the special style of description in phenomenology. Levinas goes on: "Phenomenology is the destruction of the representation and of the theoretical object. A contemplation of an object is never an abstract occurrence as a way of forgetting its truth. To perceive the object, to represent, is already a way of forgetting the being of its truth. To perform phenomenology is to qualify the direct vision of the object as naïve. … A return to the acts in which the intuitive presence of things unfold is the real return to the things".[33]

6.5 A First Creation

Neither deduction nor induction as phenomenological method will be able to defend the primacy of one fact over another. That procedure would never reach beyond the phenomenon itself. A synthesis of perception will never be finished, and the exterior world remains full of uncertainties. They make no sense without their togetherness: "the phenomenological description searches for *the meaning of the finitude in the finitude itself.* That characterizes the special style of description. Phenomenology is thus *the revelation of the revelation of beings in our being ('Sein').* That is an attempt to reach what Husserl calls an Urimpression, Urschöpfung or Urzeugung—a first creation. The search for a first creation, a "first",[34] is not feasible without special attention to Einstellung/attitude. This conclusion does, however, not belong to Levinas' patterns of thought.

During the same colloquium Van Breda described Husserl's approach in all subtlety as though he were delivering a portrait of Einstellung/attitude without directly outlining its image. He mentioned that Husserl did not perform a dialectical and certainly not a deductive method. Van Breda mentions that: "A phenomenological explanation unfolds through intentional analyses, showing the implications of hidden or forgotten significations, which the envisaged data contain. Even where he uses a method that makes us think of Kantian research (for instance an exemption of conditions that govern possibilities) or methods that are based on deductive

[33] Emmanuel Levinas: "La technique phénoménologique" in: *HUSSERL: Cahiers de Royaumont*; No. 111, Paris 1959, p. 96 f.

[34] That idea is remarkably parallel to Ch. S. Peirce, for whom attitude change functioned also at the basis of his philosophy.

reasoning, he presents them *bona fide* as analyses and explores them in a reflective attitude (!) and a mediating description."[35]

7 The Pivotal Role of "Einstellung/Attitude" in Phenomenological Meaning Research

The "Einstellung/attitude motif" accompanied *all* steps in Husserl's development of a transcendental phenomenology. Their pivotal role in philosophy and the study of meaning is our focus here. His above-mentioned essay on Kant culminates constitutes a beacon on the path to phenomenology. The *split Ego* is its central motive; it is not a split to overcome or diminish, but an essential element belonging to the stream of conscious life. A reflecting 'I' and its reflecting life with all components of the split 'I' remains in the dark as long as there is no understanding of the ever-changing Einstellung/attitude. Changing attitudes bring what usually remains concealed to the fore: "The I that I am, lives a concealed, but at anytime to be thematically revealed, life, an absolute life, a life as a stream of consciousness 'pertaining to ---'. But I have knowledge of this only in the phenomenological reflection and reduction via an absolute consciousness (a consciousness that is itself consciousness 'of ---') as its inner theme." Husserl takes it to a personal level in explaining: "My profession is not the natural sciences, my profession is momentarily not a 'natural' profession. My profession is the study of pure subjectivity. And to this pure subjectivity belongs, as it belongs to all consciousness, also a natural (a naturally experiencing), a natural sciences consciousness." It implies that this position is pivotal and unique, a pinnacle of philosophy and thus in its uniqueness not leading to any form of solipsism. "If the constitution, which operates in myself as a 'an estranged (distanced) human being' will be perceived in a purely phenomenological view, then all this is not solely in *my* system of experience including its real and possible types of empathy (Einfühlung) but *the O/other* is represented in it at the same time, in the form of pure subjectivity."[36]

7.1 Einstellungsänderung

A conclusion is the apogee of phenomenology, yes, of philosophy in general since Plato's *Cratylus*, since Kant and Freud as articulated in the sentence: *"Phenomenological reduction is nothing other than 'Einstellungsänderung'*

[35] H.L. van Breda: "La Technique Phénomenologique, Discussion", in: *Husserl: Cahiers de Royaumont*, Op. Cit., p. 113.

[36] Edmund Husserl: *Erste Philosophie. Zweiter Teil: Theorie der phänomenologischen Reduktion.* [First Philosophy, Vol. II: Theory of the phenomenological Reduction], R. Boehm (Ed.), Op. Cit., 1959, p. 429, 431, 435.

[change of attitude]".[37] In that process of ever-changing attitude/Einstellung occurs that which makes philosophy important: "(…) in it, consequently and universally, will the world of experience be seen as world of possible experience, that is as experiencing life in which what will be experienced is an experiential sense with a well-determined intentional horizon."[38] There is no doubt in Husserl's mind that this attitude change (an experiential sense) does not concern a purely individual subjectivity, although the reduction towards transcendental subjectivity embraces *my* private cogito. But it does so in another attitude: the *individual* character of my cogito is *social* in essence.

The phenomenological reduction thus meets a *renewed* consideration of what the first edition of the *Logische Untersuchungen* formulated in 1900 as follows: "The solution of a psychological analysis was clear and informative when the question about the origin of mathematical ideas or psychological forms of practical methods was posed. But no clear continuity and clarity could be found anymore as soon as a transition from the psychological coherence of thinking to the logical unity of the contents of thinking (the unity of theory) was made. (…) I thus experienced the necessity to unfold more and more general critical reflections pertaining to the essence of logics and in particular to the relation between the subjectivity of knowledge and the objectivity of the content of knowledge."[39] Precisely this relation is made clear by means of the attitude-change: the suggested *subjectivity* and *objectivity* are elements of a 'meaning making' process (which are forms of knowledge-acquiring) in Husserl's "Erkenntnistheorie" [theory of knowledge] *and each of them takes place in a specific and therefore different attitude*. There is no doubt that this approach, covered by the concept of 'phenomenological reduction' is thought to be exemplary for philosophy in general.

7.2 *Logic and Einstellung*

An immeasurable energy discovered in the center of philosophy and determined as attitude or attitude change, led Husserl in 1929 to a (again new) reconsideration of whether there can be a reliable connection between logic and attitude. His statement is short, but the consequences are many: "The objective Logic, Logic in natural positivity, is for us the first but not the last Logic."[40] So: "Logic in natural positivity" is logic in/of a natural attitude (see how 'attitude' works constitutively)—and as a

[37] Op. Cit.: p. 436.

[38] Op. Cit.: p. 436.

[39] Edmund Husserl: *Logische Untersuchungen, Band I: Prolegomena zu einer reinen Logik* [Logical Investigations, Vol. I: Prolegomena for a pure Logic], Op. Cit., Halle 1900, p. vii, p. 175 f.

[40] Edmund Husserl: *Formale und transzendentale Logik—Versuch einer Kritik der Logischen Vernunft* (FTL) [Formal and Transcendental Logic—a Critique of Logical Reason] Halle 1929, Op. Cit., p. 239.

consequence, there are more logics than this first one, because there are more attitudes possible. And if there are more logics and attitudes, then there are also more meanings!

A beginning is always necessary—it is the necessity of a natural attitude, a necessity to be and to regard a human being as being 'in' the world. Husserl explains in the midst of his 1929 publication on *Formale und Transzendentale Logik* that phenomenology is to be understood as the self-explanation of a transcendental subjectivity. That shows how deep the Kantian 'Self' unfolds into the region of attitudes. It does so in the form of an ever-split(ting) Ego. As if Husserl wishes to repeat his own words, he writes: "... phenomenology is nothing but the direct (that means: in a certain naïveté unfolding) self-reflection of a transcendental subjectivity. That subjectivity is gradually and critically directed to itself, but it always remains a scientific self-reflection—embracing the trajectory from fact to essential necessity, to the *Urlogos*, [primeval *logos*] which is the source of all logic/logical."[41]

All critical research about logical knowledge pertains phenomenologically to a subject acquiring knowledge through a large variety of reflections on its proper functions—and is thus a matter of attitude. Do not forget: if a transcendental subjectivity reflects upon the *Urlogos* and thus *has logics in mind*, it does *not* mean that it is no longer "a worldly human being". It is a *different* one, as we read in his 1935/36 *Krisis der Europäischen Wissenschaften* [*Crisis of the European Sciences*]: "As phenomenologist I can at every moment come back to the natural attitude, in the simple performance of my theoretical and other interests; I can again be active as father of the family, as citizen, civil servant, as a 'good European' etc, even as a human being in the context of humanity, in my world. I can as always—but not entirely so. *I cannot acquire the old naïveté, I can only understand it*." And, in the same context: "I know (...) that I, who was a naïve I, am nothing else but the transcendental I in a naïve taciturnity (...) I know the entire dimension of endless and continuously intertwined transcendental functions" which exists because of the human property called 'attitude' and 'attitude-change'".[42] Here is also a Husserlian re-reading of importance, because the 1929 study on *Logic* reads already: "Also as a transcendental ego (in the absolute attitude) I am determined by a most extremely external reality, which is beyond the reality of space and time. What does that externality mean and what does mean that I am determined by it? " The question leads to the O/other that determines the Self. Subjects are coexistent—they work, are effective as a common project, a social construct.[43] When the 1929 text tells us that this

[41] Edmund Husserl: *FTL*, Op. Cit.: p. 241 f.

[42] Edmund Husserl: *Die Krisis der Europäischen Wissenschaften und die Transzendentale Phänomenologie* , Op. Cit., p. 214.

[43] Husserl has, in particular in the 1950s of the twentieth century, been criticized because the transcendental attitude would isolate from reality; his philosophy would be of a lonely transcendental self, according to F. Heinemann in his *Existenzphilosophie: lebendig oder tot?* [Existentialism: alive or dead?] Stuttgart 1954, p. 53. See also: Th W. Adorno: *Zur Metakritik der Erkenntnistheorie* [A Metacritique of the Theory of Knowledge] Stuttgart 1956, p. 159: "The drowning phenomenology tries to save itself through tearing oneself by one's hair from the morass of the despised existence ...".

is not at all hypothetical but "the result of a systematic reflection on the world as phenomenon in myself, which has ontological sense in myself and from myself towards reality (...) and is really self-reflection; self-reflection as a progressing form",[44] it reads as an important re-reading of the above-quoted sentence: "Phenomenological reduction is nothing other than 'Einstellungsänderung'".

7.3 Attitude Variations

As phenomenology shows, philosophy is created by kaleidoscopic attitude-variations, Husserl's so-called 'eidetic variations' being a variation of them and part of the continuous change of parameters and varied segments of order and reality. *Mastering an attitude equals mastering the Self, as mastering the Self equals mastering an attitude*. That seems a new philosophical method to obtain a new understanding of meaning. Husserl designated a *first*—and a *final* variation; the *first* is leaving the naïve natural attitude behind, and the *last* is to actively explore a transcendental subjectivity, which is the ultimate position a philosophizing Self can reach. The entire package of variations is much richer, and its inner structure should be mapped: there is the major differentiation between a naïve-natural and a non-naïve natural attitude. And the latter has three more attitudes: a natural, a reductive and a transcendental.[45] But that *map* should become a *film*: it would be a catastrophe if the attitude variations were understood as points of no return on maps that are fixated.[46] Variations unfold with the occurrences of a human psyche's life. The not-yet-filmed map changes with the continuous changes of points. All this opens up to futures unknown and reworks pasts that now appear richer than once experienced.

7.4 The First

"The First" was not only a problem for Husserl or Peirce; *a first remains an attitude to be laid out as the perhaps richest and most radical in human history*. It is at the same time the most painful: leaving precious forms of life behind (Husserl and Peirce meant 'the naïve-natural world) is never an easy-going activity. Meanings vary with attitudes, change and shake humans because of their implicit transitions. Peirce wrote Lady Victoria Welby about that experience. He was driven by the thought that any understanding of Firstness is the awareness of an attitude change, which expresses itself. He considers whether that expression is a *feeling*, whereas

[44] Edmund Husserl: *FTL*, Op. Cit.: p. 244 f.

[45] See Jan M. Broekman: *Phänomenologie und Egologie*, Op. Cit., p. 63.

[46] See for a more general consideration of the "map"-concept, and consider here also the Peircean "diagram": A.M. MacEachren: *How Maps Work. Representation, Visualization, and Design*, New York/London 2004, in particular Part II: How Maps are Imbued with Meaning, p. 213 f.

Husserl takes the expression as a *sign* of being involved in what he calls 'phenomenological reduction', that is in active philosophizing. Peirce writes: "the typical ideas of Firstness are qualities of feeling, or mere appearances", and adds: "it is simply a peculiar positive possibility regardless of anything else (…) Notice the naïveté of Firstness."[47] Naïve indeed: naïve, because if the first is the first, then it is the first of- or amidst something that was and will be. We mentioned this in the preceding chapter in view of the concept of a "cosmic silence". The same is correct for the *last*. It means: there is a something, perhaps a history that makes the first the first, and thus existed before the first, which is also the case with the last: *the final has a future that makes it final like the first has a past that makes it first.* Peirce searches for the meaning of all that when calling it 'feeling' and thus locating that meaning in the totality of a person, whereas Husserl performs the same thought when taking it as a sign and thus locating it in 'the world of a subject'. Both are impressed by what seemed to remain concealed: the fact that neither *first* nor *last* is a concept that can be without a notion of *wholeness*. However, not unlike a *first* or *last*, this *wholeness* anticipates to be broken, ruptured, partitioned—it thus desires *another wholeness* of different dimensions, which is only perceivable *after* the partitioning took place. *Firstness* and *partition* belong together; the epistemological implications of this insight are manifold.[48]

7.5 Categorial Objects

Husserl outlined in his 1908 study on *meaning* the respects in which a change of consciousness unfolds different meanings. That correlates with reality because a 'categorial object(ivity)' becomes expressed in linguistic acts and articulations.[49] *First* and *last* are such 'categorial objects'—what Peirce called 'feeling' and Husserl 'sign'—and are linguistic articulations *in se*. In this idea one encounters a philosophical consideration that touches our common understanding of concepts such as *first* and *last* in life as well as in philosophy. It is full of philosophical and practical implications, colored by problems of logics or of 'Psychologismus' because the coherence between categorical objects and linguistic articulations appears to be decisive. This seems to be a purely theoretical problem, but it is far more than that, if one considers those coherences as constituting meaning. The revolting (but hitherto little noticed) use of the concept Einstellung/attitude has its origins in the battle against psychologism in logic. Following the Göttingen lectures in 1908, Husserl begins to read his *Logische Untersuchungen* differently. The context is no longer a matter of logics or of the relation between concept and reality. Consciousness is

[47] Ch. S. Peirce: *CP*, 8. 329.

[48] Jan M. Broekman: Firstness and Phenomenology—Peirce and Husserl on Attitude Change" in: Anne Wagner & Jan M. Broekman (Eds): *Prospects of Legal Semiotics*, Springer 2010, p. 49.

[49] See E. Husserl: *Vorlesungen 1908,* Op. Cit. p. 38; Also: F. Stjernfelt: *Diagrammatology.* Op. Cit., p. 148 ff.

losing its unique mastership of logical operations. And Einstellung/attitude becomes gradually relieved from psychologistic associations! That often unnoticed turn is also important in the relation between Husserl and Peirce.[50]

7.6 *Psychologism*

Husserl turned from "psychologistic" towards different and more radical stances, which he called "transcendental". These contain a methodology relevant for philosophy as such, and are founded in a most radical self-understanding with progressing insights into '*a split(ting) ego*'. Peirce turned to *Firstness, Secondness* and *Thirdness* as fundamentally different regions of meaning, knowledge and reflection that he had to master by means of defining them appropriately. Yet, "this sort of notion is as distasteful to me as to anybody; and for years, I endeavored to pooh-pooh and refute it; but it long ago conquered me completely", Peirce wrote 1904 to Lady Welby.[51] But Husserl re-reading and re-considering his *Logische Untersuchungen* provoked the most radical consequences for philosophy, although this turn, unfolding since 1908, remains generally unnoticed in the literature.

It would nevertheless be worth an in-depth study to profile the change in reading on meaning-intention and meaning-completion as exposed in the *Logische Untersuchungen* and then in the *Ideen I—III* or the *Krisis der Europäischen Wissenschaften* (to mention only few examples). The change is first and foremost a matter of changing Einstellung/attitude, from naïve-natural to non-naïve natural first, and within the latter attitude from natural to phenomenological and finally transcendental. *Tracking that change is showing the pivotal position of the Einstellungsänderung/attitude-change in philosophy.* In 1907, one year before the *meaning* lectures in 1908, looking back at his logical investigations from the decade before, Husserl wrote: "The *Logische Untersuchungen* show phenomenology as a descriptive psychology; one should, however, separate this descriptive psychology understood as an empirical phenomenology, from the transcendental phenomenology (…) if one does, then a transcendental phenomenology comes to the fore, which was in the *Logische Untersuchungen* already fragmentarily presented."[52]

---

[50] A Peircean link with the *Logische Untersuchungen* and a deeper insight in the commonness of Husserl and Peirce is the basis of a more general comparison, which has hitherto only been developed in the 2007 and 2014 works of Frederik Stjernfelt.

[51] Charles S. Hardwick (Ed.): *Semiotic and Significs. The Correspondence between Charles S. Peirce and Victoria Lady Welby.* Indiana UP 1977, p. 24. See also Peirce: *CP* 1, 141–353.

[52] Edmund Husserl: *Die Idee der Phänomenologie*. [*The idea of Phenomenoloogy]* Op. Cit., 1950. p. ix f.

7.7 A Law of the Human Mind

Who is prepared to re-read with Husserl the earlier texts as fragments leading towards a new transcendental philosophy? Yet, his logical investigations served the long and difficult path to queries about knowledge-formation. The desire of the transcendental is to touch or to master the general, the total, the whole. Peirce shares this desire with Husserl. But the substance of Peirce's achievements is in his eyes *not* his pragmatism or pragmaticism but rather his *tychism* (named after the Ancient Greek Goddess Tyche).[53] *Tychism* and *agapism* were for him the elementary components of the *synechistic* law of the human mind, comparable with what was the law of nature for Husserl. A total interconnectedness of things is at stake, and *signs* are just parts of it—they are *constructions* like maps, icons, plans, theories or other articulations. Peirce introduces this thought pattern under the heading of *continuity.*[54] His doctrine of *pure chance*, Tyche's capacity, shows the importance of *becoming*. The world as becoming is an *unlimited* process of semiosis, he suggests. Does Tyche show us the double-faced character of our articulations? She does, apparently. Understanding Peirce's Tyche would contribute to an understanding of Husserl's transcendence. A comparison of the two thinkers enriches immensely. A condition is, however, that one honors the pivotal function of the Einstellung/attitude-change—in Husserl's phenomenology as well as in interpreting Peirce's Firstness as a foundational method in philosophy *tout court.*

7.8 Diagrams, Einstellung

Stjernfelt's comparison focuses on the diagrammatic reasoning in Peirce related to Husserl's concern about logic, and this interest makes the Einstellung dimension unnoticed. As a consequence, the focus is on the *Untersuchungen*, and not on an eventual re-reading of that text.

Does the concept fit into the semiotic world? Stjernfelt offers an interesting list with virtual meeting points, but without the Einstellung.[55] The concept of meaning as mentioned in that list is no more than a link to meaning acts (Husserl) or types of meaning (Peirce). What if meaning appears to be highly dependent on, or perhaps determined by one of the Einstellung/attitude positions? Is that not a semiotic issue beyond the *Logische Untersuchungen*, a work of importance in philosophy of language, of semiotics, of meaning studies and—last but not least—of ontology? A challenging consequence of recognizing the Einstellung/ attitude as a constitutive moment of philosophy is to conclude that the language of the naïve natural attitude

[53] Jan M. Broekman: "Artificiality and Naturalness—The Tyche Deity" in: Jan M. Broekman & Larry Catà Backer: *Lawyers Making Meaning*, Springer 2013, p. 217 ff.

[54] Kelly A. Parker: *The Continuity of Peirce's Thought*, Vanderbilt UP 1998, p. 75 f.

[55] Stjernfelt, *Diagrammatology*, Op. Cit., p. 144 f.

cannot articulate the meanings of transcendental phenomenology. In a naïve language: one can at most offer the *road to go* to transcendence or the *map to follow*. The question what the transcendental *is* can only be met *on that road* which is a process of self-development. An appreciation of Einstellung/attitude and its multiple, continuous changes appears now in a new light. One perceives *the birth of a new theory of meaning* when the acts of a manifold reading of the *Logische Untersuchungen* unfold.[56]

Those readings find their literary form in quotations that function on the road towards transcendental attitudes. This directs us to language, linguistic expressiveness and creativity in words, texts, phrases as well as other means of linguistic nature. A transcendental attitude is thus defined as a set of specific speech-acts performed in a transcendental attitude. The language of the *naïve natural* attitude cannot directly articulate meanings of the *transcendental* in phenomenology. *All* speech-acts (those performed as well as those merely possible) are *always* involved in a diversity of attitudes; the ensemble of attitudes is philosophy itself as a process. Meaning is not identical with attitude variations, but meaning is forcefully re-energized by them. One of the most important observations in this context is that each attitude has its specific level of linguistic expressiveness—what causes meaning to be a *plural* concept within the boundaries of language *tout court*. This requires a dynamic vision of meaning and language; a non-dynamic attitude is according to Husserl a *contradictio in adiecto*, which indicates that any static understanding of meaning (and hence of semiotics) forms a serious misconception.

His very intense re-reading almost symbolizes the emancipation from psychologisms and makes us also perceive the path to a transcendental attitude and its linguistic expressivity. The latter is never a *final* destination. It is rather a path *in* life, and as such a path *of* life, so that the *Ego-variations* as discovered and carefully explored from Plato to Kant and then Husserl must be characterized as moments of an *Ego-field*. Positions in that field, in phenomenology, *reach out* towards a past and a future beyond any First or Transcendental. Do not forget: First has a history (darkened in Peirce's consideration whether First is a feeling) and Last/Final has a future. Meaning participates in all, and at all language levels, enabled by the diversity of attitudes. A theory of meaning, visible on the path between the two, tells us that an attitude does not finalize and determine, but forcefully *enables* meaning in a cosmos of variations. That insight abolishes the tendency to interpret any emphasis on attitude as another form of psychologism. There is no way to formulate sentences like: "attitude is meaning" or: "meaning is attitude". The radical positioning shows multiplicity, ongoing openings of past and future, static points of reference changing into fields of forces, as major features of any attitude. An "understanding of attitude as the beginning of a broader understanding of meaning" is the ultimate reason for

[56] It might be of interest that Husserl's 1929 *Formale und tranzendentale Logik* seems to be a prelude to this continuous reading that follows; it is a reading that gradually clarifies the unfolding of his transcendental phenomenology. The latter shows a pluralizing notion of and a methodological distancing from the naïve-natural Einstellung/attitude.

highlighting the pivotal role of attitude. This has been presented by Husserl's transcendental phenomenology—almost beyond his intention.

8 Peirce Meets Husserl on Skype

After many considerations of Husserl's concept of 'attitude' and the pivotal role of attitude in phenomenology and philosophy, and after identifying Husserl's 'attitude' with Peirce's 'faculty', their respective forms of plural included, some clarity in the form of a comparison between the two philosophers seems due. Herbert Spiegelberg wrote in 1956 an innovative article on that theme, and Frederik Stjernfelt's 2007 and 2014 publications researched the comparison more broadly, with an emphasis on Husserl's logical studies over three decades.[57]

8.1 Four Themes

Spiegelberg mentioned four important themes in his comparative study: (1) the immediately given as approached by both thinkers without presumed theories; (2) their firm indifference *vis à vis* questions of reality or unreality in their observations; (3) their fierce differentiation between psychology and philosophy, not only in view of logic but in view of philosophy in general; (4) the foundational function of phenomenology for logic.

8.2 The Importance of Attitude

However, this may not be enough. It does not suffice to construct a comparison without a conversational consideration of themes beyond the 1956 catalogue. The role of attitude or faculty is one of the most important of them, because that concept touches the method and content of the two philosophers' thoughts. The finality of their philosophies seems to be another issue in that regard. Cultural differences play a role, as the two philosophers acknowledge. They arranged for that purpose a virtual conversation, presented here as a Skype exchange. This conversation took place over two days, on the initiative of Charles Sanders Peirce. So, what follows is their (imaginary) Skype conversation in the light of their philosophies.

[57] Herbert Spiegelberg: "Husserl's and Peirce's phenomenologies: coincidence or interaction" in: *Philosophy and Phenomenological Research*, Vol. 17, 1956, pp. 164–185, and: Frederik Stjernfelt: *Diagrammatology*, Springer 2007, Op. Cit.: Part I.; Id.: *Natural Propositions*. Boston 2014, Op. Cit.: Ch. 2.

8.3 On Phenomenology

P Very happy to talk to you, Professor! Finally a face visible, a home, a room to see instead of blank or half-blank pages, book titles or reviews! We both have a daily life of conversation with our papers; we now can finally have a livelier contact …

H You are right, and welcome! I often have the feeling that once others have deciphered what I scribble everyday and want to have published, will become texts that take many, many volumes.

P And (sorry to interrupt you) what will be printed will be definitively ascribed to us—even the smallest and most deviant thought. Horrible idea. I already experienced fragments of such horror.

H You do not want to be accountable for your writings?

P What "you" do you mean?

H Hah, a great joke. As if you knew my phenomenology better than your own phaneroscopy! Remember how our use of the word phenomenology referred to a problem we had in common: the battle in logics against 'Psychologismus". You were searching for an embracing thought-pattern, which includes all possible experiences from dreams to upcoming virtual realities and I wanted (like you) to find …

P But my question …

H OK, you got me: your question about a 'who' is a 'you'! A 'you' is for me at any time a particle of the more encompassing Ego, indeed: one of the many—as we know from Occidental philosophy since Plato and Kant. *Who* is '*the one that means something*': such a *Who* is always different from another one! I like the *Cratylus* in that regard, although I quote the *Kritik der reinen Vernunft* extensively!

P Your policy, Herr Professor! Better a Kantian than a Platonist in these days, isn't it? But you were the one that coined Kant's most intimate thought on the issue. You grasped the dynamics of Ego-parts through the concept of "Ich-Spaltung", didn't you?

H Right, the "split-ego dynamism" is the major basis of my transcendental phenomenology. On the other end, many have accused me of reviving psychologism under the heading of Self-reflection. But I am still impressed by the myriads of possibilities created by so many ego-positions, which are altogether observed at a distance from psychology. They lack in the first place a methodical approach so that philosophical conclusions could finally be drawn from those possibilities.

P For me, it all began in the years immediately after the turn of the century, when I browsed your *Logische Untersuchungen*. Those days, we lived with logics in our mind! You slowly transitioned your thoughts in the direction of phenomenology. What a method, what spirit! I claimed that phenomenology is much more than only your philosophy; that it was a unique philosophical stimulus to open our mental eyes and find characteristics of what we perceive—be they the wildest of our dreams, or the most sophisticated scientific conclusions. I felt that you, when reading such lines, would have agreed.

H I did, and that is exactly what on the one hand brings distance from any psychologism but creates on the other hand a chance for logic to be founded on such experiences—but not on them as a psychological experience. You later called the seeing what you perceive 'Firstness', seeing/experiencing/feeling! You know very well for yourself, how much that is a problematic articulation. Later I heard you had named your Firstness a "*faculty of the mind*"—and then I felt deeply with you: that was exactly what I meant to determine as "attitude"—again: not in a psychological but in a methodological sense. Ego-positions were expanded when I named them "attitudes".

P I remember a 1903 lecture I gave in Harvard when I called phenomenology "*the initial great department of philosophy*". That 'initial' is closely connected with what I called Firstness—I once read you naming this Firstness, as if you were quoting Kant, "Anfang". You are right: before our eyes we perceive (a very, very special experience, a double bottom) that there must always be a beginning, and we never analyze it systematically as a factor of importance for the totality we desire to achieve in our philosophy! I did and keep doing just that! You too did, but somewhat differently and coupling it with your variety of attitudes. But I am happy to report now, that you did not miss the point!

H I know. By the way: your Harvard lecture pleased me very much; it is the lecture in which you were as near as possible to my thoughts, despite the distance caused by ocean and language. You mentioned three different faculties. Among them is the famous "first faculty", which is what I call "attitude". We both begin with perceiving what is right before our eyes, and then we go on distancing ourselves from that Firstness or naïve—natural attitude. But what importance and consequences had this initial partition!

P Was this not a later interpretation of your famous device "Zu den Sachen"? I myself formulated your slogan as: "… make out what are the elements of appearance that present themselves to us". How close we were!

H Sure; the differentiation of your faculties, presented in your paper, was more or less parallel to my three attitudes: the naïve-natural, the reductive/eidetic and the transcendental attitude, which I only later incorporated in my methodology.

P You remember my "method of methods", so nicely worked out by Bobby Kevelson in the eighties of our century?

H But your method was still tributary to logics (perhaps based on your experiences in geodesy, or even your father's occupation of his Harvard chair—the two being elements of a family tradition), whereas mine were purely philosophical and should straightforwardly lead to a final position, which I called 'transcendental'. That was the purpose of distinguishing a kaleidoscopic series of attitude-variations—I ventured myself even beyond Freud in that regard. Don't forget that the first volume of my *Logische Untersuchungen* was published in the same year as his *Traumdeutung*!

It was clear to me that a human being *freely* changes his attitude—as he does his mind. And what is more: he can freely master those changes so that I considered the pure or transcendental ego as the result of a free activity called attitude-change!

As a consequence, the *eidos* ego is thus a pure possibility of the *factual* ego; there is no distance between the two, they embrace only a different attitude. All this is a matter of exclusive evaluation, an ascription of value, an "ausschließliches Geltenlassen" which all attitudes capture in freedom. Of course, that freedom is socially embedded. Don't think I am too naïve to consider this! The channeling through social norms, values and expectations is forceful enough, but those forces direct the application of structures I am examining in my phenomenology.

I was hesitating but also feeling strong, when I called the phenomenological reduction 'a sort of "Ich-spaltung"'. The split, the partition of ego-parts, seems omnipresent and throughout constitutive in the eyes of a phenomenologist. Don't you think so?

P Hmm, it sounds and, by the way, always sounded: *great*. But can you really defend the viewpoint that what you call 'final knowledge' can be acquired by the ego questioning backwards to its ultimate sources—probably being '*silence*'? Is that possible on the basis of self-reflection? Can we really work 'backwards' from experience, and would that ever lead to a trustworthy interpretation rule? Can all this be the explication of an ego by the ego, so that your transcendental philosophy accesses knowledge through self-recognition? Is that self-recognition not in essence a form of solipsism? Does it suffice in our century of expanding wisdom in all fields of science and knowledge? How should we define such a 'Self' that it then would be our key to knowledge and wisdom? A 'Self-created transcendence'—is that possible? And: *who* defines what ego-part in what particular and privileged attitude? My pragmatism is not that broad, flexible and optimistically elastic as your ego-fragments allow you to operate philosophically!

H That's an underestimation of the wealth and unique power of the ego in all phases of its flexibility and multiplicity. Your argument would hold if we were only given the possibility of an everyday-life discourse that unfolds in a naïve-natural attitude. But there is more ...

P ... and human freedom is not only in social relations, but also in relations of the ego to itself, you would say!

H Sure, but one should, however, be very careful *not* to identify the human ego with the human psyche! This is a keystone. We are often misunderstood.

P That is true. You articulated a wonderful slogan. In fact, we both are *egologists*: your phenomenology is clearly based on variations of the ego and its parts, and you could understand mine as based on variations of faculty. My triadic contexts of signs and even reality (to start with Firstness, of course) as well as many others are egological, not unlike your reductive phases in phenomenology.

H A great thought! And a great joke! *We egologists!* Please write a manifesto on it. I'll sign it wholeheartedly. Do not make a mistake and do not write the **g** as a **c**—that will be one bridge too far …

P Talking about 'far": I propose to have a break now. We can live with our conclusions. I will Skype you tomorrow again, around 16.oo hrs your time, that is, around 10.oo hrs my time. Is that OK for you, Professor? We'll have time to reflect upon our conversation.

H Of course, it is OK! Thank you my colleague, my friend. I'm eager to see you back on my little screen and talk to you tomorrow.

8.4 *Tyche and Transcendence*

P Waiting for our Skype connection today, I was thinking: "Life seems for both of us a continuous experience of freedom—of freedom to meet the changes of faculty or attitude. Both are constitutive forces in reality, creating reality as well as meaning. That phenomenon, which is anchored in the meeting of self and reality (most often on an equal level) focuses in all regards on the human mind. Any encounter of self and reality is a process of constant change, and in that change, the attribution of meaning seems an essential occurrence."

What is there to say about all this? I am so happy that my laptop connected me with you again, verehrter Herr Professor! Did thoughts like these also occur to you? That must be the case, although you seem to concentrate far more on philosophical issues specifically attached to your 'Lehrstuhl' [Chair]. Or do I have that feeling because I myself seldom taught philosophy academically?

H Hello Peirce—yes: again we are in contact. I see your face, and parts of your room. Nice to be connected again: I do hope you are doing well today. Indeed, such thoughts are not unknown to me, but in my eyes is their *radical* character that should be accorded more importance. Phenomenology and philosophy are for me grounded in a specific activity I call in a perhaps old-fashioned manner: self-reflection. In today's mentality, such a radical approach is not easy to find or to keep going, and certainly not where reflection is in the center of our attention. But if you call that 'academic', I do not agree!

I would rather call the hesitation, or even disgust, to engage in a radical method pertaining to philosophy a feature of cultural decline, or even a bad omen nested in the general feelings of our times. As we mentioned yesterday, exactly that radical method is inspiring, yes, even determining my methodology and my phenomenology in general. So I am not living in a favorable climate—perhaps in contrast to my former student Heidegger and his fundamental ontology, which he classifies as 'Existenzphilosophie'.

P The radical character you want to achieve and to serve as a method underlines the acknowledgment that self and reality are a constant process of *change*, I think. We cannot easily accept that, or make it come true. A human mind dislikes change in general, I think, but I do not fully grasp why that is the case. I am not a psychologist! Yet, this is the key to my thoughts on continuity: not a continuity of the same, but a continuity of change fascinates me, and inspires my thoughts. I've seen this everywhere, not only in psychology or in social situations: even where I surveyed the coastal zones of my country, I was measuring their change! What is today will be different tomorrow, the high waves or perishing rocks told me emphatically.

Understand, please, that also your attitudes are in change and encapsulated in processes all the way in all time. Their process character dominates, and exactly that makes an indication about the precise quality of the process itself difficult, if not impossible. It's like my concept of faculty: the two, attitude and faculty are indicators of the power of meaning. The latter is a force that continuously explodes in all directions—and yet I see continuity rather than chaos.

H Great, Peirce! As long as we share this insight, we share a power that has immense quality. My understanding of an attitude once the changing stops is like your habit, I would say—the change then becomes repetitious and threatens to be a static power. Here is the danger of fixating articulations. Changes of habit are even less natural and therefore more difficult to understand than attitude changes. Yet, we have to emphasize change in all regards.

P But does your skilful search for transcendence not aim at a *final* issue; a final point to reach? *Is that finality not fixating?* Humans possess an infinite capacity to change, and you suggest that exactly this capacity parallels the creative forces within, or of the Ego.

H Attitude changes create meaning and thus narrate how the world is.

P Is this level of narration not a ground for new and wider limits? On the level of narration, there is most certainly an "*after* transcendental", or an "*after* Thirdness"; both might in their turn become a new dimension.

H Mind you! Be careful. It would threaten my strict method because it leads to cosmological dimensions with hitherto unknown ontological implications. But that unfolding of narrative dimensions does not fit within my methodic phenomenology.

The latter is philosophical and not metaphysical or cosmological. I do not forget this limitation, and you shouldn't do so either.

P I do not forget, but I am still fond of my Tyche! She is the 'max', and perhaps worth the title of "Goddess of Semiosis" and therefore perhaps "Goddess of Meaning". Her realm is the fertile soil of our narrations.

H Your Tyche is a sort of a Dike for me, but is she figuring the maximum you want to achieve, the apex of any faculty? Well, if that is the case, I do have my "radical" self-reflection as a 'max' of attitude change! I don't abandon the severity of my method and am constantly in search of the structure of the splitting ego that reaches its maximum result: an all-understanding, all-overseeing ego, which I like to call "the transcendental ego". You leave that position to an Ancient Greek Goddess, or to the principle of continuity, as far as I understood—in a way all in parallel to my principle of radical rationality. Agreed? Hence my philosophical attempt to forge phenomena and logics, indeed: my roots are in logics. But those roots are 'logic in change', primarily in attitude-change.

P Hm. The question arises: are we both aware that such a position (either Radical or Godly) has a past before—, and a future after its occurrence? Is our thinking in those dimensions not more cosmic than we ever will be, a sudden light, a 'Blitz" as Walter Benjamin suggested? Are we waiting for that light, and just philosophizing in the meantime? Is that our situation, the moment for us, philosophers? The "Skype"—character of this conversation would be a great symbol of that moment!

H Here, Dear Friend, I understand you without agreeing with you. Your Tyche is also a Goddess of Chance, and that is contrary to my radical method.

P That viewpoint is for me (please allow me to say so) too German, too Bourgeois, too Self-induced and for that reason you disagree here! I am happy you allow me to indicate this different stance between the two of us. We have much in common but are differently educated, differently thinking or striving for positions only philosophy can achieve.

But now, in this part of our conversation, I feel all of a sudden very pragmatically inspired by my Tyche! Did it ever occur to you, Professor Husserl, that there is no change without her, no growth, no understanding of our (linguistic as well as non-linguistic) articulations, even no patterning of thoughts that come to us philosophers? Is fate not a privileged form and energy of growth?

In Tyche's mind there is a great partition at work, which we often call a 'schism'. We experience that schism when we reach conclusions about the instability of human affairs and their politics, or about the course of history. Today we cannot deify unfortunate decisions anymore, or blame presidents and politicians because they are not Gods anymore. Tyche and Dike are operating closely together: this closeness is the heart of a science of signs and meanings, which I called semiosis.

H Would you characterize your pragmatism as a form of mastering politics, and in so doing, is your philosophy a matter of reflecting or even governing political issues? Then there is really a gap between us …

P Could we put our conversation on hold for a moment, Professor? I would like to change chair and sit on my porch for the rest of this Skype event. By the way, I still perceive the porch as the birthplace of my Firstness, and you will see a few fragments of the landscape that belong to the concept …

8.5 On Language

… thank you for your patience.

H Indeed, what a beautiful landscape I see now on my screen! I cannot offer you a comparable view, being in my study, my private library in the center of town, central Freiburg. I would say: your philosophical concept of Firstness gave Mother Nature a wonderful reward for appearing so breathtaking—your words wrote her deeply in human thought.

P Thank you! Let's come back to our conversation. Why do you want to define philosophy at this moment while the world is on fire around us? Yes, the question fits with the landscape you see now in a mysterious way! When I changed to the chair in my porch, I took a book with me from which I quote a line. Polybios, who lived between 200 and 118, wrote on Tyche: "… she is quite capable of wiping out our reasonable expectations with unforeseeable turns of events and if she gives aid to anyone and tips her balance in his favor, she will eventually, as if she regretted the help, tip the scale against him and instantly ruin his successes".

Not only individuals, but also even entire countries experienced this dynamics of change as well, and this happens today with the same vigor as it did thousands of years ago. I am aware of the limits of our thoughts. Therefore I am asking what was before Firstness and what future is there in an after—Thirdness. And you? Does your marriage between phenomena and logics come to an end, a well-defined, rationally mastered end in transcendence? *And what happens then …?*

H I think I understand what you want to say, although it sounds harsh, particularly in this beautiful scenery. My position is a position in German philosophy, and German philosophy is in my lifetime the leading one in European philosophy and culture. For answers to the questions you articulate, we German philosophers read and listen to our poets and often our novelists.

It's perhaps an interesting difference between your students and mine: philosophy students cannot study philosophy without knowing and consulting the poets and novelists of our day, and we, scholars and teachers, often quote their work in our lectures on an equal footing. That is my experience, and that is my world. We read our expressionist poets, like Grosz, Schwitters and Schickele, read Else Lasker

Schüler. Our students read novels of the Mann's parallel to our lectures. When I published my 1929 book on logics, Walter Benjamin wrote in the same year one of the Parisian Parts of his work on *Passages*, studying what you called Firstness and categorized as a 'faculty': 'the faculty of seeing what stares one in the face, just as it presents itself, unreplaced by any interpretation'. He exercised that faculty as a 'flaneur'. Such was his observation and such were objects in a Parisian passage through his faculty of perception. We were compatriots of the mind!

In my life, the ties between philosophy and literature are strong. An example is, how the poet Friedrich von Schiller (which you also read) initiated my exploration of the attitude-concept—it did not have a beginning in the works of Kant, Hegel or any other philosopher—it was in literature! And your considerations, guided by Tyche, are not in my philosophy. With poets and novelists you find the possible answers to Tychean questions about the future of an after-Thirdness, if you like, but not with me. Here is a big and culturally grounded difference between us: a cultural difference that limited or delineated all our philosophical approaches. Who knows?

P Indeed, who knows? Who really does? Most probably neither of the two of us! When talking about 'cultural' as contrasted to 'natural', as we both do, who knows its full meaning? Who has an appropriate notion of the natural—look at your computer-screen. I experienced that question when I tried to determine a special sign I called Dicisign. That's a good example. You believe I was successful? I don't!

H Please explain.

P I was fascinated by the fact that a sign can exist, which as such conveys information. And *that 'self' should represent the 'natural'*. It was first described when I prepared the Lowell lectures in 1903 and wrote a syllabus to supplement them. Especially during my work on the third part, which I myself called "Sundry Logical Conceptions", I had a dream. I thought that that a sign could indicate its object independently. Let me suppose: I possess a painted portrait of a beloved one. The painting tells me: that is her! It tells me this without my intervention. Does it? It does if you agree that the painting is a proposition without any reference indicated. That was the logic of a dream of naturalness existing in human life without any intervention. The dream was that the sign makes explicit its reference (or 'object') as if it possessed (or was) a 'self' beyond my own consciousness, knowledge or culture. What a dream! What consequences! The word 'information' I used in that text should already have taught me a different lesson.

H Who else but we ourselves decides that 'nature' conveys information? The concept "natural" in attitude or faculty rather shows that there is no natural external to any type of cultural meaning-field—excuse my spatial metaphors.

P Yes, indeed: my doctrine of Dicisigns implies an attempt to find naturalness, but I find no "natural" apart from "culture/consciousness", as neurologists sometimes suggest. Meanings of consciousness are not definable other than by that consciousness itself. Our mind tries to overcome its own boundaries with this type of search, its articulations the impossibility of expressing a "beyond". Here we are back to our earlier questions.

H That's all right for me, but we did not talk about a certainbewildering property of an attitude or a faculty of the human mind, which relates to this issue. Let me formulate it as follows: not all phenomena we encounter—phenomena that 'stare you in the face' or that 'convey information'—are perceivable or approachable at the same attitude level.

Freud already had the intuition to ascribe various phenomena to various attitudes of the human "I"—he constructed addresses from the "Ich" to the "Über-Ich" to the "Es", etc. The dependency of a consciousness articulating itself in a specific attitude is visible in the variety of linguistic forms that sustain human communication. It has hardly been understood when I once wrote, that insights of a transcendental ego cannot always be transposed in another attitude, for instance the attitude and level of naïve-natural articulations. So we should investigate the various levels of linguistic expressivity that result from equally various levels of attitude or faculty. That differentiation of levels determines meaning. In my words: a delimitation of the naïve-natural, the eidetic-reductive or the transcendental attitude is also a delimitation of meaning's expressivity, indeed, of meaning *tout court*.

P The concept of the 'natural' plays an important role in our philosophy, doesn't it?

H As your 'dicisign' demonstrates, it does! That concept is in your work embedded in sophisticated logical analyses, and the 'natural' is not easy to find there, although it plays a crucial role. I think I have used the 'nature' concept more methodologically. Remember what is generally acknowledged as one of our common interests: the transition from the rare faculty of Firstness to other regions (in your words) or from a naïve-natural attitude to a non-naïve natural Einstellung (in my words). That is often seen as the great partition, which is basic to our philosophy, even to philosophy in general. A methodological *tour de force,* however, was the attitude change towards a reductive attitude. There is no phenomenology without the first, and no methodological unfolding without the last. Both have a concept of the natural in common.

P True, but here is a point that strikes me. Our reference to a concept of the 'natural', to 'nature' or to 'naturalness' is not evident or generally discussed. The book or philosophical article about *"The Natural in Peirce and Husserl"* has still to come! But we don't know whether it will ever be the case. I would like a special session on that theme, as a follow-up of our Skype conversation of this moment.

H Let us organize that! It would be great! I would like it very much indeed!

P But, none of the publicly debated subjects of our philosophies has been mentioned in our conversation hitherto. How come? I mean topics such as sign, symbol, meaning, reference, continuity, reduction, focus, degrees of reality, and others that flourish in the Wikipedia articles around and about us. I am happy that we could let go; that we could indeed talk about what doesn't belong to the surface of our texts—neither of us has yet authorized text collections, finished and available for study! And yet, what is in our conversation today will perhaps never belong to those issues. Do you grasp the meaning of my observation?

H I think I do. I have the feeling that we tried to grasp the entirety of our philosophy—both are different in origin, and perhaps also in purpose. But many common issues are not appropriately represented by the fragments you mentioned and which have landed in the literature, such as 'sign', 'attitude', ''reduction', or 'Firstness'.

I really want to thank you, Peirce, for your challenges and participation. One of the differences between us became clearer than ever. It is that my 'Einstellungen', how pivotal in my phenomenology they may be, have always been embedded in the Self. As a consequence, I never used my reflections from the *Logische Untersuchungen* on until my last years, to enter the field of language and articulation. Those have been too much encapsulated …

P I am happy with this remark, dear Professor, Colleague, Friend: I wanted to make this remark at various occasions, but did not do because you were articulating too interestingly what indeed had be said. This is in particular the case when you spoke about the importance of Einstellung, which I call faculty. Your 'attitude' remains a product of the Self, I would say, of the Self in conversation with the Self (Plato), whereas my 'faculty'—as Firstness, Secondness and Thirdness show—includes the power to articulate outwardly: the latter being a power *of* the Self as well as a power *in* the Self to enforce a great partition.

H Indeed: the various levels of attitude and the many 'Einstellungen' I deemed possible have all their own level of expressivity and linguistic articulation. They should not be interpreted psychologically: the battle against psychologisms has evidently blinded me during various periods of my work! We image language as *one* level—that is wrong: there are kaleidoscopic quantities and levels of language. Expressivity is extremely rich—I neglected this! And in doing so, I misunderstood meaning!

P This is the apex of our Skype event today, isn't it: language and communication, yes: meanings, "stare us in the face", always … and we miss them philosophically as well as in life when they do not become our Firstness—as they are also, and always, "perfused with signs"!

9 Attitude, Partition, and Plurality

Philosophers generally agree that there exists a fundamental freedom to perform attitude changes far beyond law's determinations. A genuine difficulty is, however, that those changes are by no means always a rational decision or a conscious act.

They remain at a distance from psychological interpretations, as the battle of logicians against *psychologism* in the first decades of the twentieth century demonstrated. Husserl and Peirce successfully tried to coin concepts and theories on attitude, and in doing so provided the groundwork for a theory of meaning. However, their philosophies were inexorably linked with a broader and more determined issue, which we ontologically call "partition". So where we focus on the idea of attitude in connection with meaning, we include ties between attitude and partition.

9.1 Aspects of Attitude, Philosophically

'Attitude" is a complex philosophical concept. Many discussions of the idea are in the context of semantics and general propositions. Differences in view between Frege and Russell were fruitful in that regard, and also Peirce was not without interest in that matter, especially with regard to the understanding of signs.[58] A key focus of interest was on attitude as the standing of a subject regarded in relation to what is often articulated as a thought or a proposition. Ascriptions appear as the major form of attitude, and seem important in semantic debates. This is not without broader relevance: the question is whether semantic contents can be linked with linguistic expressions under the influence of certain attitudes, or even as the fulfillment of an attitude. Another approach to parallel questions is the consideration of whether facts can in the grip of an attitude be stated in correspondence with certain semantic contents they seem to have. In both cases, the role of attitude is very near to an everyday understanding of attitude as a particular mood of a subject. On that daily conversational level of language, attitude is often linked with a specific position, a way of carrying oneself as typical for a subject, a posture or the state of mind of a subject, her disposition or orientation in view of realities of life, in short: a stance. This shows that attitude remains in proximity to psychological interpretations, although the concept plays a role in philosophical attempts to establish a theory of meaning, which is remote from psychological considerations.

That is, however, not entirely the case with 'attitude' as the English translation of the phenomenological concept 'Einstellung' or with 'attitude change' for 'Einstellungs-änderung'. Husserl developed a subtle series of observations concerning the concept. His major profile unfolded in the last phase of his *Logische Untersuchungen* and its debates (sometimes developing into serious battles) pertaining to *psychologism.* Constituting elements of subjectivity (as if they were 'Ego-particles') work in me, Husserl remarks. Those coordinate with reflections that concern the creation of my own Self as well as a sense of Being, which is engendered in my Self. He underlines, that this insight will lead to a process of systematic self-reflection linked with the unfolding of a kaleidoscopic wealth of different attitudes. The largest part of his philosophy after his *Logic* publications is a method-

[58] See F. Stjernfelt: *Natural Propositions*, Op. Cit., 2014.

ological investigation into that specific wealth. It does not therefore surprise us that coming to understand the concept of meaning receives a new impetus when it is considered in this light.

Husserl concentrated on 'Einstellung' without precisely defining the concept. An attitude is in his thought exemplarily treated as *a move of the human mind towards a changing or changed focus on a reality fragment of any kind.* In this specification a breach, or partition is engraved. In other words, an attitude is impossible to conceive without taking a breach into account. The emphasis on change confirms this clearly. Meaning is linked with attitude: the concept cannot solely be fixated in the realm of articulations or remain identical during life, since life itself is continual change by definition. That issue was already discussed in the Skype conversation between Husserl and Peirce. It includes a challenge to unfold a deeper investigation pertaining to 'Einstellung'. It is fascinating to concentrate for a few moments on the German term Husserl originally deploys.

9.2 *Einstellung—Entstellung*

Would the German "Ein-Stellung" suggest in English "One-Position"? In the German expression is clear that the word suggests a positive selection, which is the 'taking into account' or even 'the occupation of' a position. So there is a singularity created by means of performing a breach in the totality of possible positions. This shows in what way a numerical translation of 'Ein' with 'One' is short-sighted. The specific 'one position' move is not just one free act of counting but much more than that: an activity, a performance, a forceful event willfully achieved and positioned far beyond chance or any other passivity. That dynamic property is not correctly translated with a number. As a consequence, the German 'Ein' is more adequately expressed with the English 'In'.[59] The inwards move is by definition temporary; it is an exquisite moment of perception, interpretation and understanding. What is more: there is a goal behind that activity, which is not openly articulated. The 'In' of 'Einstellung' guarantees, yes expresses the fact that breaches guarantee dynamics in naming and understanding. To develop an 'Einstellung' can serve all sorts of desired effects, no matter whether they are intended or not. Any occupied position shows that change is the key notion of a particular 'Einstellung'. To take or to develop an 'Einstellung'" demonstrates an intention or openness towards change, because the profile of the 'Einstellung' will only become clear by means of change. The latter is therefore implicit *and* foreseen in the 'Einstellung'. All those components may suggest translating the German 'Einstellung' in English as 'focus'. One can, however, develop a focus on literally everything, so that a 'focus on a something' has implicit but indefinable ontological implications—in contrast to 'Einstellung', as we will see.

[59] Not unlike in Dutch, where a correct translation of the German "Einstellung" would be: "instelling", an expression translated by the Dutch-English dictionary as "attitude".

Von Schiller, who inspired Husserl to use the word 'Einstellung', suggested a parallel with what Freud later concluded in understanding that all '*Ein'*-stellung is in fact an issue of '*Ent'*-stellung. An '*Ein*-stellung' is dynamic: it leads to diverting, and thus proceeds towards '*Ent*-stellung'. The virtues of the latter are (in contrast to the first) innumerable, as Lacan remarked in several crucial essays during his life as a psychoanalyst.[60] The "I" and the "Self" as a constitutive moment is exclusively individual and utterly social at the same time. If the two do not mutually participate in a process of '*Ent*-stellung', Lacan suggests, human identity is endangered. The human "Self", with the "I" as its continuous expressive counterpart in need of a new '*Ein*stellung', unfolds in social relations and engenders them while they are articulated and given time and place in the social continuum. It is necessary to underline the character of continuity in order to accomplish social life as a process, which is the product of *Ein*—and *Ent*—stellung in togetherness. One should be careful *not* to interpret this dynamic occurrence as an argument against or in favor of a *dialogic* philosophical anthropology, or for psychiatric schisms to be explored in human theory or therapy.[61] This is firmly stated in the experiences of Lacan, where he suggests that each ontological structure of the human world (political structures and dynamics included) needs an identification via "a specular image", which is a threshold of the visible world and which we experience the moment we embrace the *Ein*-stellung / *Ent*-stellung dynamic in the fields of meaning in life. That is even stronger in one's infirmities, projections or mirror appearances of *doubles* in which psychic realities manifest themselves.

Now, there are two places in linguistic expressivity where those doubles play a remarkable and often privileged role: these are the cases of *metaphor* and *metonymy*. Both depend on the dynamic transition *vice-versa* of an 'Ein-' and an 'Ent–stellung'. A metaphor is generally understood as a figure of speech that identifies one thing as being the same as some unrelated other. The similarities between the two are founded upon the exchange of one expression by another, one thus taking the place of the other. In the case of a metonymy we meet a comparable dynamics: here the issue is not called not by its own name but rather by the name of something associated: names are exchanged. The two forms of '*Dis*placement' or '*Ent*stellung', forms of expression and of name, fortify the *Ein*stellung. They strengthen as well as intensify the articulation required and are *not* the creation of a special word but of one specific meaning. One is tempted to understand this entire extension of articulation as an example of what occurs in the case of an 'Einstellung/attitude" in phenomenology as well as in semiotics and meaning theory.

[60] See Jan M. Broekman: "Lacan, The Mirror and the 'I' " in: Jan M. Broekman & Larry Catà Backer: *Signs in Law—A Source Book*, Op. Cit.: Ch. 16.

[61] See for instance Susan Petrilli: *The Self as a Sign, the World, and the Other*. New Brunswick & London 2013. See the nearly grotesque remarks of Th. W. Adorno on Husserl in his: *Zur Metakritik der Erkenntnistheorie*, Stuttgart 1956, p. 197.

9.3 *DifférAnce/'Ent'stellung*

Thinking back to the source of Husserl's phenomenology and its Kantian inspiration, one asks whether the Self could be acknowledged as the ultimate power that causes the described breaches? Are breaches and ego-splits parallel or perhaps identical? Any confirmation of that idea would lead for instance to Martin Buber's coherence of an 'I' with a 'Thou', which are fierce powers finding their identity after a breach or at least a deep differentiation. But the language of an attitude bringing an "I-Thou" relation to the fore is different from Husserl's more general and neutral Einstellung. Peirce experienced the latter when researching and contemplating the sign as subject of his philosophy. The breach, which seems to specify the Einstelling/attitude, intrudes on the existence of the sign, Husserl and Peirce confirm. However, the first refers to the Kantian explanation of the Ego as the source for those considerations, in particular the forceful and ongoing "Ich-spaltung". The second refers to the general human experience that we have no direct access to our consciousness, but need reflections and even refractions to reach that goal. All that is given "is mediated through hypotheses and inferences, including deductive and automatic operations where some of the premises are implied, unexpressed," Petrilli concludes following Peirce.[62]

9.4 *A Sign's Meaning*

In Peirce's view, a sign occurrence needs an interpretant—which should not be falsely understood as an interpreter, but rather as a force that bridges the breach, which belongs to the existence of the sign. In simple words: a sign on its own is not a sign, it needs a sort of compensation for the breach that happens during the birth of a sign. This includes that the meaning of any sign is always a shared meaning: there is an extension of meaning in the breach-compensation called by Peirce an interpretant. To call this "dialogal" is a bridge too far. That move would lead away from the specificity and ingenuity of the sign as accompanied by a breach—which is a Peircean discovery with cosmological consequences, as his Tyche clarifies. Colapietro underlined this reference forcefully by quoting Jose Ortega Y Gasset, that ""no human acquisition is stable". His commentary is of central importance: "whatever we have won, we are also able to lose. Thus, the term 'subject' … stands for *radical instability* of the human person." This view expresses also the opinion of Peirce who defined human consciousness and the concept of a self, while saying

[62] S. Petrilli: *The Self as a Sign*, Op. Cit., 2013, p. 259. See also the Ogden and Richards quotation on p. 260 of Petrilli's publication: "Throughout all our life we are treating things as signs…and very little of it escapes some degree of interpretation".

that "a self itself is a sign".[63] We encounter here the Kantian 'Ego-split' in Peirce's terminology, Husserl could suggest.

All this reads remarkably parallel to Jacques Derrida, who stated in his 1968 essay *La Différance*: "The sign is usually said to be put in the place of the thing itself, the present thing, "thing" here standing equally for meaning or referent. The sign represents the present in its absence. It takes the place of the present. When we cannot grasp or show the thing, state the present, the being-present, when the present cannot be presented, we signify, we go through the detour of the sign. We take or give signs. We signal. The sign, in this sense, is deferred presence. Whether we are concerned with the verbal or the written sign, with the monetary sign, or with electoral delegation and political representation, the circulation of signs defers the moment in which we can encounter the thing itself, make it ours, consume or expend it, touch it, see it, intuit its presence. What I am describing here in order to define it is the classically determined structure of the sign in all the banality of its characteristics--signification as the différance of temporization. And this structure presupposes that the sign, which defers presence, is conceivable only on the basis of the presence that it defers, and moving toward the deferred presence, which it aims to re-appropriate. According to this classical semiology, the substitution of the sign for the thing itself is both secondary and provisional: secondary due to an original and lost presence from which the sign thus derives; provisional as concerns this final and missing presence toward which the sign in this sense is a movement of mediation."[64]

9.5 The Specular Image

Derrida also underestimates the character of *breach* belonging to the sign. He stresses the *dynamics* of Husserl's Einstellung/attitude to obtain insight into the kaleidoscopic multitude of speech and articulation possibilities, including meaning. So the human Self is not the source, but rather (to use words of Lacan) *the specular image* of the breach concerned. That image repeats itself continuously in linguistic articulations, at levels of language and communication as well as discourses. The sign pool of life is the ultimate dimension of that particular image repetition.

Whorf, in 1940, extended the Sapir thesis, which shows that the sign pool as well as the *specular image* of a human being is not an individualistic feature but socially and culturally determined like all languages seem to be. He wrote famously: "We dissect nature along lines laid down by our native languages. The categories and types that we isolate from the world of phenomena we do not find there because they stare every observer in the face; on the contrary, the world is presented in a

---

[63] Vincent M. Colapietro: *Peirce's Approach to the Self. A Semiotic Perspective on Human Subjectivity*. SUNY NY 1989, p. 42, 68. See p. 104 and the argument: "the human mind in its actual operations … is an embodied form, and, as such, the mind belongs to the same genus … as the word".

[64] J. Derrida: *Marges de la Philosophie*. Paris 1972, Ch 1 p. 9 f: *La Différance*.

kaleidoscopic flux of impressions which has to be organized by our minds—and this means largely by the linguistic systems in our minds. We cut nature in pieces, (re-) organize it into concepts, and ascribe significances as we do, largely because we are party to an agreement to organize it in this way—an agreement that holds throughout our speech community and is codified in the patterns of our language. That agreement is, of course, an implicit and unstated one, *but its terms are absolutely obligatory*; we cannot talk at all except by subscribing to the organization and classification of data which the agreement decrees".[65]

This Whorf quotation makes very clear that the continuously recurring breach might be the origin of a Derridean 'différance", so that the said différance cannot be the origin of or identical with the breach, which is foundational for Husserl's attitude. Whorf's words direct us towards the last lines in the Skype conversation between Peirce and Husserl, and we have to pay more attention to them.

9.6 Attitude and Leveled Language

Indeed: "the various levels of attitude and the many 'Einstellungen' I deemed possible have all their own level of expressivity and linguistic articulation", Husserl mentioned at the end of his above-mentioned Skype conversation. This leads us to a more profound appreciation of the Einstellungs-concept. Husserl said: "We image language as *one* level—that is wrong: there are kaleidoscopic quantities and levels of language. Expressivity is extremely rich!" In his second Harvard Lecture, April 02, 1903, Peirce had already explored a comparable position. He suggested that philosophy decidedly differed from physics and natural sciences "by the circumstance that it does not undertake to make any special observations or to obtain any perceptions of a novel description". That, however, focuses special attention on what is included in the many spiritual moves of philosophy, as expressed in his First faculty to "see what stares us in the face" and sound like a variation on Husserl's "Zu den Sachen". Linguistic expressiveness, i.e. language, seems the only means that can be appreciated by both as the pre-eminent instrument for philosophy. Three various attitudes characterize the three faculties, which Peirce brings importantly to the fore while reinforcing Husserl's system of 'Einstellungen'. Hence Peirce: "The first and foremost is that rare faculty, the faculty of seeing what stares one in the face", "The second Faculty … is a resolute discrimination, which fastens itself like a bulldog upon the particular feature that we are studying", "The third faculty we shall need is the generalizing power … that comprehends the very essence of the feature".[66]

If Husserl has learned and accepted from Von Schiller, that (a) a naïve and a sentimental attitude in poetry and literature brings different categories of expressiv-

[65] B. L. Whorf: 'Science and Linguistics', in: *Technology Review* 42(6) (1940): 229–31.

[66] Ch. S. Peirce: "On Phenomenology" in: *The Essential Peirce, Vol. II (1893–1913).* Indiana UP, 1998, p. 147f.

ity and language to the fore, and if he (b) further underlines in his own philosophy that articulations stemming from an ego in a transcendental-phenomenological attitude cannot without further ado be understood in another, for instance naïve-natural attitude, then (c) we are allowed to conclude that the rich variety of attitudes/Einstellungen creates a rich and far-reaching variety of linguistic articulation with immediate consequences for the concept of meaning.

9.7 A Conclusion

This conclusion is of utmost importance. When studying the widely shared idea that a word is the smallest unit of language, one encounters linguists such as Shaumyan and semioticians like Greimas or Kristeva who suggest that language is a leveled, multidimensional and internally highly differentiated phenomenon/body. Husserl as well as Peirce did initiate a thorough research in that direction. That is why we consider the *Logische Untersuchungen, 1900,* as an eminent study in philosophy of language rather than in *Logics* tout court—perhaps more because of the conclusions that opened up after the work was finished and the many ways Husserl himself has re-read and re-interpreted these texts, than because of the immediate results on the book's pages. The 1929 *Formale und Transzendentale Logik* proves this in all regards, where in the second part of the crucial essay the theory of Einstellung is given its pivotal place.

That place leads in any case to two important insights, which were less considered in the days of Husserl or Peirce than today: one is a view on the importance of discourse and narration as prevalent bodies of language loaded with articulation forces, and the other is the strong multiplicity that characterizes human language. It needs no additional commentary that both are of utmost importance for semiotics and a theory of meaning.

A further look at the concept of Einstellung could deliver a deeper insight into both aspects. The trajectory Husserl proposed: "from naïve-natural to non-naïve natural first, and within the latter from natural to phenomenological and ultimately to transcendental", is a theory on meaning and being in its own right *and* a methodology that might transcend logics as well. Two characteristics prevail. (1) Consequences of the methodology are important for a more direct understanding of meaning in the context of language and expressivity related to attitude change. They focus on the concept of 'naïveté' in the tradition of the influential Schiller essay from 1800. (2) Consequences pertaining to being and meaning are cosmological or (if one wishes) metaphysical, so that they contain a broader picture of the implications of language and linguistic articulation in human history. In the context of this paragraph, we focus mainly on the first.

9.8 Natural—Non-naïve Natural

It is clear, that the differentiation, or even breach, between the naïve-natural and the non-naïve natural Einstellung is fundamental. It is the articulation of one of the most persistent themes in Occidental philosophy, perhaps even beyond that specific cultural awareness. Husserl has never been shy about emphasizing its importance: "It will perhaps become clear one day, that the complete phenomenological attitude and its *epoche* brings a fundamental and personal attitude change, solely to be compared with a religious reversal".[67] There is, however, a problem. The multilevel process of attitude change starts with distancing oneself from what can be characterized as 'natural'—but naturalness can only be determined *after* having created that distance and thus presumes a knowledge that does not precisely define the distancing or the breach itself. *The ontological relevance of the breach is in the name giving*. So one should consider that despite the use of the term "naturalness", the Einstellungsänderung must not be understood as a psychological concept because it is not to be understood as a fact but as an attitude, including the possibility of change. Only in the course of differentiating various attitude changes does one understand their intertwining with ontology. There is in Husserl's approach (unlike in Peirce's ideas) a method to break down the naiveté described as intertwined with the natural. For Husserl, that naiveté is solely part of the natural in a specific attitude, which is called the "naïve-natural"; it is precisely a matter of, even an element of a *necessary process* of looking back on experiences past.[68]

In the *first* place we re-emphasize the structure of reflection: only after reflecting upon the homogeneity of the naïve, can we begin to discover its essence—there is no first step to naiveté other than a move that is alien to and does not belong to the subject itself. *Secondly*, the dynamics of treating and understanding naiveté is always more than a purely psychological issue; the philosophical dimensions are not easy to find in the catalogue of traditional philosophical methods, theories or teachings. *Thirdly*, it is unclear from the beginning while staring at naiveté to say or think what any result from breaking that naiveté down could be, and what elements of this procedure of reduction or analysis would become important or deliver a fruitful new insight. *Fourthly,* naiveté is always an "only remembered" reality, not a perception of how it is, but a perception of a past possibility of specific being. So: naiveté is an expression not for how it is but for how it was. Peirce's Firstness is the description of that process from was to is, or better: he describes the "was" (being the character of the First) in terms of an "is". Diverse quotations pertaining to Firstness confirm this. *Fifthly:* Exactly this often-confused ontological motive, so typical for the Firstness or for the naïve, blurs the lines of division between the

[67] Edmund Husserl: *Die Krisis der Europäischen Wissenschaften und die Transzendentale Phänomenologie* [The Crisis of the European Sciences and the transcendental Phenomenology] Op. Cit., 1954, p. 139.

[68] See Jan M. Broekman: "Firstness and Phenomenology" in: *Prospects of Legal Semiotics*, Op. Cit., 2010, p. 44f.

natural and the cultural, as was already mentioned in the Skype conversation between Husserl and Peirce. Naiveté is a cultural datum represented in cultural context as natural! But its focus is on nature as a cultural construct; more precisely: it is a name for a necessary component of any cultural determination or linguistic expressiveness maintained in a culture.

10 Legal Semiotics (2): Training Attitude-Changes

Law students might experience once in a while in what way we step over the line between the natural and the cultural in daily life experiences. But we forget that the two remain within the domain of the cultural. Is legal education focusing on that line, and on a deeper understanding of the issue in its totality? That is seldom the case! Peirce and Husserl debated the issue, but only the latter systematized it. He called his "attitude change": a key to philosophically understand the world and all reality. *Legal education includes training in attitude changes*. How? The answer may surprise: in learning language! That sounds provocative, so its needs some explanation.

'Learning the language' is a trusted expression in legal education. Students learn step by step how to read and to write; they have extended role-plays and other social sessions to learn speaking … to learn maintain the language of law! Is writing or speaking that language so peculiar? One of the main answers to this naïve question is, that legal language articulates how law thinks, interprets, regulates and maintains reality and life. What is more: mastering legal language means acquiring the ability to function in the framework of law as a social institution. In doing so, the decision about what is law and what is not law relates very intimately to legal language as such. Lawyers must come to a performance, which is essential for the concept of meaning and its semiotic embedding: they are always on their way to identifying law's articulation with human living and striving. While doing so, they decide in the heart of society about law and non-law—a decision that is important for each citizen. In that context, advocates plea that judges *may say for law*. What is legally articulated: *is*! Legal education has to teach law in view of this articulation. We mention three examples.

A *first* example refers to a student's position at the borderline between *responsibility* and *liability*. Anyone said to be *responsible* for any occurrence is not going to pay a fine or an indemnity or to spend days in prison, even if lawyers or police officers were involved. She will also not have a record for a committed crime. The very same occurrence can, however, lead to a legal articulation pertaining to *liability*. In that case, law's rules will be said to apply and the legal qualification will show a totally different face.

The two words are a sign, semiotics would emphasize, and each is a very different sign for law in its totality—a totality being the language of law, its limits of expressivity, its institutional features, the implied economic factors, the psychological issues involved, ideological and political implications and many other articulations often being evaluated in terms of 'justice' or 'injustice'. There is no need to underline how the first word is a sign for all that is *outside,* and the second for all that is *inside,* the realm of the law. That is essential in legal education, because every legal expression begins with an implicit or explicit statement: "'saying for law' is a decision about being inside-or outside the law".

But that is not a decision caused by a speech-act, which is called "saying for law" in Courts or in the minds of judges and lawyers. The decision is encapsulated in the *meaning* of the spoken words. That meaning is the ultimate subject of legal education. Within the possible differentiation between 'responsible' and 'liable' is indeed another differentiation, the one between 'in the law' and 'outside of the law'—both are closely linked with and a function of a broader differentiation between *ethics* and the *law.* To educate about the legal means with which one decides to attribute the expression 'responsible', and not of 'liable' in a given circumstance means to decide for an ethical and not for a legal view on the facts at hand. A law student should learn to understand the intertwining of three levels of articulation, which reach out far beyond the limits of 'the law'. Those levels are relevant, and embrace different meanings that are in their turn linked with an understanding of the given occurrences. The entire complexity of the terminology expresses the importance of attitudes understood.

1. There is the non-naïve attitude to envisage responses from an actor to others in the given situation, which are not at issue where a pattern of liability is envisaged. The first excludes the second. Ethics will only be considered when those responses seem sensible in their social context.
2. The decision to apply the law and have a legal discourse functioning in full is not focusing on law as an isolated subject and its supporting power, but on law in the functioning of a society/culture. Ethical dimensions are more often associated with 'human nature' and the legal, more with the 'techniques of maintaining social life'. Law students should discuss the differences, their pro's and contra's in this case of a balance required.
3. Law students might understand the fact that the intertwining of the expressions and viewpoints in this exemplary case is a matter of the generally debated and philosophically founded idea of *legal interpretation.* Understanding the law is for lawyers in many regards identical to an appropriate interpretation of reality.

Our *second* example, another attitude-issue, can be studied in the case of *theft.* It is clear that all the above-mentioned insights are valid, but the language problem is even more complicated. A general but also most complicated issue is that the words 'theft' and 'thief' in cases of robbery or burglary belong to and are used in everyday language, as well as in technical-legal language. The attitude, which determines meaning creation in the diversity of possible contexts is decisive here. A lawyer should take care, and has to be educated time and again, to make an appropriate distinction. If I walk on a street and suddenly hear people crying: "catch the thief!" around me, I must decide how to be involved. I do certainly *not* expect to hear the *legal truth* as an argument at this moment: the escaping individual does not stand still, smile and answer the threatening mob: *I am not yet a thief*"! But he is right in a certain sense: to become a thief in a legally correct manner, there is an entire procedure to be followed, which is not (solely) possible in the street. The example shows in a simple manner what can become very complicated. Legal words explored in a natural language *also* belong to the language of the law, which is an artificial language. Their double use should be safeguarded in legal practice.

A third and last example of legal attitude and meaning being intertwined concerns the often debated issue of a person's state of being legally accountable.[69] One should keep in mind that a non-legal accountability equals the concept of responsibility. This shows how legal- and non-legal meanings are often extremely close, and are maintained without clear criteria pertaining to their differences. But that is only a part of the lesson to be learned. One also meets the fine lines between ethics and law again. Psychiatrists as experts in Court do know about it, and deliver hot topics that are often socially discussed. Ascribing accountability can silence psychiatric symptoms in a person. If he/she is legally accountable, then psychiatric or medical care is not at issue in the first place (and perhaps never)—who reads the signs of what?

Application of the law is more than a matter of interpreting the words of legal language. Law students should become aware how complex law's words are. One should not distinguish between legal activity and legal discourse—one is not activism *tout court* and the other is not a distanced philosophy. The intertwining of the two: activity and discourse, shows the importance of any *saying for law* in any attitudinal circumstance.

References

Adorno, Th.W. 1956. *Zur Metakritik der Erkenntnistheorie*. Stuttgart: Kohlhammer.

Bernouw, Jeffrey. 1988. Aesthetic for Schiller and Peirce, A neglected origin of pragmatism. *Journal of the History of Ideas* 49: 4, University of Pennsylvania Press.

Breda, H.L. van. 1959. La Technique Phénoménologique, Discussion. In: *HUSSERL: Cahiers de Royaumont*, No. 111, Editions de Minuit, Paris.

Broekman, Jan M. 1963. *Phänomenologie und Egologie,* M. Nijhoff, Den Haag, Series *Phaenomenologica* Bd 12.

Broekman, Jan M. 2010. Firstness and phenomenology. In *Prospects of legal semiotics*, ed. Wagner Anne and M. Broekman. Dordrecht: Springer.

Broekman, Jan M. 2013. The emancipation of meaning: Sign, meaning, norm. In *Positivität, Normativität und Institutionalität des Rechts. Festschrift für Werner Krawietz zum 80. Geburtstag*, ed. C.S. Aarnio. Berlin: Duncker & Humblot.

Buber, Martin. 1923. *Ich und Du*. Leipzig: Insel Verlag.

Colapietro, Vincent M. 1989. *Peirce's approach to the self, A semiotic perspective on human subjectivity*. New York: State University of New York Press.

de Haan, J.I. 1916. The essence and task of legal significs. In *Signs in law—A source book*, ed. Jan M. Broekman and Larry Catá Backer. Springer.

[69] "Accountability" has been made a key issue in legal semiotics by the Dutch lawyer, politician and scholar J. I. de Haan in his 1916, dissertation in Amsterdam. See Jan M. Broekman & Larry Catà Backer: *Signs in Law—A Source Book*, Op. Cit.: 2015, p. 73f.

de Haan, J.I. 1916. *Rechtskundige Significa*. Amsterdam: W. Versluys.

Derrida, Jacques. 1972. *Marges de la Philosophie*. Paris: Minuit.

Ghosh, Peter. 2014. *Max Weber and "The Protestant Ethic"*. Oxford: Oxford University Press.

Hardwick, Charles S. (ed.). 1977. *Semiotic and significs: The correspondence between Charles S. Peirce and Victoria Lady Welby* (Assistance of James Cook). Bloomington: Indiana University Press.

Heinemann, F. 1959. Schicksal und Aufgabe der Philosophie im Zwanzigsten Jahrhundert" [Fate and Task of Philosophy in the 20th Century]. In *Die Philosophie im XX. Jahrhundert* [Philosophy in the XX. Century]. Stuttgart: Ernst Klett Verlag.

Husserl, Edmund. 1913. *Logische Untersuchungen. Prolegomena zur reinen Logik* [Logical Investigations. Prolegomena for a Pure Logic], 1900, 2nd ed, Max Niemeyer, Halle.

Husserl, Edmund. 1929. *Formale und transzendentale Logik—Versuch einer Kritik der Logischen Vernunft* [Formal and transcendental Logic—a Critique of Logical Reason] Max Niemeyer, Halle.

Husserl, Edmund. 1950. *Die Idee der Phänomenologie*. W. Biemel (ed.), M. Nijhoff, Den Haag.

Husserl, Edmund. 1956. *Erste Pilosophie—Erster Teil: Kritische Ideengeschichte* [First Philosophy – Vol. I: Critical History of Ideas], ed. M. Nijhoff and R. Boehm, Husserliana vol. VII, M. Nijhoff, Den Haag.

Husserl, Edmund. 1959. *Erste Philosophie. Zweiter Teil: Theorie der phänomenologischen Reduktion* [First Philosophy, Vol. II: Theory of the Phenomenological Reduction], ed. R. Boehm, Husserliana vol. VIII, M. Nijhoff, The Hague.

Husserl, Edmund. 1970. *Die Krisis der Europäischen Wissenschaften und die Transzendentale Phänomenologie,* M. Nijhoff, Den Haag 1954, Husserliana Bd. VI [The Crisis of European Sciences and Transcendental Philosophy (trans.: Carr, D.)]

Husserl, Edmund. 1982. *Ideen zu einer reinen Phänomenologie und phänomenologischen Philosophie* [Ideas Pertaining to a Pure Phenomenology and to a Phenomenological Philosophy – First Book: General Introduction to a Pure Phenomenology, [1913]. (trans.: Kersten, F.) The Hague: M. Nijhoff].

Husserl, Edmund. 1987. *Vorlesungen über Bedeutungslehre, Sommersemester 1908*. (U. Panzer, Ed.) [Lectures on Theory of Meaning, Summer Semester 1908] Husserliana Bd. XXVI, M. Nijhoff, Dordrecht.

Jung, C. G. 1971. *Psychologische Typen*, Zürich 1921 [Eng: *Psychological Types*, London].

Katz, Daniel. 1960. The functional approach to the study of attitudes, *Public Opinion Quarterly* 24: 173.

Lalande, André. 1951. *Vocabulaire technique et critique de la philosophie*, 6th ed. Paris: Presses Universitaires de France.

Latour, Bruno. 2013. *An inquiry into modes of existence*. Cambridge, MA: Harvard University Press.

Levinas, Emmanual. 1959. La technique phénoménologique, Discussion. In *HUSSERL: Cahiers de Royaumont*; No. 111, Editions de Minuit, Paris.

MacEachren, A.M. 2004. *How maps work. Representation, visualization, and design*. New York/London: Guilford Press.

Pamuk, Orhan. 2010. *The naïve and the sentimental novelist*. Harvard University Press.

Parker, Kelly A. 1998. *The continuity of Peirce's thought*. Nashville: Vanderbilt University Press.

Peirce Edition Project. 1998. *The essential Peirce. Selected philosophical writings,* 2 vols. Bloomington: Indiana University Press.

Petrilli, Susan. 2013. *The self as a sign, the world, and the other*. New Brunswick/London: Transaction Publishers.

Reiss, Hans. 1978. *The writer's task from Nietzsche to Brecht*. London: McMillan.

Schmücker, F.G. 1956. *Die Phänomenologie als Methode der Wesenserkenntnis unter besonderer Berücksichtigung der Auffassung der Münchner-Göttinger Phänomenologenschule*, [Phenomenology as a Method to Acquire Knowledge about Essence in the Particular Views of the School of Phenomenologists in Munich and Göttingen] Gruenewald, München.

Spiegelberg, Herbert. 1956. Husserl's and Peirce's phenomenologies: Coincidence or interaction. *Philosophy and Phenomenological Research* 17: 164–185.
Staude, Martin. 2013. *Meaning in communication, cognition, and reality*. Exeter: Imprint Academic.
Stjernfelt, Frederik. 2007. *Diagrammatology. An investigation on the borderlines of phenomenology, ontology, and semiotics*. Dordrecht: Springer.
Stjernfeldt, Frederik. 2014. *Natural propositions. The actuality of Peirce's doctrine of dicisigns*. Boston: Docent Press.
Szondi, Peter. 1978. Das Naïve ist das Sentimentalische. Zur Begriffsdialektik in Schillers Abhandlung [The Naïve is the Sentimental. On the Conceptual Dialectics of Schillers Essay]. In *Lektüren und Lektionen* [Readings and Lectures] in: *Schriften II* [Writings II], Suhrkamp, Frankfurt/M.
von Schiller, F. 1795–1796. Über naïve und sentimentalische Dichtung. Essays separately published in the Journal *DIE HOREN*.
Whorf, B.L. 1940. Science and linguistics. *Technology Review* 42(6): 229–231.

Chapter 3
Word

1 The 'Word' and Its 'More Geometrico'

Whoever considers analyzing the concept of 'meaning' in life, law or other discourses, will encounter the expression 'word' in a variety of contexts. One of the most general among them is firmly embedded in twentieth century analytical philosophy: the word is 'the basic and smallest unit of language' and thus the predominant particle of speech, linguistic articulation and meaning. This viewpoint has even been the source of inspiration where the "meaning of meaning" was brought to the fore.[1] But the view has indeed been challenged, in particular in "legal semiotics". There is every reason to challenge that comment and to develop a new critical view from here. Three points of attention contribute to this intensification.

First, outstanding authors in that field (from Jacob Israel de Haan to Lady Welby around the beginning of the twentieth century and from Roberta Kevelson to Bernard Jackson on the threshold of the next century) clearly understood that life and law in the sign pool are intimately connected with the sign pool of everyday—Kevelson referring for that insight to Charles Sanders Peirce and Jackson, to Algirdas Greimas. The intertwining of both discourses is named "our culture", and we accept its power when thought patterns, inspirations and appropriate forms of expression in words and word-related utterances are at stake in our everyday language. The importance of this context when considering 'the word' is clear, in particular in so far as meaning is related to the word.

Secondly, meaning is not a specific quality, property, color or attitude given/glued to a thing or object, a once-and-for-all event, an occurrence or any other individual situation. The meaning of something is in the first place a particular process aiming at "*a* something". That is a difficulty when meaning is linked to reference, which is throughout a classical move in philosophy of language. No, to give meaning is not to determine single and individually conceived words. This highlights the

[1] C.K. Ogden & I.A. Richards: *The Meaning of Meaning*, London 1923.

J.M. Broekman, *Meaning, Narrativity, and the Real*,
DOI 10.1007/978-3-319-28175-9_3

fact that one needs to challenge classical philosophies of meaning: they all want to be and to become literal, to relate to or transform into a literal/verbal meaning. It throws a special light on interpretation (neither an issue of word alone or of texts alone) and on hermeneutics. Both should be perceived in relation to signs or a sign. Signs belong to the body of language and meaning.

It is an interesting question in this context whether the power of words still contributes to meaning-formation when the process of making meaning can no longer be understood as ticketing or gluing signs. The meaning of a (some)thing is always in process! *To make meaning is to enter fields of words*. Words are contextual by their nature. A word on its own is not a word. This is a major concern when meaning wants to become literal, or obtain a specific literary quality. The 'word' plays in all outlined respects the most prominent role. As the Dutch philosopher and significian/semiotician Gerrit Mannoury once proclaimed in his critical approach towards the predominant position of the word: "…philosophy … does not appreciate in a word more than a means to communicate and determine the results of its investigation."[2]

Thirdly, the fate of meaning is not only confined to literature and hermeneutics but reaches also, and most remarkably, from semiotics to quantum mechanics, from language and literature to mathematics and vice versa; never forget that 'meaning' is *not* a philosophical or scientific concept only, it is a coin in daily life's languages.[3] It is clear in the midst of all these approaches: *meaning is not a thing*. One rather discovers that meaning is a multifaceted concept that represents presence, presentation and even reference. This insight positions meaning in the center of any philosophy of language, which might be able to change its most intimate basic views and important philosophical ideas on reference. After a full century, meaning has not yet accomplished its emancipation, given the fact that meaning remains in the main linked to sounds, signs, sentences, or texts as the major component of language. Adding speech to this list can*not* lead to a more prolific understanding of meaning as long as speaking and speech are understood as 'the use of words'. An alternative unfolds a new understanding of speech because of its connection with the potential in all speech phenomena. That connection opens new ways of understanding meaning and suggests a renewal of semiotics as a multi-discipline.

---

[2]Gerrit Mannoury: *Signifika en Wijsbegeerte.* [Significs and Philosophy] Lecture in the *Dutch Philosophical Society*, Amsterdam, November 18, 1922. Published in: *Tijdschrift voor Wijsbegeerte,* [Journal of Philosophy] 1923 Nr. 1. See: Jan M. Broekman & Larry Catá Backer: *Signs in Law—A Source Book.* Springer 2015, p. 41f.

[3]John K. Sheriff: *The Fate of Meaning. Charles Peirce, Structuralism, and Literature.* Princeton UP 1989, and—Id.—: *Charles Peirce's Guess at the Riddle*, Indiana UP 1994. The history from Husserl's 'Ausdruck', [expression] and Peirce's sign, to Derrida's criticism of the logocentric attitude as well as the series of categories such as signifier-signified, expression-content, sensibility-intelligibility shows the strength of this metaphysical commitment.

1.1 A "More Geometrico" Philosophy of Language

Understanding a *sign* always includes a *meaning*—that is an experience broadly discussed in law and legal discourse under the heading of legal semiotics. But the concept of meaning in the Anglo-Saxon social sciences and philosophy of the twentieth century is not exclusively mirrored in law and legal discourse—it was also mirrored in 'ethnology' and related studies of then-so-called "primitive" cultures and languages (Malinowski). In the 1923 Preface of their famous "*The Meaning of Meaning*" Ogden and Richards characterized fieldwork in ethnology as "…the peculiarly difficult border-lands of linguistics and psychology" and then referred immediately to the issue of central importance for all linguistics and philosophy of language in those days, which was, and still seems to be, *the word.*

If a 'word' is characterized as a 'unit' or a 'particle' of language, then it is fully understandable that performing speech acts is understood as the 'use' of such units/particles. Any performer performs by means of uses. But the world around us teaches us that a word on its own cannot exist, and if we imagine such an existence—for instance in the way a dictionary does, suggesting multiple possibilities of use—then the word does not work, live, have any effect. The choice of the word for a primordial function in a philosophy of language characterizes that peculiar philosophy in all regards. An important observation would be, that the concept of 'philosophy of language' itself is also the product of a thought pattern that makes the choice of the word seem natural to all who live in the sign pool of an everyday language. That is mirrored in a variety of implications regarding the concept of 'theory of language':

1. Each theory of language is a theory about *the role of language in man's relation to the world*, the latter understood and named as *reality*. Peirce's man-word-world connotations are as significant in that regard as Searle's analyses about a performative character of certain speech acts.
2. A theory and philosophy of language is almost entirely a theory about *the internal architecture of language* (in which words function as separate and independent units). Any theory of language is a theory about the connections between those units or elements. Patterns of connectivity are contractually formed and languages structured along the lines of contract (as for instance grammars display).
3. In the Occident, a theory of language focuses on the indisputable position of *an autonomous speaker*. This position is clearly repeated where signifying is at stake, or the meaning of signs and meanings contemplated, or the features of a specific discourse explored. Freedom of contract, impartiality of the judge, autonomy of the legislator and ultimately the inviolability of the rule of law all mirror the speaker's position. Debates at the beginning of the twentieth century claimed that language barriers should be diminished so that the complexity of legal language would no longer block access to justice.
4. The latter viewpoint indicates a wider interest in Occidental law. Language can only be the preferred instrument of the speaker (the subject in society) if there is

this firm *unity between basic thought patterns that determine society*, which we characterized as *more geometrico*. Everyday expressiveness is in the chains of that thought pattern—it needs the 'subject-verb-object' schematization like all other linguistic utterances and significations to make life acceptable, as it seems to do by means of 'correct' law and 'justice'.

So there must be a close connection between law and society, between language and legal discourse. Before everyday language can compose this expressivity, it needs the 'word' as its ultimate building block in language. We learn from contemporary pedagogic and education efforts in regions with illiteracy that knowledge is enormously important and that large-scale social effects are at stake. *Everyday* expressivity illustrates the profiles of *social* expressivity; one perceives the inverse only in secondary cases. Legal discourse is an artificial discourse (like mathematics) composed with words of our daily languages (different from mathematics); the predominant position of law in society conceals that the two fortify one and the same geometric pattern.

5. A final question comes up: "What does 'understanding' really mean?" Is 'understanding' a perversion, a hidden form of slavery, honoring the *more geometrico* thought pattern as if the days of Hobbes were still here? And: is the determination as a *more geometrico* thought pattern or discourse the only one to adopt in one's analyses of modern thinking? This consideration will find its fulfillment in forthcoming pages. The question is extremely important in social issues and particularly where legal judgments became large-scale directives for social behavior.[4] It also fascinated theology, the arts, law and philosophy in the context of hermeneutics. 'To understand' has never meant a repetition of what the speaker had in mind, the lawyers, artist, priest, or philosopher. The Ancient Greek differentiated between 'thinking' (NOEIN) and 'speaking' (LEGEIN). However, we want to know the meaning of our discovery that thinking and speaking are both determined by an identical pattern. It seems that our understanding is always along common lines, which we are seldom aware of. Total freedom, including thought formation without any basic pattern or internal order, seems a phantom, a distorted image of human capacity.

1.2 The Hidden Philosophy of Language: On the Particle

A hidden philosophy of language reigns in various forms. Philosophy and linguistics embrace the 'particle' idea to determine their view on the word. Both interpret human communication in terms of a large-scaled Newtonian view on reality. This same model functions in unison for human speech: the speaker-hearer model and speech are understood as categories of the use of words. Thus, speech—in particular as a meaning-making force—remains without insight into its peculiar dynamic

[4] See: Peter Goodrich: "Historical Aspects of Legal Interpretation" in: *61 Indiana Law Review 331*, 1986.

character, and does not find a correct place in theories of meaning. The speaker-hearer relationship and its mechanistic character should *not* be understood as dialogue! Speech and its language require an integration of Newtonian and Quantum approaches to reality—approaches that are more than a physics project. All elaborate forms of social and intellectual life are indeed affected by changes in our attitude towards, and our use of, words. *"How words work"* is commonly regarded as a purely theoretical matter, and of little interest to practical persons, but as Ogden and Richards wrote in their Preface "...its disregard by practical persons is nevertheless short-sighted ... no science has been able to deal directly with the issue, since what is fundamentally involved is the theory of Signs in general and their interpretation". Lady Welby, Peirce, Husserl, and Mauthner are among the authors who contributed more attention to and analyses of *the word and our uses of words.*

Richard Rorty, in his 1982 *Consequences of Pragmatism* mentions a tendency to appreciate Charles Sanders Peirce in this context. He states: "Peirce is praised partly because he developed various logical notions and various technical problems (such as the counterfactual conditional) which were taken up by the logical empiricists. But the main reason for Peirce's undeserved apotheosis is that his talk about a general theory of signs looks like an early discovery of the importance of language. For all his genius, however, Peirce never made up his mind what he wanted a general theory of signs *for*, nor what it might look like, nor what its relation to either logic or epistemology was supposed to be. His contribution to pragmatism was merely to have given it a name, and to have stimulated James. Peirce himself remained the most Kantian of thinkers—the most convinced that philosophy gave us an all-embracing a-historical context in which every other species of discourse could be assigned its proper place and rank."[5]

Several misunderstandings are at stake. All have to do with an understanding of language. The importance of language should not depend upon a specific understanding or a specific tradition. Semiotics, as a general theory of signs, reaches far beyond debates on what language is or how language should be understood. The epistemological relevance is to be brought together with Peirce's triad: Firstness, Secondness and Thirdness, but also with the cosmological foundations of his philosophical insights, theories of chance and riddles included. And do not forget that he coined the term "pragmaticism" to avoid the use of "pragmatism" and all possible misunderstandings accompanying that.[6] Charles Morris' 1946 publication "*Signs, Language, and Behavior*" is meant to "lay the foundation for a comprehensive and fruitful science of signs. It attempts to develop a language in which to talk about signs" and "is written from the point of view first expressed by Charles Peirce, that to determine the meaning of any sign 'we have (...) to determine what habits it produces." Signs, Morris concluded, are therefore described and differentiated in terms of the dispositions of behaviors, which they cause in their interpreters. That approach embraces views of behavioral studies in social sciences as well as in

[5] Richard Rorty: *Consequences of Pragmatism.* The Harvester Press, UK, 1982, p. 160 f.

[6] See: Karl-Otto Apel: *Charles S. Peirce: From pragmatism to pragmaticism.* Amherst: Prometheus Books. 1995.

logics. Each variant of ordinary language (a sign complex with signs of all the modes of signifying ministering to a vast variety of purposes) wants specific purposes to be met. Morris' prevailing *mode-use classification* of discourses mixes a dominant mode of signifying with a primary usage—of what? The answer is: *of words*. The most effective and responsible manner of classifying discourses Morris offers occurs under the tacit condition that a discourse is defined as *an ensemble of word-uses*. This concentration on words, clearly formulated for more than a century, seems to be the real problem pertaining to the foundations of meaning. This chapter thus contains further observations reinforced by many variations on 'The Word': from Word (Lady Welby, Peirce, Searle) to Sentence (Frege, Shaumyan) to Text (Kristeva, Husserl).

2 Peirce, Semiotics & Significs

The word is in the modern history of linguistics and/or literature understood as *a lingual sign-component* in social practice and philosophy. Verbal traditions were marked in their longstanding tradition of occidental thought patterns. The word plays a dominant role in those patterns, which reach from significs (Welby) and semeiotics (Peirce) toward structural linguistics (Shaumyan) or text semiotics (Kristeva) deep into deconstructionism (Derrida) and current theories of meaning. One should not wonder about this wide range, because *whatever can be determined as a word is a component of human expressivity*—and in occidental culture the latter became came to be dominated by the verbal and its linguistically understood properties.

Any use of the expression 'word' implies the acceptance of a predominantly Latin linguistic tradition. One should be aware, that 'the word: verbum' means 'word in general' and at the same time 'the word as an active, dynamic, creative component'. In the performance of speech, 'verb' and 'verbum' display two features in one expression: the more or less passive 'word' and an active counterpart, which is also named 'word'. This Latin tradition is known in English, German, French, Spanish or Italian, but also in Scandinavian languages (the Danish 'verbet' and the Swedish 'verb'). There is exception in Dutch, where the Latin 'verbum' means 'woord' *and* 'werkwoord': the latter combining the active and the passive in one word to indicate a particular grammatical function.

One conclusion remains: the concept is considered as *the basic unit of language*. Activity-zones of a grammar, as the Dutch 'werkwoord' proves, remain a 'word', and the dynamics of language find their foundation in that basic unit which keeps its name: 'word'. It follows that activities such as speaking are exclusively understood as word-activities, so that speaking is 'the use of words'.

A direct analysis of "'the word' as such" seldom occurred in Peirce. That is already an interesting issue in view of the introductory observations pertaining to the major outlines of twentieth century philosophy of meaning and language. There are exceptions to highlight, and those are very fascinating indeed. 'The word' is in

Peirce's ideas (a) to be placed in the tension field between sign and symbol, so that (b) the role of 'the word' in significs (for Peirce better named semeiotic) determines the major features of the study of signs and language. It is no surprise that both viewpoints relate intimately to the concept of meaning. And there is (c) Peirce's concept of a "dicisign", for which the 2014 publication of Stjernfelt begs our particular attention.[7]

2.1 Sign and Symbol

> Meaning, that pivotal term of every theory of language, cannot be treated without a satisfactory theory of signs.
>
> C.K. Ogden & I.A. Richards: *The Meaning of Meaning, 1923*

Word, sign and symbol belong closely together for Peirce. Does he, however, single out the word, and place it in a predominant role like many philosophers of language used to do? Tensions between the three focus on their place and function in language as well as their ontological implications. The terms sign and symbol are primarily essential for his philosophical views in general. Robert Marty collected Peirce's sign concepts via 76 definitions and Alfred Lang later completed this list with 17 further definitions; all were published 1997 with annotations of J. Ransdell.[8] The term symbol has a comparable position in Peirce's work, but was hitherto not collected systematically. Possible tensions between sign and symbol can be noticed when a sign is characterized as *mediating* and a symbol as *representing*. The difference has immediate ontological implications: *mediating* can lead to all types of being, whereas *representing* is always chained to well-determined types of being.

An 1885 definition of a sign already reveals the mediating dimension. In his last year of being in charge of the "Office of Weights and Measures", Peirce published in the*American Journal of Mathematics* an essay "On the Algebra of Logic: A Contribution to the Philosophy of Notation" which opens with the observation that there are *three* kinds of signs. Overarching is the insight, that "a sign is in a conjoint relation to the thing denoted and to the mind." It means, a sign is never alone, there is—apart from the object—always the mind/interpretant playing a role: "the sign is related to its object only in consequence of a mental association, and depends upon a habit. Such signs are always abstract and general, because habits are general rules to which the organism has become subjected. They are, for the most part,

[7] F. Stjernfelt: *Natural Propositions: The Actuality of Peirce's Doctrine of Dicisigns*. Docent Press, 2014. See: -Id.: *Diagrammatology*. Springer 2007. p. 31 f.

[8] www.cspeirce.com/menu/library/rsources/76defs/76defs.htm; see also: J. Ransdell: "Another Interpretation of Peirce's Semiotic" in: *Transactions of the Charles S. Peirce Society*, 1976, XII (2), p. 97 ff.

conventional and arbitrary. They include all general words, the main body of speech, and any mode of conveying a judgment."[9]

Among a sign, its object and the mind exists always a triadic relation—this is the basis for overcoming traditional philosophical dualisms of all kinds.[10] *In this triangle, the word plays an important role, but is never seen as a single element* because it needs the constitutive function of the mind within the triangle. "A Sign is a Cognizable that, on the one hand, is so determined (i.e., specialized, *bestimmt*) by something *other than itself*, called its Object … while, on the other hand, it so determines some actual or potential Mind, the determination whereof I term the Interpretant created by the Sign, that that Interpreting Mind is therein determined mediately by the Object."[11]

That would already be a sufficient answer to the question whether Peirce places the word in a unique and self-sufficient position—he evidently does *not*. But before entering the field of definitions, we have to read another clarifying description of a sign in order to acquire insight in possible tensions between sign and symbol around the word. In another 1909 letter to William James we read: "I start by defining what I mean by a Sign. It is something determined by something else, its Object, and itself influencing some person in such a way that that person becomes thereby mediately influenced or determined in some respect by that Object. This being what I mean by a Sign, I must classify signs according first to their natures by themselves, second in relation to their Objects and third in their relation to their *Interpretants*, i.e. the effects on the interpreter. You see here the triplet is absolutely forced upon me by the nature of my concept of a Sign".[12] *Mediation* and *flexibility* (or *impressionability*) of the interpreter are two observations, which return in nearly every description of the foundational triad. In order to be itself "the sign", a sign has to create the influenced, determined o/Other. A sign cannot exist in itself, single, alone, in solo—it needs to stimulate someone or another mind in order to be "sign", and that irrespective of the fact that a sign also needs to be "a sign *of* …".

Before we make a step from here towards the *word*, we must face the *symbol*. A symbol possesses also a certain dependency, although different from the mediation-dependency of the sign—the symbol does not explicitly need another personal mind, but rather, more abstractly, a habit, rule or language, Peirce claims. In his 1903 essay *On Existential Graphs*, he explains that: "A *symbol* is a representamen whose special significance or fitness to represent just what it does represent lies in nothing but the very fact of there being a habit, disposition, or other effective general

---

[9] Charles Sanders Peirce: "On the Algebra of Logic: A Contribution to the Philosophy of Notation", in: *American Journal of Mathematics*, 7, 1885, p 180–202, and in: Nathan Houser & Christian Koesel, (Eds), *The Essential Peirce*, [*EP*] Volume 1 (1867–1893), p. 225 f.

[10] Marty differentiates between a "global triadic" conception (before 1905) and an "analytic triadic", but highlights that we cannot speak of the differences before underlining their unity.

[11] Peirce: Letters to William James, 1909 in: *EP* Vol. 2, p.492. Mats Bergman: *Peirce's Philosophy of Communication*, New York 2009, writes p. 93: "I believe that the increasing focus on rhetoric and communication in Peirce's mature philosophy is reflected in—and conversely influenced by—developments in his theory of interpretants and his conception of meaning …".

[12] Peirce, *EP 2*, (1893–1913), *Letter to William James, 1909*, p. 492, 494.

rule that it will be so interpreted."[13] Habit and rule are mentioned, language follows immediately *by reference to a word:* "Take, for example, the word '*man*'. These three letters are not in the least like a man; nor is the sound with which they are associated. Neither is the word existentially connected with any man as an index. It cannot be so, since the word is not an existence at all. The word does not consist of three films of ink. If the word "man" occurs hundreds of times in a book of which myriads of copies are printed, all those millions of triplets of patches of ink are embodiments of one and the same word. I call each of those embodiments a *replica* of the symbol. This demonstrates that the word is not a thing. What is its nature? It consists in the really working general rule that three such patches seen by a person who knows English will affect his conduct and thoughts according to a rule".

Peirce claims: *the word is not a thing*. It is closely related to and dependent upon a convention/habit, as De Saussure also mentioned, so that a certain materiality will cause a specific behavior. Are reading and writing, interpreting and understanding thus altogether just forms of rule following? Those who read Peirce with an analytical mind will agree. Others will not. Tensions profile themselves; they concentrate on the concept of *mind*, and with *mind* also on *communication. Mind is for Peirce a symbol in itself*: a symbol of the totality of a designating/representing capacity of mankind and its cultural dimensions, not an individual decision- or rule making apparatus located in a person's body and soul.

The distance between descriptions of the symbol and the word narrows even more if one considers a sentence from the 1866 Lowell Institute Lectures, which took place a year before he was elected to the *American Academy of Arts and Sciences*: "A symbol is a general representation like a word or conception. [---] A symbol is a representation whose essential Quality and Relation are both unprescindible[14]—the Quality of being Imputed and the Relation ideal."[15] So: a symbol is *like* a word! It is (like words) a special form of representation. The proximity of the word to the symbol was already highlighted in the 1866 Lowell Lectures: symbols "... connote attributes and so connote them as to determine what they denote. To this class belong all *words* and all *conceptions*. Most combinations of words are also symbols. A proposition, an argument, even a whole book may be, and should be, a single symbol." The word is in Peirce's thoughts never an independent entity to be treated as a unit or component of and in language, but a process in itself. The challenge of the process is in the need for a habit: to be a sign is like to be a word: both are in need of a rule, a habit, an o/Other.

Whereas a sign can become a symbol through the course of processes of developing meaning, a symbol needs a sign as its Firstness. The fulfillment of that need is the main cause for tensions between sign and symbol, which the word should overcome. In *Logics and Mathematics* one reads: "... a word is general—it occurs

[13] Ch.S. Peirce: *Existential Graphs,* C.P.4.2

[14] unprescindible = indispensible (JMB).

[15] Ch. S. Peirce; "Lowell Lectures on The Logic of Science; or Induction and Hypothesis": Lecture ix,http://www.commens.org/bibliography/manuscript/peirce-charles-s-1866-lowell-lectures-logic-science-or-induction-and-0.

often, and every time it occurs, it is the same word, and if it has any meaning *as a word*, it has the same meaning every time it occurs. … A meaning is the associations of a word with images, its dream-exciting power". Generality and specificity are characteristic features of the word in Peirce's thinking, because "the" must always be transited towards "*a* the …"[16]

All these observations, the tensions around the word between sign and symbol included, could considerably expand and thus enrich a philosophy of language by means of a general picture of Peirce's thoughts. But in the context of an investigation of meaning, we just repeat one conclusion: *'the word' is in Peirce's body of texts nowhere understood or used as a 'basic unit' of language, an independent entity or a self-contained articulation.* The reliance of sign as well as symbol upon the interpreter proves the impossibility of such independence. While mutually influencing each other, often even constituting each other, sign and interpreter (i.e. patterns of habits, rules, cultural factors) unveil a relationship that could lay the foundations of communication among human individuals, which are enveloped in processes that transcend any fixation of independent entities, and certainly 'the word' as an entity.[17]

That is one of the most essential features of Peirce's 'semiosis' defined as "an action, or influence, which is, or involves, a cooperation of *three* subjects, such as a sign, its object, and its interpretant, this tri-relative influence not being in any way resolvable into actions between pairs." One reads again the influence of the mind/interpretant/habit, and the coordination of a pragmatist approach and semiotics sparkles in the foundational idea that every concept (also, and even primarily, the word) and every thought (again, even primarily, the function and meaning of the word) beyond immediate perception is a sign. "Beyond immediate perception" is immediacy—not unlike, but certainly not beyond Firstness. Every sign belongs to a surface structure of language. A deep structure of the word would, in terms of Peirce's semiotics, be: the mind, the interpretant in the form of the o/Other. He definitely considers that: "… the most perfect account of a concept that words can convey will consist in a description of that habit which it is calculated to produce. But how else can a habit be described than by a description of the kind of action to which it gives rise."[18]

2.2 *Between Significs and Semiotics*

The main thesis on Peirce focuses on the fact that he gives 'the word' an important place in his semiotics project without having 'the word' function in the *more geometrico* framework of preceding philosophers or of social thinkers like Hobbes. With it, a geometric position of 'basic unit' or 'particle' of language is not in his

[16] Ch. S. Peirce: *Logics and Mathematics*, CP 4.56.

[17] Mats Bergman: *Peirce's Philosophy of Communication*, New York 2009, p. 92 f., 116 f.

[18] Ch.S. Peirce: *Essential Peirce,* Op. Cit., Vol. 2, p.411, 398.

semeiotic- or in later developments of *semiotics* after him. He expands insights into language while unfolding numerous expressions, and 'the word' is one of the most important among them. Hence his famous drive to create refined nominations within a system of logical expressivity relations. The 'sign' plays a major role, immediately connected with 'the word' but also at a critical distance from it. An example of all this can be read in a letter to Lady Welby from October 12, 1908: "But I wanted to write to you about signs, which in your opinion and mine are matters of so much concern. More in mine, I think, than in yours. For in mine, the highest grade of reality is only reached by signs; that is by such ideas as those of Truth and Right and the rest. It sounds paradoxical; but when I have devolved to you my whole theory of signs, it will seem less so. … You know that I particularly approve of inventing new words for new ideas."

The latter remark, a proof of Peirce's enduring interest in refining an analytical naming process, links to a letter in December 1908: "As we use the term 'word' in most cases, saying that 'the' is one 'word' and 'an' is a second 'word,' a 'word' is a legisign. But when we say of a page in a book, that it has 250 'words' upon it, of which twenty are 'the's, the 'word' is a sinsign. A sinsign so embodying a legisign, I term a 'replica' of the legisign. The difference between a legisign and a qualisign, neither of which is an individual thing, is that a legisign has a definite identity, though usually admitting a great variety of appearances. Thus, &, *and,* and the sound are all one word."[19] This is a treatment of 'the word' that differs fundamentally from the geometric attitude and its linguistic implications.

But one does not immediately find an answer to a particular semiotic consideration: how can we expand the boundaries of a language? Can we search for linguistic expressiveness *beyond* our everyday language formation? What Peirce refined terminologically remains situated within the boundaries of conversational discourse.

The above question leaves us with at least two further possibilities: (a) a search beyond everyday language forms of expressiveness *like*- or at least *comparable with* language (such as non-verbal forms of communication), or (b) expressivity in other types or levels of language (in everyday, artificial, formal etc languages). Did Peirce differentiate along the lines of those two? Did he notice this layered character of language and/or discourses at all?

Peirce's focus on changes of language level and articulation seems confined to a general concept of language. 'Beyond' language is for him always 'within' language—considerations pertaining to the word confirm that. Is 'significs' aware of this perspective, or is that awareness a privilege of Peirce's semiotics? The two do *not* place 'the word' in the position of prominence the way a *more geometrico* thinking about language proclaims. So, what does the latter consideration mean to Lady Welby and Peirce, to semiotics and significs? Both understand for instance that things and occurrences need to be encapsulated and determined as 'facts' if they are

---

[19] See also: Charles S. Hardwick (Ed.): *Semiotics and Significs. The Correspondence between Charles S. Peirce and Victoria Lady Welby*, Indiana UP 1977. p.22 f, 66. and: C.K. Ogden & I.A. Richards: *The Meaning of Meaning,* 1923, (London 1946; 8th Ed.) p. 279 f. Appendix D, § 6.

ever to become components of human relations and signs in and of life. *Signs have in their turn to be understood as facts, so that they can mean acts*. Human activity seems never directly accessible in semiotic terms; a transition of meanings is necessary before a semiotic qualification of human activity will be significant.

It is fascinating that transitions of meaning-fields and their central concepts from: (a) 'event/occurrence' towards (b) 'fact' towards (c) 'act' towards (d) 'human activity' towards (e) 'communication', unfold at one and the same language level, which Peirce would characterize as 'habit'. When this presupposition does not work, there seems no awareness of any layered structure, and it does also not come up when conversely the chain of transitions is directed backwards from 'communication' to 'occurrence'. The transitions remain observed at the surface-level of language; they seem to exclusively belong to an everyday discourse and have yet as their common deep structure the *geometric* thought pattern, which will seldom come to the surface in a clear manner. A philosophical approach to sign(s) often displays this one-leveled understanding of meanings so that any signification does not enter deeper layers of language, meaning or the signification process itself.

Lady Welby also concentrated on language and meaning. In 1892 she published in *The Monist* on "*Meaning and Metaphor*", and in 1897 in *Mind* her essay "*Sense, Meaning and Interpretation*". The major idea was an early development of "significs": there should be some 'linguistic conscience' to fight terminological confusion and therefore unnecessary polemics on philosophical insights and statements. That theme was always in the background when *signific* ideas were promoted, concentrating on forms of expressiveness and the nature of language. That attitude was later the foundation of her famous article on *significs* in the 10th and 11th editions of the Encyclopedia Britannica. She thus writes a few years before, in her 1903 book *What is Meaning?* on *significs*: "Significs, then, will bring us the philosophy of Significance; *i.e.* a raising of our whole conception of meaning to a higher and more efficient level; a bringing cosmos out of the present 'chaos 'of our ideas as to sense, meaning, and significance, and showing us that we need to use these terms in a certain order of value and range. .... In fact, for the first time we gain a glimpse into what lies 'beyond the veil,' which both our own primitive and confused idea of Meaning and our modes of applying it have drawn over the world. The criteria thus reached will vindicate themselves alike to the most opposed of our thinkers." In 1897 she had already written: "The greatest lesson the philosophical analysis of language teaches us is, that we should be above language, making words our servants, and not allowing them to be our masters."[20]

Her concentration on the word, and her battle against inadequate understandings of the word did not serve the *more geometrico* idea pertaining to social life and law. This did inspire Peirce. He wrote about his sophisticated mistrust towards the dominance of the word in a letter written on March 14, 1909: "One remark of yours I approved particularly was that 'language is only the extreme form of expression'". In the same paragraph of the quoted letter, Peirce formulates the difference between

[20] Victoria Lady Welby: *What is Meaning? Studies in the Development of Significance*, London 1903, p. 113 f.

significs and *semeiotics* in his own sense and focuses on the position of 'the word' in her philosophy and in his own: "I think, dear Lady Welby, that perhaps you are in danger of falling into some error in consequence of limiting your studies so much to language, and among languages to one very particular language, as all Aryan languages are; *and within that language so much to words* (...).[21]

Peirce thus proposed to envisage a broader science of semiotic that embraces all sorts of signs (there exists not *one* single type of sign!) and which includes icons, symbols, indices etc., as well as—on the same level of analysis and observation—the relations of signs with objects and sign-interpretants. *The semiotic project is not an issue of the word*, Peirce underlines. Word-language has indeed a most prominent role to fulfill in our daily language.

A conclusion on 'the word' is that neither Peirce nor Lady Welby placed 'the word' in a position that could serve the *more geometrico* thought patterns and its many ideological components that reign in science and society also in our day. Language is a layered phenomenon in itself, but any explanation of this feature would need the language of another planet or of another (human-like) race.

2.3 *Peirce's "Dicisign"*

If it is acceptable that the semiosis as process is layered in itself and multidimensional like language, then the question comes up whether, and if so, in what way we can expand the boundaries of language to have expressiveness be more effective and put the dominance of everyday language levels in perspective. It is the issue Nietzsche brought to the fore when writing in 1886 that one cannot stay in town and at the same time know the height of its towers: "(...) wie es ein Wanderer macht, der wissen will, wie hoch die Thürme einer Stadt sind: dazu *verläßt* er die Stadt."[22] Community is found outside the town, the 'talk of the town' must incorporate an overall view, not unlike Google satellite views can enrich daily life.

Our purpose is to suggest that Peirce approached an answer to those questions in his explanation of propositions, and among them in the *Dicent Sign* or *Dicisign*, as suggested by Stjernfelt. Publishing on a consequence of Peirce's conception of propositions recently, he states that *propositions are natural inhabitants of reality* and thus are no strangers to a naturalist world-view form. This is because propositions—Peirce's Dicisigns—contrary to most standard assumptions—do *not* depend upon the human or its intentionality.[23]

The entire weight of the question whether the given descriptions and definitions are able to expand the realm of language and of linguistic expressiveness is on the

[21] [Italics are mine, JMB.] See: Charles S. Hardwick (Ed.): *Semiotics and Significs*, 1977, p. 117f.

[22] F. Nietzsche: [what a rambler does, when he wants to know how high the towers of a town are: he *leaves* that town].

[23] F. Stjernfelt: *Natural Propositions*: Op. Cit., 2014. See: -Id._: Diagrammatology. Springer 2007. p. 31 f, 81.

word *'nature'* in this context. Are dicisigns in any way beyond (human) culture and thus (fragmentarily) a matter of nature? We do not discuss whether the nature-culture formula is applied correctly, but try to understand Peirce's reasoning: "a Dicisign … conveys information, in contradistinction to a sign [such as an icon] from which information may be derived."[24] Experimentation makes information from an icon possible—which "so to speak makes it speak", Stjernfelt writes, in "using it as material for a proposition". The proposition is, however, a sign making explicit the object to which it refers. A mere icon does not. "All in all, the idea that algebraic, formal and linguistic syntactic systems must involve iconicity in order to be able to convey information is a remarkable consequence of Peirce's concept of iconicity."[25] The quality of iconicity as embedded in the nature-culture concept should determine the possibilities for expanding the boundaries of linguistic expressivity. If that conclusion is correctly deduced from the above observations, then one touches here indeed a foundational issue for maintaining the concept of meaning. Should we ever be able to see the skyline of what Heidegger once named romantically "Das Haus des Seins" [the house of being]?[26]

3 Searle, and 'The Word'

Clarity of thought and opinion is a virtue of John Searle's famous 1969 essay on *Speech Acts.*[27] This clarity is the result of a specific choice of research subject, attitude and methodology. All three focus on 'the word'—a guiding theme in research on meaning. Considerations of Searle's theory have a double purpose in that context: to clarify 'the word' from the angle of Searle's philosophy of language, and to indicate consequences of reducing that philosophy of language (which is implicit in his speech act design) to one type of language level: the everyday language.

3.1 The 'Principle of Expressibility'

Speech unfolds in Searle's philosophy through the performance of what he calls speech-acts, and that activity is based on a "principle of expressibility". It is fascinating to experience in what way he suggests that the clarity of his method and

[24] Ch.S. Peirce: *§14L Logic. CP* 2. 309: A man cannot criticize every part of his reasoning, since he cannot criticize the act of reasoning he is performing in the criticism, it is true. But he can criticize steps whose validity he doubts; and in doing so, ought to consider in what characters the validity of reasoning consists, and whether the reasoning in question possesses those characters.

[25] Stjernfelt, *Diagrammatology,* p. 81.

[26] "Die Sprache ist das Haus des Seins." In: M. Heidegger: *Brief über den Humanismus*, 1949 [Engl. Ed.: Letter on Humanism, Tr. F.A. Capuzzi & J.G. Gray, San Francisco 1978].

[27] J. Searle: *Speech Acts. An essay in the philosophy of language.* Cambridge UP 1969, p. 21.

representation is successful: "… in our era of extremely sophisticated methodologies, the methodology of this book must seem naively simple. I am a native speaker of a language. … But everything I have ever read in the philosophy of language … relies similarly on the intuitions of the speaker."[28] His method and his speech act theory unfold deliberately at the level of a native speaker. They do not consider any expansion of the level of language, speech or articulate intention, and should therefore be characterized as "belonging to the everyday language level", which Husserl classified as a language resulting from a "naïve-natural attitude".[29]

That has its consequences for the position of 'the word' in a speech act context. All linguistic communication involves linguistic acts, and thus the unit of linguistic communication is in this view an issue of central importance. It illustrates the influence of a *more geometrico* pattern reigning in the everyday language level. At this level, the theory cannot be imagined without an overall knowledge of the smallest and hence foundational unit. A conclusion is therefore, that "the unit of linguistic communication is … the production or issuance of the symbol or word or sentence in the performance of the speech act." So the unit is not a determined *static thing* like a symbol, word or sentence would appear to be, but a *power*, an utterance *in the form of* a static and fixated thing: symbol, word or sentence. At the level of everyday language, however, one does not clearly distnguish between them. Hence the consideration that an utterance we take as a means of communication is understood as a *produced* or *issued* utterance. It leads to the conclusion that "speech acts … are the basic or minimal units of linguistic communication." If speech acts are those units, then the word as the form of that production is the unit—at least at a naïve-natural language level.

Considerations pertaining to expanding the language phenomenon are thus reduced to the knowledge needed for performing in a mother tongue. The reliance on the intuitions of a native speaker can only reach beyond the immediacy of the spoken word by means of introducing/learning new words. That restriction in Searle's approach teaches us about the enormous interest in, and the importance of perceiving language (and meaning in language) as layered and potentially infinite.

All this leads us back to Searle's "principle of expressibility". Does it express anything of this infinite character of human speech? Searle describes: "We might express this principle by saying that for any meaning X and any speaker S whenever S means (intends to convey, wishes to communicate an utterance, etc) X, then it is possible that there is some expression E such that E is an exact expression of or formulation of X. Symbolically: (S) (X) (S means X—P (3E) (E is an exact expression of X). A footnote adds 'This formulation involves an explicit use of quantifiers through a modal context; but since the kind of entity quantified over is 'intensional'

[28] J. Searle, *Speech Acts*, p. 15.

[29] This is true for the speech act theory designed by Searle, but in other contexts, the author does try to expand the boundaries of language, as is the case in for instance his *The Construction of Social Reality*, London 1995, where he studies in Ch. 3, p 59 f. how language is constitutive of institutional reality. See also Searle, *Speech Acts*, p. 51 for 'institutions' as systems of constitutive rules.

anyway, the modal context does not seem to raise special problems'."[30] Consequences for Frege's theory of sense and reference are claimed, the exactness of meaning is debated and rules for performing speech acts are envisaged.

3.2 The 'Word' as Basic Unit of Language

The word, the basic unit of communication, unfolds where act and principle come together and thus create speech. Searle formulates: *to speak is to perform the act of using words*. Since the level of everyday language provides (in contrast to for instance the artificial language levels) a perhaps unlimited possibility 'to use words', Searle can claim *on that level only* that it is "an analytic truth about language that whatever can be meant can be said" ... so that "... there are no barriers in principle to supplementing the impoverished language or saying what I mean in a richer one." And therefore, "the speech act or acts performed in the utterance of a sentence are in general a function of the meaning of the sentence. ... a study of the meaning of sentences is not in principle distinct from a study of speech acts. Properly construed, they are the same study."[31]

In those considerations, an identity between a theory of language and a theory of meaning grows—especially within the boundaries of a naïve-natural attitude or language level. The "principle of expressibility" plays a key role here. Whatever can be meant can be said, and can thus be the germ of a speech act. There is no seamless connection between what we say and what we mean, because every speaker can enrich the language she uses and bring her meanings in accordance with this enrichment. "Where there is in a given language or in any language an upper bound on the expressible, where there are thoughts that cannot be expressed in a given language or in any language, it is a contingent fact and not a necessary truth", Searle states for the sake of defending the principle.[32]

3.3 Sociolinguistic Activity: The Speech Act

So there is "a series of analytic connections between the speech acts, what the speaker means, what the sentence uttered means, what the speaker intends, what the hearer understands, and what the rules governing the linguistic elements are". In the pursuit of his analysis of the speech act, Searle investigates various types of sociolinguistic activities. In all of them the activity itself is the utterance of a word as the token of process, power, energy and unfolding speech. This is for example clear in

[30] J. Searle, *Speech Acts,* Op. Cit., p. 20.

[31] J. Searle, *Speech Acts,* Op. Cit., p. 17.

[32] J. Searle, *Speech Acts*, Op. Cit., p. 20—which makes again clear how those thoughts play solely at the level of everyday (or naïve-natural) language attitudes.

his qualification of what he calls the 'speech act fallacy'. His example pertains to the word 'good'. *Calling* something good, he states, is "characteristically praising or commending or recommending it, etc. But it is a fallacy to infer from this that the meaning of 'good' is explained by saying it is used to perform the act of commendation." So the use of words in their contextual association with other words sets the tones of meaning. In the quoted example, our understanding is once more based upon an analysis of *the word* 'good'. This example can be perceived as a basic presupposition for Searle's analysis of speech as a specific human activity.

In his defense of the proposal to introduce the concept of 'speech act', Searle defined the underlying principle of expressibility in many ways. Most fascinating is the principle's parallel with meaning. What the speaker means, what the uttered sentence means together with an understanding and with speaking as a rule-governed behavior, is determinative. Meaning is treated as 'meaning of…' and expressivity is understood as 'expression of…'. Relations between them are possible on the basis of a separation between meaning and expression. The idea of reference has been used to build bridges to explore both sides of the abyss between them. "Whatever can be meant can be said", Searle formulates—and this brings meaning together with means of speaking. Yet 'meaning' remains even in its clearest pronunciation 'meaning of…' as Peirce clarified: 'signs' as 'signs of…'.

For Peirce, this was the beginning of further research into the characteristics and ontological status of a sign, and those insights are also fruitful for meaning embedded in expressivity. They could contribute to a further emancipation of the 'meaning' concept—an emancipation, which seems urgent in the light of his philosophy. "A word", he writes after having read Lady Welby's study on meaning, "has meaning for us in so far as we are able to make use of it in communicating our knowledge to others and in getting at the knowledge that there others seek to communicate to us. *That is the lowest grade of meaning.*"[33] So other grades have to follow! Let us not forget that expression, meaning and sign are in an equal position in so far as Searle's 'what can be said' implies 'what can be said in language', therefore: 'what can be said *in words'*—both, however, at the level of everyday (naïve-natural) language. The latter leads one to define the speech act as 'the basic unit of communication'—naively perceived like words, which are generally understood as the basic unit of language.

3.4 Meaning in Speech and Language

It would be of interest to finally highlight three components that influence the search for structures of meaning in speech as well as in language in general. (a) The omnipresent importance of 'the word' as the basic unit of language makes the word appear as a natural and self-evident component of speech. Searle's theory proves the overriding influence of his preconditions, collected in the seemingly naïve sentence:

[33] Peirce, *CP* 8. 176. (Italics are mine JMB).

'I am a native speaker'. (b) This dominating position of the word is not solely a semiotic issue but characterizes human expressivity in today's occidental culture in many ways. (c) One must consider that the word is a basic constituent and final signifier at all levels of expressivity in what is called "the verbal". In the case of "the non-verbal", the word maintains signifying power at a deeper level of expressiveness (genotextual), while other signifying elements can be translated at any time into word-governed expressivity.

What a picture has to say, Searle emphasizes, is always prepared for thousand words! The existence of "non-verbal" expressivity never diminishes the dominance and power of the "verbal". The distinction between the two does not do away with the dominance of the latter. Is there a *status quo* in view of that dominance and its semiotic-philosophic understanding? Does that dominance change the character of 'the word' as perceived by Searle and other philosophers of language, in particular in the combination proposed between word, symbol and sentence?

4 Frege, and the Sentence

4.1 The Word

The latter question inspires us to consult Frege's specific attention to the sentence; perhaps he had the same approach in mind as Searle. So we consider whether words can wait and receive meanings in their togetherness with a symbol or with a sentence. Can they? One should be able to perform in a book what can be achieved in film and TV: at this moment the reader is offered any image. What is so clear here? The image is made clear, and words wait. See the Arcadian landscape, or watch the moves of the persons involved, or the series of occurrences which create a situation. No word is necessary: the situation intensifies in gestures, in glances that are reciprocal and filled with desire or disgust. The non-verbal creates, the verbal emphasizes. The verbal reinforces if it is articulated at the right moment. If the moment is not there, verbs annihilate and work destruction. Words wait. They are in the field of multiple articulation forces, but their presence at the surface delicately depends upon other words, or other occurrences. One word on its own is never a word! Contexts? Sentences? The observation leads to a further exploration of the character of the word, and the character of the word-field—with the sentence as the most primordial of all fields.

4.2 The Sentence as Unit

Michael Dummett states in his widely appreciated 1973 study on Frege: "(…) the assignment of a word, whether a name or an expression of another logical type, only has significance in relation to the subsequent occurrence of that word in sentences.

A sentence is (...) the smallest unit of language with which a linguistic act can be accomplished, with which a 'move can be made in the language-game' so you cannot do anything with a word (...) save by uttering some sentence containing that word."[34] What is at stake? The sentence replaces the position of the word in a philosophy of language by means of capturing its definition as 'the smallest unit of language'—an idea that also found its expression in Searle's theory of speech act. Is that move correct? Can a sentence replace the position of the word, or in that hypothetical case does the word loose its meaning because the word had to wait too long?

Dummett paraphrased Frege and formulated: "Definitions of the sentence such as the following are very widespread: 'A sentence is a thought expressed in words', or 'A sentence is a completed thought expressed in words', or 'A sentence is a linguistic unit which expresses a thought', etc. All of these are not definitions of the sentence in the strict sense of the word, but rather explanations of what we intuitively grasp to be the concept of the sentence".[35] Thought and sentence are united under the power and position of the word in the ideas of Frege and Dummett. Emphasizing and analyzing sentences will not change that position. And the *word* remains the proper unit in the semiotic toolkit. How? Does the 'Word' remain in its function within a philosophy of language as *Name*? Articulated otherwise: does Searle's theory and also Frege's suggestion about the sentence only persist because the idea of 'the smallest unit of language' is *given the name*: 'word', so that 'the word' and its position are both no more than *a primary element*?

Wittgenstein has discussed this issue in the context of his heavily debated §43 in the *Philosophical Investigations*: "For a *large* class of cases—though not for all—in which we employ the word 'meaning' it can be defined thus: the meaning of a word is its use in the language". He refers to Socrates debating the status and meaning of primary elements in the Theaetetus, quoting in his § 46: "… everything that exists in its own right has to be … named without any other determination. In consequence it is impossible to give an account of any primary element; for it, nothing is possible but the bare name; its name is all it has. But just as what consists of these primary elements is itself complex, so the names of the elements become descriptive language by being compounded together. For the essence of speech is the composition of names."[36]

4.3 *"Doing with" Words*

Another consideration completes the picture. Dummett suggested, "A sentence is … the smallest unit of language with which a move can be made in the language-game, so that you cannot *do* anything with a word … save by uttering some sentence containing that word." To *do* something is in this context to *say* something. Is this

[34] Michael Dummett: *Frege. Philosophy of language,* London 1973. (*Italics* are mine [JMB]).

[35] Michael Dummett: *Frege.* Op. Cit., p. 193. (*Italics* are mine [JMB]).

[36] L. Wittgenstein: *Philosophical Investigations*, Oxford 1953, p. 20 f.

restricted to the verbal? We suggest, and contemporary semiotics does also, that this is *not* the case. There is a *doing,* which is considerably wider in meaning and sense than what the verbal doing allows or holds to make sense. It can be determined by reaching further than the boundaries of a language incidentally spoken would suggest. The first issue is therefore that sentences with which something is done (Dummett's articulation) do not exist as such. They are always part of a larger entity, which we call *text.*

This is not in Searle's or Frege's motivation of their philosophy of language: the 'text' is for them not an issue, although 'the word' moves indeed from individuality to textuality before or along with becoming speech. A continuously changing context makes decisions about truth-conditions or their falsity as sentences relatively unimportant. That has also its consequences for the importance of the general idea of 'the smallest unit' of language—as if language were a unit rather than a relatively unidentifiable process.

5 Sebastian Shaumyan: Word, Dynamisms and Layered Language

J. Stalin initiated a renewal in Soviet linguistic discussions around 1950, which was a tendency confirmed at the XX Party Convention. In the years after that dictum, also years in which Structuralism developed in Western Europe and moved to Paris while referring to Moscow and Prague as moments of its own history, Soviet theoretical linguistics unfolded forcefully.[37] Publications from Shaumyan (1916–2007) form a key to several renewing insights in linguistics. He was clearly aware of the importance of the thesis pertaining to the word being the smallest unit of language: he introduced important features that characterize natural languages; he proposed the distinction between pheno—and genotype language levels, and all in all contributed to seeing meaning as an issue of a multilayered language structure.

5.1 The Structure of Language as Hypothetical Construct

A first viewpoint of importance was dominant from the beginning: the structure of a language is a hypothetical construction; any linguistic structure is a construct and thoughts about structures of language result from constructive mental forces. To speak of a "natural" language is in this light also a construct. The concept of a "natural language" is as artificial as the concept of an "artificial language". Husserl therefore never speaks of a "naïve-natural language" versus a "non-naïve natural language" but rather of a "naïve-natural-" or "non-naïve-natural attitude" which

[37] See Jan M. Broekman: *Structuralism: Op. Cit.*, Dordrecht 1974.

finds its articulation in linguistic forms/elements, among which are 'word', 'symbol' or 'sentence' as mentioned by Peirce or Searle.

This conceptual character brings with it the conclusion that structural linguistics focus on the dynamics of a linguistic synchrony, thus reinforcing the dynamic character of semiotics in general. De Saussure had sharply distinguished synchrony and diachrony in language, but structural linguistics emphasizes the intertwining of the two. The argument, that synchrony as well as diachrony are constructs and not at all 'natural data' on language is helpful. If language as a system of signs is studied as a complete system at any given point in time, as De Saussure highlighted, then this completeness and system character are artificial articulations. Their importance in language becomes visible in the movement of fragments and the indeterminacy of their positions. The profile of each (like the shape of words) is only important in that its potential (as belonging to or not yet belonging to a field of meaning) can be recognized. A synchronic relationship is one where two similar things exist at the same time. For instance, Modern American English and British English have a synchronic relationship.

5.2 A Semiotic Two-Level Structure

The dynamics in this synchrony are important in the context of this paragraph's thoughts on 'the word'. Shaumyan proposed in his 1965 book *Strukturnaja lingvistika* a 'semiotic two level structure', which is specific for natural languages.[38] He states in a later publication that the meaning of any linguistic unit (not only the word!) is "the class of linguistic units, which serve as its translations. Thus, the notion of meaning is reduced to the notion of translatability". 'Translations' is a dynamic concept; the dynamism of this operation comes to the fore by observing that "...to give the meaning of a given linguistic unit is to give the rules for translating this linguistic unit into other linguistic units."[39]

This is for Shaumyan one of the possibilities for solving the problem of meaning. Connected to it is, at first sight, the view that translations take place via rules that affect all linguistic units at one specific level. But he also states that this solution for meaning is fruitful for a semantic study of language within the framework of generative grammar. And that is clearly at another level, or even at other level*s*. There is in that latter case not a translation on one level, but among two or more levels of not always identical structure. The basis for this observation of a multi-leveled dynamics is in laid down in the thesis that in natural languages a secondary semiotic system of diacritical elements covers its primary sign system, whereas artificial languages (mathematics, physics or biology) work directly with specific sign systems

[38] S. Shaumyan; German Ed: S. Saumjan: *Strukturale Linguistik*, W. Fink, München 1965, Engl. Ed: *Principles of Structural Linguistics,* Mouton de Gruyter 1971.

[39] S. Shaumyan: "The Genotype Language and Formal Semantics" in F. Kiefer (Ed.): *Trends in Soviet Theoretical Linguistics*, Reidel Dordrecht 1973, p. 251 f.

without a primary system as basis.[40] This layered structure makes meaning description possible. The formulation of that possibility is very near to Peirce's observations related to his concept of a *dicisign* (a proposition or a quasi-proposition), where a quality of iconicity determines possibilities for expanding the boundaries of linguistic expressivity.[41] One touches here indeed a foundational issue for maintaining the concept of meaning. "A *Dicisign* must profess to refer or relate to something as having a real being" Peirce wrote in 1903: it is "a sign which is understood to represent its object in respect to actual existence".[42]

5.3 Words in Layers

Shaumyan differentiated between a surface structure (phenotype) and a deep structure (genotype) of texts. Words function in both to create a text—Kristeva exposed later. In his 1973 chapter on *The genotype language and formal semantics* he puts *the sentence* at the center of language, so that the question arises whether despite all other considerations we find here an alternative for the overall emphasis on the word. Can a sentence in a text be regarded as a basic unit of language in the same manner as Searle and even Peirce understood a word in language as such? Thoughts are expressed in sentences, and are often a product of sentences; values are presented as parallels; meaning is considered to be the central unit of sentences nurtured by an ever-ongoing translatability, and hence of language in general—all these are explorations of the question whether sentences can be seen as definite components of a series of linguistic elements: from sign to signal to word to sentence to text … and what follows in this sequence, should then also belong to the materials for our semiotic toolkit. Hence Shaumyan: "Let us note … that the notion of a genotype language makes it possible to consider the conception of linguistic relativity in a new light. The conception of linguistic relativity was most clearly formulated in the works of Sapir and Whorf. The essence of this conception is that the linguistic representations of the world are relative. That language gives a relative picture of the world is an indisputable fact. But this is only one side of the matter. The other side is that any relative picture of the world contained in the linguistic shell of a particular language must be considered as a projection of some invariant of world pictures. The genotype language functions as such an invariant. Phenotypic languages are various projections of the genotype language. Thus, the relative pictures

---

[40] Saumjan: *Strukturale Linguistik* (German Ed) Op. Cit., p. 123 f. Law would in that case be a mixture of the two structures whereby lawyers are supposed to master both languages: the language of everyday and the language of law.

[41] Iconicity = Likeness that stands for an object by signifying or representing it either concretely or by analogy.

[42] Ch.S. Peirce: *The Essential Peirce*, Op. Cit., Indiana UP, 1998, Vol 2, p. 294 f.

of the world represented by phenotypes, i.e., specific natural languages, also contain something non-relative, an invariant represented by the genotype language."[43]

Remember Frege's specific attention to the sentence and a parallel approach. Dummett stated: "(...) the assignment of a word, whether a name or an expression of another logical type, only has significance in relation to the subsequent occurrence of that word in sentences. A sentence is (...) the smallest unit of language with which a linguistic act can be accomplished, with which a 'move can be made in the language-game' so you cannot do anything with a word (...) save by uttering some sentence containing that word." So the sentence replaces the position of the word by means of capturing its definition as 'the smallest unit of language'.[44] We met that formula already at various levels and with various authors.

Shaumyan decided, however, to move in a different direction than Dummett's interpretation paraphrasing Frege: "Definitions of the sentence such as the following are very widespread: 'A sentence is a thought expressed in words', or 'A sentence is a completed thought expressed in words', or 'A sentence is a linguistic unit which expresses a thought', etc. All of these are not definitions of the sentence in the strict sense of the word, but rather explanations of what we intuitively grasp to be the concept of the sentence." So, as for meaning, it is of interest to meet the same approach in many contexts: thought and sentence are united under the power and position of the word. Emphasizing and analyzing sentences and texts will not change that position. And the word remains the proper unit in the semiotic toolkit—but what does this mean for meaning?

5.4 *Consciousness, Meaning*

"The source of the structures of sound and meaning is consciousness. Consciousness is not a passive reflection of reality. Rather consciousness is an active factor that imposes structures both on language and on our total perception of the world. The theory of grammar is concerned with the structure of meaning and the structure of sound", concludes Shaumyan in his 1998 article *Two Paradigms Of Linguistics: The Semiotic Versus Non-Semiotic Paradigm.*[45] Those two paradigms (a classical bound between meaning and sound) also inspire contemporary thought formation on meaning and indicate an important mark that is often underrated in exercising semiotics: *dynamism.* The differentiation between genotype and phenotype language (transformed in the work of Julia Kristeva into genotext and phenotext thus from general linguistic units/structures into textual structures and with them into the

[43] S. Shaumyan: "The Genotype Language and Formal Semantics" Op. Cit., 1973, p. 254.

[44] See J. Kristeva, *Semeiotikè Recherches pour une sémanalyse.* Paris Du Seuil 1969, p. 318 f. "La phrase comme unité sémantique"; Michael Dummett: *Frege. Philosophy of language,* London 1973, p. 193.

[45] S. Shaumyan: "Two Paradigms Of Linguistics: The Semiotic Versus Non-Semiotic Paradigm" in: *Web Journal of Formal, Computational and Cognitive Linguistics,* Sept 19. Yale UP. 1998.

realm of speech) is a dynamism that throws a different light on the idea of the word being the main particle of language. This light comes from expanding the boundaries of language levels and thus creating a new linguistic construct: the layered structure of language makes each layer having specific characteristics. The latter determine the large variety of meaning concepts at hand, which were originally represented in linguistics as a series of relationships between sound and meaning, which inspired De Saussure's work as well as Chomsky's generative grammar. But the laws, which determine meaning with linguistic units (constructs like 'the word'), remain of utmost interest.

So, Shaumyan notices: "True, the sentence is the basic unit of language; true, the linguist must study the laws of the generation of sentences—but it is also true that the linguist must formulate the laws of the generation of sentences in accordance with the laws of relationships between sound and meaning: these laws are logically prior to the laws of the generation of sentences. If you do not understand these laws, you do not understand the laws of the generation of sentences".

This type of understanding refers to text and speech rather than word or sentence. Word and sentence are nevertheless the two constructs that are continuously debated as well as deemed meaningful in language: what does that sign of multiple and enduring consideration mean? In other words: what significance has the discussion over the priority of word over sentence or sentence over word?

6 Julia Kristeva: Engenderment and the Speaking Subject

Julia Kristeva learned from Shaumyan that language seems a continuous structuring of sound and meaning. That was in line with Chomsky and the majority of influential linguists in those days. The power of structuring is effective in any partition between two constitutive elements. Yet, the insight exists that any language—and thus the work of overcoming such partitions—is potentially a philosophy waiting to unfold. Unfold *in* what, unfold *as* what? In and as words, we would normally say, and while articulating them we get rid of doubts pertaining to the quality of that answer. Most linguistic insights and philosophies of language find their anchor point only after having naively accepted the function and essence of the word as a basic feature of language. Structuring energies relating sound and meaning are an example in that regard.

Kristeva combines her linguistic with her psychological/psychoanalytical insights in two equally fascinating dimensions: the word overcomes partitions in the text (most often leading to speech) as well as in the speaking subject (most often leading to identity fulfillments). The first is an overwhelming issue of contemporary culture, in particular of literature, whereas the second seems an equally important issue of humanity (in particular human rights) today. We highlight those in their linkage with the concept of meaning to acquire clarity about 'the word' in language and linguistics. In view of her multifaceted work, one vital question is dominant: can the simplicity and naïveté of 'the word' guard us from the extreme complexity of 'the text'? The answer seems a surprise: *no*, because all aspects of 'the word' are as complex and as often identical with those of 'the text'.

6.1 Texts, Pheno-Text and Geno-Text

A text is never the text we read, and the text we read today is not the text our ancestors read a century ago! And, even more fascinating: reading a text is a confrontation with a moment of the life of a text rather than that of ancestors. So one enters a *life process* when reading, and becomes witness of a selected moment of a life called 'text'. Our generally accepted concept of a 'text' is thus a snapshot of a more encompassing engenderment. And a focus on surface-meanings characterizes our conventional methods of reading. They unfold without consciously engaging in deeper meanings and the text's entire process character.

Noam Chomsky stressed that the pairing of signs and their semantic interpretation corresponds with a purely structural and thus ideal speaker-hearer situation, which he couples with the idea that each language can be regarded as a particular relationship between sound and meaning. Two dualisms share that view. First, there is the system of relationships between sound and meaning, which enters a rich tradition indeed. However, his analyses focus secondly on a broad linguistic-theoretical concept, which provides a language-independent means for representing the signals and semantic interpretations that are interrelated by the force of grammars of specific languages.

A discussion of a generative grammar never directly touches the level of structures of texts or sentences; it fails to distinguish text and sentence and understands a sentence naively as a component of a text like so many others did with 'the word'. Guiding ideas of the generative grammar are, that (1) the surface structure of a sentence is a proper bracketing of the linear, temporally given sequence of elements, with the paired brackets labeled by category names, and that (2) the deep structure of a sentence is an abstract representation of grammatical relations and syntactic organizations.[46] A differentiation between surface- and deep structure is fruitful but the reference to a dualistic speaker-hearer situation is untenable, as Peirce had noticed long before. Kristeva takes on a discussion as to whether a deep structure of a text is deep because of linguistic patterns (such as "grammatical relations and syntactic organization") or because of foundational structures of culture, or because of both—or are we confronted, when speaking of a deep structure, with just another layer of language and its specific properties?

[46] Noam Chomsky: *Topics in the Theory of Generative Grammar*, Mouton, The Hague/Paris 1969, p. 12, 37.

Approximately in the same years as the unfolding of those ideas Greimas suggested,[47] that we always "… move from immanence to manifestation in three principal stages:

- *Deep structures,* which define the fundamental mode of existence of an individual or a society, and subsequently the conditions of existence of semiotic objects. As far as we know, the elementary constituents of deep structures have a definable logical status.
- *Superficial structures* constitute a semiotic grammar system, which arranges into discursive forms the contents susceptible of manifestation. The products of this grammar system are independent of the expression, which reveals them, in as far as they can theoretically appear in any substance, and, in the case of linguistic objects, in any language.
- *Structures of manifestation* produce and organize significances. Although they can include quasi-universals, they remain particular to any given language (or more precisely they define the particular characteristics of languages), or to any given material. They are studied by the superficial stylistics of morphemes, shapes, colors, etc."[48]

These observations suggest (a) how the textual deep structure appears thanks to *a definable logical status*, and (b) how we in those cases read a development *from grammar to surface* within the boundaries of a linguistic system, and (c) we also read how a text surface is in his eyes a manifestation of significance(s), a *meaning* dependent upon *specific linguistic articulations*. All ties are proposed in this analysis as beyond the process character of the text, its dynamic linguistic perceptions and schemas, which are in essence vital processes in human life. Becoming a text surface is not a matter of words or sentences, but of cultural change, historical events or individual initiatives.

6.2 Semanalysis

This insight (corresponding to the ideas of Peirce and Shaumyan) resulted in Julia Kristeva's 1969 publication: Semeiotike. *Recherches pour une sémanalyse.* Despite the various "Kristeva-Readers" offered to the public of the US East Coast in the seventies and the eighties of the last century, her main theoretical essay was never translated into English.[49] It contains a plea to perceive the dynamisms in text-semiotics and proposes to focus for that purpose on what she calls a "semanalysis".

---

47 A.J. Greimas & Fr. Rastier: "The Interaction of Semiotic Constrains" in *Yale French Studies,* Op. Cit.

48 A.J. Greimas c.s. Op. Cit., "The Interaction" p. 86f.

49 See two great examples: J. Kristeva: *The Portable Kristeva* K. Oliver, Ed.), New York 2002; and J. Kristeva: *Desire in Language. A Semiotic Approach to Literature and Art*, (L. Roudiez, Ed.) New York 1980.

The essay is entitled: "*L'engendrement de la formule*" [The engenderment of the formula] and the question comes up whether "the formula" is just another expression for "the word". But some important strains of thought go in another direction.

The essay opens with a distinction between *semiotics* and *semanalysis*, for which various definitions are used. "A text is the product of language and can thus only be perceived linguistically; texts reveal a theory of signification". The (new) concept of semanalysis is offered for more than one reason:

(a) "We use the concept of semanalysis from the very beginning to mark a difference within semiotics: we do not want to block the study of signifying practices by means of using the 'sign', but we want to decompose that concept and open a new level in the inner regions of semiotics, a new space of returnable and combinable sites: the space in which the signifying process takes place (significance)".
(b) "Semanalysis is the theory of textual signification, which considers the sign as a central element and sustains the representation of each engenderment—a process of germination, an inner process in which laws are laid down. In other words, (without forgetting that a text is a system of signs) the semanalysis accesses in the inner spaces of that sign system yet another scene: a hidden scene, that reveals *significance as an operation which embraces a structure of solely falling down and moving back again.*"(my italics JMB)
(c) "Without suggesting that one can quit the terrain of the sign entirely, the semanalysis liberates itself from the central obligation ... to combine possible viewpoints leading to something like an engenderment. ... the semanalysis protects itself from psychological as well as from idealistic aesthetic interpretations pertaining to what one calls the action of writing (Derrida). Or ... the semanalysis has nothing to do with forms of description of a "corpus", a carrier of information content, which guarantees the communication between a sender and a receiver."[50]

6.3 A Text: Not a Linguistic Phenomenon

Kristeva's conclusion is often quoted but seldom understood in its entirety: "a text is not a linguistic phenomenon". The slogan is not negativistic. Rather it opens access to a wider study of a text in the perspective of dynamic yet structural linguistics. A text, she writes, is not a fixated and definitely structured signification, and not a flat, that is: two-dimensional, body.

We therefore consider Kristeva's opinion on a text and its layered character: "A text is its engenderment: an engenderment inscribed in a linguistic phenomenon, in other words: the pheno-text, being the printed text, which is only readable if one

[50] J. Kristeva: Semeiotike. *Recherches pour une sémanalyse.* Quoted are subsequently fragments of pages 279–283 (French-English translation by JMB).

traverses through its genesis in a vertical direction (1) of its linguistic categories, and (2) of the topology of the signifying act. The meaning (significance) of that textual engenderment can thus be understood in a double grip pertaining to the tissue of the language and the engenderment of the "I" that presents the significance/meaning. The linguistic generation of the pheno-text occurs in such a vertical move. We refer to that operation as the making of a geno-text and thus unknot the very notion of a text in pheno-text and geno-text (surface and depth, signified structure and signifying production). These formulations should precisely re-orientate linguistics from static to dynamic approaches of language and meaning, and embrace therefore the totality of the signification process".[51]

It follows that a text is "an object made dynamic". Text semiotics and semanalysis become identical, and the distinction between pheno-text and geno-text become a standard for thinking on meaning. The geno-text appears to be a most fascinating issue in the new dynamic understanding of a text. A geno-text is not a first cause, but has nevertheless an engendering function in the frame of the totality of a text (a problematic issue in its own right: what is the totality of a text; what is a text in total, or: as text?).

Kristeva suggests: "The specificity of the text remains anchored in the fact that it is a translation/transformation from geno-text to pheno-text, whereby the process of signifying unfolds constantly on the line between pheno-text and geno-text and vice-versa. In other words, we present herewith a first operative definition, which we will complete and specify. It pertains to a textual meaning making, which proves that the system of signification becomes manifest via the pheno-text. We consider each signifying practice, at all levels of the pheno-text (as signifier as well as signified) positively belonging to the process of generating the signifying system itself, to be textual. Or, let us formulate shortly, the textual is each practice which forwards the Freudian slogan: "Wo es war, soll Ich werden" (Where It was should I be")".[52]

6.4 *Against Static Linguistics*

From here, *she concludes against static semiotics and the predominant position of the word as a major particle* for all linguistics: "What we call a geno-text is an abstract level of the linguistic function in general, which makes up its anamnesis while remaining at a distance from solely reflecting the structures of the phrase, and even precedes or exceeds those structures. It thus concerns a signifying function ...[53]

Our awareness of the continuous movement from pheno- to geno-text, back and forth, is not incidental or an irregular occurrence, but a dynamic that never stops functioning. Reading a text is participating in the flow of that movement. One reads

[51] Kristeva, Op. Cit., p. 280.

[52] Kristeva, Op. Cit., p. 279/280.

[53] Kristeva, Op. Cit., p. 280/281.

a pheno-text at a moment of moving into a geno-text and vice versa; the sentences and words of the text are a marker of that movement, *not a marker of a package of individual elementary units in one or another relation to each other.* The practice of signifying is importantly more encompassing then any pheno-text can suggest, but nevertheless condemned to find itself at least temporarily engaged in pheno-textual dimensions. What a geno-text injects in a pheno-text is never a single word or a set of words but an already signifying complexity, which Kristeva named 'linguistic body'. The signification process is about significations and the power of signifying, not about words and their so-called meaning.

"The geno-text is the infinite signifying that could never "be" a "this" because it is not a singular; one should better describe it as "the signifyings" in their plural form with all the infinite differentiations through which the signifying is present. The signifying as the-formula-presented-by-the-word-of-the-subject is just a boundary stone, a name of place, an accident, an approximation that adds itself to the signifying the moment it abandons its position. The plurality of signifiers in which (and not beyond which) the signified (of the pheno-text) can be situated is as such hyper-determined. The geno-text is in that regard … an ensemble of other scenes in its multiplicity, whereby any index is missing because of the hyper-determination that defines the infinity from inside."[54]

It is fascinating that this view contains a reference to the classical analytical tradition to evaluate the performance of speech-acts as a matter of a speaker's viewpoint. Her argument is: "The text presents itself therefore as a body with a multiple register, and each of its elements possesses a multidimensionality, which bestows features of hieroglyphic nature on languages and discourses alike. The text generation … is the result of a rhetorical discourse, which envisages a text production based on seeding processes and refractions weaving the text".[55]

Here it becomes clear what Shaumyan mentioned in the 1971 edition of his *Structural Linguistics*: every scientific discipline must distinguish two levels of abstraction: observation and construction. Both levels are to be understood as logical and not just as solely a psychological expressivity. The logic of observation cannot be identical with a performance at a textual surface level. It looks, in other words, as if there exists no surface without a deep structure, and some of those deep structures have indeed a stable foundational function in relation to their surface. The dichotomy of surface- and deep level, pheno- and geno-text, points with necessity to multidimensional views, and withstands any static character, as Shaumyan concluded for his structural linguistics. If that multidimensionality is not provided, no observation can take place. Observation as a scientific activity is constructive in essence and therefore needs the dimensionality of two levels of ontology, which present themselves in language—an experience of speakers as well as hearers.

[54] Kristeva, Op. Cit., p. 283.

[55] Kristeva, Op. Cit., p. 283.

6.5 The Speaking Subject

Kristeva understood that entering into a language and its patterns of social relations by means of becoming a speaking subject is equivalent to constituting oneself as a human individual in history and society. She emphasizes the importance of the speaking subject in relation to the meaning-dimensions of texts or textual surfaces: "…if language is the articulation of a heterogeneous process, with the speaking subject leaving its imprint on the dialectic between the articulation and its process, then the linguist and the semiotician should study *the ethics of each signifying process"*.[56] Notice the fact that these ethics depend on the unfolding of meanings in their engendering. That is one of her main viewpoints, which in this regard approximates Peirce and enriches the analyses of Chomsky, Greimas and perhaps also Shaumyan. Her emphasis on 'engenderment' is beyond psychoanalysis and above all a means to direct us to signifying practices that excel in the construction of text surfaces. In that regard legal texts are at the same level as poetry, myth, narrations and other language practices, which are by no means reducible to the 'language' object.[57]

A speaking subject in everyday life constitutes its proper identity in forms, which language *and* society create as 'habit' (Peirce). The Ancient Greeks understood their *nomoi* (in part comparable to 'habit') as an achievement of a linguistic nature. Kristeva characterized that speaking subject with a double meaning: "…we recognize, on the one hand, the unity of the subject who submits to the law—the law of communication, among others; yet who, on the other hand, does not entirely submit, cannot entirely submit, does not want to submit entirely… and is always in a state of contesting the law…"[58] Assigning values to elements of reality is important in occidental culture and essential for any process of meaning making. But the speaking subject, the major component of the linguistically highly profiled "speaker-hearer" distinction, is more than a representative of identity issues alone. One questions who (that must clearly be a product of linguistic abstraction) can be a speaker of words, and if so, whether those words are then more than words, for instance also sentences, texts and, in the end, speech?

The transcendental ego, Kristeva remarks, is such a philosophical construct, but we cannot imagine that construct to speak, and at the same time we characterize that speaking as: to use words. A real human being (in the role of speaker involved in a process of speech) does not "use words".[59] No, even if he/she would like to do that, she *could* not "use words"—for the simple reason that "word" and "use" are scien-

---

[56] Kristeva: *Desire in Language*. Op. Cit., 1980, p. 23, 34.

[57] Relations between specifically *legal* texts and the text theories of Kristeva are in: Jan M. Broekman & Larry Catà Backer: *Lawyers Making Meaning*, Op. Cit., p. 70 f, and :—Id.—:*Signs in Law-A Source Book*, Springer Op. Cit., 2015, Ch. 30, 35.

[58] Ross M. Guberman (Ed.): *Julia Kristeva Interviews*. Columbia UP, 1996, p. 26.

[59] It is interesting how a mid-twentieth century discussion on Husserl seems repeated here: the discussion about the abyss between a "factical ego" and a "transcendental ego". See: Jan M. Broekman: *Phänomenologie und Egologie*. Op. Cit., 1963.

tific constructs that cannot as such actively contribute to speech. This situation, reflected in the dominant position of 'the word' in linguistics and philosophy, mirrors the ambiguity of the speaking subject's position. A speaker has to leave the level of an everyday language in order to experience his 'use of words'. The verb 'use' and the name 'word' are both elements of a so-called 'natural language', often named 'mother tongue'. Despite this confidential, even familiar connotation, 'the word' seems not at home in that meaning field. The word 'word' is not a natural datum because its belonging to a natural language is not natural, but results from an artificial expressivity.

6.6 Construct and Reality

There is an abyss between construct and reality, between a speaker at the level of linguistics and a speaker at the level of everyday life/language/articulation. There are at least two levels at work here, and only one pertains to a human being as a whole. If words are constructs located *beyond*- as well as *in* language, then answers pertaining to the 'what' or 'where', and thus the 'meanings' of those words are also constructs from beyond- as well as in mind, habit, and culture. This multiplicity reigns the human condition: the speaking subject articulates that condition in and with her articulation. Kristeva brings psychoanalysis and linguistics together at this point. There are at least three issues to highlight.

First, there is the fact that a speaking subject as a human being (tensions between the two components remain) and thus as an integrated whole, is in his or her speaking confronted with the task of balancing a co-presence of gender and mind, of sexuality and thought pattern. A remarkable parallel with the classical definition of language as the well-structured co-presence of sound and meaning is noticeable. This striking precondition for speech is in itself well beyond the boundaries of linguistics and yet directly focuses on the concept of 'meaning'. What seems to be transcendence in linguistics appears as immanence in psychological perspective. The superior power of the human condition bridges the abyss between the two—Freud referred to the 'superior essence' of the human being in this regard. This energy creates 'meaning' and 'sense' in life, the latter being primarily directed to the o/Other. Socially relevant behavior seems inscribed in the meaning-making process itself. Understanding 'meaning' is not an issue of linguistics or a philosophy, but reaches beyond those boundaries as it directs towards the co-presence of other human beings.

Secondly, Kristeva's psychoanalytic orientation underscores forcefully that this unique togetherness of *meaning* and other-directed *sociability* creates an ambiguity in human life. This ambiguity directs us to consider the social dimensions of meaning making, which is central in psychoanalysis and forms a particular field of research and interest in Kristeva's work.[60] A particular set of risk factors beyond politics or law becomes visible.

One was expressed in 1916 during the defense of the PhD thesis of Jacob Israel de Haan, the first legal semiotician at the Amsterdam University, beginning that same year, who wrote: "One can never avoid metaphors. But one can diminish the risk of confusing comparative and explicative metaphors. Even this metaphor as such is comparative and risky. A word is not a living organism that possesses meanings like humans possess property. The same incorrect thought is in the expression "What is the meaning *of* this word". One should never underestimate the fatal influence of an incorrect metaphor."[61]

Metaphors retain a deep ambiguity in their relation with the 'meaning' concept. That ambiguity is, by the way, not erroneous: it is in discrepancies between sound and meaning, just as between linguistics and psychology, between mind and gender, or between the mental and the physical (a relation he calls soma-significance). Bohm suggests that these ambiguities are always "a form in which the whole of reality appears either in our perception or in our thinking. … We describe these aspects using different words; nevertheless we imply that they are revealing the unknown whole of reality, as it were, from two different sides".[62]

A further risk factor is imminent in each speaker's situation. Performing a speech-act is engaging in a (or a series of) risk(s) because there is uncertainty about the position of the other as a partner in the speech situation. However, Lacan made us understand that master discourses diminish the risk through reordering the subject's catalogue of meanings. Here we encounter a much more deeply anchored consideration. The problem is that the "reordering of the catalogue of meaning" which each of us carries in any speech-act remains grounded on a fragmentation or dissection of reality. Elementary units of meaning are thus engendered without any reference to the totality from which they originate. This seems to be a new version of the *more geometrico* pattern that serves as a basis for modern society. Alienation is therefore a basic element in the history of meaning and of what meanings represent. The engenderment of meaning in general is in this light an extremely important theme in our Occidental culture.[63] Expressions such as 'freedom' or 'liberal', 'diversity' or 'tolerance' mean different social practices, some of them clearly hidden in the deep structures of explorative social practices embedded in capitalism and its liberal ideology. Guess the many implications in a politician's speech on

---

[60] Hence her interest in theses like Horror/The Abject, Feminism, Totalitarianism or the EU background ideas. Those themes open a broad field of interpretation of the 'Meaning' concept beyond law, linguistics or psychoanalysis—a study not yet performed. See in particular: J. Kristeva: *The Powers of Horror* 1980 (Engl 1982), *Chinese Women* 1977, *Nations without Nationalism* 1993, *Crisis of the European Subject* 2000, and *Hatred and Forgiveness,* 2010.

[61] J.I.de Haan: *Rechtskundige Significa*, Amsterdam 1916, p. 14. See also: Jan M. Broekman & Larry Catà Backer: *Signs in Law,* Op. cit., Ch. 9.

[62] David Bohm: *Unfolding Meaning*, Routledge, London/New York 1985 p. 72 f.

[63] Jan M. Broekman & Larry Catà Backer: *Lawyers Making Meaning*. Op. Cit., p. 81.

'democracy' or 'equality'. There is an urgent need to elevate new 'master signifiers' to enable the subject to reorder a sense of a self and relations to others.

A *third* issue in Kristeva bringing psychoanalysis and linguistics together relates to the difficulty of knowing the influences of the master signifiers (Lacan) in a speaker's activity. Speakers consider that meaning makes one involved in a heightened semantic awareness. The latter creates an additional and specific risk. Let us take legal discourse as an example: if a Supreme Court speaks with one voice, even with a dissenting opinion, then the master signifiers utter a unique *voice*. If a legal case is engraved in decades of a culture, the master signifiers determine legal and political considerations by means of a *text* that carries a name.[64] Master signifiers order and reorder opinions, prejudices and notions of a self that indulges in fragments of cultural history.

6.7 Overcoming the Abyss

Kristeva's considerations come back to Freud's reference written in *Das Ich und das Es*, 1923, where he speaks of "das höhere Wesen im Menschen" [the higher essence in man].[65] As if that line is an indication of where to find the point in which all ambiguities begin to disappear and all risks diminish, so that freedom is on the horizon. The social consequences of overcoming the abyss between sound and meaning, gender and mind, sign and language are indeed altogether related to the concept of freedom. But our understanding of freedom, Kristeva reads in Proust, is also connected with revolt, uprising, and eventually resurrection. This reading made Kristeva extremely popular for a long time, in particular among students of all disciplines and institutions. The uprising is, however, not a political revolt but rather the exploration of freedom to change the course life's urges *in vita*.

One learns from Proust about the importance of such psychological movements, which are essential for a speaker, his or her power of linguistic expressiveness and the imminent reconstitution of memory. This power and reconstitution are actually at work when the speaking subject utters words—but the spoken words are only signals of that dynamic, not signs in their semiotic sense. The act of speaking speaks a language. The language of that act is layered. It relies primarily upon the institutionally approved surface structure to empower communication (among which meaning has a dominant position) and follows the norms of the deep structures. The interplay between those layers, its powerful tensions, its urges and drives,

[64] The practical consequences in Common Law have recently been brought together in a review of two publications on the theme: Laurence Tribe & Joshua Matz: *Uncertain Justice: The Roberts Court and the Constitution,* 2014, and: Mark Tushnet: *In the Balance: Law and Politics on the Roberts Court*, 2013. See: David Cole: "The Anti-Court Court" in: *The New York Review of Books,* LXI, 13, 2014, p. 10 f.

[65] S. Freud: *Das Ich und das Es*, in: *Gesammelte Werke,* Band XIII, S. Fischer Verlag, Frankfurt/M & Imago Publ. Co, London 1940, p. 237 f.

its secrets and secretions performed by any speaker should be accessed in the analyst's understanding. The analyst as speaker, however, should perceive the tensions between immanence and exteriorization and invite the everyday-life speaker to step over the abysses created during life's experiences (as Freud differentiated between "Erlebnis" [passing through, seeing] and "Erfahrung" [practicing, learning].

6.8 The Act of Speaking Speaks a Language

This formula could function as a slogan for understanding 'the word' in Kristeva's philosophy, linguistics and psychoanalysis. There is a clear distance from Searle's theory of speech acts. Tensions between active and passive participation of a subject in the speech process, the disposing of the constitutive power of the speaker over language and the social situation of speaking, the multiplicity of forces at work when only one word is uttered, and above all the layered structure of language as such, are issues of contrast between the two authors. Roland Barthes wrote in this context (focusing on the text and including the speaker and writer as equivalently belonging to texts): "A text is… a multidimensional space in which a variety of writings, none of them original, blend and clash. The text is a tissue of quotations… The writer can only imitate a gesture that is always anterior, never original. His only power is to mix writings, to counter the ones with the others, in such a way as never to rest on any one of them."[66]

Texts are instrumental in the languages of experience, no matter whether written or spoken. Much of what we 'know', we have read, seen, or heard. Boundaries between texts as well as between texts and the world of lived experience are blurred. The world as we know is the current representation of their co-presence in life. 'The word' has no dominance in that field of meaning, one can conclude with Julia Kristeva. The context of her theory in view of the concept of meaning is in the recognition of the layered character of language. As a consequence, multiplicity contradicts all attempts to articulate words as: "This *means* that!" We repeat: if words are constructs located *beyond*- as well as *in* language, then answers pertaining to the 'what' or 'where', and thus the 'meanings' of words are also constructs from *beyond*- as well as *in* mind, habit, and culture. This multiplicity reigns the human condition.

7 Benjamin's Word

Walter Benjamin's (1892–1940) essays on language have closer relations with the word as a linguistic component than any philosopher hitherto recognized. His works are not always considered as a genuine philosophy of language. In the context of

[66] Roland Barthes: *La Poétique du récit*, Ed. du Seuil, Paris 1977, p. 146.

studying "meaning', however, it seems more than appropriate to introduce his ideas and texts on language and to consider their consequences. This is all the more urgent because his relations with 'the word' are substantially different from the most widespread and powerful type of linguistic philosophy, the analytical approach. Amos and Fania Oz recently demonstrated that 'the word' is essential for the Jewish tradition from their reading the very first lines of the Genesis story onward—a perspective that reaches far beyond, for instance, the Anglo-Saxon view.[67] But Benjamin seems to foster a philosophical understanding that, not unlike the Anglo-Saxon tradition, gives the word a prominent priority as the major unit of language. What are the implications and significance of this priority, and what does this move mean for the concept of meaning?

The basis for considering the work of Walter Benjamin in this study on meaning is laid down in his own words: "The existence of language, however, is coextensive not only with all the areas of human mental expression in which language is always in one sense or another inherent, but with absolutely everything. There is no event or thing in either animate or inanimate nature that does not in some way partake in language, for it is in the nature of each one to communicate its mental contents. *This use of the word 'language' is in no way metaphorical ... we cannot imagine a total absence of language in anything*."[68]

7.1 The Use of the Word

Reconsider his remark: "the *use* of the *word* 'language' is in no way metaphorical". A twentieth century philosopher of language, especially in Anglo-Saxon philosophy with German roots, would claim that Benjamin's views are very much in conformity with their conventional philosophical projects. Searle would immediately refer to two expressions in his own studies on language: the words "word" (as a unit of language) and "use" (as speakers use language). So, what does compatibility mean, and what importance do Benjamin's theories have in view of language and meaning that differ from traditional philosophies of language?

The central issue in Benjamin's view on language can be read in the following: *plurality is at work in the heart of language and meaning*. This motive is the main reason to include Benjamin among the philosophers of language in the first decades of the twentieth century. That plural, he underlines, articulates itself continuously in a variety of linguistic forms. One method to explore those varieties for Benjamin as

[67] Amos Oz & Fania Oz-Salzberger: *jewsandwords*, Yale UP 2012, see also: Karl Wolfskehl: "Die Juden und das Buch" in: *Bild und Gesetz*, Berlin/Zürich 1930, and Wolfskehl: *Gesammelte Werke*, Bd II, Hamburg 1960, p. 334 ff.; as well as Avivah G. Zornberg: *The Beginning of Desire,* Doubleday 1995,—Id.: *The Particulars of Rapture,* Doubleday 2001,—Id.: *The Murmuring Deep*, Schocken 2008.

[68] W. Benjamin: "Uber Sprache überhaupt und über Sprache des Menschen", in: *Gesammelte Schriften,* (GS) Band II,1. Suhrkamp Frankfurt/M 1977, p. 140 f.; Engl. Ed.: *Selected Writings,* (SW) Vol. 1, Bullock & Jennings, (Eds) Harvard 1996, p. 62 f. (Italics are mine, JMB).

well as for Rosenzweig is to study a scale of fragments on the Ancient Greek tragedy, the tragic hero, the hero's speaking and his meaningful silence, as well as the hero's role in Greek theatre, with language as the general frame of interest.[69] For that same reason one finds a parallel in their intense understanding of the Torah's Genesis narrative, with dividing lines between languages, words and discourses that stem from before and after the Fall; one furthermore encounters complexities of relations of words and names in relations to God's words, and analyses of the expression 'Word of God' as well as the relation between speech and name-giving. All those fragments elucidate the plurality and the different types of language, which is always layered. Those fragments and themes are by no means independent studies on cultural or religious motives of the Occident. They should rather be perceived as excursions into layers of language that differ substantially from everyday language, so that they unveil meanings unknown in everyday communication. Varieties of layers are in their own right important components of a general theory of language, while demonstrating the multiplicity of human expressiveness. They are reinforced with powerful visions of space and time in language.

7.2 Multiple Languages, Human Essence

It must once more be emphasized that those fragments are not in the first instance leading to a philosophy of religion or a theology, but are excurses to reinforce a philosophy of language by means of exploring other types or layers of language/discourse. The purpose is to find a key to understanding the human essence in context, which is cosmological rather than anthropological. Oppenheim highlights this purpose in his introduction to Rosenzweig's *The Star of Redemption*: "… the text intricately weaves together, that is, addresses, some of the most fundamental human disciplines: mathematics, logic, aesthetics, philosophy, theology, world history, Western intellectual history, world religions, psychology, sociology, political theory, biblical literature, and linguistics".[70]

To reinforce this insight into Benjamin's contribution, we explore a series of observations pertaining to: (1) the importance of language, (2) what are words?, (3) the meaning of 'word', (4) the expression 'Word of God', (5) language is layered, attitudes change, and (6) space and time in language.

[69] See the fascinating parallel/contrast with M. de Unamuno, in his: *Del sentimiento trágico de la vida en los hombres y en los pueblos*, 1913 [The Tragic Sense of Life in Men and in Peoples (tr. J.E.C. Flitch), 1921] and M. de Unamuno: *The Tragic Sense of Life in Men and Nations* [tr. Anthony Kerrigan, with M. Nozick, 1972].

[70] Franz Rosenzweig: *The Star of Redemption,* (1921) Eng. Ed. Barbara Galli (Tr.). Wisconsin UP, 2005. *Foreword* Michael Oppenheim. Notice furthermore in the *Foreword*: "the text intricately weaves together, that is, addresses, some of the most fundamental human disciplines: mathematics, logic, aesthetics, philosophy, theology, world history, Western intellectual history, world religions, psychology, sociology, political theory, biblical literature, and linguistics". These remarks about *The Star* also count for Benjamin's essays on language (1916).

7.3 The Importance of Language

The importance of language, Benjamin emphasized, goes hand in hand with a distancing from any instrumental understanding of language. He thus expands the specter of those who focus on the word. For instrumentalists like Searle, language is an instrument for communication- or information that promotes the idea of "the word as the basic unit of language" as its major constitutive insight. Benjamin's position is different and fits in with his earlier critique of instrumentalism where he considered time, study and remembrance as a theme of modern youth during the first years of the twentieth century.[71] That intuition led him to naively focus on "the word"—exactly like his instrumentalist colleagues seemed to do, but differently. Such a parallel makes it difficult to directly descry the profile of his thoughts on language. Why does he focus on the word like all instrumentalists? His answer would be, that a word glints like a gem and that we need that glint to become aware of whether a word is *not* just a means to communicate. His search is for a "more", a "more" that blocks our purely instrumental use of words as if they were coins. Benjamin's focus is therefore on "what is 'the more'" and "'what path' leads" to the more.

7.4 What Are Words?

Well, *what are words?* Words are a layered phenomenon—that is an enigmatic feature noticed in De Saussure's as well as in Shaumyan's linguistics and structuralism. All instrumentalist approaches in occidental languages and culture display that prominence of the word. Benjamin shares this attitude but rejects an instrumentalist position at the same time. That leads to an expansion of, and a different position in the spectrum of, language approaches. The word is for him connected to a receptive attitude, a *hearer attitude*, which goes beyond the traditional analytic speaker-hearer model of linguistic activity and beyond the emphasis on the speaker as the acting subject in language. A word is uniquely, continuously and under all circumstances embedded in an evolving spirituality in which speaker and hearer are equivalent. Benjamin, as Herder and others before him, names that spirituality *Sprachgeist* [the spirit of language]. A word is without further ado the evident and major component of that *Sprachgeist*—hence its natural prominent position. He would not say so, but the word is for him *a sign*: most prominently a sign of universality. Hearing the word is reading that sign in philosophical perspectives, but also in those of cosmology, metaphysics and even physics.

Benjamin's essays around 1916 are on language and its foundations—texts that are witness of a new attitude, as his *On Language as Such and on the Language of*

[71] See also below § 6: *Space and time in language*.

Man illustrates.[72] A draft answer to a letter on language and mathematics from Gerhard Scholem, emphasizing language and leaving mathematics aside, inspired this text. He wrote in that same year on *Trauerspiel und Tragödie* [Tragic Drama and Tragedy] and on *Die Bedeutung der Sprache in Trauerspiel und Tragödie* [The Meaning of Language in Tragic Drama and Tragedy].

Those texts form the contexts and ground lines for Benjamin's philosophy of language as well as his entire philosophy. Notice that he never attempted to create a specialized and independent philosophy of language, because language has always to do with everything—like philosophy itself. The essays reveal an ardent desire to access the essence of man. Benjamin finds that access encapsulated in *the word*: "a human being communicates his own spiritual being *in* his language. But the language of humans articulates itself in words. A human being shares his spiritual essence (as far as it can be shared/communicated) by means of *naming* everything else".[73] Word and name, speech and naming, are key components of the human essence/spirit. That basic idea is reflected in the three essays. They contain specific terms, which function as a slumbering dictionary for his philosophical projects *tout court,* such as: time—art—historical—hero[74]—death—event—music—speech—word—tragic—source—play—lament/gloom.

7.5 The Meaning of 'Word'

The meaning of 'word' in such thought patterns is different from views expressed in the twentieth century Anglo-Saxon philosophy of language. Benjamin's position on the word should be understood as a *sign* saying that the word is solely prominent in a naïve-natural everyday language. He does not further unfold that observation, but remarks that a human being communicates his own spiritual being solely *in* his language. His language is in essence an everyday language, a "naïve natural" language in terms of Husserl's transcendental phenomenology. Benjamin is aware of the fact that the word is not only our word as speaker, but it is also our word as hearer, whereby the speaker is essentially beyond the speaker-hearer relation named: "*the (o)Other*". Hence the difficult indication for that type of word and its language: that word belongs to a non-naïve language, it requires a different attitude than we explore in everyday linguistic communication; it is reason as well as revelation; it is unfolding and challenging at the same time; it is spirit, magic, revival and adjustment. This word, a universal key to meaning, deserves ultimately the most prominent place, and is therefore named in that exceptional position: "the Word of God"—but in what type, level or layer of language is it then spoken? We don't

---

[72] An anti-nationalistic political move, a breach with his mentor Gustav Wyneken, and a new view on the task of writing: not a means of political or any other social action (as in the case of M. Buber) but coping with the mystery of language itself.

[73] Walter Benjamin: *Gesammelte Schriften* Band II, 1: Frankfurt/Main 1977, p. 142.

[74] Especially in drama and tragedy.

know, nor do we mind not knowing: it is understood, no matter how, when, and in what language, or at what layer of language. That word can therefore never be interpreted as a basic unit, because understanding is a major issue in any philosophy of language. Once proclaimed, it fills the world—if not the universe(s).

One cannot read Benjamin's essays on language without an eye on Franz Rosenzweig's philosophy of language. His famous 1921 book *The Star of Redemption* [Der Stern der Erlösung][75] should *not* be read exclusively as a philosophy of religion—the way it was categorized in Benjamin's or Buber's days, which were also the days of unfolding *significs* with Lady Welby, J.I.de Haan and F. van Eeden—but rather as a philosophy of language (language of the everyday, of religion, ethics, philosophy) with just this *WORD* as its central notion to understand religiosity and to approach through that the essence of man. Because of the difference in spiritual climate, Rosenzweig's text and view of language impressed Benjamin while he was writing his essays. Both philosophers focus on language, recognizing the restrictions of their articulations despite the complexity of involved meanings. They know that *we can treat of language only within language.* Any articulation is therefore a form of magic—a magic to share, to unveil, to understand.

7.6 The Word of God

'The Word of God' is a particular expression, which needs a special place in a philosophy of language; it cannot become dissolved in the multiple webs of speaker-hearer relations: it functions as an ultimate meaning in language and speech. It can only be heard or only (in still more exceptional situations) function in a dialogue. The word of God is a form of Being that presents and represents at the same time; togetherness determines its type of expressiveness/articulation (which should not be confused with *dialogue*). In other words: it is Existence, which unfolds at distance from communication, ethics or religion. That Word Is. It is Prominence in the form of a word and Benjamin as well as Rosenzweig reflected upon the word because they understood that extreme prominence. The being of that word is a key for a philosophical approach to language; it is religiously unbounded and experiential on a level of language that includes indeterminable spheres of articulation. It is given, naïve and non-naïve, grammarless and not in need of any syntax at the same time. *Geist* [Spirit] and *Sein* [Being] evolve into a state which demonstrates the existence of another language-level or layer at each moment of articulation: the language of Paradise, the Fall, the Tragedy, the Drama, the language of Everyday—and all of them make Meaning identify the flux of Being.

This new, non-analytic prominence of the word seems to be the result of experiencing and reflecting upon the multiplicity of language. Benjamin attempted to

[75] Franz Rosenzweig: *Der Stern der Erlösung*, Heidelberg 1921, 1954(3); *The Star of Redemption*, W. Hallo (Tr.) 1971. and B. Galli (Tr) Wisconsin UP 2005.

grasp the latter and posits his approach at the borderlines of, or even beyond the boundaries of lingual expressivity. The 'Word of God' as word has the property to (a) break the speaker-hearer duality open—that duality is an otherwise strictly closed speech situation—and to (b) awaken to a change of level of language—often imagined as a change from horizontality towards verticality—while performing language acts. Rosenzweig and Benjamin highlight the *first* property when they study specific speech situations that reach *beyond everyday positions*. Those are positions in words of Ancient Greek tragedy, in the role of the Hero in Greek drama, in recapitulations and re-readings of the Genesis story and in the connections between the Fall and the Word. They are altogether examples of changes in language level and the practices of broadening speech conditions. The *second* property excels in the breach of the speaker-hearer situation so that *hearing the word* is given highest priority above all issues of everyday life and language.

Speech beyond everyday positions is at issue in Rosenzweig's *Stern* [Star], when Creation and Revelation come together in linguistic Articulation. He makes a distinction (not unlike Shaumyan, who in 1965 distinguished *phenotext* from *genotext*) between an *under-worldly* language and an *upper-worldly* language. When a linguistic figure moves from the first towards the second, etymons (stem-words) of Creation and Revelation coagulate and sentences are spoken in two voices: men and world form an identity, singing as it were with the same breath. Rosenzweig concludes: instead of a Divine "I" which only God could pronounce, the Divine Name appears, which also men and world can carry with them and dedicate to each other—and from here should come the meaningful conclusion "all is Good".[76]

The humanization of the Divine Name is also an important component, in particular where different levels of expressiveness and changing attitudes (from Godly to Human articulation) are concerned. Hence Benjamin: "Translation is removal from one language into another through a continuum of transformation." One should notice the dynamics characterized in the center of meaning, which are reconfirmed in Benjamin's next sentence, when he writes: "Translation passes through continua of transformation, not abstract areas of identity and similarity." The power of change is articulated in the heart of the translation phenomenon, which in itself has cosmological dimensions. "The translation of the language of things into that of man is not only a translation of the mute into the sonic; it is also the translation of the nameless into name. It is therefore the translation of an imperfect language into a more perfect one, and cannot but add something to it, namely knowledge."[77] The Genesis narrative contains words that are basic for a contemporary understanding of language.

Benjamin brings to the fore that the various levels/attitudes/layers of language create a *multiplicity of language as such*: "Since the unspoken word in the existence of things falls indefinitely short of the naming word in the knowledge of man, and since the latter in turn falls short of the creative word of God, there is a reason for

[76] F. Rosenzweig: *Stern der Erlösung,* Part II, p. 185.

[77] W. Benjamin: "Uber Sprache überhaupt und über Sprache des Menschen", in: *Gesammelte Schriften,* (GS) Band II,1. Suhrkamp Frankfurt/M 1977, p. 150 f.; Engl. Ed.: *Selected Writings,* (SW) Vol. 1, Bullock & Jennings, (Eds) Harvard 1996, p. 70 f.

the multiplicity of human languages (…) so many translations, so many languages—once man has fallen from the paradisiacal state that knew only one language." The plural reigns: meaning and linguistic articulation are partners in plurality.

They are so from our human genesis on, Benjamin reminds us, and that is articulated in the more than prominent position of one particular word: *the name*. "For the essential composition of language, the Fall has a threefold significance (in addition to its other meanings). In stepping outside the purer language of name, man makes language a means [*ein Mittel*] (that is, a knowledge inappropriate to him), and therefore also, in one part at any rate, a *mere* sign; and this later results in the plurality of languages.[78]

This is a most interesting observation from Benjamin in view of the meaning-concept. The *sign* seems to result from a specific language type/level/attitude, namely from a level of impure expressiveness. It includes (a) that each sign has a counterpart at another level or enveloped in another layer of language, and (b) that this position is itself the germ for the plurality of languages as a consequence of the layered character of language in general. The contrast between "pure" and "mere" sign is in this view caused by that layering feature, and not the result of any idealistic theory of knowledge pertaining to language. All this finally includes that (c) semiotics—a theory of signs—is embedded in a philosophy of language, which recognizes that (1) the existing narratives on human genesis are a philosophically important field of articulation of language, and that (2) the layered character of language (as explored by Benjamin, Rosenzweig or by Greimas, Shaumyan, Kristeva and other structuralists) is of actual importance for any consideration of meaning.

One could venture the idea that in a "pure" language, which is positioned at the level of "the word of God" or at the level of Paradise "before the Fall", a sign is not a sign we encounter in semiotic considerations. Benjamin confirms: "…from the Fall, in exchange for the immediacy of name that was damaged by it, a new immediacy arises: the magic of judgment, which no longer rests blissfully in itself."[79] The "mere" sign of semiotics—and its meaning of "meaning"—is a matter of the layer of everyday discourse, or of what Husserl characterized as a language articulation in a "naïve-natural attitude". The proximity and parallels of Benjamin's views and Husserl's phenomenological methodology should be underlined. This is also of importance for the third consideration Benjamin writes: "The third meaning that can perhaps be tentatively ventured is that the origin of abstraction, too, as a faculty of the spirit of language, is to be sought in the Fall."—or in the structure of the narrative pertaining to the Fall. That narrative creates levels of language by means of creating a diversity of places, of localizations where events occur. The paradise—a supreme exodus narration—narrates a mapping, a trajectory where different layers of language are created, spoken and heard. The story is hence a narration on pluralities, and presents never a 'one word—one site' structure. Benjamin: "… immediacy (which, however, is the linguistic root) of the communicability of abstraction resides

[78] W. Benjamin: *SW* I. Op. Cit., p. 71; *GS* II,1. Op. Cit., p.133. Notice, how the *name* is in particular emphasized in Jewish cultural and religious tradition.

[79] Id.: *SW* I Op. Cit., p. 72 f; *GS* II,1 Op. Cit., p. 134 f.

in judgment … when, in the Fall, man abandoned immediacy in the communication of the concrete, of the word as means, of the empty word, into the abyss of prattle. … The Tree of Knowledge stood in the garden of God not in order to dispense information on good and evil, but as an emblem of judgment over the questioner.[80] This immense irony marks the mythic origin of law; … making language mediate, laid the foundation for its multiplicity; linguistic confusion could only be a step away."[81]

7.7 Layered Languages, Changing Attitudes

Layered languages, changing attitudes are thus a leading motive under the heading of *multiplicity* in Benjamin's philosophy of language; they are the result of philosophical insights and analyses and relatively independent from Jewish, Christian or other religious convictions. To consider the first chapter of Genesis is neither to submit biblical interpretation or subjection of the Torah to objective considerations of revealed truth, Benjamin emphasized.[82] He makes clear, that *any "emblem of meaning" relates to and depends for its meaning and understanding upon the relevant layer of language, speech or articulation.* The importance of this observation seems immeasurable. Not only differences between a professional and an everyday language are contemplated, but also the contrast between languages we experience as 'natural' and those we consider to be artificial or characterize as a 'meta—language'.

He writes: "… (I)t is impossible to talk about a language of music and of sculpture, about a language of justice that has nothing directly to do with those in which German or English legal judgments are couched, about a language of technology that is not the specialized language of technicians."[83]

Again: legal language is different from everyday language, and so is medical language, the language of music or of any other type of art. That differentiation concerns more than an awareness pertaining to a specific lingo. Furthermore, a professional language and the everyday language differ in their turn both from language as such—not to mention a meta—language or a formal language, which seems often difficult to categorize. Apart from those views, which include already five different layers of language and meaning fields, the layered character of language no less than its multiplicity and diversity is important for the concept of meaning. The observation that *language is layered* enables to conclude that meaning (and the meaning of meaning) always relates to a specific layer of language—each layer being a level of meaning itself. Benjamin's effort to understand language and life takes the word as a privileged access to such understanding.

[80] Notice, how "an emblem of judgment" is (perhaps even more importantly) an "emblem of meaning", the latter being the central issue of this book.

[81] Id.: *SW* I Op. Cit., p. 73; *GS* II,1 Op. Cit., p.134/135.

[82] W. Benjamin: *SW* I, Op. Cit., p. 67; *GS* II,1. Op. Cit., p. 147.

[83] W. Benjamin: *SW* I Op. Cit., p. 61; *GS* II,1. Op. Cit., p. 140.

This step has general, even ontological consequences, which Benjamin tried to articulate: "Language communicates the linguistic being of things", he wrote, and so did Charles Sanders Peirce. "The clearest manifestation of this being, however, is language itself. The answer to the question: "*What* does language communicate?" is therefore "All language communicates itself"—an *autopoeitic* reference in the sense of N. Luhmann, one could say. "For in language the situation is this: *the linguistic being of all things is their language*." Benjamin proceeds: "That which in a mental entity is communicable *is* its language. On this "is" (equivalent to "is immediately") everything depends."[84] His conclusion leads to many excursions on the tragic, the tragic character and tragedy as a form of expressiveness. The *tragic* is for Benjamin a *locus* to understand some of the metaphysical dimensions of 'the word', which go with the layered character of language and thus with its multiplicity and its inner dynamics. Every word that is spoken in Ancient Greek tragedy, he thus considers, is *tragically decisive*. The latter conclusion is enigmatic and full of layers of meaning. Judgments are dependent on their own layer of linguistic properties—their social contexts included. Yet they constitute the tragedy, and are thus an example of language creating its own forms of expressivity—not the inverse!

Remember in what way judgments are in themselves a form of meaning: the turns and twists of words filled with the power and dynamics of judgment form in the end the sign pool of Greek tragedy and of the shimmers of our contemporary understanding of 'tragic' when we think back to what remains for us today of those high forms of expressiveness. All this results from the excursion on Greek tragedy, which constitutes valuable insights into the layered structures of language and their effects on meaning. One remembers Oppenheim's *Foreword* to Rosenzweig's *Star of Redemption*, which also displays this layered feature and its consequences: "What is most impressive is, that Rosenzweig does not just allude to these topics but puts them into their disciplinary contexts, that is, narrates correlations between what may be called different registers."[85] The registers exposed stem from layers in language: "differences of register are constitutive for meaning" could be the constitutive power behind their narrations called "a philosophy of language". Words in their one-layer and temporary character may be units—but they are dynamic and by no means fixated units. They never lose their image of representing one way or another a 'pure' meaning, or 'meaning as purity'. A conclusion should be, that a context for a word is never an ensemble of other words, but a deeper language-layer, as the existence of pheno-texts proves.

---

[84] W. Benjamin: *SW* I Op. Cit., p. 63; *GS* II,1. Op. Cit., p. 142.

[85] Franz Rosenzweig: *Der Stern der Erlösung*, Op. Cit., 1921, [The Star of Redemption, B. Galli (Tr) Wisconsin UP 2005].

7.8 Space and Time in Language

Space and time in language is a theme that belongs to foundational considerations pertaining to the word—they belong therefore to a philosophy of language and meaning. Space and time are images realized in speech activity when it comes to languages,. Are they constitutive elements in a theory or philosophy of language? "Zeit erhebt sich am Ende der Zeiten" (Time rises up at the end of times], Benjamin writes. The multiplicity of language demonstrates *that notions of time and space will vary in specific cultures according to layers of unfolding linguistic expressivity.* Dynamics reign and attitudes change with them. We can understand why Benjamin's notion of time connects to *Youth*: in his eyes the living portrait of dynamic evolvements that fixates itself: in 'diaries' as today in 'Selfies', 'Twitters' and 'YouTube'; they are altogether forms of literary phenomena. These are of central importance for a theory of language and meaning also in our days.

Time and language are in fusion during conversation as well as writing. Benjamin makes them vary according to gender differences: in his essay on the *Metaphysics of Youth*[86] he distinguishes a concept of language dominated by 'silence' and another dominated by 'words'. The first is associated with the feminine, the other with the masculine. Understanding of the two is dominated by their diversity of intrinsic meaning. But there are more dimensions to clarify. In his thinking, and in thinkers of his time such as Heidegger or Bergson, the notion of 'mechanical time' plays a role when a confrontation between time and language comes to the fore.[87] A mechanical time is abstract, linear and predominantly logical—features opposed to 'historical time' as laid out in the essay *Trauerspiel.* Does youth live in a historical time, when they write or twitter? In principle, they do: "What we do and think is filled with the being of our fathers and ancestors", Benjamin wrote at the beginning of his essay on *The Metaphysics of Youth.*[88] The form of recognition entwined here will never be experienced as a mechanical occurrence. A certain concession occurs when he writes on *The Diary* in the third part of his essay on *Youth*, that young people write in an "immortal time", whereas that time finds its place and fits in a "developmental time" which is a form of mechanical time as far as clock, calendar or corporate activity are concerned. Life's occurrences and encounters, mirrored in linguistic expressiveness of multiple sorts, come together in a flux of time, which mixes types of time and language, and indicate them as the experience of a 'self': the latter a result of a transformed time, (a particular 'ray of time') which demonstrates that identity-formation and language belong together. The landscape of events profiles the traveling 'self', is irrigated by signs and other occurrences in the sign pool of life, and fortifies the fact that past things become future and create the

[86] W. Benjamin: *Metaphysik der Jugend,* in: *GS,* II,1 Op. Cit., p. 91 f,; *SW* I, Op. Cit., p. 7f.

[87] See H. Eiland & M.W. Jennings: *Walter Benjamin. A Critical Life,* Harvard UP 2014, p. 56 f.

[88] W. Benjamin: *SW* I, Op. Cit., p. 6; *GS* II,1, Op. Cit., p.91: "Was wir tun und denken is erfüllt vom Sein der Väter und Ahnen." Notice how this observation stems from days long before any awareness of genetics.

dynamics of a 'self' in the flash of a 'selfie'. Their spatial dimensions are in this process—life outside the process seems unbearable, not actual, out-modish, an unaccomplished fulfillment of a misplaced 'self', for short: *death.*

Death is for Benjamin the keyword for naming the great partition. Its fate is unfolding when the past of things and events becomes the future of an "I" time. "With the events our diary writes the history of our future existence", Benjamin concludes, "and writes the story of our greatness from the vantage point of our death … the time of death was the time of our diary, death was the last interval, the first loving enemy, death which bears us with all greatness and the manifold fate of our wide plain into the unnamable center point of time".

And there, *in the space of the plain*, "awaits us the new radiance … time rises up at the end of times."[89] We remember the features of the tragic: word and the tragic are encountered in the same space. A word carries an unmistaken meaning only if it is directly and immediately tragic. That position is spatial and also time-bound: words change and migrate from source to mouth, from sound to emotion to music. An unknown layer of language seems apparent: the level at which each spoken word is decisive, represents a judgment, for short: represents the *tragic* in its character of *effect.* Its dialogue, without which no tragic is understandable, is a form of speech with cosmic dimensions. There is no order, no physical law or universal space and no human destiny without a spoken word that is not intrinsically tragic; it will not be effective in ambiguity and will not destabilize the security of meaning. Language is marked by multiplicity, as Benjamin's focus on *the word* unveils.

Benjamin or Rosenzweig study the tragic hero to find the main traits of Ancient Greek Tragedy as different from those of a Roman Emperor as hero, or a War Hero, or a modern hero on the stock market or a heroic defender of Human Rights. There is a definitive level of language between the first and the others; the Otherness of the first marks their interest—not an interest in Greek culture, in religious attitudes, religions, wars or market mechanisms. This should be repeated when reading every page of those authors: the difference they search for is a being different because of a difference in language layer, of meaning and signification therein. In the background is the conviction that there is never *one* language, never *one* meaning or *one* signification. A philosophy of language or of religion, as mentioned in every encyclopedia under their name, is a field of practical and methodical research; the preoccupation with that field is to find meaning in multiplicity. Benjamin's distancing from the *more geometrico* thought pattern makes the question possible, whether our ability to determine a meaning is a gift of the multiplicity of language itself.

[89] W. Benjamin: *SW* I, Op. Cit., p.16; *GS*, II,1, Op. Cit., p. 103.

8 Preliminary Conclusions

Considerations about *the word as the basic unit of language* relate immediately to logics and metaphysics in philosophical perspective. That particular reference has scarcely changed in our days of a global interest in the plurality of languages, signs, symbols, particles and processes. Neither logical positivism nor structuralism nor theories of deconstruction provided us an alternate. Developments in modern semiotics uphold the distinction between the verbal and the non-verbal and do not allow any change in that regard. Moreover, the differentiation between the verbal and the non-verbal in the many recent *phenotypes* of semiotic texts appears not to affect any *genotypic* feature: in all semiotic approaches the *word* still remains the major component of the semiotic toolkit.

So, what philosopher or what philosophical insight changes that insight? Any contemporary theory of meaning must profit from the various insights mentioned above. The predominant position of 'the word' seems important in understanding meaning, independent from any acceptance or dismissal. When contemplating the broad variety of considerations in different philosophical views in equally different periods of the twentieth century, one encounters several of the following components.

8.1 *Singularity and 'The Word'*

The *singularity* determining all the focus on 'the word' does not exist on the basis of any specific factual, argumentative, spiritual or cultural motivation. 'The Word" is singled out from a larger set of possibilities including 'The Name", 'The Sentence", "The Argument", 'The (Speech) Act", "The Meaning" or even "The Absence of Meaning", which all belong to a cultural process or a 'habit' (Peirce) with longstanding tradition. They should be understood in terms of a conceptual and not of a natural order. 'Words' may be acknowledged as natural language elements, but one must explain in another layer of language in what manner they are products of the human mind and not of any type of nature untouched by human creativity.

A full understanding of this basic cultural fact needs a different level of linguistic expressiveness than that of everyday language. That level is often 'conceptual'. But the laws of grammar and syntax must in the end find adequate forms of expressiveness in an everyday life's linguistic system of communication. Such expressions, however, explain language and discourse terms, which are in essence not word-based but—as Frege and Shaumyan highlighted—mainly sentence-based.

We repeat that the singularity of the word is thus a hypothetical construction, since any linguistic structure is a construct. Thoughts about structures of language result from constructive mental forces. To speak of a "natural" language is in this light also a construct. The concept of a "natural language" is as artificial as the concept of an "artificial language". The question of the dominant position of 'the word' is a question of language as being a construct.

8.2 *Genesis and Meaning*

The creation of the singular position of 'the word' left impressive traces in the major narratives of Occidental culture. They are in the form of stories, historical and religious narratives, story-related images and many equivalent codes. What Walter Benjamin suggested in view of the ontological dimensions of language remains valid: "…language … communicates the mental being corresponding to it. It is fundamental that this mental being communicates itself *in* language and not *through* language. Languages, therefore, have no speaker…"[90] It means that languages expressing fragments of narration which are traces in a culture may report about speakers but do not contain speakers. The "speaker-hearer-situation" does not fit for those narrations. Their narration *IS* reality in the narrated perspective. One of them is based on Benjamin's enigmatic conclusion that the linguistic being of man is *to name* things. Here we have to keep in mind that Benjamin is able to refer to one of the most famous and important narratives of the Occident—the Genesis narration in the Torah—to expand his research into the essence of language.

Benjamin is perfectly clear in describing his position. As was noticed before, he did *not* refer to the *Genesis* text to open or follow religious perspectives, but to expand his insight into language. "If in what follows the nature of language is considered on the basis of the first chapter of Genesis, the object is neither biblical interpretation nor subjection of the Bible to objective consideration of revealed truth…"[91] The *Genesis* narration tells us about a paradisiacal language based on *Names* that were given, so that *meanings* (debatable and changeable in themselves) were not relevant or even known. Notice: a word has to communicate something, and often *a* something. A *named world* does not support that type of communication. Only after the Fall, Benjamin suggests, and thus after an Exodus from meaninglessness, can the word become a prevailing component of a then different layer of language. The singularity focusing on the word is in the light of this great narration a matter (a) of a breach with meaninglessness which creates the Name, and (b) of a specific historical outline concentrated on a human expansion of knowledge, an outline known as a "before and after 'The Fall' ". In that regard, there is no 'Word' without 'History' and no 'History' without 'Narrative'—the latter being a human construct beyond dimensions.

[90] Benjamin, *SW* I, Op. Cit., p. 61; *GS* II,1. Op. Cit., p. 140.

[91] Benjamin, *SW* I, Op. Cit., p. 67; *GS* II,1. Op. Cit., p. 147.

8.3 Name and Breach

The name as first bearer of meaning is, as long as it remains the first, also the sole bearer of meaning: God. Apart from the Name thereare no meanings in the sense of the languages human speak in our era. One could speculate, reading modern literature about the development of the human brain, that in the period of the Name's dominance there was no need or desire for a multiplicity of language and layered discourses. Multiplicity has to do with an encompassing consideration of the historicity of discourse and its narratives in a human culture.

An important point for any insight into the process of meaning is insight into its conceptual features. To unfold that riddle, *language* as well as *brain* should be regarded as historical processes. The state they are in momentarily (their identity) is never completely represented by their actual state resulting from factual observation. And, what is more: the conclusion should also be (Benjamin did not enter this field of meaning) that also "the Name" should be considered in a historical perspective—what theologians of diverse religions are hesitant to acknowledge.

A truly preliminary remark in view of the historicity of the meaning concept pertains to the often-mentioned *constructive* character of word or name. The emergence of concepts as products of the human mind directs us towards the mind as understood in the framework of modern neurosciences and brain research. A cluster of insights and knowledge offers a substantive, even challenging viewpoint here.

First, one encounters all varieties of "Firstness" (Peirce) or "Naïve Naturalness" (Husserl) as a point of departure for scientific articulation. Deeply encapsulated in Firstness is, spoken along the lines of the *Genesis* narration, the breach with Naturalness. The Name has two names—one before and another after the Fall. That breach plays a major but often concealed role in Occidental philosophy.

Secondly, the desire to gain insight into the functioning brain, so eminent in modern neurosciences, confronts us with the fact that that human brain has also, at least, two names—one describing the brain as it is a human quality today (in this quality fundamentally different from earlier periods of life on earth) and one at the level of language for which brain is not like a word in everyday language and can be qualified as a basic unit.

8.4 Brain and Meaning

Speaking about the brain directs us to a language level where one must articulate brain and mind, mind and brain, *in their combination,* and only the latter can be treated "as one word". On that language level, the expression 'brain' indicates the 'word': 'mind brain' or 'brain mind'. That insight is an important step in the understanding of meaning: not only does meaning mean differently in different periods of culture, but that difference is equally important at the various language levels.

This linguistic issue is particularly important once one considers that the history of the brain is an evolutionary history, with the reptilian brain, the mammalian brain and the neo-cortex, which we mostly call 'the human brain' or the mind brain. The path of evolution of humans seems to evolve from the first to the latter. Absolutely essential, however, is the observation that the *temporal character* of that evolution, and with it also of the human brain mind, is not measurable other than *in geological terms*, which are at great distance from our everyday discourse and its notions of time.[92] The map of development of the human brain is a map of geological conditions. Movements of the crust of the globe thus parallel the evolutionary phases of the brain—with the mind gradually influencing and pairing with the brain. This process is a marker of our notions about the relation between word and name, as expressed in the narration about the breach of a before and an after the Fall—to re-use the *Genesis* narrative.

The intertwining of history in cosmic dimensions and of language layers seems decisive for understanding meaning. There is, in other words, no understanding of the concept of meaning without understanding human historicity. The latter is *not* represented by scanner results, neuro-images or outlines and determinations of geological nature. Respect for human historicity in the process of conceptualization includes awareness of the multiplicity of time—all the consequences included. The before-mentioned intertwining of language and history challenges us to articulate time in a variety of language layers. This is foundational for the discovery that perhaps once the name was the bearer of meaning par excellence. Some of this awareness is still active in our ideal of and desire for unity, security and simplicity in science as well as philosophy. However, one recognizes that a deference to this desire leads the scientist and philosopher to honor multiplicity in discourse and its articulation., in other words: to honor meaning in its multidimensionality.

9 Legal Semiotics (3): Law and Language

A first address to law students was about opening one's mind to the importance of meaning as a key concept in law and legal discourse. Lawyers are always making meanings—mostly concentrating on those which fit to prescriptions about how to maintain the law and follow the lines of its constitution in society.[93] Semiotics broadens that view, most importantly beyond meaning fixations and prescriptions about *what is* and *what is not* law. The second chapter on attitude as a major force in deciding the language quality that should be linked to specific meanings, must have clarified the manner in which meanings are tied to specific attitudes. Law students should train themselves to appreciate the dynamics of different language

[92] See Michio Kaku: *The Future of the Mind*, New York 2014, p. 104, 250, 329f.

[93] See: Jan M. Broekman and Larry Catà Backer: *Lawyers Making Meaning. The Semiotics of Law in Legal Education II*, Op. Cit., 2013.

levels at which they articulate reality. The specificities of *legal* reality make this study a socially important subject of training.

9.1 Saying a Word

Thirdly, the "saying for law" was presented as an expression, which highlights the *saying* as a particular speech act resulting from a specific attitude, but also—the theme of this chapter—as an entity called *word*. That issue is often disregarded in legal training. Law is evidently a matter of managing words, and words are thus viewed as the natural components of that activity. What lawyers suggest within the boundaries of their professional thought patterns seems also valid in most theories and philosophies of language: the *word* is perceived as the smallest and basic unit of language.

The above insights, extremely relevant for the law student, introduced the idea that this view of the word is problematic and ultimately incorrect. A major argument is directly applicable to law and legal discourse: one word (as a basic entity) cannot have meaning! Words are always contextual; the meaning of a word is determined by other words and articulations. This leads to a level that is very precious to legal students: is not any text the contextual property of the word? Laws are texts; legal activity is in great measure the writing and interpreting of what was already written. A word is never on its own, just like a sign is not a sign when it is positioned on its own.

9.2 Text Structures

But semiotics explains that not only the surfaces of texts or speech play a role in the creation of meaning. Apart from what law students do encounter (that is: the pheno-textual structure; the surface they consult), there is a deep structure of language, which also determines meaning. Hence the lawyer's interest in the ways a concept (expressed in linguistic articulations) came to life. Legal history has a deep function in the language of law: law's history is packed with meanings of legal expressions and not only a matter of what thoughts or occurrences happened in time. Law students should learn to be constantly aware of those two different dimensions when they are performing their function through speaking and acting legally—and give a thought to legal history.

Semiotics explains to each student of law that there are at any time two dimensions to respect in a text. There is first of all the *horizontal* dimension of texts. Texts do intertwine continuously and that intertwining creates (legal) meanings that words pretend to indicate. And there is furthermore the *vertical* dimension of texts (and languages in general) showing us a surface, which belongs to our daily life—the surface of the sign pool—and an often precariously concealed deep structure in which values, norms, habits and related social powers are influential, even before they are properly articulated (Peirce's "feeling").

9.3 Signifiers

Now, legal discourse—and its meanings—is a cautiously and severely regulated and controlled entity, with special attention for the proper places and roles to assign to the *signifiers* in a case. It is especially important to have constantly an eye on the *surface-text signifiers* in the study of law.[94] They not only allow the construction of the so-called "Greimasian Square", an outstanding explanatory instrument,[95] but primarily prove that law students should be trained *to observe most attentively the positioning of activities in a specific field of legal meaning*: in an advocate's opinion, a jury's consideration, a judge's decision, in often contrasting interpretations of relevant legal texts. Signifiers are centrally positioned to determine meaning in the message *tout court*. They illuminate Court opinions as well as general argumentative strategies of participants in law. However, the interest in the "surface-text signifier" does not complete and finalize our attempts to envisage legal discourse in a semiotic manner. Semiotics in law also focuses on questions that remain without a definitive answer. At least three must be mentioned.

First, *a signifier is not a sign*. Each signifier *carries* a sign, and thus functions implicitly as what Peirce called an "interpretant". Both signifier and sign are in need of a third!

Secondly, *carrying a sign* is only observable when the sign is indeed *effective*. Non-effective signs are forms of silence we do not discern—not even in semiotics.

Thirdly, "meaning" and "functioning sign" are not separately understandable; one can rarely identify one without the other. Their appearances reach from 'fixation' to 'process/total change'.

The three lead to a philosophically interesting conclusion: *a signifier always needs a third.* Peirce encountered here the *triadic* character of sign relations, which expresses the need described. He writes for instance in 1903: "Not only will meaning always, more or less, in the long run, mould reactions to itself, but it is only in doing so that its own being consists. For this reason I call this element of the phenomenon or object of thought the element of Thirdness. It is that which is what it is by virtue of imparting a quality to reactions in the future." And in this context, he wrote 1909 to William James: "A Sign is a Cognizable that, on the one hand, is so determined (i.e., specialized, *bestimmt*) by something *other than itself*, called its Object (…) while, on the other hand, it so determines some actual or potential Mind,

[94] Broekman & Backer: *Lawyers Making Meaning.* Op. Cit., 2013, p. 204 ff.

[95] Broekman & Backer: *Lawyers Making Meaning,* Op. Cit., 2013, p. 57 ff, 182, 201 ff.

the determination whereof I term the Interpretant created by the Sign, that that Interpreting Mind is therein determined mediately by the Object".[96]

9.4 Firsts, Dialogues, and Triads

One conclusion, however, should *not* be made. The *triad* Peirce had in mind, as a foundational feature of all sign relations and thus for semiotics in its entirety, cannot be interpreted as a *dialogue*. In other words: the need for a third (as mentioned above by Peirce: an other than itself) differs from the need of an o/Other. Petrilli concluded: "The meaning of sign is constructed as a *response*, an interpretant that calls for another response, another interpretant. All this is connected with the presupposed *dialogic nature of sign and semiosis*.".[97]

Will our critique of the theory that "a word is the basic unit of language" ultimately bring an insight into the *dialogic* character of signs? In that case, "signs in law" must lead the law student to *openness* for dialogue and for *recognition* of the other in law's discourse. Are signs a concealed outcry for a Third, particularly for a Third Person? That would be a charming and most convincing conclusion: ethically, sociologically as well as politically, and all of that on a global scale.

But the conclusion does not fit—the Third is needed in a different manner when sign relations and signifier functions are at stake (the triad) than when speech- and face-to-face relations are concerned (dialogue).[98] The difference between the two should be studied, in particular in law. It is fundamental to distinguish legal discourse as an ensemble of speech acts from discourse as an open-ended chain of signifiers. The first view accepts that Peirce mentions "a First" or "Firstness" as being a human quality while interpreting reality (the breach). The second is at distance from human occurrences and leads to cosmological theories or speculations. The study of semiotics in legal education might embrace the speech-directed view but not the open-ended chain view, the cosmological perspective. The problem of this difference remains even where Petrilli suggests: "… dialogue and semiosis converge, not only in the sense that *dialogue is semiosic* but also in the sense that

[96] Ch. S. Peirce: *Lowell Lectures on Some Topics of Logic Bearing on Questions Now Vexed.* Op. Cit., 3rd Lecture. http://www.commens.org/bibliography/manuscript/peirce-charles-s-1903-lowell-lectures-some-topics-logic-bearing-questions-0 and: *Letters to William James* http://www.commens.org/bibliography/manuscript/peirce-charles-s-1897-1909-letters-william-james-l-r-224

[97] S. Petrilli: *The Self as a Sign, the World, and the Other*, Op. Cit., p. 27f.: "Each time there is a sign occurrence including the "first Sign", there is a "Third", (…) something mediated, a response, and interpretive novelty, an interpretant. It follows that a sign is constitutively an interpretant. The fact that the interpretant (Third) is in turn a sign (First), and that the sign (First) is in turn an interpretant (already a Third) places the sign in an open network of interpretants: this is the Peircean principle of infinite semiosis or open-ended chain of interpretants".

[98] See Jan M. Broekman: "Faces Face to Face" in: Jan M. Broekman & Francis J. Mootz III (Eds): *The Semiotics of Law in Legal Education.* Op. Cit., p. 21ff.

semiosis is dialogic".[99] But, one should ask, is there indeed an emergence, a beginning, a First possible in an infinite semiosis? It may not be the case, because signs are in this view not actions but reactions, already pre-formatted interpretations of earlier formatted interpretations. The latter, the interpretations, are by no means only speech-acts or fundamentally linguistic by nature.

9.5 No Surface Alone

There is, however, a final remark to consider. The totality of analyses of the sign and the signifier, exemplary for semiotics as such, concerns the *surface structure* of language, or in other words: they concern *language in its surface articulations only.* Theories to explain sign and signifier do *not* consider any aspect of the deep structures of texts, speech and language. Notice that they did not study any *geno-textual* features, although these are at least as important as the *pheno-textual* ones. What does specifically belong to deep structures of language, text or speech that we must consider?

Greimas, one of the Godfathers of semiotics, observes that *deep structures* of language "define the fundamental mode of existence of an individual or a society, and subsequently the conditions of existence of semiotic objects."[100] Apart from a surface- and a deep structure, he also mentions a specific *structure of manifestation*, which produces and organizes the signifiers and their products, significance/meaning. The latter: the various manifestation of signifiers and the meaning process that follows from their activity, is of utmost importance for functioning as an actor in legal discourse. The creativity required from lawyers starts from kernels of meaning, Greimas said, and from there operates from the general to the particular (often "the case"), from the simple to the complex (legal argumentation, law's logic, legal positivism are catchwords here).

9.6 A Conclusion for Law Students

The processual character and the layered structure of discourse are essential—the two bind law and language, which makes them into a unique social and institutional force. Again: its formula is concentrated in a "saying for law". Meaning is quality here; signifiers cooperate to construct what Lacan has called a "master discourse". He thus underlined that a "discourse" is a social bond founded in inter-subjectivity. The latter highlights the trans-individual nature of language because speech always

---

[99] S. Petrilli: *The Self as a Sign(....)* Op. Cit., p. 29.

[100] A.J.Greimas & F. Rastier: "The Interaction" Op. Cit.,, p. 86ff.; Also: Jan M. Broekman & Larry Catà Backer: "Layered Discourses, Dynamic Semiotics" in *Signs in Law—A Source Book.* Op. Cit., p. 125 ff.

implies another subject. In one of the reigning powers of linguistic deep structures is the 'other subject': the master. Even a concealed master must be obeyed … no justification is given for this power: *it just is*. It shows no weakness, hides the fact of its linguistic depth structures as well as the effects of its symbolic castration: the split between conscious and unconscious brought on by the signifier is the secret of any master discourse—legal discourse is such a master discourse in occidental society. Its major realm is in deep structures of language, which are generally acknowledged *as a text*. One important conclusion can be drawn from these considerations that appeal to a law student. Only a text, which is understood as *a unity of surface- and deep structures* can access an understanding of signs in action and signifiers in the functioning of a legal discourse. Once that unity is neglected, understanding the dynamics of meaning in law seems incorrect.

References

Apel, Karl-Otto. 1995. *Charles S. Peirce: From pragmatism to pragmaticism*. Amherst: Prometheus Books.

Barthes, Roland. 1977. *La Poétique du récit*. Paris: Ed. du Seuil.

Benjamin, Walter. 1977. Uber Sprache überhaupt und über Sprache des Menschen. *Gesammelte Schriften,* (GS) Band II, 1. Suhrkamp Frankfurt/M 1977 [Engl. Ed.: *Selected Writings,* (SW) Vol. 1, Bullock & Jennings, (Eds) Harvard 1996].

Bohm, David. 1980. *Wholeness and the implicate order*. London: Routledge & Kegan Paul.

Bohm, David. 1985. *Unfolding meaning. A weekend of dialogue*. London: Routledge & Kegan Paul.

Broekman, Jan M. 1963. *Phänomenologie und Egologie,* Den Haag, Series *Phaenomenologica* Bd 12.

Broekman, Jan M. 1974. *Structuralism: Moscow, Prague, Paris*, Synthese library, vol. 67. Dordrecht: Reidel.

Chomsky, Noam. 1969. *Topics in the theory of generative grammar*. The Hague/Paris: Mouton.

Cole, David. 2014. The anti-court court. *The New York Review of Books* LXI: 13.

de Haan, J.I. 1916. *Rechtskundige Significa.* Amsterdam: W. Versluys.

de Haan, J.I. 2015. Essence and task of legal significs, 1916. In *Signs in law—A source book*, ed. Jan M. Broekman and Larry Catá Backer. Springer.

de Unamuno, M. 1913. *Del sentimiento trágico de la vida en los hombres y en los pueblos* [The Tragic Sense of Life in Men and in Peoples]. Trans. J.E.C. Flitch, 1921.

Dummet, Michael. 1973. *Frege. Philosophy of language*. London: Duckworth.

Eiland, H., and M.W. Jennings. 2014. *Walter Benjamin. A critical life*. Cambridge, MA: Harvard University Press.

Freud, Sigmund. 1940 *Das Ich und das Es*. In: *Gesammelte Werke,* Band XIII. Frankfurt am Main/London: S. Fischer Verlag/Imago Publishing Company.

Goodrich, Peter. 1986. Historical aspects of legal interpretation. *Indiana Law Review* 61: 331.

Greimas, Algirdas J. 1976. *Sémiotique et sciences sociales*. Paris. [The Social Sciences: A Semiotic View. Trans. P. Perron and F.H. Collins, Minnesota University Press, 1980].

Greimas, Algirdas J., and François Rastier. 1968. The interaction of semiotic constraints: pp 86–106 in *Yale French Studies* 41.

Guberman, Ross M. (ed.). 1996. *Julia Kristeva interviews*. New York: Columbia University Press.

Hardwick, Charles S. (ed.). 1977. *Semiotic and significs: The correspondence between Charles S. Peirce and Victoria Lady Welby.* (Assistance of James Cook). Bloomington: Indiana University Press.

Heidegger, Martin. 1949. *Brief über den Humanismus*. [Engl. Ed.: Letter on Humanism. Trans. F.A. Capuzzi and J.G. Gray, San Francisco, 1978].
Kaku, Michio. 2014. *The future of the mind*. New York: Doubleday.
Kristeva, Julia. 1969. *Semeiotikè Recherches pour une sémanalyse*. Paris: Éditions du Seuil.
Kristeva, Julia. 1980a. *Desire in language. A semiotic approach to literature and art*, ed. L. Roudiez. New York: Columbia University Press.
Kristeva, Julia. 1980b. *The powers of horror* (Engl. Ed. 1982).
Kristeva, Julia. 2002. *The Portable Kristeva*. ed, K. Oliver. New York.
Mannoury, Gerrit. 2015. Significs and philosophy (1922). In *Signs in law—A source book*, ed. Jan M. Broekman and Larry Catá Backer. Springer.
Ogden, C.K., and I.A. Richards. 1923. *The meaning of meaning. A study of the influence of language upon thought and of the science of symbolism*. London: Trubner & Co.
Oz, Amos, and Fania Oz-Salzberger. 2012. *Jewsandwords*. New Haven: Yale University Press.
Peirce, Ch.S. 1958. *The collected papers of Charles Sanders Pierce*, ed. Charles Hartshorne and Paul Weiss, vol. I–VI; 1931–1935, ed. Arthur W. Burks, vol. VII–VIII. Cambridge, MA: Harvard University Press.
Peirce Edition Project. 1998. *The essential Peirce. Selected philosophical writings,* 2 vols. Bloomington: Indiana University Press.
Petrilli, Susan. 2013. *The self as a sign, the world, and the other*. New Brunswick/London: Transaction Publishers.
Rorty, Richard. 1982. *Consequences of pragmatism*. Hassocks: The Harvester Press.
Rosenzweig, Franz. 2005. *Der Stern der Erlösung*. Heidelberg 1921, 1954(3); The Star of Redemption. Trans. W. Hallo and B. Galli. 1971). Wisconsin University Press.
Searle, John. 1969. *Speech acts. An essay in the philosophy of language*. London: Cambridge University Press.
Searle, John. 1995. *The construction of social reality*. London: Penguin.
Searle, John. 2015. *Seeing things as they are*. Oxford/New York: Oxford University Press.
Shaumyan, Sebastian. 1973. The genotype language and formal semantics. In *Trends in Soviet theoretical linguistics*, ed. F. Kiefer. Dordrecht: Reidel.
Shaumyan, Sebastian. 1998, September 19. Two paradigms of linguistics: The semiotic versus non-semiotic paradigm. *Web Journal of Formal, Computational and Cognitive Linguistics*. Yale University Press.
Sheriff, John K. 1989. *The fate of meaning. Charles Peirce, structuralism, and literature*. Princeton: Princeton University Press.
Sheriff, John K. 1994. *Charles Peirce's guess at the riddle*. Bloomington: Indiana University Press.
Stjernfelt, Frederik. 2007. *Diagrammatology. An investigation on the borderlines of phenomenology, ontology, and semiotics*. London/Dordrecht: Springer.
Stjernfelt, Frederik. 2014. *Natural propositions. The actuality of Peirce's doctrine of dicisigns*. Boston: Docent Press.
Tushnet, Mark. 2013. *In the balance: Law and politics on the Roberts Court*. New York: W.W. Norton & Company.
Welby, Victoria Lady. 1903. *What is meaning? Studies in the development of significance*. New York: Macmillan.
Wittgenstein, Ludwig. 1922. *Tractatus Logico-Philosophicus*. London: Routledge.
Wittgenstein, Ludwig. 1953. *Philosophical investigations*. Oxford: Blackwell.
Wolfskehl, Karl. 1960. *Gesammelte Werke*. Hamburg: Bd II.
Zornberg, Avivah G. 1995. *The beginning of desire*. New York: Doubleday.
Zornberg, Avivah G. 2001. *The particulars of rapture*. New York: Doubleday.
Zornberg, Avivah G. 2008. *The murmuring deep*. New York: Schocken.

Part II
Particles and Partitions

Chapter 4
Particles

A not-so-modest smile was on the face of the French philosopher and psychoanalyst Jacques Lacan, when he read the line. The profession had characterized him as "the most controversial since Freud".[1] His discourse theory had profiled four types: a *master* discourse, a *university* discourse, a *hysteric* discourse and an *analyst* discourse. The latter was prominently challenging his professional circles; the first was most generally recognized and globally quoted. We are all shaped in our thoughts, it said, guided in our expressivity and determined in our articulation by a discourse that hovers over the sign pool we consider as our life. Legal discourse is a powerful example,[2] other discourses often fill the gaps of the former; no one can express herself beyond any such determination. And now, all of a sudden, Lacan reads a line about a "*master*—master discourse". Is that an exaggeration? No, it is not. It might stylistically be an impure articulation, but it is the proper theme of this chapter, because we indicate with the word "particle" the particular issue with which any theory of meaning will be confronted.

Indeed, the *master—master discourse* is the most powerful story about particles, or: about the concept called 'particle'. The latter is thought to be present in many cultures over the globe today, as well as innumerable years ago. It is considered to be identical with the story of human life and its civilizations based on that idea. One could venture the thesis that the word 'particle' is approximately in the same position as the word 'ego': both arc at home in nearly all languages, effective in all types of explanation of reality, and determining all formations and applications of meaning in scientific as well as non-scientific reasoning. Each master discourse has in this perspective a master: it is most frequently the discourse of 'particle'. And, one thing is clear: *a particle is not a thing*, but an articulation of whatever type of reality.

[1] See the excellent general information in: Elisabeth Roudinesco: *Jacques Lacan*, *Esquisse d'une Vie, Histoire d'un Système de Pensée*, Ed. Fayard, 1993, La Pochothèque Paris 2009, p. 1994 ff.

[2] See Jan M. Broekman: "Master Signifiers, Master Discourses" in: Jan M. Broekman & Larry Catà Backer: *Lawyers Making Meaning.* Op. Cit., p. 67 ff, p. 80.

J.M. Broekman, *Meaning, Narrativity, and the Real*,
DOI 10.1007/978-3-319-28175-9_4

That discursive power is in its turn not easy to manage—certainly not in a philosophical context, as Ogden & Richards experienced in their well-known 1923 study *The Meaning of Meaning*. Philosophers "hypostasize their definiendum" they state (in this case Meaning), "either by inventing a peculiar stuff, and intrinsic property, and then saying let everything which possesses this be said to possess meaning, or by inventing a special unanalysable relation, and saying let everything related by this relation to something else be said to have meaning."[3] The idea of 'the particle concept' being created under the power of a *master-master discourse* seems to approximate the second type of experience without letting go the charm of the first. However, a continuous drive to partition feeds our desire for meaning: there is no meaning if there is no particle to detect. And there is no particle that is not the result of a partitioning process. That desire and its partition seem essential in every sign pool on the globe. Knowing 'what this means' is a pillar of human understanding—the particle fulfills its predominant role in that context. Life as carrying an ultimate meaning is safeguarded only when it is understood and experienced as a construction of particles.

The particle story is too complicated for a single book publication and will never produce a reliable outcome via one particular research project only. Can its story be articulated at all? The question remains unanswered. Instead of "a world history of the particle concept and its influence on human cultures through the ages" we offer solely an *illustration* from very different regions of the arts and sciences.[4] One region is *poetry* (Celan), a second *physics* (Bohm) and a third *painting* (Cézanne). These concern the particle three times at the center of interest in an artistic or scientific context; they include three different authors of the twentieth century and represent three attempts to cope with questions raised in this short introduction.

1 Particle Flurry (Celan)

We first focus on a poem of Paul Celan (1920–1970) to illustrate the relation between poetics and the particle-story (alias the master—master discourse) in twentieth century. Occidental literature is challenging: the selected poem entitled "Engführung" begins aggressively with lines that deliberately cause disorientation. That disorientation is embedded in a remarkable parallel (entirely at a theoretical level) between the poetically presupposed Newtonian position of the reader, and the particle's quantum physics insight that physical processes cannot be predicted with certainty because they are not determined as such. In both discourses, the poetic and

[3] C.K. Ogden and I.A. Richards: *The Meaning of Meaning*, London 1923, p. 185 f.

[4] See L. Wittgenstein: *Philosophical Investigations*, 1953, par. 133: "The real discovery is the one that makes me capable of stopping doing philosophy when I want to (…) Instead, we now demonstrate a method, by examples; and the series of examples can be broken off.—Problems can be solved (difficulties eliminated), not a *single* problem. There is not *a* philosophical method, though there are indeed methods, like different therapies."

the quantum mechanical, a reader is, thanks to the different underlying character of theory, brought into a position which is on the one hand trusted and well known and on the other completely alienating.

Characteristic for Celan's poetic discourse is his continuous reference to the cultural and existential situation shortly after the Second World War in Europe. The poem we read was written in 1958 and opens with three lines in fragment (a)[5]:

VERBRACHT ins	DEPORTED into
Gelände	the terrain
mit der untrüglichen Spur	with the unmistakable trace

The unmistakable trace leads to or comes from concentration camps and other places of crisis or death—several of them all around us, often right in view of what we daily experience, for instance in dense and dangerous traffic situations. The reader is put in position and torn away with those opening words. Peter Szondi concentrated on the poem "Engführung", emphasizing that the reader is left without any explication of meaning from the first words on.[6] This makes it even more necessary to highlight the prominent position of the word "particle" and its historical as well as philosophical reminiscences. If, as was said before, the poem's feelings are familiar from the beginning, they nevertheless lead immediately to misunderstanding and disorientation. The poem's title does not help to clarify this in any regard. Title and first words: 'verbracht' [deported, spend] and 'führung' [guided] are expressing a situation of leading/guiding the reader, but there is no further explanation of their meaning. Is that necessary? The reader is confronted with a "dark" text, Szondi notes. "What words mean becomes clear when we perceive the specific use that is made of them, and yet often with our first glance taken away from us". The enigmatic title lights up: *if* "Engführung" can be understood as 'guidance with intensified togetherness through narrow passes', then: *who* guides? The contrast between 'particle flurry' and 'opinion/meaning' (in the sense of Kant's "Meynungen" [Opinions] that have chanced to arise here or there) suggests an answer: it is the master—master discourse of the 'particle' and not the poet or the reader. That emphasis on the 'particle' is exactly the reason why we introduce a short analysis of the poem in the context of this book on 'meaning':

Geh, deine Stunde	Go, your moment
hat keine Schwestern, du bist—	has no sisters, you are—
bist zuhause.	are at home.

Where are we at home? The title suggests: in the *master—master discourse*, the discourse of the particle inscribed in this exceptional poem. The words in the titles of the poem and the collection are but an approximation of the German original in

[5] All translations German—English in this chapter are by the author (JMB).

[6] Peter Szondi: *Celan-Studien*, Suhrkamp Verlag Frankfurt/M. 1972 [Bibliothek Suhrkamp Bd. 330] p. 47 f.

the poetry of Celan. A translation of, and commentary on all the titles in the collection—inseparably in their literary context—brings us to the 'particle' concept at its level of "Engführung", the level of the last poem in the collection "Sprachgitter" published 1959.[7] The poem eventually unveils some features of the evoked master—master discourse. With the 'particle' as the leading actor, the reader is given no attention. Where is she/he at home?

1.1 Engführung

"Engführung" seems parallel to English expressions such as "Bottle-neck" or "Narrow Pass", but these are most probably too spatial; the title could also be translated as "Without Fail"—an expression near to "Precision", indicating the severity of following the rules of composition. Spatial dimensions have their own meaning-reducing consequences in the realm of poetic metaphors, which are in their turn philosophically decisive.[8] The poem is like an outline for the reader, a road to go without prefabricated knowledge and an unknown context, which will become clear and knowable, *through the act of reading only.*

But that suggests more. Peter Szondi published his interpretation in 1971 in French in an essay with the title *Strette.* His text was published in its German translation several times with the title "Durch die Enge geführt" [Guided through Confinement], then eventually: "Through Straits".[9] It is not unimportant to consider whether the emphasis remains for him entirely on *reading* and *text*—an observation that fits with a closing line of the essay: "Who has learned to read the writing of Celan", it says, "knows that there is no focusing on a decision about one of the many meanings, but rather to understand that those meanings are not separated but one."[10] The question arises: do we *only* have to learn to *read* those lines? The importance of reading linguistic particles diminishes when confronted with the non-dimensionality of their meaning that governs the sign pool. Reading the poem makes us perceive a comprehensive *sign* of the human condition as well as the Universe(s).

1.2 Ground Lines of the Poem

This perspective is already visible during a first reading of the poem, if one ventures to perform that reading at a distance to the many interpretations one encounters on the Internet and in book publications on modern literature. It comes to us in eight

[7] Paul Celan: *Sprachgitter* [Language Grid], S. Fischer Verlag, Frankfurt/Main 1959, p. 57 ff.

[8] See: Pajari Räsänen: *Counter-figures . An Essay on Antimetaphoric Resistance: Paul Celan's Poetry and Poetics at the Limits of Figurality*. Helsinki 2007.

[9] Peter Szondi: *Celan-Studien*, Frankfurt/M. Op. Cit, 1972 see "Anhang" by Jean Bollack, p. 129 ff.

[10] Peter Szondi: *Celan-Studien*, Op. Cit., p. 47 ff.

parts, whereby the quasi-mysterious word "Partikelgestöber" is mentioned twice in the sixth part. The relation between this word and the poem's title "Engführung" is in its turn anchored in the manifest repetitions of words and fragments throughout the poem in its totality. The order of the poem's fragments seems, apart from any possible in-depth analysis and at distance from further interpretations, to comprise eight fragments:

(a) First, the *subject* of the poem finds its articulation: a wheel and its spokes is perhaps a symbol or sign for stability;
(b) But those components do not have a name anymore, and are not orderly connected, as the randomly spread spokes illustrate;
(c) The 'I' as redeemer is introduced, but there is nowhere any reaction, so that
(d) The search for an understanding goes on, although
(e) There is no word to hear, but we did not give up.
(f) Reality thus challenged, unveals a deep partition between a notion of stabilized reality on the one hand and just a groundless opinion on the other.
(g) Psalms, Hosanna's, replace circles, squares and other scientific issues: perhaps nothing is lost;
(h) Traces of groundwater, sign pools, grasses are left to go on.

That pattern represents the human condition in the same way "Engführung" is constructed. That construction is interesting: Szondi understands the title as representing a *musical* concept. That advances a reading of the poem beyond exclusive links with literature. A musical notion is empirically related to the German word "Engführung", in French: 'strette'[11] or in Latin: 'strictus', in English: 'without fail'—there is no musical performance without strictly following rules of a special togetherness. Szondi describes the musical features by using words from three different encyclopedias (which together offer an outlook on a musical theory in the strictest sense of the word) as follows: "the closely, if possible simultaneous, contrapuntal bringing together of themes. More precisely, it is the third (last) part of a fugue in which the beginnings of canonic themes follow very shortly after each other, so that the various voices form a dense interconnection of the counterpoint composition."[12] The themes (a) to (h) in the poem just form such a pattern: "Engführung" as a counterpoint composition. Does the music of J. S. Bach voice the master—master discourse?

[11] This text was originally written and published in French, in the literary journal *Critique*, Nr. 288, May 1971, Paris, under the title "*Strette*".

[12] One encounters a composition of texts from the German "*Der Große Brockhaus*", the French "*Dictionnaire Littré*" and the French "*Grand Robert*".

1.3 Atomism Articulated

Any reader should listen and, while doing so, elect expressions, which relate to an articulation emphasizing the "particle flurry". Do not forget, that our major focus is still on the concept of meaning. Celan's poem leads exactly towards the borderlines of meaning and to questions philosophy seldom stresses.

The "particle flurry" in the poem confronts us with material reality understood as composed of undivisible units (units no more to be partitioned) the way Leucippus (fifth century BCE) suggested. He was probably the earliest Greek philosopher to develop a theory of atoms: everything is in that theory an issue of imperishable, indivisible elements. Do not, however, forget: if indeed *everything* is an issue submitted to "the master—master discourse of 'the particle'", then any linguistic articulation (a word, for instance) is *a fortiori* submitted to that discourse. Little is known of Leucippus' views and his specific contributions to an atomist theory, so that most discussions refer to Democritus, who wrote in a more fashionable manner. It is fascinating to read how "in the atomist system, change only occurs at the level of appearances: the real constituents of being persist unchanged, merely rearranging themselves into new combinations that form the world of appearance". That is "Engführung" understood as 'particle flurry' in a specifically musical context. Also here, "… like Parmenidean Being, the atoms cannot change or disintegrate into 'what is not' and each is a solid unit; nonetheless, the combinations of atoms that form the world of appearance continually alter".[13] Meanings are in this perspective like atoms and also do not change into 'what is not'. The experience of the particle-hurricane, as a consequence of epistemological nature, does not accept 'meaninglessness' as a genuine component of 'meaning'. 'Meaninglessness' should not be understood as 'nonsensical' or 'without meaning'. Celan noticed that silence can be a mark of 'meaning not yet articulated', but his attempt to articulate in words of poetry what is beyond linguistic meanings did not succeed. Walter Benjamin pointed out that the 'word' is generally understood as particle but observed the contrary, which is, that focusing on 'Your' *presence* diminishes the importance of the *word* "You", perhaps even the importance of the word in general. [14] Linguistics step aside in that case, and prioritize social presence. Human encounters often articulate reality beyond grammars. What does that mean—did this inspire the poet? Is there a partitioning, whereby word and presence do *not* totally fill out reality but reach out to the silence that reigns *before* articulation transits towards what we call reality? This would perhaps invite to an awareness of the way meaning and meaninglessness belongs together—they not only *belong* together, they *need* each other.

A partition between 'reality' and 'opinion' as suggested in the poem challenges the concept of meaning. Every decision about meaning finds a 'particle-hurricane' as its context: as a storm or at least as a 'flurry'. That is the case when 'words' are

---

[13] See: *The Stanford Encyclopedia of Philosophy* on: *Leucippus*, by Sylvia Berryman, 2004; 2010 at <sberrym@interchange.ubc.ca>.

[14] As exposed in Chap. 3; notice how deeply this idea is engraved in Jewish culture and religion.

viewed as the 'basic unit of language' and thus as particles. There are two motives here.

1. The tension between 'reality' and 'opinion' leads one to reconsider the importance and structure of inter-subjectivity. If particles do not bind together, do hands or words perhaps do so?
2. The corruption of order, cohesion and stability displays the limits of any human articulation.

The two motives underscore the point that meaning-formation is a process beyond the material and the social world and leads to an encompassing process called Universality. *Articulation seems no longer an exclusively human, subject-bound occurrence but a cosmological process in which the human subject functions amongst a bewildering plurality of signifiers.*

1.4 Particle and Opinion

The wheel (of material reality) was nowhere, as fragment (e) suggests, and no name or word could help out. Even the Redeemer, the Subject, the 'I', did not succeed. Then, in the midst of repetitious suggestions partaking of sameness in articulation, unexpected and like an unforeseen cosmic storm, the clash between reality and opinion occurs (fragment (f)):

Orkane,	Hurricanes
Orkane, von je,	Hurricanes, as always,
Partikelgestöber, das andre	particle flurries, all the rest
du	you
weißts ja, wir	know that well, we
lasens im Buche, war	read it in the Book, was
Meinung	opinion

Reality is reduced towards what is considered as an original yet complex insight. Meaning is opinion; nothing stable, as the Book informed. Democritus. The master—master discourse manifests itself in one word: the word 'particle'. It unveils a combination of bottomless neutrality in view of human conceptions and shows an unrestricted power over the human mind as such. It does not hide away where it comes from; in contrast to the human condition as described in the poem, it has names: Leucippus, Democritus, Ancient Greek Atomism. The foundational concept with a name: 'particle', does not belong to one of our often-groundless chats, nor is it prone to interpretation: it is power—a hurricane announced by initial flurries. What is more: this hurricane is an attitude /Einstellung (the 'guidance', "Führung" in the title) in the sense of Husserl,[15] which was already suggested by the speaking subject. This can be read in fragment (a):

Lies nicht mehr—schau!	Don't read anymore—look!
Schau nicht mehr—geh!	Don't look anymore—go!

Or in (b):

Der Ort, wo sie lagen, er hat	The place they had, has
einen Namen—er hat	a name—it has
keinen.	none.

It is important to stress that each possible attitude/Einstellung has in the end no longer a sense where that story reigns. Even the scattered spokes of the wheel, also in (b), do not break that power.

Sahn nicht, nein,	Did not see, no,
redeten von	were talking about
Worten. Keines	words. None
erwachte, der	woke up, the
Schlaf	sleep
kam über sie.	came over them.

Since Hegel sleep has been the preferred metaphor for 'not-Being'. Is the role of articulation ever finished? Democritus' view that "there is nothing but atoms and empty space: everything else is opinion" prevails.[16] Szondi concludes that in this poem "there is only reference to the creation of the world, a re-creation by the word." The 'particle flurry' not only refers to Democritus, but also to Dante, he claims.[17] What to say about *Meinung/opinion*? Kant had already posed that question. Celan repeats it. Its reality-character seems too different from the powerful atomistic particle story. That is especially the case when 'opinion' is understood as a 'word without reality' and randomly uttered in human relations. There is still this drive to re-create the world, to repeat the Creation, to have the Word coming back to humans in its Full Meaning. The contrast to 'opinion' reinforces that drive continuously, as the reality of the human body ('hands' in the poem, fragment (d)) illustrates:

[15] See Chap. 2, on Husserl.

[16] H. Diels & W. Kranz: *Fragmente der Vorsokratiker*, Berlin 1935, p. 399, § 7.

[17] Peter Szondi: *Schriften II*. Suhrkamp Taschenbuch Wissenschaft 220, Frankfurt/M. 1978, p. 366. See Dante: *Inferno*, *Book V*, 138: "…on that day we did not read further" relates for Celan to his: "…we/ read in the Book." (Fragment (f)).

… ein Finger	… a finger
tastet hinab and hinan, tastet	gropes down and near, gropes
umher:	around:
Nahstellen, fühlbar, hier	close spots, touchable, here
Klafft es weit auseinander, hier	is it yawning greatly, here
Wuchs es wieder zusammen—wer	did it grow together again—who
Deckte es zu?	covered it up?

And (e):

Deckte es zu—wer?	Covered it up—who?
Kam, kam,	Came, came,
Kam ein Wort	Came a word

The body as metaphor for social togetherness, which counters a dominance of physical (particle-oriented) reality seems to be sustained by the repeated desire to perform a 'common reading' (as the Book, the Torah, suggests) in which the word of the dialogue plays a central role.[18] In this context there is a contrast between 'truth' and 'particle flurry' clearly fulfilling a key role. But does this free us from the master—master discourse of the particle?

That question provokes us while we read the Celan poem. The attempt of the poet to re-create reality by means of an achievement of the word includes the concept of meaning. Indeed; but it remains unclear whether the 'word' as viewed in Democritus' atomistic theory as playing the role of a basic unit of language can indeed generate a concept of *meaning* that reaches beyond its linguistic articulatory character.

1.5 The Spoken Word

A spoken word is like a touching hand. But read in (d):

… ein Finger	… a finger
tastet hinab and hinan, tastet	gropes down and near, gropes
umher:	around:

or in (f):

… Wie	… How
faßten wir uns	did we take hold
an—an mit	of each other—hold with
diesen	these
Händen?	hands?

[18] See Gilda Encamaçao: *'Fremde Nähe' als poetisches und poetologisches Prinzip bei Paul Celan*, 2007, p. 168 ff. confronts *Truth* (as episteme) and *Particle Flurry* (as doxa).

There is an interesting aspect in the relation between hand and word. A spoken word always breaks a silence. What the word said before, within an actual context of speech, represents always a breach. Patterns of meaning that occur *before* a particular speech act is performed are seldom completely known. Peirce's ideas on 'habit formation' are difficult to apply to speech. We also fail to know whether they influence the further life of that expressive act. Theories of reference should perhaps be revised in the light of that breach. What are the *archai* in this context of our epistemology? They remind us to acknowledge the fact that every reference has a history. In other words: each speech act refers to other speech acts, and each reference is linked to an unknown, yet *prior* field of meanings, which are seldom fully clarified. Priority is not enough to count on them. They all do, however, determine the context of a meaning transferred by linguistic utterances. A word resembles a hand most closely in a dialogue. Word and hand only act within a field of certainty: the word is in the dialogue less certain about the field of expressed meanings than the hand is about the fact that the other body is located there. Participants in a dialogue know most of the contextual components (or are supposed to know: "did you not say …"). But performing a speech act remains a breach of silence, and that breach delivers insecurity of meaning, as Peirce experienced at his *Arisbe* porch. One is, when one speaks, never fully aware of what quality of silence is broken. Here is perhaps a contrast: a hand is aware of another body that will be touched. Celan's lines illustrate that uncertainty always characterizes the quality of such awareness. A hand touching another body located and perceived a body, and has therefore a view on what was before and is now at the very moment of the touch. Hence the question in the poem: how did we do—do hands touch like words?

Do they? If that is the case, then they are *not* beyond the master-master discourse's influence. The poem shows this in all clarity. "Engführung" is a counterpoint *composition* along musical standards and a *name* in literary standards. The title reveals that all elements of the composition belong to the particle flurry, which organizes the poem by carefully mastering its parts. Reading a flow of word repetitions and variations of verbal motives makes one experience its dynamics as well as listen to tonal expressions. The reader/listener is allowed only one direction: that of guidance through the narrow path until the end of time, life and universe.

How incomplete is this unfolding view! Celan or Szondi did not consider the limitations of being guided by particles and their flurry—an epistemological constraint in itself. Can we imagine another type, another way, another meaning, or perceive other materials of composition? Celan was clearly not aware of the determination provoked by the master—master discourse, which is so straightforwardly articulated by the poem's title. And Szondi did not notice, that Democritus is decidedly *not* the Father who explained all matter and universes—the conception of meaning included—with his theory of atoms.

1.6 The Meaning of Meaninglessness

The meaning of meaninglessness is a component of meaning-fields. In what way do we detect its significance and understand its position in the multiple theories of knowledge embedded in Occidental culture? An answer to that question could be regarded as a translation of what the poet wanted to achieve into the language of philosophy. We, the poet's readers, experienced that his contrapuntal work of art did *not* succeed in articulating reality *beyond* linguistic means. The poem did not arise above repeating, mirroring and executing what the title "Engführung" means. Yet, the poem as a sign or message should originally lead to an existential understanding of human expressiveness. In other words: "what do words say, what meanings do they convey successfully?" functions next to "how and where do words find their place in the poem?" The poem's title is until now honored by understanding whether the meanings of words and their strict composition into a contrapuntal work have a sign function in culture. But security about the meaning of a sign and its referential activity were not achieved.

In that regard there exists a striking parallel with the *Chandos Letter*.[19] The letter and the poem pertain to the trustworthiness of words and their meanings. Problems inherent in a lack of trust based on a loss of reference are their major subject. Not a single composition can repair that breach of reference. A Self lacks its voice as well as its language and written words, and can solely represent an elusive alienation with the loss of a fixed meaning of signs. Norms can in that case no longer be formulated nor can they function as a social beacon. The disjunction between *signifier* and *signified* opened a vertiginous prospect where the limits of language and linguistic articulation are at stake. That is what the Chandos letter as well as the Celan poem indicates. But there exists a difference between them. The letter *describes* a situation in modern culture; the poem *represents* that situation by means of coordinating its own construction plan and our particle-story bound epistemology. An imperfect articulation of reality is at stake in the letter, a shortcoming of our theories of knowledge in the poem.

A complementary lesson from reading the poem is, however, grossly neglected. It is on the importance given to the meaning of meaninglessness. We neglect that constitutive issue in the poem as well as in our theories of knowledge in general: when words break a silence, they do not tell us anything about what existed before that breach and what was broken during that breach. Nor do they show any influence on the meaning-making process and the consequences for the meaning of the word in its many tonal and other expressive utterances. We are acquainted with that philosophical concern from theories pertaining to the *archai* and their Ancient Greek beginnings until today.

Should we not revise our theory of knowledge, including its theories of meaning? Our epistemology must *particularly for the sake of meaning* consider a number of cosmological perspectives, which were hitherto excluded. What damage did this

[19] Hugo von Hofmannsthal: *The Lord Chandos Letter.* Op. Cit.; See also Chap. 1 of this book.

do to our considerations of meaning? Any revision of epistemology remains within the field of meaning; meaninglessness is a specific condition. It is therefore important to understand that the particle story obfuscates broader epistemological considerations.

The dynamics of 'partitioning' characterize the particle story and thus veil any other, eventually fuller or more complete view of the human condition. In the jargon of our theories of knowledge, meaninglessness is regarded as a form of 'silence'. No matter whether that designation is correct, our theory of knowledge causes that silence to remain excluded from any theory of meaning. Democritus' dictum reins deeply in the twenty-first century. But there are many more characterizations of 'silence' than our particle-bound epistemology ever could suggest. Silence is evidently not a 'non-speaking', 'no-words' or 'no-noises' occurrence. Any discussion about the *archai*-bound meaning of silence exemplifies the shortcomings of our epistemology. Is a poem meaningful when it remains only a poem? We remember F. Hölderlin's "*Was bleibet aber, stiften die Dichter*" [What lasts is created by the poets]. Such a bewildering authority and independence of the poem creates silence, because it relegates the poet's words from the realm of speech-acts. This insight pertaining to silence implies a fruitful challenge to renew, broaden and integrate a constitutive role of insights, uncovered by highlighting that the master—master discourse took possession of the *archai*.

Celan's "Engführung" does not succeed in doing so, but initiates that suggestion.

2 Particle: Theory and Experiment

It appears even in poetry and literature that the particle-reined master—master discourse has formatted Occidental philosophy in a powerful manner. Traditional sources confirm that the 'atom' was from the Ancient Greek on at home in physics while its concept also unfolded in philosophy. Theories in physics always led to extended philosophical exposés.[20] We observe this today in quantum theory as well as in Einstein's theories, in the viewpoints of the Copenhagen School, in Bohm's quantum mechanics and his holism, not to mention contemporary experiences with recent nano-, IT- and other technologies. And we repeat that because of the underlying character of theory a reader is, in the poetic as well as the quantum mechanical discourse, brought into a position which is on the one hand trusted and well known and on the other completely alienating from his usual interpretations regarding the reality of everyday-life.

---

[20] As the important texts on this subject show for instance in: Paul Edwards (Ed.): *The Encyclopedia of Philosophy*, London/New York 1967 Vol. 7, p. 41–49 (N.R. Hanson, Yale) or the 389 documents in the *Stanford Encyclopedia of Philosophy* at http://plato.stanford.edu/entries/ written in various years by a wealth of authors.

2.1 Theory in Physics

At least four types of physics rely upon one specific experiment, called the "double slit" experiment. Experiments shaped by that thought pattern were already arranged in the nineteenth century. Most famous was Thomas Young's experiment published in 1803. At issue was the status of the concept of particle in our understanding of light. Ever since Newton's *Optics* light had been considered a corpuscular phenomenon (i.e. of particles), but the view was formulated in few words: Young forced a change towards wave theories of light and thus distanced it from a particle-bound interpretation. Today, we recognize that light and matter can be defined as waves and particles together; with this conception we display the probabilistic nature of quantum phenomena. A wave is in modern physics understood as 'a disturbance or oscillation of a physical quantity that travels through matter or space, accompanied by a transfer of energy'. If a wave is split into two waves and later reunited, then a phase shift and the creation of an interference pattern takes place. An 'interferometer' to measure such interferences was already developed in 1887, so that the 'double slit' experiment could play a key role in modern physics. A wall with two vertical slits and another wall or screen behind the first (nothing definite about sizes, measures or materials) suffices for the experiment that changed physics from Young to Bohr and Bohm. That experiment was on light passing through the slits and forming patterns on the back screen. The experiment provoked a new branch of physics and also a new language in which being and universes could be articulated.

The pictures in a 2010 Hawking publication entitled *The Grand Design*[21] confirm what we called "the particle story" and characterized as the "master—master discourse" in Occidental culture. The Geneva CERN opened its renewed facilities in April 2015 and confirmed in its turn our current interest in those theoretical foundations. At the same time, it is fascinating that the 'concept of theory in physics' always involves considerations pertaining to 'the particle'. As if there exists at this point no difference between philosophy and physics. The double slit experiment underscores this.

But there is another issue: does a theory necessarily distance itself from observations, and if so, what does that say about the position of an observer? It appears that a theory build solely upon observable facts is not correct. The "double slit" experiment, with its first observations in 1803, embraced the perhaps most intimate encounter with the particle. Feynman wrote that it contained all the mystery of quantum mechanics. It formed the basis for theories and techniques in today's CERN and elsewhere; this appeared even to be the case when unraveling the riddle of the famous Higgs particle.

[21] See: St. Hawking & L. Mlodinow: *The Grand Design*, New York 2010, p. 63 f. See also Jubogroff: *Wave-particle_duality.ogv* 2012. (Compare Thomas Young's two-slit diffraction from 1803, and the more recent history of the wave-particle duality since that year, at: http://en.wikipedia.org/wiki/Wave%E2%80%93particle_duality.

2.2 *Particles, Balls*

Sometimes it appears to be a soccer field. Descriptions of the double-slit experiment are always couched in a naïve-natural, everyday language.[22] The same applies to the situation of fields and particles, not to mention their surroundings. Players are positioned along the ground lines of the game, and their effects on the ball are caused by their bodily activity. Any description of what happens here is determined by implications of a naïve-natural language pattern: gravity, time, space, causality and the like. Does all of this also determine the slit experiment? In that case, the saying that the balls are *like* the particles or the kicks of players *like* sources of energy indicates in essence the distance between the meaning-fields of the two languages: the naïve-natural distinguished from the language of physics, that of quantum mechanics in particular.

Participants in the famous Solvay Congress in Brussels 1927, among which were Einstein, Bohr, Heisenberg, Planck and others, had expressed their ideal that ordinary language and the language of quantum physics would remain close together. Only then could the importance of the new insights in physics, in particular the unfolding of quantum mechanics, be understood and accepted at all levels of society.

Remembering this opinion gives birth to at least two questions. First: here an idea is forwarded that touches the relations between two levels of language: the ordinary and the specifically professional level. Was the opinion expressed during the Solvay conference—that these should stay as close together as possible—a unique phenomenon? Second: if a foundational experiment, a key issue for the emerging quantum mechanics, can be described as a soccer game, is that then a true realization of the described ideal of linguistic clarity? To place the first question in correct perspective, we consider the second first. What does it mean to propose a view on the slit experiment as a soccer game? There are at least three components to consider during a closer look: the ball(s), the field and the players.

2.3 *Double-Slit*

A player would perhaps deny it but soccer balls are neutral and have no individual properties; they belong to the game simply to be kicked. The game is rather defined and controlled by international institutions, and the balls move according to such rules via the players and their energy. If those rules do not fit the game, there is no game. And the balls sustain the definition of the game exclusively during its play.

[22] See the wealth of data and descriptions in the *Wikipedia.org* texts and pictures. See Al-Khalili, Jim: *Quantum*, London 2003, p. 132: ", while the formalism of quantum mechanics is not in doubt, nobody has yet found a satisfactory explanation, or interpretation, of the theory that is agreeable to everyone" … and … "to translate what is essentially advanced mathematics into words that make sense."

Hawking has beautiful pictures, and offers one on a two-slit soccer event and one on a two-slit molecular event. The pictures indicate a classical field position that defines the experiment: there is the player, a wall with two vertical slits, and a net/screen on the far side behind the wall parallel to the wall. [23] That structure is not a subject of debate or critical consideration.

The authors of *The Grand Design* intensify their parallel between molecular particles and soccer balls by referring to a 1999 Austrian experiment in which soccer-ball-shaped molecules were fired to and through such barriers. The molecules were named 'buckyballs' after the British architect Buckminster Fuller, and were each made of 60 carbon atoms. If a soccer player were to stand before the wall, Hawking suggests, he would have to kick the balls consistently at a pre-determined speed. Most of his shots would hit the wall and bounce back; some would go through one of the two slits and then into the net. In addition, it should be considered that the wider the slits are in relation to the size of the balls, the more the two streams of balls in the net will fan out. If one of the two slits is closed, the stream pattern through the other slit does not change at all.

It follows, that what we observe when both slits are open is the totality of what passes trough each of the two slits. That's life! What is so special in this experiment? Nothing that belongs to our daily experiences of soccer balls or their imitations is special here. But firing molecules differs from firing soccer balls. Yet, a firing of molecules does *not* take place outside of our life (in that attitude soccer balls do not differ from molecules)—it only concerns *a different level* of life, as philosophical explorations of the 'attitude'-concept in the sense of Husserl, made clear (see Chap. 2). "Einstellungsänderung", change in attitude, delivers the possibility of changes in meaning. They depend upon the outcome of physical experiments; double-slit experiments demonstrate the relevance of that insight.

As a consequence, one should remind Hawking and his companion observers of the double-slit experiment, that the latter shows the multi-level character of our universe. Exactly *that quality* becomes clear in the double-slit experiment, which produced a new theory of physics. Soccer balls and buckyballs appear now, thanks to the experiment, as *different signs* of different *levels of the universe(s)* we live in. This basic semiotic fact created quantum mechanics and stimulated the emergence of its new field of meaning. Equality and inequality of balls has a meaning to be discovered only on the basis of awareness of the multileveled character of life in the universe. To insist that soccer balls and molecules are equal or unequal is a too bold venture if one disregards the foregoing observation.

Hawking describes our intuition pertaining to the existence of various levels of out understanding of reality: "As we improved our technology and expanded the range of phenomena that we could observe, we began to find nature behaving in ways that were less and less in line with our everyday experience and hence with our intuition, as evidenced by the experiment with buckyballs. That experiment is typical of the type of phenomena that cannot be encompassed by classical science but are described by what is called quantum physics, (…) a framework for understanding

[23] St. Hawking & L. Mlodinow: *The Grand Design,* Op. Cit., p. 63 ff.

how nature operates on atomic and subatomic scales".[24] Meanings ascribed to nature as an active subject ('how nature operates') and as an object ('nature is found to operate') obfuscate the semantic dimensions at issue. These are important in understanding the role of particles—a role, which is in the double-slit experiment not profiled or considered as a constitutive factor. The experiment is silent on any semiotic specificity of our concern pertaining to the particles.

This becomes clear when we look at the fact, that *the specificity of the particle was never a separate item in the experiment.* The 'wave-particle duality in function' became a generally accepted concept not as a consequence of observing the particle as such but of its path. Remember where the path of the soccer balls and the quantum particles were no longer parallel. They did not follow a single definite path but took every possible path, often altogether simultaneously. The discovery that *matter particles behave like a wave* was a surprise. A puzzle concerning identity forced itself upon us: spots were detected on the screen when only one of the two slits was open but not when both slits were open. Will opening an additional second slit cause fewer particles to come to certain points? The actual patterns were never the sum of the patterns caused by opening one slit. They were of interference, of interfering waves; 'wave-particle duality' became for that reason easily accepted as expression in a new theory of physics.

In other words: the meaning of the concept of a particle as well as (on another scale) the change in physics from Newtonian to quantum theories, remains in the hands of the master—master discourse. That becomes visible where the experiments do not study the particle but solely its functions, path and orientation. Consequences of a deeper insight in the master—master discourse's dynamics are the subject of the next chapter on *partitions*. Hawking inspires us in that regard, because for him a particle in quantum physics can adequately be indicated with the word 'object' that stems from our naïve-natural language, yet it "... dictates a completely different schema, one in which an object's position, path, and even its past and future are not precisely determined."[25] The latter are solely at issue when the particle is seen as the "object" in experiments, measurements and theoretical imaginings in which waves, time units and related particle dynamics are observed.

2.4 *Wave-Particle Duality*

A wave-particle duality shows that even quantum physics is what the master—master discourse aims at: a manipulation of meaning. Particles are macro- and microscopic fragments or quantities of matter, whereas quantum physics has not solved the question whether particles form an ideal, an abstraction or a distinct entity. The above-mentioned duality is in that regard not providing a solution. Very much contrary to physical theories about our intuitive everyday life, quantum mechanics

[24] Cf. St.Hawking & L. Mlodinow: *The Grand Design,* Op. Cit., p. 66.

[25] Hawking & Mlodinow: *The Grand Design,* Op. Cit., p. 67.

suggests a model of reality inspired by an observation in the first double-slit experiment performed in 1927 by Clinton Davisson & Lester Germer, who studied a beam of electrons interacting with nickel crystals. They concluded that particles on the scale of their experiment, the electrons, behave like water waves. That *light* behaves like waves was no surprise, but that *particles* could do so was highly surprising. Thomas Young showed already in 1803 that a beam of light on the two slits makes two waves emerge and meet on a screen at the back of the slits.

Our explicit focus on particles leads us to conclude that the quantum expression "wave-particle duality" may aim at the very limit of the master—master discourse's power of expressivity. Its wordings could be read in the proximity of Heisenberg's "uncertainty principle" formulated 1926: there are limits to the simultaneous measurement of data such as the position and speed of a particle. The question "what is a particle" is not answered univocally in that zone of expressivity. A quantum entity/particle exhibits the property of a wave as well as of a particle; there is no '*or*' in the expression: 'particle or wave', because a particle and a wave form a duality *beyond our everyday language's use of the words.* This reveals the inherent meaning of the Heisenberg 'uncertainty'—his uncertainty is uncertain in the context of expressing quantum mechanics in naïve-natural language (a difficult translation on its own), though perhaps not in other forms of linguistic expressivity. It is even doubtful whether one can conclude here about a difference between "the *world* of quantum mechanics" and "the *world* of our everyday life", because the two meanings of the word "world", might reach beyond their limit of expressivity in this context.

2.5 The Third

It will be clear that we are not outlining a *history* of quantum mechanics in the twentieth century, nor searching for decisive issues that would shape such a history of physics and worlds or universe(s). The 'double-slit experiment' showed the *semiotic* relevance of the particle concept, but without explaining that relevance or considering it as a constituting factor in quantum mechanics, and that is what inspires to write and read these lines. It became once more clear, in what a powerful fashion the master—master discourse formats scientific thoughts at the limit of expressivity. That issue is at stake in the double-slit experiment, as it facilitates a *new* type of physics and a new language.

Philosophical remarks about the role and function of the *signifier* have been mentioned more than once. We come back to this theme because the slit experiments (also in its later versions, for instance in the interpretations of Richard Feynman developed since the 1940s) have treated the particle as a signifier only implicitly. What does this mean, and what relevance does it have for understanding meaning?

Focus on *the particle as a sign* approximates the famous question *whether there is something rather than nothing*, which is the basis for reference. The 'particle as sign' in quantum mechanics tells us beyond everyday naïve-natural existence in what ways that sign-function transcends the linguistic and/or expressive barriers of a naïve-natural language. An observer observes how it 'is there' only within the limits of his existence in that 'there'—not beyond those limits. Also not when the limits are just limits of levels of language! Here is the point where physicists perhaps decide differently, although the plurality of language remains at issue in their theories.

In other words, physicists focus on the observer, or on the process of observation. They thus observe in what way and under what circumstances each signifier *carries* a sign, and conclude that meaning and signifying are equal because of their need to carry a sign. The double-slit situation forms no exception here. Particles do not exist in the experiences of daily life and its naïve-natural language. Those who live a daily life know about the existence of particles via education and are trained to understand the world accordingly, but have never experienced the particle. On the other hand, there exists no particle (a fortiori not a quantum particle) without the culturally embedded observations and activity of an observer. Those are mostly described and institutionalized as a 'theory'. An observer is hence playing a role in constituting a meaning called 'the particle concept' and called a 'theory' without which observation and meaning seem impossible. Observer and theory fulfill their role in a close togetherness, and as a consequence can be considered to be *a third.*

A 'particle' concept is always linked to a subject: a speaker or writer, but within the boundaries of everyday language never to an observer. A 'particle' concept on the level of physics (in particular quantum physics) cannot find its expression without an observer and/or observation. So we must conclude that there '*is*' no particle without an observer/observation. We already mentioned that we live in a highly differentiated *sign pool*. That pool exists because of a *third,* enabling us to experience and profit from the multiple signs around us: a multiplicity causing a high degree of differentiation often appreciated as a wealth of signs and choices. We discussed in the last section of the preceding chapter whether that leads to the recognition of a dialogic character of human life. The answer was not clear: on the one hand—particularly when mainly living in the everyday naive-natural consciousness—we do live dialogically but on the other, as quantum mechanics shows, there are levels on which we do not!

We know about the existence of particles thanks to leaving the naturalness of our lives behind and accepting that physics and its observer/observations unveil a 'reality' of particles together with its dependence upon a *third.*

That situation is (as the double slit experiments over the centuries show) an example of what Peirce called 'the interpretant'. However, to understand the interpretant only as a third person with whom one must dialogue is incorrect. Einstein formulated this in a 1926 conversation with Werner Heisenberg. He suggested: "… it is completely erroneous to ground a theory exclusively on facts from observation. In reality, it is inverted. A theory decides what one can observe. You see: an observation is in general a very complex process". He then describes the long way from occurrence to conceptual fixation, which structures our consciousness: "if we want to understand how nature works, we have to gather practical knowledge about the laws of nature if we want to claim that we observed something. Only the theory, only knowledge of laws of nature allows us to conclude from sense impressions to fundamental occurrences."[26]

The observer/observation is apparently a complex issue, a part of consciousness, human intelligence, techniques and culture in general, a complex *third,* without which an occurrence (such as a particle) cannot become articulated. Do not forget, Einstein seems to suggest, that each instrument which forwards an idea or fact in the world, embraces a specific history. Peirce named this an *interpretant*—around 1905 he emphasized that an interpretant is a sign legitimately and purposely determined by a sign. There are therefore *three* kinds of signs to distinguish. The overarching point is, that "a sign is in a conjoint relation to the thing denoted and to the mind."[27] This means: a sign is never alone; there is—apart from the object—always the interpretant playing a role, so that among a sign, its object and the mind there exists always a triadic relation. This insight is the basis for overcoming traditional philosophical dualisms of all kinds. The relation between sign and interpretant is, however, not appropriately understood in terms of question and answer, initiative and response, for short: in terms of dialogue. There is a lively network of interpretants in which meaning emerges. Participation in that network is of utmost importance. But one must keep in mind, that those meanings are not equally valid at all possible language-levels. This is clearly highlighted by the difference between the level of articulation at the naïve-natural language level and at a quantum mechanics level.

Einstein would have greatly appreciated Peirce's consideration of the long road from fact to fixation in which a third is always engaged: "A sign stands *for* something *to* the idea, which it produces, or modifies. Or, it is a vehicle conveying into the mind something from without. That for which it stands is called its *object*; that which it conveys: its *meaning*; and the idea to which it gives rise: its *interpretant.* The object of representation can be nothing but a representation of which the first representation is the interpretant. But an endless series of representations, each representing the one behind it, may be conceived."[28] He would have classified all issues in a (physics) theory with the Peircean word: an "*interpretant*" and perhaps: a "*third*". Without this third: no theory, and without theory-observer connection: no particle, we conclude. The triadic character, in which sign-relations are embedded requires the same language-level as particles. Meaning in general appears to be a truly multi-level phenomenon, and relativizes tensions between an exclusively dialogical or triadic character of relations.[29]

---

[26] Werner Heisenberg: *Der Teil und das Ganze. Gespräche im Umkreis der Atomphysik* [The Part and the Whole. Conversations on Atomic Physics]. München 1969, p. 92 f.

[27] Ch. S. Peirce: "On the Algebra of Logic: A Contribution to the Philosophy of Notation", 1885. In: *The Essential Peirce. Selected Philosophical Writings,* Vol. I, Indiana UP, p. 225 ff.

[28] Ch. S. Peirce: *Collected Papers (CP)* Vol. 1, 333.9.

[29] This comes very near to what David Bohm writes in the introduction of an essay on the relations between mind and matter, signaling the possibility of "a new way of thinking, consistent with modern physics, which does not divide mind from matter, the observer from the observed, the subject from the object." See D. Bohm: "A New Theory of the Relationship of Mind and Matter" in: *Philosophical Psychology,* 1990, Vol. 3, No. 2, p. 271 f.

A theory is a frame for decisions about observations regarding a specific subject, a special method or technique and a specific time slot, Einstein suggested. This is for him a major argument for qualifying a theory as a "Vorgang": a process, history or technical complexity that shapes the consciousness of a scientist as well as an average citizen. Notice that the position of an observer is located within the boundaries of expressivity which are (more often than we are aware of) unfolding at different levels. Ask a physician to reflect upon the language he explores to describe a complex clinical picture; ask a lawyer to give her thoughts about a difficult legal case; ask a civil engineer about the constructions of a hazardous project—all will tell tales in different words and will have difficulties in stretching their expressivity into the fields of ordinary language. It means that we are where we were in the fields of our considerations: the "*is*" of the particle must be understood at various levels and in the frame of more than one 'regional ontology' (Husserl). In other words: *the "is" depends on the speech and expressivity potential of the ontological discourse concerned.* Quantum mechanics shows the dynamics and the necessities, but also the difficulties of this particular understanding.

2.6 Bohm

David Bohm (1917—1992) makes an important contribution from the viewpoint of a physicist to the discussion about the 'Third'. His theory also shows how many related issues are at stake—they reach into cosmological dimensions. We concentrate on reading what is central in this study on meaning; we cannot open here a full debate on his new approaches to quantum mechanics. It is clear: the case of the particle is a case of interpretation as understood within quantum mechanics. The interpretation at hand is unmistakably a matter of observation from the side of a scientist and a matter of the behavior of the particles concerned in the double slit experiments and related experiments, instruments and techniques. The focus is essentially on simultaneous positions and moments of the particles. Heisenberg's conception of an *uncertainty relation* rules out *the measuring* of position and momentum at the same time. Two insights compete here: particles either *do not have* simultaneous position and momentum to be measured, or particles *have* those, *but it is impossible to measure them simultaneously, so that they remain unknown.* Not even a CERN experiment could help decide about the correctness of one of them.

The Bohm interpretation adopts the position that particles have indeed position and momentum. This is only possible in terms of theoretical physics and philosophy if one agrees with two presuppositions: the first is, that a 'particle' '*is/exists*' in one way or another, and the second that observers are *excluded* in Bohm's quantum mechanics.[30] Tensions between the two as well as between them and related quantum theories are challenging.

Heisenberg already suggested that the theoretical correctness of concepts and images in the realm of the atomic and sub-atomic reality is in what he called "the secret of the emission of light". And *in* that secret another secret is enfolded: the fact that particles and waves are *all* matter, they are at the same time *all* light beams, and *all* are a space-time structure. Finally, for *all of that* is an observer or observation crucial. De Broglie took a first step towards a deeper realism and Bohm has come back to this hypothesis that the wave function may actually represent an actual wave guiding particles along paths. They enhance the question of meaning.[31] We suggested that 'speech' is not simply a matter of rhetoric and rules of rhetoric but rather of a real (physical, cultural and spiritual) presence. Words in speech are thus like particles in waves: guided by a force field, which is cosmic and social at the same time.

The two types of articulation, 'word-speech linguistic' and 'particle-wave cosmic' articulation, are at unison when *not* observed or observed from *outside* any realm of naïve-natural conditions of actual articulation.[32] Bohm did what linguistics has not considered in parallel: he freed the ontological question "whether a particle *is*" from naïve realism in its traditional ontological context. This is accompanied by an observation, which would deserve a positive echo by Heisenberg, on the role of an observer (human or mechanical) and the uncertainty concept. Bohm writes: "… that the properties of matter do not, in general, exist separately in a given object in a precisely defined form. They are, instead, incompletely defined potentialities realized in more definite form only in interaction with other systems, such as a measuring apparatus. The wave function describes all these potentialities, and assigns a certain probability to each. This probability does not refer to the chance that a given property, such as a certain value of the momentum, actually exists at this time in the system, but rather to the chance that in interaction with a suitable measuring apparatus such a value will be developed …"[33]

It is clear that this leads definitively away from the classical realisms embraced by philosophy in many past centuries. When it comes to Bohm's matrix formulation of quantum theory, we are confronted with a still deeper philosophical step. He stated that "… an observable may be in part a potentiality [which] suggests a really striking difference between the nature of matter, as implied by quantum theory and that implied by classical theory. For each observable corresponds to some physical

---

[30] These have been, and still are, subject to intense discussion in physics and philosophy. The debate on the so-called "hidden variables" theories, focusing on the (perhaps) definite positions of particles, forms an excellent example.

[31] See the discussion of "the word as particle" and "speech" as waves in articulation in the above Chaps. 2 and 3.

[32] Indicated in Chap. 1 as B, C & D, from whence it appears for instance normal to confront meaning v meaninglessness.

[33] David Bohm: *Quantum Theory*, New York 1989 (Prentice-Hall New Jersey 1951), p. 175, see also pp. 100, 132, 609.

property in terms of which the system can manifest itself. (…) When one of the observables is measured, the system of categories associated with another observable not commuting wit the measured observable is literally dissolved, since as we have seen, the measurement of any one observable causes the system to spread out over a range of values of a non-commuting observable. Such a behavior is in striking contrast to that described in classical theory."[34] The system of categorization, one concludes, never changes in classical theory, in contrast to quantum theory, where the categorization of the system depends on either definite momentum or definite position, never in both together. Particle-like *position* categories and wave-like *momentum* categories are only possible among infinite numbers of categorization.

2.7 Quantum Potential

A related issue with philosophical relevance is to understand in what way Bohm's quantum mechanics is connected with a *quantum potential.* As always, the question leads back to a view on the double-slit experiment(s). In the expression 'wave-particle duality', an expression that emerged in the slit-experiments, is the idea of 'duality' more than challenging: is there *only* a duality to be considered? Does this idea support a level of articulation that fits Newton's physics, but not a quantum mechanical view? In the wave function there is information to be unveiled. Bohm suggested that the wave function suggests the existence of a form of energy he called "the quantum potential". That potential is effective in so far as *it propagates the particles through space, and guides them on paths.*

There is more than one issue relevant for philosophical insight. We mention only a few. (1) If a potential propagates the particles throughout space, they will never spread through the slits of the double-slit experiment without that potential. (2) The potential will permeate both slits, and its power will be effective on both sides of the slits. (3) That is the (new) context for particles in the experiment; questions about the 'being'/'is' of particles or their path through one or more slits are differently positioned now. (4) The Copenhagen discussion about the role of the observer/observation (and its certainty or uncertainty) seems superposed by the quantum potential. (5) Patterns of particles on the screen are a result of how the quantum potential in its entirety (and not the particles alone) behaves, once particles and potential have passed the slits. (6) It is impressive, that these patterns come into existence only if many atoms go through. The patterns disappear when one observes only the atoms, closes a slit or causes another change in the totality of the experimental situation. (7) As a consequence, any disturbance of the quantum potential taking place anywhere modifies the potential in the whole of space.

It is of interest from a philosophical viewpoint that these considerations underline the importance of Husserl's suggested "local ontology" (see the foregoing

[34] Bohm: Op. Cit., p. 385 f.

Chap. 2) and they support a form of holism, which is already mirrored in the conclusion that any disturbance of the quantum potential modifies the potential in the whole of space. Remember, that it is unclear from the beginning to say or think what the result can be from breaking down a naiveté in view of vested opinions and theories, and what elements will become important, or deliver a fruitful new insight. Naiveté is "only remembered" reality, not a perception of how it is, but a perception of a past possibility of specific forms of being. Naiveté is thus an expression not for how it is but for how it was. Peirce's Firstness is the description of that process from was to is, or better: he describes the "was" (being the character of the First) in terms of an "is". Exactly this often-confused motive blurs the lines of division between the natural and the cultural. Notice, that naiveté is a cultural datum represented in that cultural context as natural! Its focus is on nature as a cultural construct, more precisely: it is a name for a necessary component of any cultural determination or linguistic expressiveness maintained in a culture.

A difficulty in turning from a *regional* ontology towards another, for instance an *interregional* ontology (is there a still higher level of ontology?) lies in the change itself. Change is engraved in social habits, in education and inherited forms of applying principles, and not in novel forms of thinking created by an individual. Peirce would speak of 'habit' and not be shy to extend its meaning to the creation and application of thought patterns.

One should therefore, in the context of our analysis, focus on the word 'particle' in the grip of the 'word' as articulated in ordinary language, and its ontological basis. The parallel with a quantum potential is most striking. Its connotations focus on an analytical thought pattern, on divisible substance, on components of a larger totality, on matter build with atoms. These aspects are at home in a *regional* ontology and sustain analytical developments with an occidental metaphysical background.

But Bohm's view can be expanded: *speech* (an effect of articulation) *precedes words, and makes them pass the slits of any interaction*. But what do words contribute to meaning when they are not understood as basic units of language? Can they mean anything if they aren't manifestations of a speaking subject? If a subject cannot maintain its position thanks to the shadowing hand of the object, it can only submit to a larger entity. An articulation beyond the subject-object duality would then occur. The subject finds herself in a force field that propagates her voice. A spoken silence becomes the main event—a silence beyond any need of hearer, a silence that 'is', a silence often sounding cosmic.

The word 'word' excels in being a witness of an ontology, a historically enduring type of metaphysical thought in which ensembles are broken down along the lines of their composite particles. This type of thinking is no longer tenable in the context of a quantum potential, and certainly not in a parallel ontological context named 'speech'. The cohesion of 'word' and 'particle', in modern semiotics as well, is a clear sign of the power of those thought patterns, which are deemed 'natural' in everyday language.

These patterns are different in quantum mechanics. Consider the particle in that ontology. Confront it with the double slit experiments. They demonstrate that particles do not occur on their own but always in a force field. When subatomic particles are studied in a Newtonian and in a Quantum field of knowledge, one can conclude in what sense their behavior differs from our expectations unfolded in daily life. But we maintain our *regional* ontological meaning concept to articulate that, and do not ask what we experience with them in our daily life, nor feel the need to open up to an *inter*regional or even cosmic ontology/meaning (if that could exist). Bohm's thoughts contrast a regional ontology by means of constituting a quantum theory without observers, a theory not formulated in terms of what is perceived but in terms of occurrences. With that formulation, subject and object are in that context not the only form of acquiring and understanding knowledge. Ontological issues also no longer depend exclusively on them. The classical subject-object distinction no longer seems appropriate.

2.8 *Multileveled Articulations*

It does not, because we live our lives in multileveled spheres of articulation. As was mentioned before, the particle story involved a new branch of physics (quantum mechanics) and provided a new language for the essentials of ontological and cosmological nature. The latter embrace our concerns about meaning. "In daily life, we do not mix up inches with seconds or miles with days", the physicist Freeman Dyson writes in an essay about a recent Einstein biography.[35] He stresses that the story of the particle leads to the story of quantum physics and the latter to the story of languages that differ fundamentally between everyday life and quantum physics. This includes for Dyson the point that "as the result of Paul Dirac's elegant equation describing the quantum behavior of the electron, the mixing of space with time in the electron's movements would be clearly visible" if we lived in that layer of articulation; but "the mixing is hidden from us". This seems a firm confirmation of Husserl's thesis (as explained in Chap. 2) that our "Einstellung" [attitude] is decisive for what we can experience and express. Meaning and understanding depend upon the attitude we have appropriated.

Many will agree that a dualistic philosophy came to the fore with quantum thinking. The dualism is the unmistakable consequence of the particle story and the reinforcement of the master—master discourse. Dyson stated: "The dualistic philosophy seems to me to represent accurately our present state of knowledge. It says that the classical world and the quantum world are both real, but the way they fit together is not yet completely understood."[36] There are thus three ways to explain the universe(s) in a meaningful manner: Einstein's way, the quantum way and the combination of the two, whereby their connections remain unexplained.

[35] Freeman Dyson: "Einstein as a Jew and a Philosopher", *New York Review of Books*, Vol. LXII, 8, 2015, p. 14 ff.

[36] Dyson, Op. Cit., p. 17. The essay is on: Steven Gimbel: *Einstein: His Space and Times.* Yale UP 2015.

Philosophically speaking, Dyson reinforced the master—master discourse with his preference for a dualistic philosophy, which "gives a natural frame for the new sciences of particle physics and relativistic cosmology that emerged in the twentieth century". This dualism does in a certain sense underestimate the importance to be given to quantum theory. Dyson mentions those appearances and uses of quantum physics, which propagate a "quantum only" view. Dualism does not fit with the "quantum only" approach, since that approach, in the form of a more recent 'decoherence theory', states: that as a "consequence of quantum theory that affects virtually all physical systems", and viewing the "unavoidable interaction of these systems with their natural environment" it can be explained "why macroscopic systems *seem* to possess their familiar classical properties", and "why certain microscopic objects ("particles") *seem* to be localized in space" and "microscopic systems are usually found in their energy eigenstates (and therefore *seem* to jump between them)". All this "explains why there appeared to be contradictory levels of description in physics (classical and quantum)". As a consequence of this decoherence view, it is said that "There are no particles; there are no quantum jumps; there is but one basic framework for all physical theories: quantum theory."[37]

It is clear that a consequent decoherence viewpoint does *not* share enough elements with classical physics and quantum physics to be positioned in- or beyond a dualism as formulated by Dyson. A decoherence theory still adheres to formulations, which reign in the master—master discourse: the particle (even when declared 'to not exist'), and the possibilities of articulation (which declare what *seems* and *seems not* to be the case). A triad expanding Dyson's duality (classical physics—quantum physics—decoherence physics) encounters the same difficulty. Also a division into three languages is a semiotic issue and a sign that reality requires a multileveled articulation. That feature can only be articulated at the borderlines or even beyond the master—master discourse; it shows the profile of the town only once one has left it—as Nietzsche described. As suggested, it is a sign of an *attitude (Einstellung)* as a condition for articulations of ontological nature.

[37]The discontinuous "wave function collapse" postulated in the Copenhagen interpretation to enable the theory to be related to the results of laboratory measurements now can be understood as an aspect of the normal dynamics of quantum mechanics via the de-coherence process. Consequently, de-coherence is an important part of the modern alternative to the Copenhagen interpretation, based on consistent histories. De-coherence shows how a macroscopic system interacting with a lot of microscopic systems (e.g. collisions with air molecules or photons) moves from being in a pure quantum state—which in general will be a coherent superposition to being in an incoherent mixture of these states. The weighting of each outcome in the mixture in case of measurement is exactly that which gives the probabilities of the different results of such a measurement. See www.wikipedia.org/wiki/Quantum_decoherence dd. 05.05.2015.

2.9 *Interaction and Participation*

This is why Bohm distinguishes 'interaction' from 'participation'—the two indicate a difference in attitude. In *interaction*, the role of a subject seems understandable. Subjects interact, aware that there are related objects without which they cannot function. Particles do not move in accordance with any such command-like effect, the wave functions govern the motion and thus the positions of particles—a behavior that is the central theme of Bohm's quantum mechanics.[38] It is clear that *participation* is a requirement in view of particles, which has not to do with interaction, since the latter is a dualistic performance in contrast to the first. The actual positions of the particles are specified according to a 'guiding equation', which expresses the velocities of the particles in terms of the wave function. Goldstein concluded: "… the particles are described by their positions, and Bohmian mechanics prescribes how these change with time. In this sense are the particles primary, or primitive, while the wave functions are secondary, or derivative. (…) It is the positions of the particles in Bohmian mechanics that are its 'hidden variables'". Bell is quoted in this context: "… it is not in the wave function that one finds an image of the visible world … Of course the variables are not confined to the visible 'macroscopic' scale … to admit things not visible to the gross creatures that we are is, in my opinion, to show a decent humility, and not just a lamentable addiction to metaphysics."[39]

Bohm had already in his 1980 publication *Wholeness and the Implicate Order* introduced (as linked with the distinction between 'interaction' and 'participation') the notion of *the unfolded.* To some degree, everything enfolds or implicates everything, notwithstanding that there is a great deal of relative independence of what seems to exist and thus is articulated. It is crucial that the enfoldment relationship is neither passive nor superficially active but it is essential to the being of things. All things are internally related to the whole, and in that sense to everything else. This implicate order is dynamic in the sense that there is a constant process of change and development.

Bohm called this form in its totality the "holomovement".[40] Everything unfolds in it, emerges from it and falls back into it. Meaning is nothing but a part in this entire process. It is a substantial part in the underlying participation process, and contrasts with the eventualities of interaction. A participation zone unfolds before exact articulations come to the fore. Meanings are often a substantial component of a 'matrix participation' before they can ever become an element of analysis—this causes the multiplicity of the meaning concept. Meaning never remains statically on a specific level; it is always on the move and functioning as if it is encapsulated in the complexity of wave functions.

---

[38] See Sheldon Goldstein: "Bohmian Mechanics" in *Stanford Encyclopedia of Philosophy*, 103 (2nd rev. art. edition) at http://plato.stanford.edu/entries.

[39] J. S. Bell: "On the Problem of Hidden Variables in Quantum Theory" in *Review of Modern Physics*, Vol. 38, p. 447 ff, 1966 (reprinted 1983 and 1987). See also J. S. Bell: *Speakable and Unspeakable in Quantum Mechanics*, Cambridge UP 1987.

[40] David Bohm: *Wholeness and the Implicate Order*, London 1980, p. 150 ff.

A consequence is, that the world (alias reality) cannot be analyzed through partitioning into self-sufficient, independent and separate sections. Not words, not particles, nothing can adopt such a quality—even not the atoms that have formed since the Ancient Greek world a source of inspiration for Occidental thinking. It should be a source of inspiration for a study on meaning, that the theory called 'quantum mechanics' does not form an exception here.[41] No theory or system can be regarded as separate. All participate in all; participation does not delete but rather includes interaction. The latter will always unfold in the former—there is no inverse direction to be experienced here.

3 Cezanne's Brushstrokes

In the poetic as well as the quantum discourse the reader is brought into a position, which is on the one hand trusted and on the other alienating. If an enigmatic title like "Engführung" is translated as: "a guidance with intensified togetherness through narrow passes", *who* guides us through life's multiple slits? A contrast between 'particle flurry' and 'meaning' suggested an answer: it is the master—master discourse, also called the 'particle-story', and not the poet or the reader as an acting subject. If indeed *everything* is at issue in the master—master discourse (as the preceding sections suggested), then any linguistic articulation is *a fortiori* submitted to that discourse. The foundational concept with the name: 'particle' does not belong to one of our often-groundless chats, nor is it experienced in our daily discourses and prone to interpretation of daily life in the sign pool: it is a power-field that guides and masters our understanding of reality. It is truly a hurricane announced by first flurries, as Celan suggested poetically. Did the master—master–discourse take complete possession of our *archai*? We have already approached a poet and a physicist, and now we introduce a painter to illustrate the issues at hand.

3.1 The Particle in Painting

Life, sciences and the arts are filled with narration, speculation and other verbal efforts. Persuasion has always been a branch of the arts in occidental culture; the Ancient Greeks thus evoked their rhetoric. It is clear that language inspires and shapes the need for all sorts of communication. It characterizes an energy unfolded by each artist. With each artist's act emerges a self-understanding; the latter unveils the fact that all forms and styles of art fulfill a need for interpretation on the basis of participation. They join different facts by means of suggested, experimented, and ventured articulations that focus on relations. A work of art establishes relations between different worlds, always represented in different discourses. And, what is

[41] David Bohm: *Unfolding Meaning. A Weekend of Dialogue.* London/New York 1985.

more: alliances of words can lead to clusters, which we perceive as *names of a particular style*: consider positivism, pragmatism or functionalism in sciences and philosophy; expressionism, cubism or realism in painting. At issue is the fact, that they indicate more than a certain style—they also represent specific ideals and methods of approaching reality. Painters do have their own definitions of their work and their subsequent social roles.

A search for 'basic units' that compose works of arts can therefore be found in modern painting, forming parallels to poetry or physics. One is immediately tempted to remember two mainstreams of pictorial modernity: pointillism/divisionism, and cubism. The first are styles of neo-impressionist painters like Seurat and others who tried to create individual dots or patches through the separation of colors. A related and more widely known manner is the style called pointillism, where colors are not mixed but visual impressions were created by putting dots together. Seurat and Signac, among others, have shown that the perceiving eye is able to do what a painter's hand normally performs on its own initiative.

The influence of cubist contributions to twentieth century Western culture and its emphasis on conceptualization underlines the connections between cubism, literature and daily discourse in important epistemological regards. They all serve the master—master discourse or what we called the 'particle story'. The word takes refuge in the visual, dissolves its ties with grammar and syntax in order to ultimately find a freer expression and independent meaning formation via colors without loosening its ties with the particle-idea.

In this line of development, words change into a sign or a meaning via images, which witness the power of cubist (re)-presentation, and from there they refer to literature again. When a poem or a prose line fails, a picture accesses image, subjectivity, time or the visual. Integrating word and image is a cubist ideal, as Braque, Schwitters, Marinetti or Apollinaire showed, or a new typography: an *écriture automatique* (Breton, G. Stein, Williams James' psychology), or Ezra Pound's ideogram writings. Beyond such new conceptions of writing are daring architectural forms and cubist constructions of architects who had a "cubist town" in mind, as Ames, Loos, Rietveld or Van Doesburg showed.

Cubism provided a style and with it also an example of the ways in which a (re)-construction of meaning can initiate the exploration of new dimensions in modern life—always without cutting ties with the master—master discourse. The path of this example leads via, and often solely towards, abstraction. Only a few years more than a century ago, Picasso, living in a small village in the Pyrenean alpine mountains, showed some of his intimates a painting that would become world famous and classified as the first constructed along cubist principles. The art dealer and philosopher Daniel Henry Kahnweiler tells us that a complete silence fell during this confrontation until Matisse started to laugh out loud.[42] The title Picasso proposed for this canvas, still within traditional frames of reference, was "Le Bordel d'Avignon" but moral motivations, exhibition strategy and commerce changed it into "Les

[42] Kahnweiler Daniel H.: *Der Weg zum Kubismus* [The Road Towards Cubism] Stuttgart. 1920; Id..: *Juan Gris; his life and work*, Paris, London 1947.

Demoiselles d'Avignon". Prehistoric Iberian statues and African masks inspired the contrasting forms, colors and images of the five female figures. The images of Cezanne, in particular his large canvasses with bathing women, were still in everyone's mind when they saw the painting. The influence of Cézanne was more intense than we often consider. We know today that the silence of the spectators had meaning relevance. A canvas *proposing itself as a sign* provokes silence—an occurrence specific for a painting and the forwarding of a pictorial style, but also an experience for other discourses.

But one should go back to what *can become* a sign. The tension between the fixed "is" and the process of "becoming" is a challenge. Only signs understood as a temporary power to create meaning function in the sign pool of daily life. Peirce emphasizes the human situation as *being in process*, and he introduces the subject as a way of perceiving reality. The anthropologist Geertz emphasized the relation between sign systems and their various modes of implementation, and suggested: "If we are to have a semiotics of art (or for that matter, of any sign system not axiomatically self-contained), we are going to have to engage in a kind of natural history of signs and symbols, an ethnography of the vehicles of meaning (…) This is not a plea for inductivism, but for turning the analytic powers of semiotic theory (…) away from an investigation of signs in abstraction toward an investigation of them in their natural habitat…."[43]

Such a natural habitat is not only a specific culture but can also be a specific style of life and art. One can distinguish various *semiotic subjects* in different cultures, discourses and styles. The semiotic subject as a way of looking at the world can be known as segmenting the universe and thus coupling semantic units with expression units: this labor causes it to continuously destroy and restructure its social and historical concretions.[44] Could we appreciate the painter as a semiotic subject in that manner? This seems highly appropriate, in particular when we take a Cubist painting and its environment as a model. Two issues characterize cubist activities: (a) the specific labor of the meaning-making subject (segmenting and coupling semantic units) and (b) the activity of destroying and restructuring those units. Those two lead, however, to a third consideration: (c) what are those units in view of cubist approaches towards reality? Do we encounter the particle story once more? We most certainly do!

3.2 *The Painting Subject*

Cubism and the cubist style in painting relate to unsolved questions in French Fauvism. The latter was dated by expositions from 1905 to 1907 with Van Gogh and Gauguin as sources of inspiration and afterwards leveled to a deeper intellectual

[43] Cl. Geertz.: *Local Knowledge: Further Essays in Interpretative Anthropology*, In: *Art as a Cultural System,* Basic Books, New York 1983. p. 94 ff.

[44] Geertz: Op. Cit., p. 351.

approach by Cézanne and, more forcefully, Matisse who declared: 'J'ai à peindre un corps de femme; je vais condenser la signification d'un corps en cherchant ses lignes essentielles' ('When I have to paint a female body I condense the signification of the body through my search for the essential lines'). It is important to envisage here the profile of a complex activity hidden in that sentence: (a) the search for the *meaning* of a body, and (b) the search for access to *reality as a process*—in this case the female body as a living entity.

In the perspective of Cubism is the activity of the painting subject first of all a *conceptual* activity. In other words, cubist painters no longer perceive reality 'with their eyes' but rather with an activity of their 'mind'. They do not strive for representing and unveiling an appearance but rather for grasping an essence. Hence the close ties between life and painting, as is the case with Cézanne. This attitude dominates Cubism and that very attitude appears to be in hindsight a formidable revolution in the light of Renaissance traditions. Cubist painters take a lead in pictorial transformations, although Literary Cubism (Gertrude Stein), Film and Architecture, not to mention Music (Schönberg) also embraced the principle of playing with complex motives and styles to create a new entity. The idea of a "conceptual painting" dominates the wane of the twentieth century by means of concentrating on the problem of in what way to access reality: by means of representation, by reflection, or by both. An initiative to paint in a different mode might have important consequences of a philosophical nature!

Painting in another mode was not a matter of just painting, it was rather *a mode of activity*: first of all an activity of the painter in relation to his or her sub-/object, (the classical painter's job performance and attitude) *and* an activity (nobody knows when and where) as 'the viewer of it all'—both relations differ considerably from the simple dualistic pattern 'painter—painted object'. All this has important implications for the concept of meaning. Cubism emphasizes that changes and variations in the process of activity lead away from the traditional 'sender-receiver' communication. To paint in another mode equals the unfolding of new visions of the sign pool called 'life'. If painters create signs, then visual activity produces the dynamics of those signs and their formation, the latter being a *process* (the perception) as well as a *process-result* ("Cézanne's Ste Victoire mountains"). "Activity" dominated all occidental philosophies of art for centuries with a focus on representation.[45] But the word 'activity' entails today also emancipation, which is a gain of independence for all painting elements and their inner dynamics.

This connects with Lady Welby's and Wittgenstein's analyses of language and their striving for an emergence of meaning in language contexts. Analogous to Wittgenstein's 'proposition,' Welby's 'pictorial symbol' and 'representative action' are *high level signifying units*, which are constitutive for 'activity in the Cubist sense. These units contribute to observing complex levels of signifying (of expressive as well as communicative processes) without reducing them to the mere status of information transmission and message exchange in a dualistic sense. Each of

[45] Jan M. Broekman: *Malerei als Reflexion* In*: Jahrbuch für Aesthetik und Allgemeine Kunstwissenschaft*, 1966, Vol. 10. p. 35–65.

those authors calls our attention to the importance for the signifying processes of iconism, of otherness, which are altogether relations among signs beyond systemic restrictions. This also helps reveal the dialectical-dialogic nature of interpretive and translational processes in the relation between the categories of 'unity' and 'distinction' or between the 'centripetal forces' and the 'centrifugal forces' operating in language, as Bakhtin highlighted in 1975. Thus they focus on monologism *and* polylogism, monolingualism *and* plurilingualism as emerging from 'a logic of identity' as well as 'a logic of otherness'. Knowledge and truth thus appear as open to investigation and subject to modification in the continuous work of adapting to and generating new contexts and communicative practices—all are inherent in the Cubist 'activity'.

3.3 A Painter's Activity

Painting does not solely depict fragments of a so-called concrete reality. This becomes clear from perceiving the intense psychological engagement which occurs when Cézanne shapes his canvasses guided by a strong self-criticism: "Cézanne at his easel, painting, viewing the countryside: He was truly alone to the world, ardent, focused (…) and sometimes he would abruptly quit the site, dispirited, abandoning his canvas on a rock or in the grass," and Larguier witnesses in 1925: "I saw several (abandoned canvasses) under the trees of the Château Noir".[46]

A painter's activity unfolds at a distance from the heroic act of autonomously representing an object or a landscape by means of painting. We know and perhaps understand what a painter like Cézanne made move: also, a painter can only be creative in the context of a culture and of many forms of interactivity. A neurological counterpart is that we not only see with our eyes but with our brain as well, which means: as a complete person. Perception is a total engagement and therefore a matter of conceptualization, of mind, of rhythm. Cézanne knew what Bohm later called *proprioception* by experience long before such socio-philosophical and neurological insights shaped modern life.

Cézanne's behavior and his paintings are components of one and the same complexity, which we call 'interactivity'. That word underscores that a person's specific activity can only become realized within an encompassing structure. Cubist artists experienced this and understood their art as an activity in its own right far from any exalted individualism of a genius! This feeling of experiencing a high tide of activity is also the ground for often sophisticated theoretical explanations of their artwork, as is the case with Braque, Gris, Gleizes or Metzinger—all of them fascinated by multiple views and experiences of the visible world around them. They felt challenged to expose the truth of the human mind, which should be a truth without idealist connotations. This attitude encountered principles later understood in

[46] R. Shiff: *Lucky Cézanne (Cézanne Tychique)* in: J. J. Richel & K. Sachs: *Cézanne and Beyond* Philadelphia Museum of Art, Yale UP, New Haven/London, 2009 p. 55 f, 83.

structuralism, a cultural and philosophical mainstream of the mid-twentieth century. Activity was in structuralism the key to understanding reality as an active process and not just an idea to be applied. Roland Barthes asserted in 1964 that "the structural mind gets hold of something given, dissects it, reduces it to its component parts and puts these parts together again—this seems to be little, but this little is, observed from another viewpoint, decisive (…); creation or reflection are here not a reprint of the original world but a real creation of a world, which resembles the first, does not copy or reprint it, but makes that first understandable."[47]

Painting is an event that unfolds in many fragments of reality, with a different function, surface, line, circle, volume, color, sphere or mood. What is more: all have an equal chance to become a substantial component of a specific activity. *A painter creates in the milieu of a segmented interactivity*. Matisse expressed this when writing: "For me, the subject of a picture and its background have the same value, or to put it more clearly, there is no principal feature, only the pattern is important. The picture is formed by the combination of surfaces, differently colored, which results in the creation of an "expression". In the same way that in a musical harmony each note is a part of the whole, so I wished each color to have a contributory value. A picture is the co-ordination of controlled rhythms."[48]

Beware: it is not philosophers or scientists who have unveiled these important (in essence cosmological) changes in our consciousness of 'all there is", but painters—those who were at work in the frontline of recreation, reproduction, repetition and reconsideration of everything. Cubist painters were not philosophers, but they achieved insights of important philosophical and above all meaning relevance in view of life in the sign pool. Are there lessons to be learned and conclusions to be drawn? The 'relevance of meaning' seems an expression easy to formulate but difficult to explain and even more difficult to prove.[49]

This unfolds at various levels. (a) We mention first the call to be aware of the fact that reality is always involved in a process of achieving a *sign value* in life. (b) Then there is this relevance in understanding the basic structures of human *activity*. (c) That activity, whatever character it has, culminates in the dynamics of *meaning making*. (d) It occurs that an understanding of *painting as activity* in a Cubist style requires a strict *equivalence* of all segments or elements that compose the painting—a direct reference to the embracing master—master discourse. (e) This goes to the understanding of *meaning* in general; meaning seems to be the result of a human activity directed towards the *order* of things rather than to any *essence* they might possess. (f) The question remains whether those ideas of a specific style of painting, will achieve importance beyond the cubist scheme of thought. (g) Cubism made

[47] R. Barthes: *Essais Critiques,* Paris 1964 p. 191; see also Jan M. Broekman: *Structuralism. Moscow-Prague-Paris*. Dordrecht, Reidel Publ. Cie., 1974 p. 70 ff.

[48] G. Geffroy: 1895 *Paul Cézanne* in: Geffroy: *La Vie Artistique*, Vol 6, quoted in Yves-Alain Bois: *Cézanne and Matisse,* in: J. J. Richel & K. Sachs: 2009 *Cézanne and Beyond* Philadelphia Museum of Art, Yale UP, New Haven/London p. 113.

[49] J. Elderfield: *Picasso's Extreme Cézanne,* In: J. J. Richel & K. Sachs: *Cézanne and Beyond* Philadelphia Museum of Art, Yale UP, New Haven/London 2009, p. 915 ff.

clear that issues of human consciousness are active beyond philosophical representation. Creative activity is always *inter*activity and thus focuses on *meaning as a matter of order*. Order needs to articulate those components, which are to be ordered. This desire for articulation reinforces the power of the mind as well as social structures beyond simple acts of reflection or theory formation.

3.4 Reflective Painting

A 'brute' or 'wild' artist, who, as some imagine, paints without any reflection, does not exist. Cubism surpasses this romantic image of artistic activity unfolding beyond any criterion of human nature. The moving hand or the wandering eye does not activate an orientation in the world beyond precision and consciousness; each stroke on the canvas is premeditated. One must say, there is no 'art brute' (fr.) or 'brute art' (Engl.), and certainly no painting without consideration. 'Art brute' may be a style of painting but it does by no means determine a painter's character. Yet, a tension between painting and reflection exists. One often encounters the idea that painting is a form of reflection limited to pictorial means. Gertrude Stein, contemporary of cubist painters Picasso, Braque and Gris and inspired by automatic writing (écriture automatique), did not talk to painters about what they painted, because "painters, real painters, never really ever talk about that". Did they remain silent because their pictorial activity unfolds at a distance from any reflection? Apollinaire once stated about the art of Juan Gris, one of the founding painters of Cubism: "This is the man who has been thinking thoroughly about everything modern, the painter who searches new connections between everything, because he wants to draw and paint purely new forms…" and "…the art of Juan Gris is innermost intellectual art…".[50]

It would be of interest to keep in mind, that while considering reflection in painting and art many artists stress that they themselves did not completely understand all the dimensions of their work. That could also be important for the philosophy implied in that work. Artists should have a certain liberty to use philosophical arguments when talking about their work. Alfred Barr recalls dialogues with Picasso, and writes: "…art does not enter into philosophic absolutism. If cubism is an art of transition I am sure that the only thing that will come out of it is another form of cubism. Mathematics, trigonometry, chemistry, psychoanalysis, music and whatnot, have been related to cubism to give it an easier interpretation. All this has been pure literature, not to say nonsense, which brought a bad result, blinding people with theories. Cubism has kept itself within the limits and limitations of painting, never pretending to go beyond it. Drawing, design and color are understood and practiced in all other schools. Our subjects might be different, as we have introduced into painting objects and forms that were formerly ignored. We have kept our eyes open to our surroundings, and also our brains. We give to form and color all their individual significance, as far as we can see it; in our subjects, we keep the joy of

[50] G. Apollinaire: *Les Peintres Cubistes.* Paris 1913, p. 25.

discovery, the pleasure of the unexpected; our subject itself must be a source of interest. But of what use it is to say what we do when everybody can see it if he wants to?"[51]

It is clear that cubism is an important movement in the cultural history of the beginning twentieth century. Juan Gris writes: "Le cubisme doit avoir forcement une correlation avec toutes les manifestations de la pensée contemporaire…" [Cubism must have a correlation with all manifestations of contemporary thought] and Kahnweiler suggests that cubism around 1915 shows an important breach and reorientation in West-European art and culture. *A word painted as raw material on a Braque canvas is a semiotic novum*, just as Proust highlighted how his prose approximated the same type of complex paintings. When a word represents neither grammar nor discourse but strives for a newly found independence in the realm of expressiveness (not being the most profitable 'basic unit' or 'particle' of expression), then artistic action and scientific reflection are tied together and thus change art and linguistic communication. Marcel Proust thus concluded: "… the exclusive use of the Chinese scale, cubism, futurism or what you will, differs outrageously from all that occurred before.[52] We stress that Cubism became famous for its consistent search for *the defining pictorial composition*, an issue that was also central for structuralism at the level of sciences, arts and philosophy. It is widely known that cubist *painting* took the lead, with Picasso, Juan Gris, Georges Braque, and Delaunay, Duchamp, Léger, Picabia, Gleizes or Metzinger, although interesting parallel developments in literature, music, architecture or psychoanalysis also took place.

3.5 Cézanne's Defining Unit

Cézanne's defining unit—is it his life, his painting, his view, his temperament, his ideas and views on life? One question remains: the unit-idea is based on or refers to *representation*. Is there a painting that exists *beyond* representation or reference? This is a deep consideration about change. Cézanne knew the implications of change when he lived a life full of painting!

Could it be that Cézanne's life, his greatness and exceptional position in art, relates to his unique and perhaps revolutionary appreciation of the basic unit of a canvas: the brushstroke? This question, more or less of a philosophical nature, is a central one in a keynote essay of Richard Shiff in the catalogue of the 2009 Cézanne exhibition in Philadelphia. Robert Herbert described this essay as "the catalogue's star turn".[53] Shiff analyses the *diverse meanings of Cézanne's paint-marks*—they

[51] A. Barr Jr: *Picasso. Fifty years of his art.* New York 1946, p. 271. See also: M. Antliff & P. Leighten, (Eds.): *A Cubism Reader, Documents and Criticism 1906–1914.* Chicago UP 2008.

[52] Eric Karpeles: *Paintings in Proust. A Visual Companion to 'In Search of Last Time'*. Thames & Hudson, London 2008, p. 91.

[53] R. Herbert: "Godfather of the Modern?" In: *The New York Review of Books*, Vol. LVI, 2009 No. 13.

are predominantly at issue in his brushstrokes. Brushstrokes are Cézanne's basic units, which form in hindsight a decisive moment in the development of modern painting and are also important for a philosophy of art and modern culture. Herbert mentions Shiff's analysis of Monet's marks as compared to Cézanne: Monet's brush strokes are suggestive of a separateness, but that suggestion diminishes when shape and direction change with the imagined object. Where Monet's strokes remained subordinated to the illusion of representations, Cézanne's strokes *seem autonomous*, Herbert insists.

One should understand the importance of this conclusion. It is because of this observation that *one must grant Cézanne priority over Picasso as the Godfather of Cubism.* Picasso's path-breaking *Demoiselles d'Avignon* could not have been conceived without Cézanne's various groups of bathers as an example—canvasses which Cézanne painted with autonomous strokes but yet under the spell of *representing* his subject.[54] Picasso's words from 1963 illustrate that clearly: "He was my one and only master!"[55] There are probably two levels for understanding the essence of Cézanne's work: one pertains to the technicalities of the foundational unit: the brush stroke in his paintings. The other pertains to the much-debated character of the artist and his view on life. Both show, however, that Cézanne's development reveals *a challenging emphasis on meaning*.

This said, we concentrate on how the first level of understanding is of interest when we grasp the meaning of Cubism, the second when we focus on its broader context.[56] Consider the technical features of Cézanne's brushstrokes. *Their autonomy is not a symbol within the painting but rather a renewal of the entire activity called painting*. Shiff described in 1984 in reference to *Madame Cézanne in Blue*, how "segmented strokes that define the wooden sideboard turn a gentle corner, change color, and become the shoulder of the figure's dress; elements of the collar connect to a lozenge from the wallpaper. Such effects are to be expected in compositional painting but not to the degree that they diffuse the spatial illusion, as they do here. We imagine Cézanne concentrating on the painted surface to such an extent that he could not resist moving with its movement once the basic image had established a few points of compositional reference."[57]

---

[54] See Joseph J. Rishel: "Cézanne, Virgil, Poussin" in: J.J. Rishel (Ed.): *Gauguin, Cézanne, Matisse. Visions of Arcadia.* Yale UP, & Philadelphia Museum of Art, 2012, p. 163 ff.

[55] See Note 8, p. 217 ff.

[56] Jan M. Broekman: Zur *Philosophie des Kubismus* In: *Actes 5e Congrès Internationale d'Esthétique,* Amsterdam 1965: Id.: *Malerei als Reflexion* In*: Jahrbuch für Aesthetik und Allgemeine Kunstwissenschaft*, 1966 Vol. 10. See also: Anton Ehrenzweig: *The Hidden Order of Art*, California UP 1967, p. 67 ff.

[57] R. Shiff: *Cézanne and the end of Impressionism.* Chicago UP 1984, p. 190 f.

3.6 *Cézanne's Brushstrokes*

A viewer is impressed by the dynamics of meaning as made visible by the strokes in the painting, whereby brushstrokes embody feelings beyond any reference. They form an encompassing activity in Cézanne's case and by no means just a method. His strokes and their motives, so passionately appreciated by friends and colleagues "could not be … regarded solely as a concept or an ideal", Shiff writes: "it was instead a movement associated with a particular experience … as this experience played out in an active process of painting. Although sensation needed to catch up with itself, it would be wrong to expect that a stable image would result if it did, for living, human sensation is not divisible into moments. It merely feels like an instant or moment, that is, it feels momentary, transient, changing. …What Cézanne understood of the changing aspect of Mont Sainte-Victoire he understood of apples and human figures. … Look at (a) figure's hands. … Those hands are moving, but by what source of energy?"[58]

The strokes, each being an independent corpus of/in painting, seem the fruit of passionate precision. They require perfection on their own, self-sufficiency, fullness. The stroke *is* what it is: it is, in context and yet without reference, and a *sign* of the artist's intrinsic individuality, expressing his life, his savageness and the unfinished character of whatever is represented. For impressionists and symbolists, Shiff remarks, *distortion* is a familiar quality: "yet the varieties of *gaucherie* seen in Cézanne's paintings may have been unusually convincing in the manner in which they seemed to constitute the image from its inception rather than to deform an image already given or created."[59] The path to Cubist deformation was opened in the painting strokes of Cézanne.

The latter are a composite of *self-sufficient* strokes. That cubist drive reinforces the dynamics of analysis and synthesis in art. One could in addition interrogate Cézanne about the precise character of reference he wants to achieve with each of his strokes. Confront him with the question whether an absence of reference in the context of a painting is possible at all? His answer would claim an independence of *temperament* and a comparable independence of the painter's object: call it '*nature*'. *Strokes* are *signs* in this context.[60]

The meaning and sense of brushstrokes in the painting are a matter of each stroke independently and thus with no direct reference to other strokes. It is not the fluidity of strokes that determines the situation in that case, but rather the fact that the strokes (the basic elements of painting) are *ordered* within the identifiable complex we call a painting, a canvas or a painter's achievement. The painting may refer to an event, a situation or a subject, but the strokes, the constitutive elements of the painting, do not.

---

[58] R. Shiff: *Lucky Cézanne.* Op. Cit., p. 59, 80.

[59] R. Shiff: *Cézanne and the End of Impressionism,* Op. Cit., p. 190 f.

[60] M. Merleau-Ponty: "Le Doute de Cézanne" [Cézanne's Doubt] (1945) in: *Sens et non-sens*. Paris 1966, p. 30.

This is the riddle in post-impressionist painting: strokes contribute to representation without themselves representing! That riddle is relevant for the study of meaning. *Brushstrokes are signs belonging to a painting but existing beyond reference.* They are signs, which only receive a referential meaning through their belonging to a totality—the painting itself. In other words, they are signs without manifesting Peirce's triadic structure, being 'sign-object-interpretant'. Did not Peirce's most quoted definition around 1897 say: "a sign, or representamen, is something which stands to somebody for something in some respect or capacity"! A sign is here a single basic element of meaning and all imaginable other triads of greater complexity are reducible to this basic element. Does a cubist painting escape reference at one level only to find its *nexus* within the *plurality*, the *order,* of the painting as a whole?

3.7 Particles in Painting

The Cubist attitude forms an appropriate climate to uncover traces of the particle story in modern painting. Cézanne's brushstrokes may not *be* particles in the context of painting, but they *are understood* as such. Philosophical implications of particle traces fascinate and—as always—lead to often to vague considerations of cosmological relevance. The particle story is indeed at home in modern painting. In order to become acquainted with the story, we concentrate once more on Cézanne's works. His "post-impressionist" paintings had a direct effect on the viewer because of his much-appreciated colors. Those colors were, however, reinforced by the pulse of the strokes. They became a central issue in the appreciation of Cézanne's work, from the second half of his life time on: from Paul Signac's 1899 remarks on Cézanne's techniques to the unique analyses of Richard Shiff in our day. The strokes enhanced the color effects, not the inverse: not the colors, the strokes. His mark-to-mark technique, highlighted by Signac, made those brush-strokes pure, self-determined, direct, quintessential, and unsusceptible of interpretation.[61] Here is a difference from the dots of pointillism: Cézanne's strokes are neutral, indifferent in view of the subject of his paintings, never touched by textures of things or landscapes, nor by sentiment or interpretative feelings. Issues like texture, thing or sentiment follow only *after* the strokes were realized. They must have been a reason for Cézanne's feeling that his works were *incomplete*.

In the context of meaning and modern painting, *the meaning of the painting is determined by strokes, not by the subject represented*. This is clear in the secondary literature from Signac to Shiff where one finds abundant commentaries on Cézanne's brush strokes. They formulate that "...figurative elements exist only in their interconnection ... compositions are an addition of details to those already defined ...

[61] Paul Signac: *D'Eugène Delacroix au néo-impressionisme* (1899), Paris 1979 (See: R. Shiff: *Lucky Cézanne,* Op. Cit., p. 543, and Shiff, *Cézanne and the End of Impressionism*, Op. Cit., p. 118, 167, 204).

the strokes leaving directional quality in the painting … representing uniformity of interest in detail of the visual field … individual forms and structures dissolving back into a uniform field, the pattern of color … strokes that become parts of a single set of warm tone … strokes that *make* a *found* quality rather than discover it." Most fascinating is where strokes serve the transformation of a *naïve vision* into *a pictorial work* (which is of course non-naïve). That is a direct homage to Husserl's theory of attitudes (Chap. 2), one would say!

All these remarks do NOT consider whether they describe the fundamental lines of the particle story, but illustrate that the basics of Cézanne's art are embedded in the master—master discourse of the particle. Cézanne did perhaps not compose his works uniquely by strokes (like writers are thought to compose texts with words) but his strokes do decidedly sustain the particle story in modern painting, and thus obey the rules of the master—master discourse.

The concept of reference, which is clearly important for meaning, seems to be on the basis of *order* rather than of *parallels*, *likeness* or a simple *repetition*! That idea fits Peirce when writing earlier (c. 1873) "a sign has such a relation to an object as to bring the two latter into a certain relation within one another". *A sign became sign in the painting in the order of strokes!* A philosophy of Cubism is in essence a philosophy of order.[62] One could understand this in Peircean terminology, saying that in Cézanne's paintings, precursors of Cubism, the brushstroke is only a sign if one stroke within the painting is an *index* for another. This feature seems to be in an exemplary manner decisive for Cézanne, who mentioned how his strokes did not necessarily relate to each other. Painting for the sake of painting and in no way for illustrating or other forms of representation follows this stroke motive. That is *an extreme Cubist viewpoint*—and a special technique to cope with life in the sign pool as ceaselessly changing.

Cézanne, Picasso and other friends were widely admired because they displayed a unity of life and work. "A general theory of human consciousness, a theory of life, would be needed to determine the relation of Cézanne's manner of painting to his lived experience", Shiff noticed. Maurice Merleau-Ponty wrote in the 1945 essay quoted above: *Le doute de Cézanne*: "it is true that the life of an author does not teach us anything, but if we could learn to read him, everything could be found because of the openness of the work".[63] The same essay with the same topic does, however, read: "The significance of his work cannot be determined by his life" and referring to Greco, he stressed Cézanne's "freedom of the solitaire" which showed "a morbid constitution", "schizoid like El Greco". So there is hardly any uniformity in the perception of life and work as an issue in itself, generally exposed in biographies and theories about pictorial art.

---

[62] Jan M. Broekman: "Zur Philosophie des Kubismus", in: *Actes du 5me Congres International d'Esthetique*, Den Haag, Mouton 1968, pp. 223–226; and: "Filosofie van de Kunst als Filosofie van de Ordening", In: *Algemeen Nederlands Tijdschrift Voor Wijsbegeerte En Psychologie*, 1965, Nr. 2.

[63] M. Merleau-Ponty: "Le Doute de Cézanne" [Cézanne's Doubt] (1945) in: *Sens et non-sens*. Paris 1966, p. 18 ff.

3.8 *Tyche*

Tyche is the Ancient Greek Goddess of fortune, of chance, providence or fate, and she determines an *order of things* to emerge. Brushstrokes in their order do not refer to each other, but they are orderly in Tyche's eye. It will fascinate lawyers that the same Goddess was understood as *the constellation Virgo*, the *Dike* who took care of Justice.[64] Tyche confronts us with vision, feeling and spontaneity in the case of Cézanne. She is for Peirce important in the context of understanding his personal fate and of his evolutionary cosmology, which colors his lifelong interest in logic. His own biography leads him to the meaning of human consciousness, with the major conclusion that the self, indicating the existence of that consciousness, is characterized by itself as a self.[65] One should not misunderstand this: the characterization is a *structure*, an *order* in itself, and the self itself is for itself a *sign*. This structural self-understanding is based on insight in order to expand itself in the form of accelerating reasonableness. Peirce drafts a theory of identity while focusing on the cosmic dimensions of human life. Tyche brings meaning and order together; she inspired Peirce to find the traces of how this particular constellation emerges.

Philosophical considerations have accompanied cubist concepts in almost all regards, in particular in psychoanalysis and literature—sometimes the two are intermingled in explanations of for instance the literary prose of Gertrud Stein, or the poetic approaches of Ezra Pound[66] or T.S. Eliot, not to mention French writers such as Appolinaire, Mallarmé or Rimbaud. Many commentaries from philosophers such as Gehlen and Gadamer focus on Cubist principles; they also mention Peirce's semiotics in the same context as well as the psychoanalytical approach of Jacques Lacan and his insights in the emergence of a subject's identity. A reference to German Neo-Kantianism as a foundation for Cubist approaches to reality completes this range.

Gadamer, famous for his stimulus toward new forms of hermeneutics in his 1960 *Wahrheit und Methode* [Truth and Method], wrote important essays on art, painting and Cubism. In view of Cézanne's brushstrokes, we highlight only one point in Gadamer's discussion with Arnold Gehlen concerning conceptual painting and Gehlen's book *Zeit-Bilder.*[67] The book suggests that Cubism is founded in a Neo-Kantian philosophy. Objects and reality are declared to emerge from human thought

[64] See: Jan. M. Broekman: "A Goddess for Semiotics of Law and Legal Discourse" in *DADA – Revista di Antropologia post-globale*, (Antonio Palmisano, Ed.) Trieste 2011, p. 7–24; Id.: "Artificiality and Naturalness—The Tyche Deity" in Jan M. Broekman & Larry Catà Backer: *Lawyers Making Meaning. The Semiotics of Law in Legal Education II*. Springer 2013, p. 217 ff.

[65] Peirce, Ch. S.: *The Collected Papers of Charles Sanders Pierce* Vols I – VI, Ed. Charles Hartshorne and Paul Weiss, Cambridge Ma, Harvard University Press. 1931–1935, Vol. V, Par. 314.

[66] Jan M. Broekman: "Philosophischer Versuch über Ezra Pound" [A philosophical essay on Ezra Pound], in: *Text+Kritik,* 1965, Nr. 10/11, pp. 1–11.

[67] A. Gehlen: *Zeit-Bilder* Frankfurt am Main, 1960; H.-G Gadamer,.: *Wahrheit und Methode* Tübingen 1960, Id.: *Kleine Schriften II: Interpretationen*. Tübingen. 1967, p. 220.

processes so that the Kantian categories of space and time are purely conceptual and thus products of the mind. Gadamer replies with strong philosophical arguments, that the "…cubist facet style should not be understood and presented as the practical application of Husserl's idea of shading or fine distinction of the perceptual object! It would be absurd to suggest that Cubism highlights the synthesis of apperception and that an anything but revolutionary Neo-Kantian philosophy, just before fading away, would have caused the greatest revolution in European painting since Giotto".

Gadamer considers two features in the originality of Cubism. One is the *constructivist* component, which is widely perceived and lauded, and the other a safeguarding of a maximal transparency of the Cubist technique. The conceptual character of Cubist painting does not, as Gehlen suggests, advance a scientific approach in the art of painting, but rather a *purely spiritual use of the elementary units of the pictorial composition.* Focus on sorting out the basic unit of painting was therefore highlighted in the work of Cézanne, Gadamer suggested without reference to the particle story involved. Any philosophy of Cubism excels in essentially being a philosophy of *order* pertaining to signs and pictorial units as the basic materials for *ordering* as an artistic activity.

All these remarks stem from a wealth of philosophical considerations concerning Cubist art. They could, however, be presented with more precision, expanded and deepened for instance into the logic and semiotics of Peirce, the Lacanian vision of human growth, Gadamer's hermeneutics at work in pictorial art and above all, Cubist achievements as a substantial contribution to contemporary occidental culture. One question would nevertheless remain a central issue in all those contexts: the question of how these philosophies and their inherent notions relate to understanding the complex realities of meaning? The shift from *verbal* to *visual* expressiveness and the completion of *words* by *images* is decisive here.

Changes of meaning include changes of material elements available for articulation, which perform in terms of communication. Does verbal expressiveness suffice to understand the reality we have in mind? Or should a cubist painting inspire us to continuously reconsider our proper articulation? Consider that the character of our language levels changed under the influence of the completion of words by images, so that communication in the sign pool is no longer restricted to words or other linguistic entities. The slogan that "an image is worth a thousand words" has indeed communicative weight. "Finally, … reality depends on the ultimate decision of the community" Peirce noticed,[68] and he could have added the suggestion that *community* also means *culture*! A culture presents itself in a variety of images in public places; there is, however, no visual component in the arts, sciences or literature that fulfils a defining function. This inspires three coherent but general conclusions:

1. There is *no meaning separated from cultural values*, styles, norms and ideas—cubism is an excellent example of *intertwining meaning-creation*, which always plays a role in cultural complexities.

[68] Ch. S. Peirce: *Collected Papers*, 5. 317.

2. There is *no fine line to be maintained between literary and visual meaning*: Cubism has demonstrated via the surfaces of its paintings how literary motives can become visual, carrying important consequences for the sign-pool we live in (Braque and others).
3. What is *important for art is also important for life in the sign-pool*: there is a central place for the functioning image of a human being. Peirce and Lacan, Cézanne and Picasso, Juan Gris and Gertrud Stein all paid attention to this motive.
4. Many aspects of this summary conclusion underscore the importance of *the master—master discourse*. The search for basic and deciding units in the sign-pool is a source of fascination in *communication processes* where emancipated participants can make decisions.

Peirce's idea that the human subject is an *order* in itself, and that the self itself is for itself a *sign*, is a free basis for an observation that combines literary and visual meanings, a correct realization of elaborated *citizen participation* as explored today in the social and legal system of the European Union. Is it not the ultimate goal of social life, sustained by meaning analyses, to create an emancipated opinion, combining visual and verbal elements of discourse? Indeed, one needs an emancipated opinion in order to worship Tyche.

4 Legal Semiotics (4): Theory in Law

At last they are in touch—the poet, the physicist, the painter and the lawyer. Is any one of them, or perhaps someone else, prepared to take the floor and formulate a final word? Is a law student prepared to do so? If so, it will most probably not be a legal professional. The heading 'semiotics and law' will not inspire any practitioner of the law. The latter will rather be irritated and ask what all the foregoing ideas and analyses concerning the concept and the making of meaning as demonstrated in the cases of a poet, a physicist or a painter have to do with him. Indeed, they were examples for a theory that might encompass dimensions we are used to considering in the sign pool of daily life. Recall the discussions concerning the structure and the essence of theory. Do law and legal discourse embrace a theory—are they concerned with the essence of law? What might the lawyer or the law student remember from impressions gathered during the above-mentioned explanations? Perhaps no more than this: at last in touch again! But how?

4.1 Articulation

Indeed, there is a very good reason for a sight of relief. When the law student feels herself to be in touch with the basic issues examined in the above texts, she might consider whether law is thus submitted to the master—master discourse like poetry, physics or painting? Or do law and legal discourse possess other features and a different, perhaps more specific identity? The answer causing the sigh of relief is: "no": law remains within the lines of the master—master discourse, and is structured in accordance with its norms and values. The relief has to do with the fact that law is (although generally recognized as a 'master discourse' itself) safely anchored in our everyday sign pool.

Law and legal discourse are outstanding forms of articulation in social life—but *what* do they articulate? The question has been debated over the course of many ages, mostly in the more or less primitive sentence: 'what is law?'. Yet, occidental culture unfolded law since Roman days without a precise notion of its essence. Legal practices were not hindered by such an articulation gap. Does a law student know? Is she informed about what is said when lawyers speak? That consideration not only concerns what is spoken, ordained or codified in words and texts, but also concerns the content and structure of the oral as well as the written communication it masters. The tendency is to practice law as if those questions do not need an answer, or seem irrelevant: law's communication is a part of legally safeguarded provisions, and so is its inherent field of semiotics.

The latter, a careful study of sign and meaning, reveals that a lawyer's inclination to speak about his activity in terms of a specific practice (if he will ever do so), is to emphasize that *'legal practice' is a theoretical concept.* Why would lawyers need more than this delineation to sustain the primacy of practice? The well-known semiotician J. Greimas sustains this impression, saying "(…) legal practice is a production of law, its rules and new legal meanings. But legal practice is at the same time a procedure of recurring verification of the validity of institutional legal language."[69] There is seldom a reflection on this particular viewpoint in legal education in Europe or the US. Any attitude supporting the idea relates to the impression that 'law and semiotics' will not fascinate a law student. And she will in this light eagerly embrace the thought that she performs a legal practice under the heading of the outlined master—master discourse. That makes considerations about semiotics as a component of legal discourse and the determination of law itself superfluous. Is that correct?

4.2 Legal Semiotics

Semiotics has changed the lawyer's situation in an unexpected manner. It shifted the attention from the content of articulation (what was said) to the structure and essence of articulation itself (how it was said and under what sort of conditions). In that regard Roberta Kevelson attested that: "…the basic concepts of rights, resources, and reality take on new dimensions of meaning in correspondence with

[69] A. J. Greimas: *Sémiotique et sciences sociales.* Paris 1976, p. 91. [The Social Sciences: A Semiotic View. Trl P. Perron & F.H. Collins, Minnesota UP 1980, p. 102 ff].; See also: Jan M. Broekman & Larry Catà Backer: *Lawyers Making Meaning,* Op. Cit., p. 57 ff.

n-dimensional, infinite value judgments or truth-like beliefs which one holds".[70] As a result,

1. lawyers became more aware of the importance of language and also of their own linguistic activities. They
2. often looked back at rhetoric in law to find support for their views, even in Roman law. But they
3. encountered also a need for linguistic expressivity beyond their own mother tongue, in particular as global law came up. And
4. they experienced that any meaning formation, which specifically focused on law (and was named 'social understanding of professional language') also affected political forms of social life.

Greimas noticed that a legal text is part of a legal semiotics, is produced by a particular grammar and is the manifestation of a specific meaning-universe.

Peirce's idea that the human self is for itself a *sign* became one of the first semiotic insights that convinced the lawyer to develop some thoughts in that direction while practicing law. Literary and visual meanings characterizing law furthered a large-scale realization of citizen participation. That social renewal seemed no longer to be an issue of balancing rights and diminishing suppressive forces in society. It led rather to a hitherto unknown interest in and freedom of articulation. A most powerful example is how the 1992 Maastricht Treaty confirmed citizen participation and a renewal of free speech in the socio-legal system of the European Union. Is it not an ultimate goal of modern social life to develop an embracing articulation for emancipated opinion sustained by analyses of the various levels of meaning? That is truly the modern sense of the lawyer's field of activity. Semiotics is a key to this contribution of law and legal discourse in the sign pool of today.

One should understand that citizen participation is not a well-circumscribed and socially isolated goal but, on the contrary, it is itself a new form of communication. It is deeply influencing political decisions and constitutes the master planning of social life. Forms of communication shape forms of self-consciousness, and thus influence the quality of discourses on law or social psychology as well as economy or engineering. That powerful participation is an extension of our modern array of articulations, which is also encountered in legal discourse. It can be difficult to accept this new form of sociability in the heart of legal practice.

Law's practice should in the case of reinforced citizen participation come to be evaluated at a theoretical level as a specific form of linguistics, including particular meanings, signs and social techniques. Citizen participation, which focuses directly on the traditional concept of 'legal subject' (predominant in Civil Law) is in this light no more and no less than the improved ability to articulate and share norms and values, extending common goods and opinions. Semiotics and (legal) education are now nearer to each other than ever, and appeal to legal performance and opinionating in important social dimensions. That proximity shows the virtues of a semiotic approach: citizen participation created a sign of extending commonality while legal

[70] R. Kevelson: *The Law as a System of Signs*. Plenum Press, London/New York 1988. p. vii.

practices sustain that extension by deeply understanding their own commitment towards a process of multi-leveled articulation in culture.

4.3 Texts and Discourse

It is clear that the contribution of semiotics of law to legal practice has a complex structure. There is no straight answer to the question 'what is law' because law is a specific articulation, and the result of a specific set of institutionally anchored speech acts—a *process* and not an fixated *object* to be determined with traditional instruments. There are two features to distinguish: a linguistic and thus *articulation* component (law as a discourse) and a value-oriented and thus *meaning* component (law as a norm, a value and a set of expectations about future behaviors). Both play, in their specific coherence, a role in social and legal discourses and show a complexity, which we approach as *leveled* by its nature.

But there is another observation to add. Is it possible to be aware of specificities of a discourse while positioning oneself within that same discourse? Say the word. Articulate what is the case! Any answer would reveal that only a word from *outside* the discourse could do that. Here is the reason that law as a discourse cannot be studied without perceiving law as a text: *a legal text is in law's practice the 'outer province' of law's discourse*. This may be an example of a general constellation since the close, institutionalized and constitutive relation between discourse and text is specific for law. Speech and writing—two force fields meet continuously, but seldom in perfect synchrony. They are institutionally forged when law is at stake.

Sharpen your mind and visit a Courtroom, a law firm, or participate in a Law School lecture. At every moment of your visit words are spoken that display constitutional bounds with texts. Lawyers consult books while speaking, papers are exchanged among participants during Court sessions, libraries are continuously at hand or at laptops, students complain that they are only trained in two abilities the law apparently requires: reading and writing. It is often the writing that requires most of their energy and intelligence. Legal texts are perceived as prescriptions for legal arguments. Do students dedicate their lives to those two fields of articulation? The defining feature of law is that there is no spoken word in legal practice without relevance for, or a foundation in, a written text. And there is no text without an encompassing discourse. Law seems not to exist without those intertwining forces; without them, social institutions would deny any interest in law. The question: 'what is most important' in law will be ridiculed—there exists no hierarchical relation between them. Texts and speech serve the master—master discourse on an equal level and in doing so, they produce strictly mastered levels of words. Each incidental importance of one level or another appears to be problematic.

4.4 Law and Theory

A lawyer's way of speaking about his own activity confirms many of the above remarks on the essence of law as well as the legal view on theory. Predominant is of course that a lawyer's words as well as his acts show the formative power of the master—master discourse. There is no discussion of these fundaments at whatever level of performance research is done. But one observation should guide us most clearly: a lawyer's activity has no specific profile, which she would cherish in her speech activity. To describe a lawyer's activity as legal practice is in her eyes a theoretical conceptualization beyond her practice, often misleading her in her striving for opinions and solutions. 'Legal activity as legal practice' is not only too theoretical but also a sign of misunderstanding a lawyer's professional activity: the wealth of inherent possibilities or the weight of responsibilities and the large scale of moral and social values at stake. A deep misjudgment is evidently on a par with a deep insult when non-lawyers characterize that activity as 'practice'. An outsider to the profession would notice the inverse: if a lawyer were not able to define what law is, would he then nevertheless be able to define what he practices?

Yet, both views are relevant where the meaning of law is concerned. In the development of quantum mechanics since Einstein, Heisenberg and Bohm a central position has been given to the question 'what is a theory' and 'what should a theory deliver?' Is that question relevant for law and legal discourse? We now see that there is in legal discourse no preparedness to explore deep structures of speech and text. The master-master discourse determines the limits of discipline and discourse, but provides no freedom to raise questions and in-depth analyses beyond its borderlines.

Does law *have*, and does law *need*, a theory? The distance between a practitioner and a theoretician of law makes it very difficult to answer this question straightforwardly. The question whether law has a theory is not in the hands of theoreticians, who treat the legal specificity of discourse as a directly accessed issue of social, metaphysical or general philosophical stature. But that is not the *milieu* in which to answer such questions, which have in fact little to do with an evaluation of legal positivism, pragmatism and other isms. *The needlessness of theory in law is a legal conclusion in its own right.* Law decides always about what law is and what it is not—the appreciation or non-appreciation of the 'appeal' modus is a proof to consider. The idea that law does not need a theory (including all its values, importance, social appreciation and moral values) is a strictly legal view. The organization of institutionalized speech characterized as 'legal' expresses itself as a multi-meaning discourse. To say in this context that law does not need a theory is in itself a theoretical conclusion, lawyers claim, and parallels the idea that speaking about law's practice is theoretical. The 'non practice' verdict is identical to the 'non theory' verdict.

4.5 Theory

We mentioned before that Einstein discussed in one of his talks with Heisenberg whether a theory provides us the framework for perceiving facts. The 'non-theory' of law is clearly an ultimate force to decide what legal facts are and what legal discourse has to embrace. Judges refer to facts related to the prescriptive power of relevant texts so that their speech bridges gaps between word and action. They are indeed aware of what Einstein formulated: bridges and related instruments for reaching a judgment are complicated processes *in se*. They have their own history and tradition, qualities and values. They created and still create new occurrences, views and appreciations to ultimately find the long path to a final word, a fixation and a fact. And yet, they are but instruments in law … the 'non-theory' of law seems an efficient but complex theory for legal practice, marked by its special (legal) efficiency.

It is as if this efficiency blinds the subject of law in the first place through its authoritarian character. Words of law are repetitious because of their submission to special instrumental features, some of them called 'text'. The master—master discourse makes the lawyer believe that he does not need to explore deep structures of the legal text. The latter operation would uncover the master—master discourse and show that it is in itself the servant of one and only one leading idea: 'the particle story'.

That story unifies the physicist and the lawyer in a most remarkable manner. The first aims at uncovering what nature-in-itself is and in what ways its processes unfold, the second at uncovering the multiple meanings of social life (the sign pool) and ultimately of human activity in general. What appeals, what criteria, what analyses must the lawyer deliver in law? The question is all the more urgent when it becomes clear that the meaning of 'theory' affects all types of meaning including all sign-bound levels of human life.

4.6 Deep Structures

Word and text, conjoint in legal discourse, are processes. They are presented to the reader, to the law's subject or to the legal actor who functions as lawyer as if they were the basic units or particles of law and legal discourse. But an analysis of the meaning they participate in, shows how they are processes, organized as strings of signs. If, as Peirce claimed, a sign on its own cannot be a sign, then a sign is a sign due to its relations with other signs—that which creates a complex totality often indicates that *string* as *culture*. We should remember that texts in law possess a *surface* structure, which is manifested, printed, read, communicated, and functions as an authority; and a *deep* structure, which indicates that texts are always generated, historical and never without pedigree—an element that conveys authority. Texts are never instantaneous but always bound to a specific constellation, and also not without claim for a future. On this basis, a legal text or discourse has, in Husserl's terms, a non-naïve natural character.[71] But what is 'deep' here? 'Deep' means in law in the first place: not 'naïve—natural' and thus different from everyday language; 'deep' means therefore in the first place: *in* law. That is the depth as aimed at by the metaphor 'deep'. The latter indicates that each level of manifestation is a step in descending towards a hypothetical origin. That origin is what is commonly perceived as 'deep layered', no matter whether it is empirically tangible. The meaning of the metaphor 'depth' in law has two meanings: first, it refers (as said) to an origin, and second, it presupposes that origin beyond its manifestation. In other words: depth in law means that a meaning of a legal text is always a matter of *difference* caused by a re-placement. All meaning results from replacement. Meaning and activity called 'legal' focus primarily on that replacement. Hence the strong belief of lawyers (particularly in the US) in the great and unmistakable function of an 'origin', which laws and related legal texts are supposed to possess. *The in-depth meaning of a legal text is always a text*; that meaning will never reach beyond what is institutionally anchored as belonging to law and/or expressing legal discourse: Can law be 'deep' beyond the boundaries of its discourse, which confirms the principles of the master—master discourse? That does not seem to be the case, since law has confined its theory, its linguistic universe, its metaphysical anchors and its view of reality to its proper defining power—and no more than that! [72]

4.7 The Culture of Particles

The latter insight makes clear that a legal culture is confined to itself—that 'self' being a sign of its self-referential potentiality. Questions about the character and being of its basic elements are *instrumental* within, and *destructive* beyond law's discourse. Words, names, expressions are given a *legal* meaning, which are sometimes embarrassing when the naïve-natural level of language mixes with the non-naïve-natural of law, as the example of the word 'thief' showed.[73] As we suggested before: shout: "Thief!" on the street! That has a fundamentally different meaning and consequences than the word shouted by a police officer. It means that one has to highlight legal meaning as belonging to an institutionalized, well defined linguis-

[71] This has to be understood in the more general context of semiotic analyses of the commons, history, mythology, narratives and their grammar, stories, proverbs and other linguistic occurrences, in: A. J. Greimas: *Du Sens. Essais Sémiotiques*. Paris 1970. More explanations are in: A. J. Greimas: *Du Sens II. Essais Sémiotiques*. Paris 1983, and specifically for law in: A. J. Greimas: *Sémiotique et sciences sociales*. Paris 1976, p. 79–129; See his analytical remarks on p. 88 f.

[72] N. Luhmann became famous by bringing all this together in one expression, which functions as the basis for his extended theory of law: the word *autopoiesis*. See N. Luhmann: *Soziale Systeme. Grundriß einer allgemeinen Theorie*. Frankfurt M 1984; and: G. Teubner (Ed.): *Autopoietic Law: A New Approach to Law and Society*. Berlin/New York 1988; G. Teubner: Recht als autopoietisches System [Law as autopoietic system], Frankfurt M 1989.

[73] See Chap. 1: *Silence,* Semiotics in Legal Education (1).

tic and legally ruled level. *Names* and *name giving* are important in that context[74]; they are a sign for the techniques and mechanics of maintaining a *valid* legal discourse. Law is not recognized as law when those techniques are not correctly applied and the mechanics of legal speech and legal writing disrespected. It becomes clear how important those technicalities are if one considers that name-giving in legal cases is qualified as "a matter of legal style" for Court documents, opinions and decisions. *Meaning* is connected with *style*. Law has no esthetic criterion at hand, other than the criterion of legal validity. That criterion entails man-made decisions and is a discursive issue articulating social and cultural values of mainstream society, Oriental as well as Occidental. *Names* name legal cases, and through this naming provide a legal identity to cases. One should not forget that *via naming* cases become truly *legal* cases. The legal naming will give sign-characters to cases, which thus become colored as acceptable for law. The 'being law' is a matter of legal decision making, one has to stress.[75] The names of cases (in Common Law as in Civil Law) may stem from a naïve-natural, everyday language level, but they decidedly belong to a non-naïve natural (artificial and professional) level of linguistic articulation. The *legal* meaning of a case name is at a distance from any name in everyday language. If the case is a matter of solving a conflict legally, then the case indicates that this solution is legal as it is determined to be by legal decision. To read the names of cases is reading a legal discourse, and reading what legal discourse accepts as being law.

4.8 Partition

The laws for composing law are legal laws—the misunderstanding that they should be social or political is widespread. It is true that composing law is highly relevant socially, but they are not in the hands of anyone apart from jurists. This is the reason that law and legal discourse must be considered as performances on *a non-naïve natural level of articulation.* In the heart of this understanding functions an implicit answer to the question how law belongs to the master—master discourse, alias 'the particle story'. The lawyer will, in sharp contrast to the poet, the physicist and the painter, decide at the non-naïve level of articulation what has to be termed and

[74] Jan M. Broekman:" Cases, Names" in: "The Legal Semiotic Modus Operandi: Names" in: Broekman & Backer (See Note 1) "*Lawers Making Meaning*", Chapter 16, p. 212 f.

[75] See the *World Legal Information Institute*, presenting itself as an independent and non-profit access to worldwide law. The institute presents 1258 databases from 123 jurisdictions via 14 Institutes, with special attention for *legal education* as well as *Courts* and *Case Law, International Law*, and a variety of *publication channels*. The references are *not* solely informative; they also present a mixture of citing and name giving, thus rigidly maintaining legal rules and legal discourses. It interests how diverse *jurisdictions have their own toolbar*: a sign of transferring legal power within the boundaries of law itself. See: www.worldlii.org. Those boundaries and verbal prescripts are also indicated in: "Preambulatory Clauses and Operative Clauses" on the *United Nations Association of the USA* at www.unausa.org/Page.aspx?pid=509.

treated as a 'particle' of legal discourse. That particle does not exist by nature, not because of the linguistic features of human communication nor because of the 'laws of painting' or of representation—the particle in law exists because of a legal decision. This sounds like 'decisionism', a chapter in legal theory and legal philosophy, which concerns by extra-legal ideas definition.[76] What was highlighted here does not refer to the decision of a subject (as is the case in Schmitt's theory) but refers to a fundamental structure of an articulation process of law and legal discourse. That structure tells us that the legal particle exists because law decided it to be: it is not a philosophical or metaphysical reality, but an encompassing technique for maintaining law; it is rather an innermost secret of law, including what is called 'legal practice'. *To name something as 'law' is of the essence.* If that naming-decision is wrong or has no value, law does not exist. The fundamental issue behind it all relates to *the partition between law and non-law.* The law student has to focus on at least this particular semiotic issue during his training: acquiring an awareness of the fact that he has to live in two worlds, two language levels, two sets of meaning and—above all—to manage in his life to bring those two together when it is needed, and to separate law from non-law when law requires it. A particle is a sign of his situation in law and an index of his partition between naïve-natural and non-naïve natural level of articulation. Law succeeds to be a discourse that obeys human measures—subjectivity, rationality and causality—and avoids following physical theories or cosmological lines of thought. In the end they will never meet!

References

Al-Khalili, Jim. 2003. *Quantum*. London: Weidenfeld and Nicholson.

Antliff, M. and P. Leighten (Eds.). 2008. *A cubism reader, documents and criticism 1906–1914*. Chicago: University of Chicago Press.

Apollinaire, G. 1913. *Les Peintres Cubistes*. Paris: E. Figuière et Cie.

Barr Jr., A. 1946. *Picasso. Fifty years of his art*. New York: The Museum of Modern Art.

Barthes, Roland. 1964. *Essais Critiques*. Paris: Éditions du Seuil.

Bell, J.S. 1987. *Speakable and unspeakable in quantum mechanics*. Cambridge: Cambridge University Press.

Bell, J.S. 1966. On the problem of hidden variables in quantum theory. In *Review of modern physics*, vol. 38, 447 ff. (Reprinted 1983 and 1987).

Bohm, David. 1980. *Wholeness and the implicate order*. London: Routledge.

Bohm, David. 1985. *Unfolding meaning. A weekend of dialogue*. London: Routledge.

---

[76] See the *Wikipedia* article on Decisionism: as "a political, ethical and jurisprudential doctrine, which states that moral or legal precepts are the product of decisions made by political or legal bodies. According to decisionism, it is not the content of the decision, but rather the fact that it is a decision made by the proper authority, or by using a correct method, which determines its validity. In legal theory, decisionism had a notable proponent in the German law scholar Carl Schmitt. Schmitt held that it is not the actual precepts of the law, which determine its validity, but rather the fact that it has been made into law by the proper authority. See www.wikipedia.org/wiki/Decisionism and: Carl Schmitt: *Politische Theologie: Vier Kapitel zur Lehre von der Souveränität*, München 1922.

Bohm, David. *Quantum theory*. Mahwah, 1951/New York, 1989: Prentice-Hall.
Broekman, Jan M. 1965a. Filosofie van de Kunst als Filosofie van de Ordening. In *Algemeen Nederlands Tijdschrift Voor Wijsbegeerte En Psychologie*, Nr. 2.
Broekman, Jan M. 1965b. Philosophischer Versuch über Ezra Pound [A philosophical essay on Ezra Pound]. In *Text+Kritik,*, Nr. 10/11, p. 1–11.
Broekman, Jan M. 1966. Malerei als Reflexion. In *Jahrbuch für Aesthetik und Allgemeine Kunstwissenschaft* 10: 36–65.
Broekman, Jan M. 1968. Zur Philosophie des Kubismus. In *Actes du 5me Congres International d'Esthetique*, p. 41f. Den Haag: Mouton.
Broekman, Jan M. 1974. *Structuralism: Moscow, Prague, Paris*, Synthese Library, vol. 67. Dordrecht: Reidel.
Celan, Paul. 1959. *Sprachgitter*. Frankfurt am Main: S. Fischer.
Diels, H., and W. Kranz. 1935. *Fragmente der Vorsokratiker*. Berlin: Weidmann.
Dyson, Freeman. 2015. Einstein as a Jew and a philosopher. *New York Review of Books* LXII: 8, p. 14 f.
Ehrenzweig, Anton. 1967. *The hidden order of art*. Berkeley: University of California Press.
Encamaçao, Gilda. 2007. *'Fremde Nähe' als poetisches und poetologisches Prinzip bei Paul Celan*.
Gadamer, H.-G. 1960. *Wahrheit und Methode*. Tübingen: Mohr.
Gadamer, H.-G. 1967. *Kleine Schriften II: Interpretationen*. Tübingen: Mohr.
Geertz, Cl. 1983. Local knowledge: Further essays in interpretative anthropology. In *Art as a cultural system*, p. 94 ff. New York: Basic Books.
Gehlen, A. 1960. *Zeit-Bilder*. Frankfurt am Main: Bonn.
Gimbel, Steven. 2015. *Einstein: His space and times*. New Haven: Yale University Press.
Goldstein, Sheldon. Bohmian mechanics. In *Stanford encyclopedia of philosophy*, 103 (2nd Rev. art. edition) at http://plato.stanford.edu/entries.
Greimas, A.J. 1966. *Sémantique Structurale*. Paris, Editions du Seuil, [Engl.: Structural semantics: An attempt at a method, 1983].
Greimas, A.J. and François Rastier. 1968. The interaction of Semiotic constraints. In *Yale French Studies*, Vol. 41, pp. 86–106.
Hawking, Stephen and L. Mlodinow. 2010. *The grand design*. New York: Bantam Books.
Heisenberg, Werner. 1969. *Der Teil und das Ganze. Gespräche im Umkreis der Atomphysik* [The part and the whole. Conversations on atomic physics]. München: R. Piper.
Herbert, R. 2009. Godfather of the modern? *The New York Review of Books* LVI:13.
Kahnweiler, Daniel H. 1920. *Der Weg zum Kubismus* [The road towards Cubism]. Stuttgart: Delphin-Verlag.
Kahnweiler, Daniel H. 1947. *Juan Gris; his life and work*. Paris/London: H. N. Abraham.
Karpeles, Eric. 2008. *Paintings in proust. A visual companion to 'In Search of Last Time'*. London: Thames & Hudson.
Kevelson, Roberta. 1988. *The law as a system of signs*. London/New York: Plenum Press.
Luhmann, N. 1984. *Soziale Systeme. Grundriß einer allgemeinen Theorie*. Frankfurt/M: Suhrkamp.
Merleau-Ponty, M. 1966. Le Doute de Cézanne [Cézanne's Doubt] (1945). In *Sens et non-sens*. Paris: Nagel.
Ogden, C.K., and I.A. Richards. 1923. *The meaning of meaning. A study of the influence of language upon thought and of the science of symbolism*. London: Kegan Paul, Trench, Trubner.
Peirce, Ch. S. 1958. *The collected papers of Charles Sanders Pierce*, ed. Charles Hartshorne and Paul Weiss, vols. I–VI; 1931–1935, ed. Arthur W. Burks, vols. VII–VIII. Cambridge, MA: Harvard University Press.
Peirce, Charles Sanders. 1998. On the algebra of logic: A contribution to the philosophy of notation. *American Journal of Mathematics* 7, 1885; Also in: Nathan Houser and Christian Koesel (Eds) of The Peirce Edition Project, *The essential Peirce. Selected philosophical writings*, 2 Vols. Bloomington: Indiana University Press.
Rishel, J.J., and K. Sachs. 2009. *Cézanne and beyond*. New Haven/London: Philadelphia Museum of Art/Yale University Press.

Rishel, J.J. 2012. Cézanne, Virgil, Poussin. In *Gauguin, Cézanne, Matisse. Visions of Arcadia*, ed. J.J. Rishel. London/New Haven: Yale University Press/Philadelphia Museum of Art.
Rotenberg, Joel (Ed.). 2005. *The Lord Chandos letter and other writings. Introduction by Banville, John.* New York: The New York Review of Books.
Roudinesco, Elisabeth. 2009. *Jacques Lacan, Esquisse d'une Vie, Histoire d'un Système de Pensée*, ed. Fayard. Paris: Ed. La Pochothèque.
Schmitt, Carl. 1922. *Politische Theologie: Vier Kapitel zur Lehre von der Souveränität.* München: Duncker & Humblot.
Shiff, R. 2009. Lucky Cézanne (Cézanne Tychique). In *Cézanne and beyond*, ed. J.J. Rishel and K. Sachs. New Haven/London: Philadelphia Museum of Art, Yale University Press.
Signac, Paul. 1979. *D'Eugène Delacroix au néo-impressionisme* (1899). Paris: H. Floury.
Teubner, G. (ed.). 1988. *Autopoietic law: A new approach to law and society.* Berlin/New York: W. de Gruyter.
Teubner, G. 1989. *Recht als autopoietisches System* [Law as an autopoietic system]. Frankfurt am Main: Suhrkamp.
Wittgenstein, Ludwig. 1953. *Philosophical investigations*. Oxford: Blackwell.

Chapter 5
Partitions

Can one think and speak outside of and at distance from the master—master discourse? The answer is a forceful: "*no*", perhaps followed by a "we can't", which might express the feeling of a shortcoming that is our fate. We cannot unfold our capabilities for articulation beyond the boundaries of the particle story.[1] That feeling of an overall limitation is reinforced by the leading thought of this chapter: *partitioning is a powerful operation of the human mind that reigns over life in the sign pool*—it reigns *in*wards during the many travels into our psyche, and *out*wards during our explorations of social life-forms.

1 Particles and Wholeness

1.1 The Power of Partitioning

That partitioning power is ours when we answer whatever question comes up or whatever challenge we are confronted with. Analysis and its partitioning seems to come before judgment: their naturalness is self-evident. We substantiate when we think and do not consider in what sense it is merely a *form* of our thinking—on the contrary, we consider the form as in essence *our thinking itself*. The natural appearance of that form conceals a wealth of possibilities for articulation: we divide,

[1]As L. Wittgenstein wrote in view of the boundaries of logic, in a sense remarkably near to Ch. S. Peirce: "We want to *understand* something that is already in plain view. For *this* is what we seem in some sense not to understand" in: *Philosophical Investigations*, 1953, Par. 89. Peirce formulated: "... that rare faculty, the faculty of seeing what stares one in the face, just as it presents itself, unreplaced by any interpretation, unsophisticated by any allowance for this or for that supposed modifying circumstance". In: *2nd Harvard Lecture 1903, The Essential Peirce,* Vol. II, Op. Cit, p 147.

J.M. Broekman, *Meaning, Narrativity, and the Real*,
DOI 10.1007/978-3-319-28175-9_5

separate, compartmentalize, explain, oppose, differentiate, split, cut and slice, disjoint and even alienate: they are all together partitions.

1.2 Partitioning and the "I"

A deeper and more fundamental partitioning is exposed in phenomenology, in Husserl's characterization of the Kantian "I": the "Ich-Spaltung" [the splitting of the Ego]. Various remarks illustrate the self-evidence and importance of the partition(ing) concept:

1. Partitions were already characterized (in Chap. 2) as a foundation for philosophy and for phenomenology in particular.
2. An all-important attitude-change[2] expressed the layered character of language and a seemingly unlimited multiplicity of meaning.
3. The latter reaches far beyond the boundaries of the meaning of a single word or any other unit of expressivity (such as a sentence) in a language or a language family. In general, meanings reach beyond those boundaries, as we see how they can be partitioned off in the innermost regions of the human psyche.
4. The intimate proximity of thinking and partitioning is a strong *sign* of the fact that the unity of body and soul is a basic human property. It is as if a *partition* between body and soul emphasizes the *wholeness* of a human being. In other words: the separation of the two possesses the power to experience them as a whole.
5. Two thoughts dominate: (a) the unbroken dominancy of the *particle*-concept and its master—master discourse, both guiding the process of partitioning, and (b) a relatively undefined concept of '*wholeness*' created by all partition genres. Those two are continuously intertwined in the process of granting meaning to totalities as well as to parts and particles.

1.3 Wholeness and the Particle

One can observe a remarkable relationship in the process of partitioning between the concepts of a particle on the one hand and of a totality (or the philosophical idea of holism) on the other. Their proximity, a major mark of our thinking, surprises and stimulates us to obtain further insights in the concept of meaning.

"*Partitions unify*", one could say. An unfolding energy of meaning correlates with this penchant. The thought that partitioning has a unifying power is because there are no parts that do not come from somewhere. A part is always part of a total, which in its turn may be or may become a part of some other whole. A musician is

---

[2] The often-quoted original German expression "Einstellungsänderung" is intended here.

part of an orchestra, the totality, which is part of a larger geographical region—musical life in a cultural and often also geographical region, and finally all these totalities are parts of culture. So are molecules in the root of a plant, which is as a totality itself a part of a landscape, a totality that is, as a part itself, part of life on earth.[3] Philosophers see partitioning indeed as the division of a *totality* into its *components* to detect, on a scientific basis, the participating musician or the growing roots. They often underestimate the importance of the fact that a part always has a totality as its ancestor, so that a totality belongs to the history of a part. It does not mean that 'a totality' is exhausted or evanishes after partitionings. There are always different parts, which in their turn and in another attitude will be recognized as belonging to other totalitiess. But, on the other hand, philosophers seldom pay attention to the ways individual components *create* the specific meaning of a totality. They make indeed an exception in the case of a *logical* division of a *genre* and its sorts, so that the body and its members, such as hands, legs or fingers are a different partition than cultural forms like the Greek, the Romanticists, the Left-Wing voters, etc. Each direction (from part to totality or *vice versa*) constitutes in itself a parallel to a major partitioning, which is repeated at every moment of human life in the Occidental world: the partitioning between a 'You' and a 'Me', between two individuals separately profiled, notwithstanding their often-common culture and education. That partitioning is a continuous creation of meaning, which seemingly never ends and—above all—a social phenomenon perceived as natural. *What* is partitioned (*totality*) determines the characteristics of *parts* as the totality's acknowledged, determined and meaningful components. The parts result from the partitioning of a totality; a totality seems to precede any partition. Does that view deceive us?

There exists, philosophically speaking, a variety of meaning-determinations—a variety that intensifies with the multiple attitudes producing specific layers of language (professional, artificial, formal etc). Their unfolding is complex. But during this precious process, it becomes clear how powerfully and at how many levels of articulation the partitioning fixates. That fixation feeds our passion for the particle, because the latter became understood as a sign for correctness and justifiability. The latter are a foundation for meaning—it is as if there is no meaning at all without a successful fixation, which always takes place in the shadow of a totality. The

[3] Read a consideration of the Swiss painter Paul Klee (1879–1940) in which he underpins the basics of his painting activity: *Exercise* on Monday, July 3, 1922, [German-English transl. JMB]: "Die Organisierung der Verschiedenheiten zur Einheit": "The organization of differences into a unity, the unification of organs into an organism was, in all its variations, always the purpose of our theoretical research.

For instance: we see everyday, every hour, human bodies, and perceive them either as a totality (for short: a human) or as a composition of head, torso, arm, leg.

As a totality one calls this a synthetic view, as organization, an analytical. The final result is the same: simply human—only the attitude is different.

The analytical attitude is profitable because it enables us to know the parts as they are, and their coherence. Each work is, however, not a priori a product, not a work that *is*, but in the first place genesis, a work that *is becoming*. No work is a priori determined, but each work begins somewhere amidst motives and grows beyond the various organs towards an organism."

See: Paul Klee: *Das Bildnerische Denken*, [Pictorial Thinking] Basel/Stuttgart 1964, p. 449.

Ancient Greek spoke about the *Holon*. When we *perform speech acts*, the totality that conditions and characterizes each act bears the name 'language'. When we *behave*, the totality that characterizes each action within our behavioral pattern is called 'nature', whereby we make its laws relate to, for example, Newtonian ideas or quantum mechanics. When we consider what *is*, the totality that determines our considerations and judgments is called 'being' in naïve-natural language. What do we learn here?

As was said, there are two directions in any thought formation: one is from the totality to the parts or the components, another from the parts or the components to a totality. Both directions intertwine, and there is clearly no hierarchy among them: the two change continuously. It is fascinating to ask whether it is correct to say that a major tendency in our contemporary thinking is to take automatically the path from part to totality and not from totality to part. In other words: *do we come to an understanding of a whole/totality other than along the ground lines of the particle story?*

1.4 A Coagulation of Parts

Any whole seems to be a coagulation of parts. We experience again (a) the unbroken dominancy of the *particle*-concept and its master—master discourse supporting the process of partitioning, and (b) the emphasis on a relatively undefined concept of '*wholeness*' as the outcome of all sorts of partitionings. The two are intertwined in the process of granting meaning to totalities and to parts.

But this description itself is also just a fragment of a larger totality, for which we have no other words than 'nature', 'history' or even 'life'. The two above insights (described as dominancy and relativity) seem to be interrupted, distorted, and fragmented according to what can be perceived and what not. Neither nature nor human history develops along clearly visible and harmoniously designed lines. Hence the strong desire to see life unfolding gradually, from the simple towards the complex, from a part to the totality and carefully guided through the disquietudes of life and nature. That is exactly what the master—master discourse brings. A continuously unstable equilibrium among living forms justifies its guidance; the picture of that discourse in its entirety displays an all-embracing energy of interactions between organism and milieu as well as an interdependency of meanings.

But one should consider that those developments comprise exclusively components of theoretical and artificial character. Theoretical constructions on man and nature were seldom in concordance; one would rather say that since our eighteenth century the two were never in unison. A causal theory about man and nature encountered great skepticism even in our twenty-first century. The question of how the two above-mentioned lines expand (one representing the particle story, the other the concept of a totality) is not posed in vain.

Modern painting, fragmentarily described in the preceding chapter, illustrates the unfolding from parts to a totality and vice versa, as well as the careful consideration of whether, in what ways, or in how far-reaching manner a painter should fixate his thoughts and perceptions. Would a painting not be an ideal 'totality' and the brushstroke an ideal 'part'—if not a counterpart? But that is too simple: any painting has parts that do clearly show in what ways the parts are managed, and other regions where this is not so clearly the case. Pointillism, to mention an example, illustrates that consciously constructed parts of paint, placed to influence our vision to direct itself to contextual, equally constructed parts, never leads via straight lines of perception and/or causal vision to the painting as a whole. On the contrary: feelings of randomly spread attention for combining colors or paint may dominate. This is not at the surface of Cézanne's paintings; we characterized his brushstrokes because deep in those strokes was performed what the principles of cubism later brought to the fore. The strokes were, in the high days of his art, partitioning miniatures of the painting itself, the totality incorporated in the parts. Frequency, direction and interlinings are seldom perceived separately. To speak about parts, particles, regions or fragments that introduce in painting a notion of totality, is perhaps solely a linguistic tradition or a specific form of articulation.

The constitution of a meaning does not depend upon one specific point of departure but upon our recognition that the particle is a constitutive element *in both directions* and never via a straight line of unfolding. We thus conclude that in approaches to a whole as exhibited in 'meaning holism', a number of issues must be left to further analysis:

(a) The particle is predominantly a *common component*. That feature creates the possibility of deciding about meaning differently from when it is considered as an individual, unique and solo element, as is the case in any one-to-one relationship between word and meaning.
(b) The particle story and its master—master discourse overpowers the entire process of meaning formation as *a consequence of partition(ing)*. If partitioning unites, as was suggested before, then the unification and striving towards any form of holism is marked by the overreaching discourse. Each case that comes to the fore will demonstrate, in whatever variation, that it is a component of the above-mentioned story.
(c) There can*not be any meaning* without the particle-protecting master—master discourse. The power of being master over all masters reaches deep into cosmological dimensions; cultural patterns and key stories in various cultures will always illustrate the position and power of partitioning as well as the eminent role of the particle-idea/concept in world history. Even if we study the basic plots of that universal story pattern, we cannot escape from the overwhelming influence of the necessity to think in term of particles and partitioning.[4]
(d) Each and every idea of *'a whole'* is in this perspective determined by the acceptance of the idea of *'a particle'*. But can one discuss the existence of the 'particle' at all? Einstein, Heisenberg or later Bohm debated that question in the

[4] See Christopher Booker: *The Seven Basic Plots. Why we Tell Stories.* Continuum, London/New York 2004.

context of quantum mechanics. They considered its artificial character and the insight that a particle could just be the creation of a linguistic tradition or a specific form of articulation. It could be one of the few essential questions to ask one self eye-to-eye before venturing to explore thoughts, to unfold scientific thinking or to let one become inspired by philosophical sources. Are 'particle' and 'whole' compatible ideas, and what function touching the borderlines of our power of articulation has the concept of a 'whole'?

No matter what precise direction is in operation, the particle remains decisive. The concept of totality is understood as particle-dependent, one has to conclude.

2 Meaning Holism

The interdependency of the meanings of a word was in mainstream twentieth century philosophy given the name "meaning holism". Willard V. Quine claimed in 1951[5] that a unit of significance mirrors the whole of science, so that—as Hempel had acknowledged—a specific meaning in a naïve-natural language will be reflected in the totality of its relationships to all other words and sentences in a language. Jackman explains this in 2014 while writing that an interdependence of words usually follows from the meaning of each word (or sentence) being tied to its use, as Wittgenstein had already formulated.[6] He thus defines 'Meaning Holism' as "the understanding of the determinants of the meanings of our terms" which are "interconnected in a way that leads a change in the meaning of any single term to produce a change in the meanings of each of the rest".[7]

A general presupposition in this particular holism is the interconnection of words. Each word carries its own meaning, so the issue is in what ways these meanings interrelate in a language.[8] Jackman explicitly mentions a 1:1 relation between meaning and word: "the function from the determinants of meaning to the meanings themselves is one-to-one". This needs more explanation, because "not only does any change to a word's meaning require some change in the determinants of its meaning, but (…) any change to the determinants of a word's meaning must [also] produce a change to its meaning." There are apparently no single and one-directional relations here. This will "require something more like a 'direct' argument, since it is unlikely that one could argue that the function from use to meaning had to be one-to-one without some sort of substantial account of how use determined

[5] See above, Chap. 3.

[6] L. Wittgenstein: *Philosophical Investigations*, Op. Cit., Par. 43.

[7] H. Jackman: "Meaning Holism" in: *Stanford Encyclopedia of Philosophy*, © *<hjackman@yorku.ca>* 2014.

[8] L. Wittgenstein has given this issue many thoughts. See his *Philosophical Investigations*, Op. Cit., Par. 120: "You say: the point isn't the word, but its meaning, and you think of the meaning as a thing of the same kind as the word, though also different from the word. Here the word, there the meaning. The money, and the cow that you can buy with it. (But contrast: money, and its use.)"

meaning."[9] If one word has more than one meaning within the totality of a language, then that word is noticed as many times as a word carrying a different meaning. The meanings of all words in a language are interdependent—that idea is the essence of meaning holism. As a consequence, the latter denies a rigid *individualistic* as well as an exclusively *social* view of meaning.

But we add that *the very act of displaying interdependency is also a form of partitioning*. In other words: interdependency is subjected to the master—master discourse. It creates, however, a more complicated picture of how relations between parts (or particles) and totality unfold. But the determinative influence of the particle story and its discourse remains. Two-way directions become multiple, various crossings among meanings are made possible, a patterning of meanings instead of one-to-one relations appear realistic. Interdependency needs to provide a more precise knowledge of WHAT *is interdependent with* WHAT: 'particle' and 'total' are only two answers to those manifold "what's" in question.

Insightful knowledge of components seems therefore necessary. Parts or particles on the one hand, and a totality or wholeness on the other must be treated as equal and identical in view of the realization of the meaning-concept. Interdependence—basic for meaning holism—tends to display only its surface structure; its deep structure remains mostly in the dark. The concept of a "text" and of an "interdependent 'word-meaning' complex" are differently defined but treated as equal. It means that *the semiotics of a text and the semiotics of meaning-holistic entities are considered equal and treated in parallel.* Theories of meaning holism have hitherto not paid any attention to those semiotic connections. The dynamics of partition and partitioning are always a *particle-related basis* for a discussion about holism—even if semiotics is introduced! This reaches further than explaining meaning and meaning-holism by referring exclusively to words in a word-language. Meaning is more than words can say or can connect with.

2.1 Quantum Thinking

The ways in which a particle determines 'its' mechanics, and (quantum) mechanics 'its' particles, are illustrated (but also restricted) by mathematical theories supporting quantum theories. Quantum mechanics predicts the behaviors of particles through its mathematics. But on that basis we do not achieve a more equivalent and higher level articulation of the world we live in, nor of its language patterns or sign-pools. The leveled character of language plays a role. We know what the theory's components are, how they are put together, and why their coherence seems to perform. We know how the information is brought in and is converted into what comes out. "The question of what kind of a world it describes, however, is controversial; there is very little agreement, among physicists and among philosophers, about

[9] H. Jackman: "Meaning Holism" in: SEP, Op. Cit., at *hjackman@yorku.ca* 2014.

what the world *is like* according to quantum mechanics", Ismael writes. "Minimally interpreted, the theory describes a set of facts about the way the microscopic world impinges on the macroscopic one, how it affects our measuring instruments, described in everyday language or the language of classical mechanics. Disagreement centers on the question of what a microscopic world, which affects our apparatuses in the prescribed manner, is, or even could be like, *intrinsically*; or how those apparatuses could themselves be built out of microscopic parts of the sort the theory describes. That is what an interpretation of the theory would provide: a proper account of what the world is like according to quantum mechanics, intrinsically and from the bottom up".[10]

One should perhaps try to describe the reason, or the multiple reasons for this gap between the qualities of our articulation of the world we live in and the refinement of the mathematical means in quantum mechanics, which inspire meaning holism. Much of the implicit discussion of this peculiar form of holism relate to what was discussed in the thirties of the last century: how far has quantum physics developed its own language, indeed beyond (although with support of) the language of mathematics, but not yet understandable in the language of the everyday, in our naïve-natural language?

2.2 *Meaning Holism Reconsidered*

One should notice in this context, that a representation of meaning holism at least does *not* mention a number of issues, which are crucial for understanding the complexity of the meaning concept. Is 'Meaning Holism' indeed a form of holism—one could ask? We dedicate a few thoughts to the main themes in that question.

(a) The often-mentioned *layered character of language* is one of the most important factors to underline the complexity of the meaning concept. An articulation's meaning will play out at an everyday-language level. But other levels, such as professional- and other group languages, may not embrace that very same meaning. Such differences deeply divide: what a logician or a mathematician articulates may not at all parallel the language level of a poet or a painter. And a humming musician means the utterances of his words at a different level than the same words mean for a judge in a Court session. Children on the school's playground have to learn and to understand utterances of other children by means of entering a complexity of meanings ascribed to words that are loudly shouted all over the place. Words and other verbal utterances have different levels—but the same is the case with sentences and related text fragments articulated via speech acts in word language and in body languages. One has furthermore to mention the different levels in speech, which parallel differences

[10] Jenann Ismael: "Quantum Mechanics" in: *SEP*, 2000/2015, Op. Cit. at *jtismael@U.Arizona.EDU*.

in levels of texts: there are surface levels and likewise deep levels active in all examples. Both are differentiated among themselves: each surface has particular depths. The depths of surface structures differ from those of deep structures. Each depth has its characteristic surface structure. Meaning is never a unison, or univocal; meaning-jumbles are involved in complex articulations. Perceiving language as a leveled phenomenon reveals extreme differentiations in articulation. A conclusion is that meanings change with the level of language, the perfection or imperfection of expression and the verbal and/or linguistic context of specific fields of articulation.

(b) The *differences of languages within a language family* are another issue to put holistic views on meaning in perspective. A word is not a word in the psychological context of all speech acts and speakers or hearers in the world. For some of them, a word is not what is considered in West-European languages as 'word'—for others it is more, for others less. And, as we will consider later in this chapter, there are words, which are not accepted in languages because they do not make conventional sense. Some appreciate the grammatical and syntactical determination of a 'word' indeed as a word, within that category even as 'the basic unit' of language. But that is not universal; it is not the case for everyone on the earth's surface! Not only locations and their subsequent history will be different and thus create different meanings, but also family ties and their history will have such an effect. All those factors create limitations, as borderlines determine the validities and the communicative power of meanings. An 'I', we will argue, is acceptable like a 'You', but an expression of ultimate closeness between them will not be expressed with the one word 'IYou'. Is it not bewildering that our thoughts and emotions are allowed to create the meaning "I and You' but not 'IYou'? To mention another example: there is no necessity to underline in today's world that not everyone on the globe has the exact and same meaning of 'peace', 'justice', equilibrium' or 'responsibility' at work in his or her sign pool. Politicians may work on that, and strive for a universal meaning of key words in a few dominant languages. There is, however, no theory of meaning that supports their strivings.

(c) The *non-translatability of languages* is another difficulty in meaning-holism. What is necessary to translate one language into another? It would take various extended theories to answer the question appropriately. That makes any one-to-one relation between meaning and word impossible. One specific feature is a deep-understandability. The latter evaluates the meaning of a word as embedded in its language, history, culture and the variety of its uses in the sign pool. Such a deep-understandability would not be conditional if one-to-one relations between word and meaning are decisive. Communication problems would never bother any translator if such a pseudo-mathematical security were the mark of meaning making. Non-translatability is decisive in the dimensions of meaning because words (to refer to just one example of linguistic and communicative components) are, together with all other means of articulation, deeply and essentially rooted in the wealth of multiplicities characterizing human culture and history.

(d) The *differences between attitudes,*[11] for instance between a naïve-natural language and all other non-naïve languages, make a meaning-holism difficult to maintain because of the fact that any one-to-one relation between word and meaning requires an extension of the traditional analytical way to acquire insight into the complexities of meaning and meaning-formation in the field of linguistic articulation. A major extension was explained in Chap. 2 where differences in attitude were described in their relation to the manifold levels of articulation. It means that learning a language only focuses on a restricted domain of expressivity: *the language-in-use idea is the sign of a larger totality of human culture.*[12] There are perhaps many ways to master the major fields of meaning within a specific culture. They accompany an acquired knowledge of linguistic means, and often become integrated in a sign pool's life. However, the various attitudes (from naïve-natural to all non-naïve) will always display differences, which sometimes cause alienation.

(e) The idea that *mastering a language is a perfect means to communicate* seems seriously doubtful if one considers the above features. Linguistic expressiveness does not serve a strictly determined set of meanings and rules of meaning-application as suggested by the idea of meaning holism. In view of the immense variety of values, norms, expectations and other basic features of human culture, there is no large-scaled sharing of beliefs, attitudes and desires upon which linguistic articulation can focus. No one could mean the same if there was not a preceding concordance to direct the necessary utterances. Truly understanding someone else is *not* solely a matter of language acquisition and the application of appropriate linguistic means.

(f) A certain tendency to emphasize *individualism* while maintaining meaning holism is not only embedded in the relations between word and meaning. It is rather the result of neglecting the time-issue in that theory. Anything at a social level changes over time, and the observation of a spreading effect presupposed in meaning holism seems not to be appropriate. A change in one element produces not always foreseeable changes in others. What meaning holism suggests is difficult to accept; if the suggestion of holism is correct, most of our terms will change their meaning daily and, expressed beyond coherence or interdependency, cause an instability in all possible sign pools. Meaning holism is not successful in explaining any social determination of meaning. It leaves the tensions between a theory of language and a social theory unsolved. It is a great credit of meaning holism—although it is a credit in the negative, a warning rather than a solution—that it provokes us to tackle the tensions between the two types of theory.

[11] For instance those maintained in most of the SEP contributions. The article written by Jackman <*hjackman@yorku.ca*> 2014 must decidedly be completed by a relevant social philosophy and a philosophy of language, including semiotics.

[12] This should block a purely technical understanding of Wittgenstein's idea pertaining to a 'meaning-in-the-use' approach in his *Philosophical Investigations,* Par. 43.

That same warning unveils any concealment about how the word functions as a form of particle thinking and as the basic unit of language. To leave that presupposition behind includes the necessity to develop a new theory of meaning. The latter will have a direct influence on our understanding of the master—master discourse and its particle story, in particular when 'holism' is reconsidered. A discourse in meaning holism is understood as a multiplication and an enlargement of the speaker-hearer structure. But the quality of a speaker-hearer relation changes when speech acts between a 'You' and a 'Me' transform their setting from dialogue to discourse. Among the changing qualities is the commonality between those partners in speech. With that change their commonality and cultural presuppositions will become visible in another light. The 'I—Thou' relationship at the basis of this very special particle of understanding will thus differ because *the partitioning of their roles in speech* changed. With such discoveries we acquire insight into issues of *partitioning related to meaning* beyond the usual presuppositions about language and particle. They also disqualify meaning holism in a philosophical sense: the holism-concept in this type of holism does not inspire any discovery, guidance or deliberation about what can be grasped *beyond* the particle story and its discourse. As a consequence, one does not approach any new, enriching thoughts on meaning.

3 Thinking Axes

A word on its own is not a word. Words are contextual by their nature. That consideration creates an ardent desire for a deeper and better perception of holism. Yet it does not deliver any particular insight to help us proficiently focus on the axes of meaning research. There are many topics to profile that research, but one does not find an answer that makes us expand our expressiveness *beyond* everyday language formation, which seems an issue of importance in our context.

3.1 Five Topics

There are at least five topical considerations to characterize our meaning-research as it was hitherto unveiled and discussed. We mention: (1) plurality in the meaning concept, (2) the multifaceted interpretation of the 'word', (3) the continuous power demonstration of the master—master discourse, (4) the tendency to understand meaning as a specific particle or as particle-related, and (5) the enticement to understand meaning through fixation.

Those topics form altogether the axes for the understanding of meaning in our days. It is true that the rich tradition and subtle methodology of what is called 'analytical philosophy' was described in the negative during our explorations. There is, on the other hand, no reason to conclude that phenomenology, structuralism, pragmatism or positivism would contribute adequately in the positive. This may lead to the wishful thought that there exists perhaps some form of *holism* which turns all negative associations in the framework of meaning research towards the positive. If that is a sign of progress in the articulation of the research, the five axes are worth keeping in mind—they appear to have their appropriate domain mostly in the cosmic phases C and D, so that the holism issue might direct us to a deeper study of meaning as related to phases A and B.[13]

MULTIPLICITY is a key word in meaning fields, because the latter is a concept deeply rooted in language: layered, leveled and full of multiple life phenomena. Life's articulation takes place in plurals and never in one singular concept or idea. Hence its dependence on attitudes and above all on attitude-change: the latter is absolutely not a source of arbitrariness in questions of meaning. Attitudes parallel (not cause) other forms of articulation (among them: linguistic), so that the plural character of expressivity seems broader than for instance the difference between phenotexts (surfaces) and genotexts (depth texts), which Shaumyan and Kristeva proposed. *To mean*, one concludes, is therefore in the first place *to engage in a level of articulation.*

THE 'WORD' is subject to elaborate considerations. Its strongest position is when it is declared to be the basic unit of language. But how far is that correct? In the naïve-natural languages of everyday life, it seems clear. One can hardly imagine or exploit a language and/or linguistic communication without words. But apart from an element a word is also a sign of an encompassing articulation in process. That element withstands the one-sided and instrumentalist conclusion about the word as an independent entity. The suggestion of identity between the word and the particle is catastrophic for any conceptualization of meaning. It has a one-to-one relation between word and meaning as its consequence—as meaning holism demonstrated.

THE MASTER—MASTER DISCOURSE and its *more geometrico* thought pattern are closely related. The two types of discourse are counterparts, which have their foundation exclusively in the particle concept. One could venture the thought that the latter type of thinking had a shorter duration in the ages of Occidental thought and was a more stable and powerful patterning of meaning within the boundaries of the first. Thanks to the ongoing process of globalization the master—master discourse bridges more and more language differences. It exercises a power beyond the norms and articulations, beyond the boundaries of natural languages, and constructs non-naïve natural (such as scientific, economic, IT, political) languages to realize its purpose of partitioning and particle dominance. The overwhelming power of this discourse, mainly dominating—as have we already formulated—the cosmic phases C and D, should be a point of departure for a socio-cultural analysis of twenty-first century Occidental culture on a world scale.

TO UNDERSTAND MEANING AS A PARTICLE is one of the major building blocks of that powerful philosophy. Our preceding pages illustrated through the theory called 'meaning holism' the ways meaning in the course of the last centuries became s individualized (from the seventeenth century on) and more or less identified with the word. The basis for all this was the desire to understand meaning as a fixated and

[13] For the distinction between phases A through D, see Chap. 1.

exchangeable entity that functions as a stable component in social patterns. Exploring this interpretation favors the feeling that arbitrariness in cases of meaning discussion could be suppressed. Security pertaining to values and norms resulted, and the probabilities of fulfilling expectations in social life supported pragmatism and instrumentalism on a large scale.

Meaning fixations have indeed a wide-ranging effect. It resulted from the breaches of silence at the borderlines of cosmic silence. If meanings are fixated, they do not show or react upon their process character. It has become a sign of intolerable weakness and uncertainty if someone in our Occidental twenty-first century does not directly express an understanding and an assignment of meaning, and instead seeks attention for the fact that every meaning is ultimately an element of a universal unfolding, which takes place at the very moment in which the question is uttered. Understanding meaning as a particular fixation robs our contemporary theories of meaning of any connotation of universality. Is this one of the legal-philosophical issues for our maintenance of global concepts like 'justice', 'peace', or 'humanity'? Indeed: in the midst of and at the hottest point of such political and juridical considerations must be shouted loudly: "Meaning is not a Thing!" or: "Meaning is not a *Some*-thing!" It seems difficult to keep in mind that meaning is an articulation offered for active participation: he, who does not take part, will die. Does taking part mean: partitioning?

This leads back to the insight that any theory of meaning has to be a dynamic theory, a process analysis, and tackle complicated and multilayered meaning articulations. A repudiation of one-to-one relations between meaning and reality, and in particular to their power of fixation, is necessarily a sign of respect for the multi-leveled character of the rich and all but global variety of meanings.

The five topics we mentioned have one decisive feature in common—a feature that forms the axes of any theory of meaning. That feature is, however, difficult to express in conclusive words, because it should be words characterizing diverse processes within one meaningful articulation. Hence the suggestion to formulate the feature at stake as: *partition(ing) unifies, partition(ing) fixates*—two meanings are, at a first reading, contradictory in a complex way. Meaning *is created* in partition, although often with a result that could not be strictly intended, because meaning must always be the meaning of a thing, of a some-thing or of something else we do not fully grasp—all of these go always with a particle, which functions as the source of security and stability.

In our globalizing Occident, the particle is the carrier of meaning since we know or are conscious of our peculiar awareness. Does the concept of 'holism' express and support this, or does it contain meanings against this fixation by the particle story? The two axes of the meaning process might, as a consequence, appear in another light: *holism* and *evolution*. But how do they appear in what light? Could holism be viewed as a new understanding of meaning, and: can we locate meaning in the evolution from cosmic silence to hyper- articulation?[14]

[14] As accentuated in the cosmic fazes A through D in Chap. 1.

4 Bohmian Holism

So: could any form of holism be viewed as the path to a new understanding of meaning? Quantum mechanics, in particular the version of David Bohm, is important in this context. Statements of the Copenhagen School were constantly in the background while he developed his new quantum insights. But also Bohm did not entirely deny and diminish particle thinking. The role of the particle in physical theories always raises the question whether particles 'really exist'. Ontological implications of the particle-concept contain ideas about holism; should physics, instead of philosophy, design the road from the particle to the whole? This road map was initiated in Bohm's observation that wave functions are not a simple mathematical entity. They are a real physical presence, he stated, and completed this view by the suggestion that all particles are guided by a force field. So, when according to the Copenhagen School there 'are' no particles without our measuring instruments, he concluded: there 'are' no particles without their force field. Who says 'particle' says 'field'. This statement dissolves any partitioning between existence and perception—a cherished philosophical theme—because the 'field' takes over some of the roles perception fulfill. In the words of, but in contrast to the spirit of the Copenhagen School: we can indeed raise questions about nature reliably 'when we are not perceiving, observing, experimenting or simply looking'. Remarks about the force field can be transformed into a thinking that might end in a new holism: the force field can function as a quantum potential, which is guiding particles along certain path through space. Physical experiments and their mathematical theories lead to the insight that we should not be too fascinated by the particle, because force fields illustrate a *non-locality* of particles. The accent on their non-locality could be understood as a first step in the direction of an insight into a holism that reaches beyond the master—master discourse.

A drive called "return to the particle" is everywhere essential. But phenomena should not be reduced to constitutive particles or components. Bohm opposes the idea that human knowledge pertains to ever-static, never-changing entities—neither in space-time nor in quantum states or in any other appearance. He is consequently opposed to the Cartesian, the *more-geometrico* or the master—master discourse position as a foundation for analysis and a description of reality. With this rejection he is against any partitioning between reality and thought, which leads to a general philosophical view and to holism in particular. An undivided whole with its implicate order is the theme of one of his publications in 1980. In this key text he criticizes his colleagues in physics: "there seems to be an unshakable faith among physicists that either such particles, or some other kind yet to be discovered, will eventually make possible a complete and coherent explanation of everything".[15] Atoms, particles, subatomic particles, quantum states and the like are all understood in terms of autonomous and independent sub-totalities that ground discourses like those mentioned before. This position is deeply philosophical and envisages a road

[15] David Bohm: *Wholeness and the Implicate Order*, London 1980, pp. 173, 11, 81.

to holism. Holism is a great challenge to understanding human knowledge and its all-embracing, globalizing culture.

4.1 Holism in Debate

Debates on holism illustrate new trends in physics, in particular quantum physics, for deepening a theory of meaning. The contribution of quantum theory to meaning cannot be underestimated. This leads to the insight that *quantum theory is decisive for linguistics and language articulation*, the more so because meaning is the most important concept in that realm of articulation. Discussions about the Holon only confirm this view. They do so at two levels: at the level of traditional philosophy, and at the level of intertwining philosophy and physics.

Any concept of holism has various dimensions, and the ways it is criticized and catalogued in Occidental philosophy of the twentieth century seems extremely meaningful. When we think through its axes, we encounter holism as a powerful idea filled with contrasts to traditional forms of thought. This is particularly clear when Bohm introduces his concept of *holomovement*—prioritizing the Holon as the dominant feature of "all there is". "… in its totality, the holomovement is not limited in any specifiable way at all. It is not required to conform to any particular order, or to be bounded by any particular measure. Thus, the holomovement is undefinable and immeasurable."[16] Those words are powerful and do not have any power at all. They seem powerful within an unknown totality of cosmic character, and powerless once the borderlines of the master—master discourse are exceeded. The concept of a *whole* remains central in epistemology and philosophy. Yet, there are serious philosophical problems about the idea of a 'holomovement'. Bohm wrote a commentary on it 10 years after and concluded that the expression functions as the most general form of the dynamics of nature, its processes of change and development: "All things found in the unfolded, explicate order emerge from the holomovement in which they are enfolded as potentialities and ultimately they fall back to it."[17] He thus describes a dynamic causality in which the holomovement seems to be a factor within a broader process of unfolding. This is remarkably parallel with what was developed in '*significs*' during the first years of the twentieth century. Lady V. Welby considered in her 1903 publication on *Meaning*[18] how the expression '*significance*' could function as a holistic concept embracing *motion* as well as *sense* and *meaning*. She does so at the basis of what in those years was explained by Husserl as *attitude change*: "we must raise language, as we have ourselves risen, from the so-called instinctive to the volitional and fully rational plane." This could find its place

---

[16] David Bohm: *Wholeness*, Op. Cit., p. 191.

[17] D. Bohm: "A New Theory of the Relationship of Mind and Matter", in: *Philosophical Psychology*, Op. Cit., p. 272.

[18] Lady V. Welby: *What is Meaning? Studies in the Development of Significance*, London 1903, Ed. Bibliolife 2012, p. 50 ff.

in an elaborate qualification of attitude-change, but also in a broad appreciation of the 'kitsch' of many holistic interpretations and the equally powerful attempts to put the dominance of the *more geometrico* thought patterns in sciences and philosophy in perspective. We have to find out whether that is the case in Bohm's theory.

There is every reason to explore within the framework of *traditional philosophy*: while thinking the *whole,* one inevitably seems to express the *elements,* which constitute our speech and knowledge concerning that *whole*—and no more than that. Holistic considerations do not support this type of constitution. An often complex and confusing discussion results: individualism is seen as the key and also as the opposite of holism. Reductionism is applied as an analytical form for our epistemological operations. Holism is thus interpreted as a constant but not very realistic remainder. From the standpoint of individualism and reductionism, holism becomes more or less identical with vagueness: metaphysically and in concrete analyses. That identification transforms holism into the often ridiculed prophecy that we will, at last, be led out of the Unholy Land of the Renaissance heritage, i.e.: the codified *more geometrico* thought-patterning.

Beyond this philosophical battle lurks the truth that philosophy in its struggle to express and to articulate reality is always confronted with antithetic metaphysical perspectives. They occur in all stages of the history of the human mind in Occidental culture. Such a formulation seems at first sight most satisfactory. But the formula is too unspecific and too shallow. There is one basic question in the debate concerning the relevance of the concept, which is not retraceable in that formula: does Holism cover a general human experience? In other words: do we ever experience 'the whole'; do we ever experience this 'whole' in a naïve-natural attitude and its layer of language articulation? Or do we rather experience 'the whole' as the totality of all the elements of our complex relational patterns? Such questions concern philosophy in general, long before quantum physics and in particular quantum mechanics came to the fore. Reductionism is one the most outstanding among them.

4.2 Reductionism

Reductionism seems generally accepted in our Occidental world. A holistic perspective remains in the background. Its approach has hitherto not played an important role in science and philosophy, but one should be aware that reductionism accepts holism on its own terms. This is a challenge and a warning that if reality is understood analytically and as a reductionist option, one should nevertheless remain aware of the original and persistent totality that forms the basis of any analytical attempt. Several arguments are important in this regard. They are quite concrete arguments, which dominate in laboratories, hospitals and industrial research rather than in a philosopher's mind.

The main argument is that we should understand the reductionist approach as a *method* and not as an articulation of the *ontological state of reality.* This is grounded in the human experience that the totality is not observable: 'you cannot observe everything at the same time and as a whole'. That is the reductionist argument. Cultural patterns as well as scientific demands make us selective in our observation. We have to make choices, we have to differentiate and to weigh; we are unable to observe the whole without these preceding analytical operations. The totality of reality, or: reality as a totality, is supposed to be the background of all analytical activity. But it remains rather an idea than a reality.

It is as if the reductionist argument suggests that an ontological foundation is given together with the concept of wholeness. That particular notion of totality is not interpreted as a concept in its own right, since it is regarded as not being operative: a totality is in this view the metaphysical and ontological *background* for reductionism and analytic epistemology. The background and praxis of science or philosophy are, however, different. Our everyday praxis shows clearly that this partitioning is neither naive nor harmless: the recognition of the holistic argument and its characterization as a founding ontology serves for legitimating a large number of reductionist operations. Modern science and technology demonstrate this function quite clearly. Yet it leads even to ethical approval of an unlimited technological development in terms of reductionism and of analyticity. That is not only perceivable in the sciences and technology but also in human sciences, the law or politics. The reductionist argument is often transformed into a more primitive statement that goes as follows: "We can be, and have to be, reductionist as long as we acknowledge that there is the totality which transcends our analytical and reductionist approach!"

4.3 Thinking Risks

An interesting variation on this theme is the idea that reductionism is and should be an *accepted risk* in science and technology, in law and philosophy. The story of the great technological successes in the last century of our civilization is the story of what is called an *accepted risk*. The role of pharmacology in medicine and psychiatry, the recognition of biological factors in psychiatric illnesses, the world-wide acceptance of the doctrine of human rights are in essence examples of the manifestation of this *risk*. Scientific mechanisms of partitions and com-partitions do not prevent us from 'knowing' that there are always other elements, other types of observation and other scientific and philosophical categories, *but* we have 'chosen' in favor of the reductionist approach, and cannot change this value orientation arbitrarily. So we remain in what is called the 'position of the observer', and know that this position is implicitly a choice, a value. We continue to speak about 'perspectives' on reality, about discovering the 'new' and about analyzing our own 'references' in legal and scientific speech acts, despite our rejection of any pretention to come to ontological foundations and a holistic appreciation of all these operations.

It is true that *experience* is involved in those formulations. It is also true that the experience of the scientist, the technologist, the lawyer and the philosopher may result in underlining the qualification of reductionism as a *methodological* approach only. This implies indeed an ontological modesty with regard to holism. But, as has already been said, this modesty functions as a justification for an unlimited technological exploitation of reality. A warning was already formulated in the writings of so-called 'holist philosophers'. Besides that, we can perfectly well conceptualize reality in reductionist operations *and at the same time forget* that such operations do not imply any ontological foundation of reality! In other words: technological results tend to suggest having implemented ontological definitiveness. They tend to present themselves as possessing a sufficient ontological basis concerning reality. The holistic argument has developed its most powerful rhetoric against this type of analytical pragmatism. Was it successful?

4.4 Parts and Wholes

Another general philosophical argument tells us about the debate between holism and reductionism, which refers to the pertinent observation that any human existence demonstrates most clearly how 'there are' parts and wholes. This differentiation brings certain dominances into life, and it is said that these dominances are only understandable and acceptable within the framework of reductionism.[19]

This problem of the parts and the whole does not legitimate a mechanistic monism or vitalism. It is of their essence, J. C. Smuts has suggested, that all forms of being strive towards totality.[20] The most concrete totality is in his eyes the human person, either in the Kantian sense—the moral personality—or in the Hegelian sense—as the person in the State. But is this enough?

Modern anthropological investigations do not take that direction. The dominance of the State or of Morality is not so effective in this regard as, for instance, the question whether human life should be regarded as entirely or partially identical or isomorphic with animal life. The concrete question would be: to what extent is the biological concept of life a determinant of human life? The philosophical problem here is that those dominances of particular life-structures are embedded in a reductionist view *before* they can obtain their final expression in scientific research. This

[19] Consider an example: a *syndrome* in medicine suggests wholeness and identity. And it suggests a natural ontology: it is as if the syndrome is a natural entity, specific for the state of health of the patient. That state of health has, according to our daily experiences and patterns of thought, only to be determined by medical investigations. But any observer of the dialogue between the medical practitioner and his patient can easily come to the conclusion that the patient is regarded as the 'owner', that is the 'bearer' of a syndrome. Those two components of meaning might precede as well as determine the application of the concept. The holistic notion of 'the totality of human life' remains present in this concept, but has already been given a reductionist meaning. That meaning is the subject of a semantic transformation, which does not appear at the surface structure of medical terminology. The conclusion is that a medical scientist, or even a general practitioner, does *not* refer to 'human life as a whole'.
See: Jan M. Broekman: *Intertwinements of Law and Medicine*, Leuven UP 1996, p. 173ff, Ch. IV;—Id.: "Holism, Law, and the Principle of Expressibility" in *Rechtstheorie,* Vol. 21,4. 1990, p. 419.

[20] J. C. Smuts: *Holism and Evolution*, New York 1946.

is a challenge to the concept of holism itself. Is holism not completely dependent on the reductionist conceptuality of science and philosophy? One could even imagine the following argument:

'Holism is in itself a form of reductionism, namely in so far as the differentiation, the dominance and the structural account of these processes is denied or reduced in favor of the concept of totality'. The reductionist component of holism is clearly observable in this argument. Totality is an abstract concept, which is reductionist according to its own account.

Let us still stay on a general level of thought. Love, food, sex, tiredness, tension, or sleep, are important as totalities of human life. But the reductionist argument was that we could always trace some forms of dominance in these phenomena. Reality is understood according to them. The biological factors of love, food, sex, tiredness, tension, or sleep are *explanatory dominances*. A holistic view *underestimates* them and this view does not do justice to the factors involved. Holism does not *break down* its own presuppositions and its proper framework, and it does not lead to an articulation of its imperfection, its negativity, or its proper incompleteness. This observation already leads to a conclusion and a hypothesis.

The relation between wholes and parts cannot be described in terms of holism or of reductionism.[21] Holism and reductionism are to be considered as mutually supplementary views. The necessary intertwinement of the two annihilates a choice between them—an opposition between them as well as the reductionist binary situation in which philosophical debates tend to become entangled.

4.5 Metaphor and Metonymy

The opposition between holism and reductionism implies a most striking parallel with the opposition between two well-known literary figures: *metaphor* and *metonymy.* The holist thought pattern is directed to metaphorical thinking, the reductionist to metonymic thinking. The first tends to contextualize the facts of life, the second to hypostasize and to ontologize them. But holistic and metaphorical thinkers explore the experience that things are always different according to the relevant type of discourse. Changes of discourse provoke different perspectives. So there exist no such things as a first meaning or a first and founding discourse, as for instance Charles S. Peirce may have had in mind.

This raises problems in connection with the holistic thesis: reductionists tend to understand 'the whole' or 'the totality' as a *first meaning.* Is this acceptable, or does one have to transcend the reductionist view in stressing metaphorically that 'the whole' or 'the totality' *precedes* meaning? In this case, it would seem obvious that the only possibility for us to understand holism in a reductionist tradition is to concede that the problem of precedence is a problem of *time and causality.* The constant

[21] See already E. Husserl: *Logische Untersuchungen*, 1900/01, II, Op. Cit., Par. 22–25, on *Parts and Wholes*.

interplay of arguments pro and contra holism or reductionism leads us erroneously into the process of hypostatizing such a dualism. But the dualism is not so much an ontological problem as it is a problem of metaphor. Dualisms belong, generally speaking, to the realm of narrative structures, which are developed for scientific and philosophical purposes, for instance particular and identifiable articulations and conceptualizations of reality. The problem of dualism is redundant within the discussion of the holist thesis. A metaphorical element can never be excluded here. The challenge of this discussion is that one has to keep the metaphorical character alive in order *not* to transform it into a problem of causality.

The problem of 'holism' in opposition to 'reductionism' is in a deeper sense a problem of time and, one could add, of historicity. This is the more so, since holism tends to suggest general simultaneousness. It tends to deny the fact that history consists of fragments and of 'decoupages' (Foucault) and that even the stream of human consciousness and the awareness of historicity express this 'decoupage'. Phenomena and processes are, as far as their time-structure is concerned, certainly not simultaneous. The contrary seems to be the case. The functioning of vital organisms, the light of the stars that strikes us in our observation (and awakens, according to Kant, moral and esthetic feelings in humanity) as well as legal acts and law's qualifications, do by no means involve simultaneity, although that may seem to be so in everyday reality and its naive consciousness. Holism tends to forget this because of its counter-position to reductionism. It is, for that reason, in danger of becoming an a-historic vision of reality. That follows from its specific interpretation of the concept of the whole. Its philosophical consequence is clear: even our *understanding* of the holistic intention is dependent upon our 'naïve-natural', in other words: 'everyday-life'-reductionism and individualism!

There is, in this regard, a firm pattern of knowledge, which is offered as holistic and touches upon the understanding of society as well as nature. Social phenomena, but also the human body or narrative unities of discourse, are in the holistic perspective not such autonomous, proper and multi-level entities as contemporary science and philosophy would have us believe.

A general idea is that reductionism and atomism are at the end a serious threat to our contemporary culture. That argument is formulated against philosophers (such as Hayek, Rawls or Popper) who formulate their theories in terms of social contract and *more geometrico* patterns. Holism should call for invisible powers and dominions, which are impersonal entities of understanding and explanation.

The final philosophical problem of holism is apparently *not* the one, which is involved in the opposition between holism and reductionism. The problem is elsewhere, that is: the problem has another place; it is re-placed by the implicit semiotic differentiations, which surround the problem and are inherent in the problem itself. Analyticity is not enough to grasp the philosophy of holism. Neither the reductionist nor the holist approach is successful in determining the philosophy, which characterizes holism. Philosophical problems have always to do with philosophy as such, and *that* cannot be found in the traditional opposition between holism and reductionism. The *justification* of a philosophical standpoint is never identical with its *solution!* The re-placement of the problem has to become clear: holism is philosophically a problem of *representation* (Hegel, Feuerbach, Benjamin). According to Hegel, only *representation* unifies, the activity of various forms of thought on the one hand, and their criticism regarding the development of knowledge on the other. But how can we give a meaning to the concept of representation within the scope of the debate on holism?

The recapitulation of our considerations regarding this theme embraces two aspects: Holism, as it is opposed to reductionism, is in itself a reduction of any philosophy of the holon. It is this reduced meaning of holism, which is regarded as political liberalism and conservatism, as a vague notion, or as epistemologically deficient. What is more: holism as a philosophy of the holon refers to quite different problems, such as the internal structure of metaphysics and of human expressivity or human capacities to participate in the cosmic process of articulation.

5 The Quantum Challenge

David Bohm challenged already in his 1951 *Quantum Theory* the narrowness of the frame in which fundamental questions about articulating reality are envisaged.

This leads us back to what has been formulated on "Holism in Debate" several pages back. They are about intertwinements of philosophy (in particular the field of articulation) and physics (in the first place quantum mechanics). The particle and the Holon both lead to the thesis that *quantum mechanics causes deep and more complete insights in a theory of human articulation and meaning in particular.* Tensions between a holistic and a reductionist approach are caused by the limits of their exploration—limits, which by no means represent a genuine philosophical vision.

We should notice that none of the requirements, which were qualified as decisive for approaching holism are met in the preceding pages. No reductionism or any of its philosophical opponents takes into account what importance the role of the particle is given in this frame. Bohm already concluded in his 1951 publication about *wave* properties compared to *particle* properties: "The quantum properties of the electron differ from those described in classical theory not only in that they are latent potentialities, but also in that these potentialities refer to developments the precise outcome of which is not related completely deterministically to the state of the electron before it interacts with the apparatus."

The reference to an electron as a particle with a latent potentiality is important. One could translate this reference as: 'Parts are by definition on the move'. This seems to be the basis for a further explanation of the reality of the wave properties of matter: "…the wave aspects of matter are just as real as the particle aspects. But we are so used to thinking in classical terms that we have an almost irresistible tendency to revert to making the implicit assumption that the electron is really a particle having a definite momentum and position that cannot be measured simultaneously.

We tend to deemphasize the physical reality of the wave aspects, which show up in the importance of the phase relations in determining interference".[22]

The criticism and opening of the strictly closed frame of reductionist—holistic contrasts focuses on what we discussed in the second chapter as "attitude" and the Husserlian "attitude-change". They are here read in expressions like: "we are so used to …" or "we tend to …". Could one suggest that the Bohmian quantum mechanics originated in the dynamics of an attitude-change? In that case, the path to holism could have various complicated trajectories.

If our understanding of the matter-particle is of consequence, then the nature of that understanding has implications for our conceptualization of matter. Do we partition human consciousness into knowledge-capacities and knowledge-objects as we do with matter-particles? That would support the highest tides of partition, and confirm the role of the particle in accordance with the power lines of the master—master discourse. This is *not* the purpose of the just quoted words introducing quantum theory. Again: the pertinence of a Subject-Object relation in acquiring knowledge or in experimenting, a Speaker-Hearer structure in communication, or a knowing 'I' versus an unknown 'It' seems to not be desired. That structure is simply not applicable to the Holon: no subject that is not the Holon can know the Holon. Bohm wrote: "… the properties of matter do not, in general, exist separately in a given object in precisely defined form. They are, instead incompletely defined potentialities realized in more definite form only in interaction with other systems …", and concluded: "… classically, every particle can have its physical state categorized in terms of the values of its position and momentum. This system of categorization never changes; only the values of the quantities associated with these categories will change. But in quantum theory, the system can either be categorized in terms of a definite position or a definite momentum, but not in terms of both together."[23] Thus, "the electron may be regarded as an entity that has potentialities for developing either its particle-like or its wave-like aspects, depending on the type of matter with which it interacts." He then concludes that his quantum theory *presupposes* the classical level and its concepts. In other words: "without an appeal to the classical level, quantum theory would have no meaning."[24] What does this tell us about approaches to the Holon?

5.1 Wholeness and Knowledge

"If we try to use the prevailing world view based on the notion of particles" Bohm writes 1980, "we discover that the 'particles' (such as electrons) can also manifest as waves, that they can move discontinuously, that there are no laws at all that apply in detail to the actual movements of individual particles … If on the other hand we

[22] David Bohm: *Quantum Theory*, New Jersey 1951, pp. 132–134.

[23] Bohm: *Quantum Theory*, Op. Cit., p. 175.

[24] Bohm: *Quantum Theory*, Op. Cit., p. 385 ff, 609.

apply the world view in which the universe is regarded as a continuous field, we find that this field must also be discontinuous, as well as particle-like, and that it is as undetermined in its actual behavior as is required in the particle view relation as a whole."[25]

A fascinating conclusion dominates those considerations. If a human consciousness wants to exploit its knowledge capacities, it needs for this activity a notion of reality, and with that notion another notion of totality. This need is detected in the context of a quantum theory, which shows that the attempt to describe and follow a particle in detail has little meaning, as the fifth chapter of Bohm's *Wholeness* demonstrates. The behavior of an atomic particle is like that of a wave—both thus depend completely on their *whole* environment, with *all* observation instruments and (human) minds. Observer and observed are merging and interpenetrating all aspects of one whole reality, which is invisible and un-analyzable. Here is what we mentioned as an axial consideration: the *total/whole/holon* precedes every *reality/universe/cosmos*. A quantum theory is not just an assortment of linguistic articulation layers and not a combination of naïve-natural and various non-naïve-natural articulations. In maintaining this physical theory, one experiences that *there is nothing to observe that is not the observer*. The *holon* is not an *external* reality related to a human consciousness. Bohm explores the metaphor of *the fold* and suggest that all is in an unfolding—an unfolding we mistook analytically when we made the *holon* into an *object of knowledge formation*. Indeed, the *holon* is not an external reality. What does it mean for meaning? Is there a link to discover between Meaning and Holon? There is, indeed.

5.2 The Quantum Challenge and Articulation

Thinking the Holon is perhaps the most radical and ultimate form of partitioning and its implications. It requires that we observe the boundaries of discourses, which present themselves as natural. In that regard, quantum physics may be an ultimate articulation of reality reaching far beyond the particle story.[26] The theory delivers hitherto unknown insights in articulation processes in which human beings are embedded. The challenge is clear.

A most ambitious focus is on articulation processes referring to insights in the universe(s), which were hitherto veiled behind the particle, its stories and its discourses. That focus was accompanied by a more or less dogmatic interest in the concept of totality (Holon) to help unveil those concepts. Particle and Holon can indeed not be excluded from any process of articulation. But the language for such articulation is not based on a speaker-hearer model or any theory produced by the

[25] Bohm: *Wholeness and the Implicate Order*, London/New York 1980, p. xvi.

[26] The master—master-discourse also pretends to create holistic powers. One of the examples it produced is the inclusion of the Cartesian way of thinking. But that pretension is very limited, although it is a basic element in Occidental culture and is currently spreading all over the globe.

more geometrico thought pattern, nor its master: the master—master discourse. Where Particle and Holon belong to the realm of language, they guarantee expressivity tied to a speaker and a hearer. Their role of reaching beyond these well-known boundaries is clarified in quantum experiences. On the basis of classical physics, quantum theories have demonstrated that particles can deliver equal layers of articulation: those of the particle and those of the waves are specific. Their equality is here more important than the traditional subject-object-verb linguistic schemes will ever unveil. Before recognizing equality between the level of articulation for particles (a theme of the preceding chapters) and the level for waves, language was based on fragmentation rather than on equality.

This is, of course, most essential for any insight into the concept of meaning. A Holon cannot appropriately be articulated without a quantum-experienced particle/wave understanding. A major defect of classical linguistic articulation profiles the problem. Its multiple modes of expression were partitioned, became ascribed to specific social roles (speaker, hearer etc) and were lacking any possibility of intertwining or other forms of togetherness. Words are uttered as individual entities; verbal functions are performed as individual acts; semiotic connotations are considered as applicable linguistic means of communication, and not of forms of communication as such. Quantum mechanics causes deeper and more complete insights into a theory of human articulation and meaning. That has its consequences. What have the physicists' quantum theories, and in particular quantum mechanics, to do with our language or with our usual linguistic articulations? The question and its possible answers are a challenge when the answer is: "everything!"

Quantum holism X-rayed the grammatical and syntactical structures of most Occidental (naïve)natural languages. Bohm radically investigated how languages contribute to the process of partitioning in mind, thought and articulation. In doing so, the meaning concept is placed within *language as a particular field* among all other fields of reality. Meaning closely relates to, and often can be described as the result of the function of, a dominant subject-verb-object scheme. It imposes itself in our speech, Bohn notices "even in those cases in which some attention would reveal its evident inappropriateness".

A question comes up: "Is it not possible for the syntactical and grammatical form of language to be changed so as to give a basic role to the verb rather than to the noun?"[27] That would liberate us from separations, breaks and other forms of partitioning. By means of experiment he calls such a mode of language the "rheomode" (The Greek verb 'rheo' means: 'to flow'). He stresses that this mode concentrates on the true function of language and linguistic articulation: to assist and guide the flow of life. Language creates awareness concerning its proper function, which is not to separate words and linguistic parts with individualized category-nominations. Bohm thus condemns each 'use of words' and in particular what has been outlined in our foregoing Chap. 3 as the habit of seeing/using the word as 'the elementary unit' of language.

[27] Bohm: *Wholeness*, Op. Cit., p. 43.

An important element of this view is that in the latter the word-constructions are introduced as if "they have no bearing at all on their meaning. In the rheomode, however, the word construction is not fortuitous, but plays a primary role in making possible a whole new mode of language, while the activity of word construction is continually being brought to our notice because the meanings depend in an essential way on the forms of such constructions."[28] The relation between *word* and *meaning* is renewed, one could say. The word is in the majority of linguistic and philosophical theories a unit, an element, an individual datum and the result of an omnipresent partitioning process. In Bohm's proposal, the word is no longer such an indivisible and unchanging atom of meaning but rather a marker in the entirety of movement that specifies language. "Meaning" fulfills a key function in all of this. There are several commentaries to this turn proposed in quantum views.

First, the concept of meaning plays an even more vital role than in Bohm's explanations. His remarks are essential, but not sufficient. Meaning is a central concept in human articulation, and reaches back to the first words uttered in the entire story of Creation.

Second, meaning does not solely relate to words and speech but is molded in accordance to the specificity of each layer of language. Within a language are many words, and many of them sound and are written identical, yet have another meaning because they stem from words in specifically different layers of language.

Third, the concept of meaning illustrates the importance of understanding language: not only as a continuously unfolding flow, but also as a layered phenomenon, so that 'the' language, or 'a' language cannot exist. The partitions between those layers are as such problematic, and their coherence-in-partaking in an all-over articulation should be studied seriously.

Fourth, the imminent order in attitudes, which creates the decisive multitude of attitudes that form meaning, delivers a special access to the various layers of language and linguistic articulation. The important partition between a naïve- and a non-naïve natural attitude (see Chap. 2) is neither a 'once-only' nor a fixated event to characterize the course of human history.

Fifth, what happens with words happens with speech. Instead of understanding speech as a collection of *speech-acts in activity* (Searle), the question of meaning urges us to perceive speech as a *field-activity.* Quantum physics inspired us to look at speech as an occurrence in a force field with boundaries far beyond those of a simple communication among individuals. Those five remarks may deepen our insight into a quantum challenge to articulation, which reaches even beyond Bohmian theory.

Bohm's diagnosis was powerful enough to make us understand how important it is to become aware that we repeat without interruption the 'subject—verb—object' scheme. In all Indo-Germanic languages and in many others we thus obey the strict laws of the master—master discourse. With that obedience we not only create a reliable communication, we believe, but also stable patterns of thought. In them we

[28] Bohm: *Wholeness*, Op. Cit., p. 51 ff.

cherish our fixated managing of meaning. There is no gap between the basic structure of our linguistic articulation and the confirmation of meanings related to the well-articulated reality. The power of this pattern cannot be underestimated. Bohm's proposal to understand and apply language differently, in particular his 'rheomode' manner of articulating reality, was not strong enough to challenge the master—master discourse and to change the basic schemes of our expressivity: linguistic and other form of expression alike. There is no turn towards the rheomode signaled that leads away from subject-verb-object in linguistics. Theories of meaning did not even mirror any of the motives included in that mode. This book has illustrated the degree to which every new theory of meaning has to begin with a critical understanding of the particle story, the more geometrico thought pattern and the master—master discourse. And there is no critical understanding that does not have to fight the all-embracing meaning typology based on the interpretations of reliability, certainty and trustworthiness inherent in that typology, and practicing at any moment the necessary processes of a foundational partitioning.

6 Meaning as Constellation

Pick a "Post-it" note, was suggested in the first lines of the book, write on it and fix it somewhere as "… Y". So, where it sticks, 'Y' is its meaning. Is this not *the* basic feature of any theory of meaning? But we keep silent about the implicit theory of meaning of our "Post-it" act.

What we learned and experienced from a deeper insight into the process and activity of meaning is, that meaning is *not* the fixation of an A to an X, or Y but an occurrence at distance from any fixation, partition or segmentation. Meaning is a constellation within the large dimensions of articulation—a human activity par excellence. As a constellation, meaning has a multitude of determining factors such as: attitude level, layer of language, process of role-divisions in social life, habit formation within diverse perspectives on it, changing positions in the sign-pool and attempts to reach beyond. To determine what something means is a complex process with diverse tasks and responsibilities of participants.

Vested interests, fixated opinions, legally bound doctrines can altogether form a pattern of elements to establish a meaning, but those can never pretend to any duration or fixated form of articulation.

The past is plural and the present has equally multiple forms: a judgment is like a rainstorm, looking suddenly as if there is nothing else anymore, but after some time every bit of reality has changed its face and seems the same. But time has gone by and meaning was an historical event: it determined other constellations in an important way and yet did not change the universe. Meaning is always contextual, but the multitude of its contexts will never be completely known. Yet, meaning does not leave the human mind untouched. Each author knows by experience and deeply in his or her feelings how meaning-creation is loaded with specific responsibilities. Maintaining meaning is an ethical action. But it does not unfold fixated activities or activities that result in any fixation. The sentence "meaning is…" is therefore misleading and treacherous. Meanings *are* not; they *occur* and have their own functionaries as socially mediated executors. In this perspective, one can never say: "I mean …" but should always be minded to say: "I participate in the occurrence to mean …". Meaning becomes rich, and a still richer expression if its linguistic articulation allows this minimum of self-knowledge; "I do *not* mean to mean …" would ultimately be an act loaded with ethical substance. The meaning of meaninglessness must be *performed.*

6.1 Meanings Layered

It is clear that fixation is not appropriate for meaning, although the master—master discourse supports that suggestion. The security and reliability, which meaning is supposed deliver does not come from any fixation. On the contrary: wherever meaning is the product of fixation, it constitutes a semiotic and social danger-zone. The layered character of meaning that contradicts fixation is clear in three dimensions: the linguistic, the social and the cosmological. Among them the linguistic articulation is the most generally regarded. The socio-cultural is as it were a shell around meaning articulation in a wider sense and the cosmological is mainly narrative. The three are adjacent in their plural connectivity.

The linguistic articulation of meaning is dominated by a partitioning, which Edmund Husserl formulated and characterized at its clearest in terms of "attitude" or "attitude change".[29] It concerns the partition between a *naïve-natural* and a *non-naïve natural* attitude. The enormous importance of this differentiation *within the boundaries of naturalness* was been a creative guess in Peirce's thoughts as well as the occasion of a more systematic exploration in Husserl's phenomenology.

His diversifications deliver a challenging insight into the relations between word, speech, meaning and articulation. The two attitudes, the naïve and the non-naïve natural, are both in essence plural, so that varieties in each of them concern a field of naturalness in attitude and articulation.[30] A truly fundamental observation can be made: words can sound or be written with a meaning that differs in accordance with their attitude. Husserl suggested that self-consciousness and a resulting self-knowledge are basic for this important partitioning that causes meaning pluralities. But it is partition only in the sense of a distinction within a process, a flow, a development, or an unfolding of reality and the human capacity to articulate—not a separation, fragmentation or the path to one-to-one connections between word and

[29] See Chap. 2: *Attitude as Phenomenological Issue.* Peirce experienced this change has when he became aware of the social and epistemological dimensions of the train whistle, and spoke of a 'breach' introducing a 'first'.

[30] A discourse evolving in the naïve-natural attitude is never *purely* or *exclusively* naïve, but the naïve-natural dominates for example expressions of scientific, professional or other character. Each naïveté of *meaning* is and will remain being witness of a natural attitude.

meaning. The naïve-natural attitude in articulation represents a pre-reflexive attitude, which expresses itself entirely in naturalness. The non-naïve natural attitude is reflexive within a different naturalness, the naturalness that first explores reflexivity. Changes among the two within the zone of naturalness are important for meaning. Meanings of words, speech and other forms of articulation are determined by their origin and emergence; those are not meaningless at all! Words can be read, heard or said in sameness and yet have a different meaning because of their original attitude. That is an additional argument against *more geometrico* one-to-one relations between meaning and word: the meaning of a word depends greatly on its emergence as well as its actual context. Both determine meaning at distance from any fixating or determining activity, because the meaning of a word (if ever a word on its own 'has' a meaning, which is seldom the case, and in certain attitude-levels or language-layers never ever) is a dynamic process.

There is indeed a gap between naturalness in a naïve, and in a non-naïve sense. Many issues of that non-naïve attitude are unknown in a naïve-natural attitude. Husserl suggests clarifying differentiations in the non-naïve natural attitude. The latter comprises first of all its proper natural attitude, indicated as 'non-naïve natural'. The non-naïve natural attitude can in its turn, as a consequence, be understood as an ensemble of distinguishable attitudes. Following Husserl, after the breach between a naïve- and a non-naïve attitude level remain a *natural*, a *philosophical* and a *transcendental* level or in the latter, non-naïve, language layer. This interesting topography of meaning evolves out of the variety of attitudes that enable a human mind to articulate reality. These are by no means uniform and in unison, but respond precisely to the criteria of the *layered* or *leveled* character of language. This insight is uniquely important for understanding (not to mention a 'theory') of meaning. First, one should be fully aware of the differences that are given. The main one is, to begin with, the difference between naïveté and non-naïveté that constitutes the difference behind the immediate word appearance.

6.2 First Person Singular

One can, for example, speak 'I' as (grammatically speaking) the word indicating the first person singular in the naïve attitude without an accompanying awareness of that grammatical position and its meaning. This word, often spontaneously introduced, will also be repeated in other attitudes, including those of a non-naïve character. They show many meanings unfolding along with their emergence from a specific attitude. And one can pronounce 'I' in non-naïveté and simply focus on a grammatical or even discursive positioning. An 'I' can also be meant to pertain to the speaker's consciousness, self-knowledge, reflexivity and other meanings related to a non-naïve philosophical position to be articulated, which is no longer attached to the non-naïve natural level of attitude.

The latter meaning of the word 'I' is often the most elaborate position of the word. One distinguishes the influence of a transcendental level in other non-naïve attitudes, which tend toward abstraction as well as fixation and reach beyond everyday language. It is the attitude in which professional and related artificial languages with their specifically defined meanings are settled. These are signaled in law, and ultimately lead to the level of logic—a level in which the 'I' of naïveté can no longer be found. The one simply spoken and written word 'I' has thus numerous meanings, depending on their subsequent level of emergence. All those meanings remain within the boundaries of languages, of linguistic expressiveness; they illustrate the layered character of language *tout court*. That illustration demonstrates the enormous distance from any one-on-one relation between word and meaning. A differentiated reflexivity seems necessary to be aware of meanings in the diversity of sign pools and their surface as well as deep level—a reflexive awareness far beyond the conversational level of daily life.

6.3 Psychologism

There is a peculiar argument that 'meaning dependent on attitudes' is ultimately a matter of psychology. The strong reference to the constitutive 'self' is a leading motive in this classification. In the second chapter, while studying the relation between logic and attitude, we met this consideration under the heading of *psychologism.* The central question was: how could one appreciate a differentiation between psychology and logic/philosophy without transforming it into a meaningless fixation? With that question, the function of 'attitude' came to the fore: it requires the greatest possible distance from psychology. We mentioned, that the exploration of the concept 'attitude' had its origin in the battle around the position of psychology versus logic. The close relation between meaning and attitude is a matter of mastering the possible varieties in articulation—in other words: an issue of a semiotic nature. We know from his Dream Interpretations how Freud analyzed dreams to determine the position of an "I" as emerging from one of the many possible attitudes functioning as a basis for self-articulation, and that new meanings in the 'I' concept came from attitude-changes. That guided his explorations in understanding how meaning emerges with multiple attitudes. It is important to note that changes of attitude can *always* occur: there is no limit known in a human life that prevents the performance of an attitude change. The unfolding of meaning is not limited to certain specific attitude changes. A philosopher must stress (in contrast to a psychologist) that the emergence of meaning is relatively independent of ego-related attitude contents. Ego-logical structures, one could add, are continuously changing and perform dynamically. The word 'attitude' often conceals the vital importance of the word 'attitude-change'.

6.4 Force Field Meaning

The latter takes account of the constitutive forces of attitudes within the layered structure of language. This makes meaning focus on speech. The first consideration one has to honor is that meanings in relation to words differ from meanings in relation to speech. The reason for this is not in the different definition of word or speech, but in the fact that those two create absolutely different contexts, which can be defined as *fields*. Kurt Lewin researched those issues a century ago, but his terminology and methodology are still to be appreciated in the context of studying signs and meanings. He suggested that we should interpret the field of *naïve-naturalness* as a matter of *folk psychology*.[31] The proposal to perceive meaning and its emergence as a matter of *field* theory is central (and also acceptable for us today).

Meanings originate in group-life, the latter being a composite of specifically differentiated social fields. Those fields show their own internal drives and forces, which relate continuously to varying coexisting social entities. Opinions and meanings are prominently visible among them. They occur in an often *naïve natural* articulation: 'we'.

Speech is another social field among those meaning-fields. Words, meanings, speech-acts become visible and demonstrate how articulation fields coexist. The individual components (words etc.) are less important then the coexistence in itself, which reinforces the cohesion and effectiveness of *speech as field*. That field of mainly *non-naïve natural* articulation pertains in the first place to reality as resulting from such an articulation, initiating a language reference to an 'it'.

Those considerations illustrate that meaning is always implied as a function in a *force field* in terms of Kurt Lewin's social psychology. It includes the fact that meaning is structured like a language—language is understood in this case as a power of articulation—so that a transition from a narcissistic ego stade towards social life is never impossible. The infant is, like any adult, continuously enforcing access to social relations by means of always again and anew becoming a speaking subject. Language is a heterogeneous field of multiple forces, which determines often-inconsistent meanings, with the speaking subject searching for his path in meanings present as well as unfolding. Meaning has therefore to be studied as present and as possibly forthcoming: the two are formative forces in the sign pool. And, one concludes: meaning is a feature for completed but also for forthcoming articulation, not to mention the past of each meaning playing a role in its actual interpretation.

[31] K. Lewin: "Frontiers in Group Dynamics" in: *Human Relations,* 1947. Vol. I, 1. p. 5 ff.;—id.: *Field Theory in Social Science,* Harper 1951, and:—id.: *A Dynamic Theory of Personality*, New York/London 1935. That is a stimulating approach of the naïve-natural attitude and the level of meaning connected with it—but there is a double problem: on the one hand, it seems correct to view the naïveté of naturalness in terms of folk-life in as far as *directness* of knowledge and emotion is concerned; it characterizes the surface structure of the everyday-life sign pool we already mentioned. On the other hand, we cannot accept any forcing in the line of naïveté and folk-life because of its possible racist connotations.

Lewin explained the sign pool and its impact on meaning in terms of a force-field: "(…) the social happening is viewed as occurring in, and being the result of, a totality of coexisting social entities [characterized by] the relative position of the entities, which are part of the field." It is important to understand that "what happens within such a field depends upon the distribution of forces throughout the field" as well as "the ability to determine for the various points of the field the strength and directions of the resultant forces." The force field is consequently a "constellation of forces directed toward one region". An example is the social force field caused by an autocratic leadership, as Lewin described extensively under the impression of then recent political circumstances during WW II. Linguistic articulations appear to represent a specific field with distinct forces and force directions. That view provides a remarkably new insight in, for instance, a 'verb': the 'verb' in a force field—the latter has holistic properties—is no longer understood as a single, monolithic and static component of speech, but is in itself a dynamic and dynamics-creating, non-binary component of language.

What in the force field of a word or expression contributes to the determination of meaning? There are in each verb many components, such as synonyms, parallels etc, but also metaphors and sayings, manners of speaking as well as texts and rule-fields belonging to grammar or syntax. All can generate meanings. At a somewhat larger distance from the center (but immediately prepared to become active overall) are sounds and sound fields, specific for a language family. That insight reaches the geno-level of word(s) in a field. A word is never alone, and has never a meaning in solitude! The dynamics of the appearing of a word belongs to the crucial meaning-making force.

6.5 *Word and Words*

Those insights are not relevant if only a one-to-one relationship of meaning and word is accepted as the basic unit of articulation. On the contrary, meaning and word demonstrate their value and importance when studied as field forces, although each in a very different way. To experience articulation in the sign pool of everyday life is a basic force for understanding meaning in its multiplicity. Speech generates identity, speaker situations enforce meaning fields and position which is not only an 'I' but also and equally an 'O/other'. There is no meaning without articulation, and there is also no meaning without social life. Personal development and maintenance of meanings are closely related, they concern a closeness engraved in the naïve-natural as well as a non-naïve natural attitude. The being-spoken-to is more important than any initiative to take the floor or utter the first word. Is there ever a *first* word?

An example is in two famous words: *Mind* and *Brain*. Many philosophical considerations are dedicated to the relation between mind and brain—many debates on their coherence have fascinated laymen as well as neurologists or specialists in brain studies. History often reads as a history of the evolving brain and its consequences for the human mind. In the context of our research on meaning, we should consider that such debates unfold (a) on the basis of *partitioning* (two separate words create the question), and (b) at a *specific level*: the research encounters most often an unfolding non-naïve-natural language level, which progresses in three attitude levels. There are furthermore three positions involved at this level or articulation: the position of the brain, second of the mind, and third of the mind-brain. Those three, with their three levels of attitude, have *different meanings,* although they frequently overlap.

The history of what is indicated with the word 'brain' is (as we mentioned in Chap. 3) an evolutionary history based on physical and medical, even paleontological data. In parallel, the history of what is indicated with the word 'mind' is a history based on philosophical and psychological data. But the third possibility suggests another view: the two histories are not forged together or intertwined while forming one word, but a history of an issue indicated with the words 'mind' and 'brain' separated. The simple word 'mindbrain' or 'brainmind' is not in our dictionaries. Those two suggest a remarkable specificity, and we repeat that there is no philosophical view or other document on the 'mindbrain'/'brainmind'. That word, if it should exist, is an articulation in another attitude. Notice, that the famous mind—brain problem seems to remain without a solution, because it does not support any consideration (which is explored classically) of 'mind' and 'brain' as two independent entities. The problem starts in fact not with the word 'brain' or 'mind', but with the 'and'. Mind and brain are so strongly intertwined, that the 'and' disturbs their deep connectedness. If 'mind' and 'brain' belong to a non-naïve natural attitude, then 'mindbrain' would belong to a non-naïve philosophical attitude (or, as Lady Welby formulated it: "the fully rational plane"). The mind-brain problem will apparently not find any appropriate solution if the multiplicity of meaning and the layered character of linguistic articulations are not recognized. The problem illustrates that it surpasses expressivity as long as this recognition is not achieved.[32]

6.6 *Words, Layers, Meaning*

We thus indicated the wealth of meaning when we let go the separation of linguistic articulations into specific units of language. Knowledge and insight, as well as meaning, broadens importantly when we accept parts to form a totality, which was unnoticed before.

---

[32] Even Lady V. Welby could not liberate her thoughts from the 'word' as the basic unit of linguistic expressiveness: "Let us beware in sense, meaning and significance of allowing the old antithesis 'matter and mind' to coerce us", she writes 1903, "This (…) cannot yet be adequately formulated in our present terminology, which is cramped on every side by the outgrown shells of controversy once protective, now mere sources of danger to intellectual and moral life." See: Lady V. Welby: *What is Meaning?* Op. Cit., 2012, p. 50, 51 ff.

'MINDBRAIN' OR'BRAINMIND' may be a conceivable solution for diverse layers of the mind-brain problem. All is in conceiving a different word. In any theory of meaning are words on the notion of the body, the *human* body in the first, but not unique, place. Keep in mind: words not only *bear* meanings (as we criticized in '*meaning holism*'), they also *oblige* us to maintain certain meanings. When words change, the realm of meaning is enriched. The classical 'mind—brain' problem, itself a product of partitioning, will take a different direction once the notion of a possible 'mindbrain' is accepted. The layer of expressivity of that new word clearly does not have the character of a naïve level: it is even beyond a non-naïve natural level and has entered a further unfolding of that level's naturalness, focusing on a reductive, more formal and artificial, even transcendental language level. In other words: it pertains to a level in which the simple expression 'body' is maintained but explored in deeper and more complex and specified manners. It has ultimately as a consequence, that the human body in its specific meaning-context with a 'mind-brain' will formally be indicated as 'B^{mb}', underlining its specific meaning that results from words of a naïve-natural language level, but which has decidedly left that level.

'BODY' AND 'MIND' would be susceptible to the same approach for their famously debated relation. The two words are, like all others, bearers of meaning only thanks to a preceding partitioning. A naïve-natural language layer takes them as natural *after* the partitioning, but a change of level brings them back to a level *before* any partition. The word 'Mindbody' or 'Bodymind' (M^b, B^m), composed with their naïve-natural language components, is different in meaning and clearly a concept from a non-naïve natural level. The latter has, as suggested above, more than one non-natural level, and one could consider that the meaning of this word "bodymind" is more complex. That is most certainly the case if one admits another variation, speaking of a 'Bodymind-brain' and a 'Bodybrain-mind'. A B^{mb} or a B^{bm} would thus possess an enriched meaning, which is for instance open to questions pertaining to the neurological or neurophysiological conditions of performing specific speech acts (such as a command, a plan, a decisive commentary etc.). The (human) body is at this level of articulation no longer the separate physiological unity that could in specific cases relate to psychological acts (such as a smile) or to psychosomatic events (such as a depression), which are decidedly not fully understood in terms of separated composites. For that purpose, the level of reflection has to be heightened and a further complexity of meaning enjoyed.[33] It is fascinating that this B^{mb} level has its own history, which has often a *narrative* character in the first place, a level that changes in the course of history. New questions come to the fore, such as: at what level is B, or B^m, or B^{mb} when narratives about the universe, or

---

[33] See Friedemann Pulvermüller c.s.: "Brain Signatures of Meaning Access in Action Word Recognition" in *Journal of Cognitive Neuroscience*, Vol. 17, No. 6, 2005, p. 884ff.; M. Garagnani and F. Pulvermüller: "Neuronal Correlates of Decisions to Speak and Act" in: *Brain and Language*, 2013 [at: www.mg421@cam.ac.uk] See also Fr. Pulvermüller, M. Garagnani, Th. Wennekers: "Thinking in circuits: toward neurobiological explanation in cognitive neuroscience" in: *Biological Cybernetics* 2014, Vol. 108, 5, pp. 573–593.

narratives about the cosmos unfold? Do not forget that the components B, M and B do not invite any explanation of the B^{mb} to proceed with meanings that are fixated as belonging to B, M and B *individually* and thus *separately*. The notion and meaning of 'body' is for that reason different in a naïve-natural language compared to the non-naïveté of body, mind and brain in the B^{mb}.

This change is important in the force field of meaning as well as in various research fields, such as neurology, psychosomatics and other social sciences; it should even be noticed in law.[34] Fascinating challenges to more precisely determined meanings unfold, once the language layers and levels of articulation are considered as decisive for meanings. The neurologist will for instance focus on the *mind* beyond any naïve-natural expressivity. His interest will accentuate the *mind* of the *mindbrain* as integrated in the *body*, which leads to his formula $M^{(MbB)}$. A psychologist will focus on the *mind* as in unity with the *body* which in its turn unites with the *mindbrain*, so that his formula would rather be $M(B^{bmb})$. A criminologist might focus on the *body* as a component of a *mindbrain* unified with that *body*, so that his formula to indicate that meaning would be M^bB^{mb}. And that is only a beginning: who will formulate the precise meaning determination when the physiological component is given due respect in its role within 'mind-brain' totalities? In that case, physiological differentiations join mind- *and* brain differentiations, complicating the physiological properties of the brain, as the neurosciences illustrate.

'I' AND 'YOU' is all in all perhaps the most remarkable parallel, based on the same experience of attitude and linguistic articulation. The parallel is known in philosophy and the social sciences as well as in psychology or medicine in words like "the 'I—Thou' relationship", as 'sociability', as 'dual identity', as 'dialogic philosophy' or as 'philosophy of encounter'. We approximate the above observation: the word 'I' is strongly present in the two natural levels of attitude (the naïve- and the non-naïve). The word 'you' is, thanks to its relation with the 'I', present in social encounters, in language or in speech (in naïve as well as non-naïve) attitudes. The human reality named 'IYou' or 'YouI' is neither translatable in a 'we', nor in our dictionaries, nor articulated in any of our attitude levels: one does not find an I^y- or Y^I -word. It is as if there is no language in which any 'IYou' can function or be articulated. That problem approaches cosmological dimensions. Its absence is felt in the basic narratives of cultures around the globe. Martin Buber, in his famous *Ich und Du* [I and Thou] 1923, tried to approach the 'IYou' or 'YouI' reality while focusing on the *inter*-relations of the two. The striking parallel is that his publication should have been entitled *ITHOU*, but that was almost tragically not the case, just

[34]Various meanings involved in a process of change between language layers are important to observe. The expression (or 'word') B^{mb} refers to what at a naïve-natural level would be indicated as *body* in relation to *mind* and to *brain*. This reference is only partially valid, because there is in the first place reference to the *body* being a totality with the *mind* and the *brain* (B^{mb}). That remains intact for a variation of the viewpoint, whereby the *mind* forms a totality with the *body* and the *brain* (M^{bb}). The same is true for the *brain* in totality with the *body* and the *mind* (B^{bb}). And there is the meaning to be distinguished of a further differentiated attitude level, in which the *body* forms a unity with the *Mindbrain* (or, in other words, the *Brainmind*), which is a different meaning-character from the *body* just correlated with *mind* and *brain*, and would be expressed as BM^b.

like there is no language and no text on the Mindbrain.[35] The 'and' as a symbol of a plurality of articulation levels did not guide the elaboration of an appropriate meaning. The most problematic issue in Buber's explication is the word 'and'—one should understand its failure and its necessity.

6.7 *Meaning Complexity*

The complexity of the meaning-concept is its clarity. There are meaningful terms that do not find their way into our dictionaries. A complexity of layers of linguistically expressed meaning illustrates the fact that any renewal of a theory of meaning is not a matter of reference or fixation, but of broadening our regions of articulation. Those have cosmological relevance.

In the course of this book, especially in Chaps. 2 and 3 and the above paragraphs of this chapter, we mentioned a Husserl-inspired scheme that seems to order the multiplicity of levels in which meaning originates. Meaning unfolds from either a naïve, or a non-naïve level of naturalness. The criterion to differentiate between them is in the degree of reflection, self-consciousness or self-knowledge. The first fills the daily sign pool spontaneously, and the latter requires a second view on the emergence of meaning. The non-naïve attitude generates three more levels, themselves important layers of linguistic articulation: a naturalness that knows and exercises reflection, a philosophical plane that focuses reductively on essentials within the reach of that level and a transcendental one which strives for abstract, logical and final insights. The three create meanings circumstantially; they differ in subtle manners in science, thought and the arts or literature. The application of this scheme through constructing meanings for individual cases or circumstances would lead to an infinite research. It would, above all, fail in one particular respect: meaning has been characterized as an ever-renewed constellation. That feature does not fit any schematic application or construction of meaning. Words, as we concluded, do not 'have' a meaning but incite meaning in constellations. That energy is the source of the dynamics of the unfolding of meaning without which we could not exist—an energy that opens cosmological perspectives as soon as the non-naïve layers of articulation are affected. Bohm teaches us: "… the field of meaning can refer to itself, and of course, it also presupposes the context of the universe to which it also refers. Meaning, though, has nevertheless been regarded as peculiar to our own minds and not as a proper part or aspect of the objective universe."[36]

---

[35] M. Buber: *Ich und Du*, 1923; see also: Jan M. Broekman: "Bubers grondwoord—een college-fragment" in: *Wijsgerig Perspectief op Maatschappij en Wetenschap*, XVIII,3, 1978 p. 51 ff.

[36] Bohm proceeds: "However if there is a generalized kind of meaning intrinsic to the universe, including our own bodies and minds, then the way may be opened to understanding the whole as self-referential through its 'meaning for itself'—in other words, by whatever reality is. And the universe as we now conceive it may not be the whole thing." See David Bohm: "Soma-Significance and the Activity of Meaning", 1985, in: L. Nichol (Ed.) *The Essential David Bohm*, London/New York 2003, p. 176.

7 Legal Semiotics (5): Law's Expressivity

This chapter exposed the complexity of the meaning concept. Is that complexity supportive of law's discourse and its practices? One would expect the contrary: lawyers are obliged to focus on meanings, and meanings should therefore be handsome in semiotic as well as social contexts. If that is not the case, legal practitioners proceed within the boundaries of their own institutionally protected understanding and maintenance of what they and their clients determine as 'law'.

One should not forget: even the most recent definitions of law and legal theory are a creation of lawyers. Their ideas are firmly anchored in professional habits, institutionally controlled denominations, as well as social values and expectations. What complicates or restrains the function of law in society will be neglected or silenced. This tendency among practicing lawyers was already described by Judith Shklar more than half a century ago[37] when she concluded, that "law is endowed with its own discrete, integral history, its own 'science', and its own values, which are all treated as a single 'block', sealed off from general social history, from general social theory, from politics, and from morality". A semiotic approach to law also suffers today from this isolationist tendency in the legal profession. So there is for any lawyer and law student the danger of isolation and silencing when analyzing the concept of legal meaning. 'Law' is most frequently understood as *the* law, which firmly supports the lawyer's position, setting aside that what does not. Court sessions illustrate this tendency in Common Law as well as in Civil Law systems: the opposing party asserts his or her position and the judge or jury determines what side to support. The chosen positions stand. The legal cycle thus continues as before. Revealing the complexity of meaning aggravates any possible form of the practice of law.

7.1 Partitions and the Power of Understanding

It will perhaps surprise a law student that his or her power of understanding is strictly limited to a level of non-naïveté. That understanding always has its starting-point within the bounds of everyday language, a naïve-natural life situation. The decision to study law is, as mentioned in the first chapter, a step into another layer of language dominated by a non-naïve attitude, which characterizes each artificial language. As a consequence, studying law is a matter of training and skills formation in social complexities determined by institutionally fixated decisions on meaning. The language perspective is closely tied to this particular form of socialization. Saying, that "learning law is learning a language", as was said above, is thus a

[37] Judith Shklar: *Legalism. Law, Morals, and Political Trials*. Harvard UP 1964, 1986[2], p. 3. See parallel experiences of Law Students in: Jan M. Broekman and William A. Pencak (Eds): *International Journal for the Semiotics of Law*, Vol. 23, No 1, March 2010 *Special Issue* "Signs of Law", p. 3 ff.

remark that embraces many layers. Learning to master the power of understanding, a multi-layered task, seems limited to the above-mentioned attitude and language.

Mastering the legal profession as a matter of attitude-dominated language implies a careful and continuous application of partitioning. Partitions result from reductive analyses, which direct the flow of our knowledge moving from parts (paragraphs, sentences) to wholes (texts, declarations, manifestos) and thus initiate the legal craft. That is what law students learn, and a semiotician points out. Those analyses are a matter of attentive listening, reading and writing in the first place. In a legal context *the other person* is always linked to or represented by *texts*. Understanding is in this view a narrower concept than the professional understanding of a psychologist or an economist. There is, simply speaking, no 'other' in law than an "'other' with text."[38]

The power of understanding in law seems to be a power to interpret and manipulate texts. That remains a central issue our days of electronic mail, of computer knowledge reigning in student minds, and of worldwide webs as the most important and efficient channel of information. That understanding applies all the requirements of the master—master discourse and its guidance by the particle story. Electronic forms of communication cannot replace legal knowledge and legal skills; the two tend to clash because of the incongruence of their discourse patterns. Electronics find its way in law and institutional discourse only hesitatingly and without much enthusiasm from the side of the lawyers. The *more geometrico* approach of legal meaning is basic for law and legal activities; it remains to be adapted by the law student. He or she will not be made aware of this determinative force behind legal fact-finding and interpretation. But those basics of law in no case fit our knowledge concerning the general complexity of meaning in culture. One consequence is clear: the power of understanding the sign pool of life encompasses more than lawyers in their profession are ever prepared to grasp. That fact is a consequence of the bewildering complexity of meaning. A meaning is always folded in another. Legal meaning is folded in a broader and ultimately universal meaning; it seems a fruitful and rather unique approach for the law student. But can it, realistically speaking, be conceived?

7.2 Meaning Complexity

The complexity of meaning is not an unchangeable, fixated and all-embracing independent issue. It is rather a source of creativity: the particle received its unique profile; texts and related documents play a dominant and decisive role; different layers of language and specific levels of understanding evolve—in other words: meaning-complexity creates legal hermeneutics. But what type of hermeneutics resulted? In the form of law, complexity reigns the performance and understanding

---

[38] No wonder that theology and jurisprudence are in the context of hermeneutics treated as neighbors.

of our social roles in the sign pool of the everyday. The priority of legal rules and their interpretation in life became a trusted value. The existence of those rules became experienced as 'natural' and their interpretation not only a strong guidance but also life's 'big business'. This cannot be contested. However, another fascinating question is left for a law student to cope with. 'Complexity' also stands for neighboring expressions: 'multiplicity', 'plurality', and often more precisely 'leveled' or 'layered-', 'surface-'and 'deep structures'—all are features of another discourse than law's master—master discourse. What does that mean?

There are two lines of thought responding to this question. One is based on the evoked master—master discourse and its clear picture of the foundations of law and legal discourse. That would suppress considerations pertaining to language levels creating various types of meaning, as was effectively illustrated in the case of 'mind' and 'brain' or 'I' and 'You'. Another is the creation of an alternative discourse, perhaps never realized but possibly in the minds of humans belonging to a culture other than our Occidental one. An interesting exercise for the legal student is to engage in a comparison between the two and thus become confronted with the limitations of maintaining 'meaning' in law. It will also illustrate how the complexity of meaning will despite its limitations unveil deep layers of articulation and the continuing changes within them. And that is not yet all about meaning in law!

7.3 Modes of Discourse

As was said many times before, the master—master discourse maintains a continuous process of partitioning and realizes its articulation power again and anew. Partitioning creates particles without which we cannot articulate reality. *Any* realty is concerned—the above Chap. 4, above illustrated that, for instance, poetic and literary reality, the reality of modern physics, and the reality of painting are equally involved in the particle story. All signatures of meaning, every determination of meaning, each application of the meaning concept necessarily articulates a reality embedded in this particle story and its supportive discourse. Would lawyers be able to perform another articulation? They certainly are not! Are they semiotically imprisoned because they cannot? No, they are not. But they share with the other inhabitants of sign pools the fact that their language cannot be re-established on different principles and gravitate toward different articulations. Global law illustrates this fundamental limitation. The dominant 'subject—verb—object' scheme, which determines all of us to perform speech and thoughts, is at the same time our limitation.

And this is what legal courses teach: detect the subject and find any issue that can be regarded as functioning as the subject in the case, in the argument, in law! The same for an object; and, again: the same for a verb. Verb, subject and object are products of partitioning; everyone knows that subjects or objects, and most certainly verbs, do not exist on their own. When words on their own, isolated, fixated, out of con-text, are never really words, then the same is the case with verbs, subjects and objects, notwithstanding their categorization in grammars or syntaxes. Meaning has to cope with this restriction.

Yet, law students are instructed to build the case with the triad, and to not consider whether verbs or words or other materials have a different background or implication. A lawyer's use of linguistic articulations is a distraction from meaning as the concept is generally appreciated, because only the prescribed legal meaning of words, verbs and other expressions counts! In other words: a legal discourse is not allowed to be powerfully reflexive. It does not need to pose background questions pertaining to meaning because the law as an institution provides meanings. A legal mode of thought does not reflect on its own function, so that—as we suggested in Chap. 4—a theory of law will never reach a realm of theory beyond the master—master discourse. Observed from a semiotic viewpoint, a law student will during his legal education refine only knowledge within the 'subject–verb–object' scheme and its discourse. She is, however, not supposed to switch to another scheme of articulation, because that leads to non-legal articulations, the loss of law and of legitimacy.

So there is a tension between a 'rheomode'-type of discourse (Bohm) and the master-master type of discourse, which determines legal discourse. In the latter, physics, psychology, sociology, economy, literature, as well as law are communicating as separate and independent entities. The law student studies law without connoting related fields of knowledge. Science fields are the product of partitions; these fields are distinguished and hypostasized *more geometrico*. For centuries they were represented as a 'Faculty' in schools and universities of "the old world". Partition and division generated them; they were treated as elementary units of a General Science, without understanding the historical and philosophical features that characterize Occidental culture and its impulse toward science. Furthermore, they were treated as bearing their own independent and fixated meaning, which was not, could not and should not become influenced by others. Law and legal science are a strongly positioned witness to this mode of discursive articulation. So, if legal discourse can be characterized as an 'anti-rheomode' articulation, in what way should lawyers then cope with that position? There is more than one answer to this consideration.

A first, swift and understandable reaction would promote an all-embracing change: "change the law by adapting a new language!" An alternative is perhaps a worldwide debate over the two modes of discourse: "Let's talk about our talking!" But a combat between a Cartesian view engraved in Occidental culture (the particle story) and the rheomode story does not work. It would make participants switch from *inside* the law and its discourse to *outside* the law—and eventually back! That move is unthinkable and socially not practicable because those switches presume the possibility (even temporarily) of a situation of lawlessness during their performance.

A second reaction deals straightforwardly with the meaning concept. If lawyers are confined in their articulations to legal meanings, then a layman's meaning embedded in the same word can deviate significantly. That difference in significance is challenging: "who knows what?" The challenge is more intense because what occurs in the fields of meaning making, unfolds mostly outside the realm of law. A legal meaning included in a word that also functions in other social fields, is *not* a legal meaning in the eyes of the lawyers. This provides insight into a fascinating situation pertaining to meaning. The one-to-one relation between meaning and word, and the same type of cohesion between individual words and meanings appear to be untenable. Law illustrates the fact that meaning seems to be determined by context and attitude, and instrumental in the flow of change. If meaning were predestined, determined and fixated, there would not be meaning, one can conclude. Legal meaning is an exceptional case of determination, which is by no means in conformity with meaning in a universal sense of the word. Law students have to understand this particular situation while managing meaning within the boundaries of their profession and its thought patterns.

A third consideration pertaining to the differences between a legal discourse and a rheomode discourse is in the understanding and positioning of the concept of interpretation: in other words, in the hermeneutic component of the meaning field. That component is in difficulties where legal discourse is concerned. Legal meanings are the product of categorization, fixation and decision-making. Their interpretation is fixated in law as if it were by a ritual. This procedure is, apart from all other consequences, a source of powerful positivism in maintaining meaning in law. But it also illustrates why in legal argumentation and other forms of reasoning, for instance, the word 'justice' is mostly absent. It seems not a meaningful word in the center of legal language, whereas the layman—as politicians often demonstrate—from outside legal discourse strives for the opposite, and identifies 'justice' with 'law'.

This clash of meaning is socially important in, for instance, social activism and theoretically important in view of the tensions between naïve- and non-naïve natural language levels. A smooth transformation from one to another is seldom the case. Will 'justice' ever acquire the meaning of 'an elementary unit of legal language'? That would be a great topic for a paper on legal semiotics! That unwritten paper would have to explain why the answer is in the negative. With that, it delivers a truthful contribution to the status of interpretation in law (or legal hermeneutics) as compared to other non-naïve discourses. Speaking in a general sense: interpretation only occurs in a language where meanings are not fixated and function as markers in the flow of life in the sign pool. If that is not the case, then interpretation is like a game of chess: only the genius of calculation survives.

7.4 Word, and Legal Meaning

A final remark in address to the law student should again be on meaning in relation to word. Legal discourse makes clear how vital the discourse is when it is qualified as an ensemble of words. Meaning can only be understood if this ensemble is actively present in the awareness of the observer. Meanings are considered as united with words, and identified with them because of the presupposition that words *have* a meaning. On the other hand, and less often noticed, we have to notice that words function in the fields of meaning without losing their specific character. Words are a mark, deeply engraved in traditional and habit-related articulatory activities. Focal points of a word-related activity are *texts*, and *speech* as well as *discourses.*

The three function mainly at the *surface* of meaning and articulation. There is, however, no understanding of meaning if one restricts the study of meaning to surfaces. All three: text, speech and discourse have their surface *and* their deep structure functioning in the totality of universal articulation. Holistic philosophies made a great effort to understand this in a non-analytical manner. Approaching meaning presupposes an awareness of these efforts, although the role of the deep structures is difficult to clarify. Meaning itself is an example of the vital fact that discourse, text and speech are each of them confronting us with their engenderment. That process is a significant component of meaning in itself. Memories, associations, or metaphors reach deeper than words. Yet we remember, think, articulate, experience 'in words'. We do so although reality has changed in the time we contemplate a word, a memory or a fragment of understanding.

Words create a surface world that does not exist in the physical sense of that expression; there is no science, or physics with that world as its object. Any differentiation and fixation of a science pertaining to that world failed. How can a change of surface in which words are folded, be a *deep* change?[39] Depth cannot manifest itself entirely in the surface, because the depth is no more there, and already changed, when the appeal to embrace her occurs. Semiotics illustrates these dynamics too often as a shortcoming of our articulatory expressivity. Peirce understood this, when he ventured to see science as 'a dialogue with nature', and wrote: "… nature follows general laws, in other words, has a reason. Successful research—say Faraday's—is a conversation with nature; the macrocosmic reason, the equally occult microcosmic law, must act together or alternately, till the mind is in tune with nature".[40] The spreading and effect of the word is larger, deeper and far more relevant than we presuppose in the often nearly frozen cataracts of the sign pool we try to meaningfully live in.

---

[39] Notice that the word "deep" has been mentioned many times. In Chapter 3, linguists, semioticians and philosophers are quoted: Peirce, Lady Welby, Greimas, Kristeva all mentioned it; in Chapter 1, Wittgenstein was mentioned exploring the concept. See his *Philosophical Investigations* Op. Cit., Par. 583: "As if what were happening *now* had no deep significance.—What does it mean to say: "What is happening now has significance" or "has deep significance"? What is a *deep* feeling?"

[40] Ch. S. Peirce: *Collected Papers* Op. Cit. 6. 568.

7.5 In the Shadow of Meaning

We all live in the shadow of meaning: our presence and the sun cause it. Days and nights are shadows reigning in our universe. Celestial bodies are said to have them. But there are several considerations to respect: if I live my life in the sign pool of the everyday, what causes a shadow to be the most clearly profiled? What happens when I change position, come together with another person, with an object, or when the sun suddenly disappears behind clouds? A shadow's profile does not reproduce the complexities and multiple factors in life. Shadows are always the shadow of another reality—without, however, losing their own specifics. Is a shadow based on a selection, a choice, on partitions and interpretations or a change of attitude? Yet, there is nothing without a shadow; meaning and its shadow accompany each phenomenon, each reality, body as well as soul. Shadows transmit meaning. Their power of intertwining is important. They intertwine and integrate: nothing is without shadow, and we perceive reality only when we include the often-ignored shadow. This embraces an essential social dynamic. Suddenly in your shadow, what is mine has traces, impressions, and meaning from you: as if perceived in another light and no longer solely my property.

In 1903 Lady Victoria Welby published her book "*What is Meaning?*" and demonstrated not only the power of her philosophical interest but also her sympathy for social activism. Meaning is the shadow of reality, she suggested: "Reality is monistic so far as ultimate division or separation or sunderance goes, but dualistic from one point of view and triadistic from and in another, pluralistic in and from yet another. The unity thus reached cannot yet be adequately formulated in our present terminology, which is cramped on every side by the outgrown shells of controversy once protective, now mere sources of danger to intellectual and moral life". Neither reality, nor its shadow can precisely determine a meaning or its articulation in a word. She quoted in that context a contemporary opinion, from 1892, saying: "… our words have only confused meanings, to which the human mind has been accustomed for so long a time that it now possesses a perfect insight into hardly anything."[41] Do problems with reality cause problems with its shadows, or the inverse? Peirce stressed that Lady Welby demonstrated actually the existence of *three* modes of meaning: *motion* (force, activity, function), *sense* (in all senses) and *meaning* (intention, purpose). With them, she distinguished meaning as a 'holon' and meaning just as a purpose or intention.

The latter is most important for understanding *legal* meaning, because that meaning is restricted to purpose or intention. Lawyers accept perhaps the above threefold differentiation of the meaning concept. But they also share the outlines of Peirce's commentary on Welby's book: "… besides the consequences to which the person who accepts a word knowingly commits himself to, there is a vast ocean of unforeseen consequences which the acceptance of the word is destined to bring about, not merely consequences of knowing but perhaps revolutions of society. One cannot tell

[41] Victoria Lady Welby: *What is Meaning?* Op. Cit., p. 50 f.

what power there may be in a word or a phrase to change the face of the world; and the sum of these consequences makes up the third grade of meaning."[42] Lawyers cope with the 'vast ocean of unforeseen consequences' through their institutionally anchored determination of meaning, the power of a word—its shadow included.

In a lawyer's eye, the power of a word and hence its possibility to initiate social consequences is more effective when it is protected against all unforeseen occurrences. Of course, a word cannot carry that protection around in the discourses of the sign pool and its language cannot be changed to enforce another meaning. So the solution is that law has unfolded and sustains its own discourse. In it a strict regime reigns. Its major criterion is admissibility: if institutionally accepted, a meaning is legally accepted and *is* selected to be a legal meaning—if not, then not! In that process are the three—sense, intention and meaning—brought together. It is worthwhile for a law student to look at the meaning concept in law with a semiotic eye: even the shadow of a meaning-reality teaches us about the exceptional quality of legal meaning.

7.6 Partitions and Parallels

The shadow of a meaning is always the shadow of reality represented by a linguistic expression—in the majority of cases a word. Words have been since the development of a legal semiotics at its center of interest, and law has from its primal sources on been focusing on words. The expression: 'words of law' has all too often evoked a nearly ritual climate. Already before the art of reading and interpretation was wide spread, words had a shadow of meaning no one could disregard. The latter had always a holistic connotation. Tensions of diverging contexts are sometimes a clearly recognizable shadow profile.

An example that has influenced international legal conventions, such as the UN Human Rights Declaration, illustrates this complexity and multiplicity of shadows produced by legal words. The Declaration speaks legally of 'everyone' as an individual, also in cultures with less focus on and understanding of individuality. 'Everyone' is envisioned in that Declaration as a person uniquely valuable in himself—a uniqueness that does not exist in any sign pool. The Declaration as legal document focuses on a legal meaning of 'everyman', which is at distance from any real-life meaning. Not only is a human being living absolutely on his or her own unthinkable (just like a word on its own cannot exist) but each meaning of 'everyman' also emerges from the common good and a common interest. The text of the Declaration contains three separate references to what it calls the 'free development of one's personality'. That freedom is a legal image, which does not mirror any component of human life. It remains therefore incomprehensible at any level of linguistic expressiveness. This legal freedom is a non-naïve natural/artificial articulation, which conforms to the logic of legal reasoning: the subject of the

[42] Ch. S. Peirce: *Coll. Papers* Op. Cit., 1.615.

subject-verb-object scheme must be able to act within the boundaries of legal discourse and in every direction that law's totality of meaning provides.

Here is a consequence to evaluate for each law student: 'everyone' is expected to act towards others in a spirit of brotherhood: also lawyers do. With this, they refer to a non-individualistic social situation and a real-life relationship of mutual dependency. Legal discourse aims to cover everyday life meanings, lawyers always say. Sign pools all over the world embrace often contradictory but basic values.[43] Also lawyers cannot forge those values into one word and one legally acceptable meaning. The very most they can do is to mention them in textual parallels and use rhetorical techniques to have them appear as equivalent despite their powerful partitioning. Texts illustrate what they are: words and their shadows are a challenge for meaning, a task to unfold for lawyers, enriching semiotic perspectives on meaning.

7.7 A Summary on Semiotics

Law students are invited to discussions and considerations, analyses and modes of understanding in an everyday language, which was characterized in semiotic perspective as a naïve-natural level of articulation. A short summary of the preceding five sections on legal semiotics creates an opportunity to expose some fundaments for studying meaning and the meaning concept in law and legal discourse in particular. The existence of other language levels, with different features and various types of meaning, are *not* taught in legal education. The latter proceeds in everyday language; the specific language of law is proposed only as a specialization of that natural language. To tell the law student to 'learn the language of law' is therefore a suggestion with a double meaning. The language of law, semiotics illustrates, emerges from a naïve-natural language level but is only functional at a non-naïve natural level. Many regions of law openly work with an artificial language they call 'legal'. The decision to study law is a step away from everyday language. But studying law includes also skills in understanding social complexities through institutionally determined legal meanings and meaning-decisions. In other words: learning to master the language of law and its specific package of meanings promotes a lawyer's power of understanding social issues. The latter are transformed into legal problems through the application of legal language. Lawyers understand social issues while dealing with them in *legal* and not in everyday language, including law's well-determined sets of meanings.

---

[43] This remark has far-reaching political and juridical consequences. Soros wrote in a recent article: "While the US is founded on the principle of individual freedom, China has no significant tradition of such freedom. It has had a hierarchical structure since time immemorial and it has been an empire throughout most of its history. In recent years the US has led the world in the innovative development of social media, while China has led the world in finding means to control it. … This is best seen by looking at the way information is distributed." G. Soros: "A Partnership with China to Avoid World War" in: *The New York Review of Books*, LXII, No. 12, 2015. p. 7.

This approach reinforces the importance of meaning for performing any job in law. An interesting question is whether law and legal sciences can refer to a specific theoretical discourse for support. That does not seem to be the case: the legal profession determines decisive features of law, questions of a theoretical nature are decided institutionally. Law students should pay attention to this particular attitude toward 'theory' in their discipline. They study texts and structures of legal institutions before entering debates with a theoretical approach. The latter are not acknowledged to be legally relevant—but this reinforces rather than weakens the importance of meaning. A form of decisionism governs legal meanings, and the machinery of decision-making can only function adequately when meanings are indeed treated as law's treasures. Those treasures are *linguistic* by nature; they are in words, expressions and other types of expressivity. No wonder that semiotics of law, studied since the first years of the twentieth century, stresses the importance of language and its signs as well as meaning.[44]

No wonder that the study of law can be characterized as studying in order to participate in a specific discourse. Because that discourse is supposed to consist of *words*, one must learn to appreciate a *word* in its major characteristics. Two properties of a word come to the fore: (1) a word is never a word if it is perceived alone, single, unique, independent, as a specific unit, as an neutral and exchangeable datum; and (2) a word does not carry its own particular and unique meaning, but is contextual also at the level of meaning itself. A word's meaning belongs to a triad of 'sign, norm and meaning' so that legal speech can become transparent thanks to existing meanings included in the meaning of a word at hand. Meaning is folded in a process whereby the dynamics of surface and depth play a role, particularly where words are embedded in texts. Surface and depth are important examples for the multi-layered properties of all language. Law students seldom take account of the fact that they are mainly confronted with, and work at, the surface level—so that depth meanings can surprise them unpleasantly: the latter do not always automatically fit the first. That observation leads, as a consequence, to another outstanding issue in the five sections on semiotics in this book. Without explicitly saying so, legal education includes training to cope with a diversity of attitudes at the level of linguistic expressivity. Lawyers always build, or presuppose, a bridge between a human being's living and striving on the one hand and their own articulations of life on the other. While they do so, they implicitly decide what is law and what is not-law for each citizen.

All participants—lawyers as well as ordinary citizens—are *signifiers* on an equal footing. What does it mean to be signifier? Some answers are clear: a signifier *carries* signs; signs are of importance when they are effective (there are no secret signs); meaning and sign are not separately understandable; signs are always meant by the signifier and interpreted by the signified, so that they (re)produce a social relation which includes a *third*. That relation with a *third* is often irritating for a lawyer, who wants and needs to control both dimensions of the signification process.

[44] See Jan M. Broekman & Larry Catà Backer: *Signs in Law*, 2015, Op. Cit., Part II.

This is an important feature of a semiotic approach to law: if one creates attentiveness to meaning and sign in a lawyer's professional approach to all that occurs in the sign pool of the everyday, one shifts the attention from the *content* of legal articulation to its *structure* and *essence*. The emphasis is in that case not on *what* is said but on *how* it was said and under *what* (also epistemological) *conditions*. One of the traditional conditions appeared to be anchored in what this book called the "particle story".

It seems most useful to grasp the connection between the structures of this story and the character of legal language. The latter is a non-naïve natural, in particular, artificial, language—largely composed of words as units from an everyday language, a naïve-natural linguistic expressiveness.

This is a surprising conclusion for a law student, who expected to 'learn the language of law' and thus is challenged to understand his or her profession in terms of a language made, sustained and controlled by the law. That is the reason why it is worthwhile for the law student to cast a semiotic eye on the meaning concept in law and its exceptional features involved.

References

Bohm, David. 1980. *Wholeness and the implicate order*. London: Routledge & Kegan Paul.

Bohm, David. 1989. *Quantum theory*. New York. (Prentice-Hall, New York 1951).

Bohm, David. 1990. A new theory of the relationship of mind and matter. *Philosophical Psychology* 3(2): 271–286.

Booker, Christopher. 2004. *The seven basic plots—Why we tell stories*. London/New York: Continuum Press.

Broekman, Jan M. 1996. *Intertwinements of law and medicine*. Leuven/Leuven University Press.

Buber, Martin. 1923. *Ich und Du*. Leipzig: Insel Verlag.

Heisenberg, Werner. 1969. *Der Teil und das Ganze. Gespräche im Umkreis der Atomphysik* [The Part and the Whole. Conversations on Atomic Physics]. München: R. Piper.

Husserl, Edmund. 1913. *Logische Untersuchungen. Prolegomena zur reinen Logik* [Logical Investigations. Prolegomena for a Pure Logic], 1900, 2nd ed. Halle.

Jackman, H. 2014. Meaning holism. In *Stanford Encyclopedia of Philosophy*, © *<hjackman@yorku.ca>*.

Klee, Paul. 1964. *Das Bildnerische Denken* [Pictorial Thinking]. Schwabe & Co. Basel/Stuttgart.

Lewin, Kurt. 1935. *A dynamic theory of personality*. New York/London: McGraw-Hill.

Lewin, Kurt. 1947. Frontiers in group dynamics. *Human Relations* I(1): 5–40.

Lewin, Kurt. 1951. *Field theory in social science*. New York: Harper.

Nichol, L. (Ed.). 2003. *The essential David Bohm*. London/New York: Routledge.

Peirce, Ch.S. 1958. *The collected papers of Charles Sanders Pierce*, vols. I–VI, ed. Charles Hartshorne and Paul Weiss. Cambridge, MA: Harvard University Press. 1931–1935; Vols. VII–VIII, ed. Arthur W. Burks. Cambridge, MA: Harvard University Press

Peirce Edition Project. 1998. *The essential Peirce. Selected philosophical writings*, 2 vols. Bloomington: Indiana University Press.

Pulvermüller, Friedemann c.s. 2005. Brain signatures of meaning access in action word recognition. *Journal of Cognitive Neuroscience* 17(6): 884–892.

Pulvermüller, F., M. Garagnani, and Th. Wennekers. 2014. Thinking in circuits: Toward neurobiological explanation in cognitive neuroscience. *Biological Cybernetics* 108(5): 573–593.

Shklar, Judith. 1964. *Legalism. Law, morals, and political trials*. Cambridge, MA: Harvard University Press.

Smuts, J.C. 1973. *Holism and evolution*. London: McMillan & Co (1926). Reprint Greenwood Press, Westport, Connecticut USA.

Welby, Victoria Lady. 1903. *What is meaning? Studies in the development of meaning*. London: Macmillan; Reprint: Bibliolife, Lexington, USA, 2012.

Wittgenstein, Ludwig. 1953. *Philosophical investigations*. Oxford: Blackwell.

Chapter 6
Meaning in a New Key

It may be somewhat bewildering to read in Michio Kaku's 2014 publication on "*The Future of the Mind*" about the nineteenth century German philosopher Ernst Haeckel's idea that "ontogeny recapitulates phylogeny". The remark refers indeed to a future unfolding of the brain and to the consequences for the human mind and thus for the concept of meaning. At issue is the development of a human brain, but no longer solely in the sense of the particle story. Evolution is the catchword and its focus is on the unfolding of life in the coherence of body, mind and brain: "In some sense, the human brain is like a museum containing remnants of all the previous stages in our evolution over million of years, exploding outward and forward in size and function. (This is also roughly the path taken when an infant is born. The infant brain expands outward and toward the front, perhaps mimicking the stages of our evolution)".[1] Kaku's 'mimicking' equals Haeckel's 'recapitulation'. The term 'recapitulation' transmits the issue of meaning into regions far beyond actual or incidental behavior patterns. Concepts like 'Firstness' or 'cosmic silence' are relevant in those dimensions, and meaning is an issue embracing folds of our universe that bring human imagination and its power of articulation to the outermost boundaries.

This illustrates that meaning's new key embraces a number of features debated in the preceding chapters. Most of them are based on the distance to atomistic views on reality as expressed in the particle story. But reality, nor language or meaning, is not a sum total of combined basic units. This observation has far reaching consequences of historical and even cosmic relevance. A non-atomistic, not particle-bound view is important for the totality of human knowledge. When knowledge unfolds at distance from the master discourse, new ways to characterize meaning as a human capacity to articulate reality arise. An important province of that knowledge is history itself: the process of articulation will be viewed in another light. Causal and logical relations are apparently no longer causing the engenderment of meaning. Peirce's notion of a breach of silence must again receive attention: during

[1] Michio Kaku: *The Future of the Mind*, New York 2014, Op. Cit., p. 20.

J.M. Broekman, *Meaning, Narrativity, and the Real*,
DOI 10.1007/978-3-319-28175-9_6

cosmic silence, as exposed in the first chapter of this book, articulation will enforce itself towards new forms– linguistic articulations will become the home of meaning.

It also inspires to differentiate the Creation story and the Paradise story as narrated in the Torah. The latter is clearly a story of human origins and understanding, whereas the first is the narration about an omnipotent Divine power. The dynamics of the Fall leads to a new linguistic structure of the Divine Presence in the question "where are you?" That occurrence is generally misunderstood as a first cause for meaning through its differentiation between good and evil. But it must be re-interpreted in the light of non-particle bound knowledge – it is not a cause but an event with narrative features.

Accepting that a variety of articulation levels determine meanings in their specificity is a crucial key to understanding meaning in general. That is particularly true for linguistic articulations, which require the formation of unities that are larger and deeper than words or clusters of words. It pertains forcefully to the famous slogan of Haeckel, paraphrased in the Kaku lines above.

1 Haeckel's Slogan

1.1 Recapitulation Writ Large

Ernst Haeckel (1834–1919) was famous as a biologist, philosopher, artist and many other disciplines; his fame and attitude were illustrated in *Die Welträtsel* 1895–99 [The Riddles of the Universe, 1901]. The theory summarized in the above-mentioned slogan was based upon French predecessors around 1820; they focused like Haeckel on zoology, embryology and comparative studies on evolutionary processes, which could be observed around the globe in animals and humans alike, especially in Asian countries. One of his other contributions to Occidental culture was to bring Charles Darwin and his theory of evolution to the attention of the German public. But he was neither politically nor scientifically a dogmatic Darwinist; on the contrary, his evolution principle brought him to enhance meaning while grasping the outer dimensions of the universe. It impresses one to see how his evolution principle brought him to observations of life in a world that expands outwards in order to see and understand life inwards—ultimately to the inner regions of a self in which distinctions between body and brain as well as mind and brain seem irrelevant. All evolution, he suggests, focuses on a cosmic synthesis, and only unifying (not: unified) sciences can achieve that moment of synthesis.

We refer to Kaku in the light of meaning inspired by a non-particle story. It is extremely important in this context, that the 'future of the mind' delivers views on brain evolutions behind the development of non-particle meanings, and doesn't pertain to a separate organ of the human body, but rather to 'the bodymind's brain' (symbolized as $B_0M^{br)}$.

Those who did not accept Haeckel's recapitulation-idea embraced the particle story as a foundation for their dismissal. Recapitulation is, however, not a simple repetition of identical factors, facts or matters. The term indicates rather the direction and destination of a process: to recapitulate is a special form of enrichment, which includes the possibility of what Husserl called "Einstellungs*änderung*", attitude *change*. Not all recapitulations have the same meaning merely because the word happens to be the same. The attitude-level of language on both sides of the partition between naïve-natural and non-naïve natural language determines the meaning of recapitulation: the latter is the determination of a force that unfolds in nature, and thus belongs to the power-lines of Creation. An infant's brain development showing those lines in its proper growth must be accepted as an extra-linguistic articulation of life's unfolding in B_0M^{br}. What is there to say about our need to partition, when the growth of an infant illustrates a powerful embodiment of mind and brain as a whole? The question is a challenging one and requires a deeper consideration of the $B_0M^{br,}$ which undoubtedly creates a greater distance to the level of daily conversation, but clarity at other language levels.

1.2 B_0M^{br} and $MB_0{}^{br}$

The bodymind's brain at issue (often in another order: the mindbody's brain) is not just the brain—a true challenge to those who suppose that brain means what the word says: an organ called the brain! Only within the context of the particle story as the dominant paradigm does the brain in itself have a meaning; *other meanings of the expression 'brain' refer to other brains that may not be enveloped in the particle story and its patterns of knowledge.* The growth of an infant brain is a unique process: it is the growth of brain material in various directions: outwards is the first, and to the front is the second—all directions of brain material create a specific B_0M^{br} which in their turn lead to a $MB_0{}^{br}$ and vice-versa. The observed growth is primarily an extended folding/unfolding of a major human brain sector.[2] Here is the basis for Haeckel's slogan: the infant's growth, characterized as *ontogeny*, follows the ground lines of the species to which the infant belongs: a *phylogeny*. The slogan's emphasis is not on any material elements hidden in two neologisms. We should, however, not forget: the great partition is not only in effect at the level of our ontogeny but also at that of our phylogeny: *the partitioning creates us individually as it created human reality in its entirety.*

[2] An inside-out ordering seems characteristic for the development of the (human) cerebral cortex. The layered structure of the mature cerebral cortex is formed during development. The first pyramidal neurons migrate out of the ventricular zone from the preplate. Next, a cohort of neurons migrating into the middle of the latter divides this layer into the layered one of the mature neocortex and the cortical plate. Later-developed neurons migrate into the cortical plate past the deep layer neurons, and become the upper layers. (See Wikipedia: *Cerebral Cortex*).

That dual process is a major component of Haeckel's idea. It illustrates an important feature of the neocortical brain in so far as meaning is engendered by the bodymind's brain. The latter is initiated by the neocortical area, without which our knowledge of any brain type or brain area would not be possible. To repeat in other words: *without the neocortical brain, we would never be the way we are, and never know a B_oM^{br} or MB_o^{br}*. In this special self-determination[3] reigns clarity concerning the fact that the neocortical brain is a matter of constant evolution, so that any meaning in this context is exclusively based on evolutionary insights into *the Self of the B_oM^{br} or MB_o^{br}*. What is said here about the diverse brain areas is also valid for the 'Great Partition' in itself. It is *the 'Self' of a B_oM^{br} or MB_o^{br}* that originates a breach with silences in brain and cosmos. That unfolding 'Self' is named: its name is "a linguistic articulation effectuated by the brain". But in our everyday language it includes a total emphasis on the participation of the neocortical areas in consciousness created in and belonging to the B_0M^{br} or MB_0^{br} respectively without specifying the latter dimension. It is clear that these specifications would have little to do with a naïve-natural level of linguistic articulation, so that the above-mentioned meanings of Self-consciousness never correlate with everyday expressivity, as Husserl was clearly aware of but did not come to the appropriate levels of linguistic articulation.

An evolutionary understanding of meaning rejects any 'one-word—one-meaning' concept. The neocortical brain, substantially dominant in the bodymind's brain, illustrates this clearly. There exists simply no meaning if it does not emerge from the coherence of flow and function. That coherence relates most intimately with the continuous expansion of the neo-cortical brain in existing lobes by means of folding. It is remarkable how the development through the millennia from a reptilian brain to a mammalian and from there to a neo-mammalian brain illustrates an increasing complexity of life, in particular of social life, as supported by neocortical folds. One should honor the idea that life in the sign pool of the everyday is in unison with an ever-enlarging (and thus changing) B_0M^{br} area at time-scales that do not fit our experiences in the pool. Not only evolution in general, but more specifically the continuous evolution of the neocortical B_0M^{br} focuses on particular fields of brain activity and its meaning-making results within specific measures of time.

It is beyond doubt philosophically important to become aware of the broadening and expanding dimensions of what Husserl claimed as being central for his phenomenology, and what Peirce equally embraced: the *egological* insight and its multi-leveled language. Especially the latter could become an important contribution to many discourses that require a clearer profile of articulation. The language of psychology, psychiatry, neurologists or general physicians, not to mention the language of caregivers and related professions with a key function in human relations could be more efficient thanks to that profiling. That is first and foremost because of the increased precision of the self-articulation of the speaking subject, which unfolds at a variety of language levels.

[3] See E. Husserl on Self-reflection, as mentioned in Chap. 2, and the varieties of Self according to a specific attitude, and the meaning of a Self as a result.

Haeckel's suggestion about ontogeny and phylogeny is in harmony with important discoveries of contemporary neurologists. The understanding of the latter is no longer that one brain-field enables to hear or read words (the Wernicke area) while another builds responses in words (the Broca area), and nerve fibers between them finally make language possible. It is no surprise that until quite recently, and even today, neurologists and other brain researchers have understood language along these lines of thought. Their focus was and is on language as we described it in the third chapter: words are the basic units of language; brain studies look at language as build out of single words.

Speech, in coordination with specified brain areas, remains in that view a coagulation of words. There is hardly any mention of the fact that the concept of evolution includes the process character of the human brain and therefore strives for integration. More recent research suggests nevertheless, that language expression and reception occur in many more areas than just those mentioned.

2 Neocortex and Narrativity

The neurological view of the human brain has changed radically, however, since the determination of the *inferior parietal lobe*: the lobe's various soma-sensory areas allow a more complicated view of the unfolding of language—beginning with language acquisition, and from this beginning on deeper towards issues of meaning, although they are generally formulated and understood in terms of a naïve-natural attitude.

2.1 Neocortex, Brains and Language

The parietal lobe of the left hemisphere is one of the four lobes of the cerebral cortex, speaking in terms of mapping at the junction of auditory, visual and soma-sensorial cortexes and supported by multimodal neurons. Knowledge of the lobe, acquired during recent decades, not only changed the picture of our knowledge pertaining to the Wernicke- and Broca areas. It unveiled other features of philosophical interest: this lobe seems to be the last and most recent result of evolution. In particular the inferior parietal lobe with the neocortical brain area is the most recent and the most effective for language. This supports the idea that language itself, in all its forms of articulation, is *a late evolutionary product.*[4] That observation is not without importance for meaning. It is also philosophically important that the parietal lobe did not engender by means of *new*, but by *changes in already existing* neural networks. All these observations illustrate that the functional organization of language (also of different attitude levels) varies for the same individual,

[4] In particular written language, which goes back some 4000–5000 years.

depending also on its life occurrences at different stages of his life. Haeckel's slogan comes again to the fore as emphasizing a 'flow'.

Applied to an infant's late linguistic- and speech capacity, one perceives a correlation with the late positioning of language in evolution. Freud noticed this delay in a peculiar manner: "What a child has experienced and not understood by the time he has reached the age of two he may never again remember, except in his dreams … in later years, they may break into his life with obsessive impulsiveness, direct his actions, force him to like or dislike people, and often decide the choice of his love-object by a preference that so often cannot be rationally defended.[5]" The delay is in this light a meaningful directive and not an incident. This goes immediately to the B_0M^{br} expansion. In the course of that expansion, prejudices, wishes or interests enter the field of a human's consciousness. That complex interplay of forgetting and remembering has its roots in this remarkable delay in development that marks an individual's specificity in the sign pool of life. Its marks will forever belong to a person's movements or sense of communication. A most remarkable meaning-component is a consequence of these considerations: the 'human Body as being one with the human Mind' and perceived from 'human Brain' developments will only be functional in consciousness *after* acquisition of a language, which occurs in a late phase of its unfolding.

That change is deeper than neurological discoveries about the parietal lobe make apparent. Data on meaning-making must focus on the B_0M^{br} as an evolutionary occurrence and not, for instance, on a partitioning neurological discourse that identifies the management of a single basic 'word' with language acquisition, language capacity or linguistic articulation. Linguists and philosophers were scrutinized in Chap. 3 of this book, and it seems that neurologists often share the viewpoints that were dismissed in that chapter.

Their discussions pertaining to the predominant position of the word—of a single word, of a word on its own, of the word as a basic unit of language, of language consisting of the individual as well as the social 'use' of single words—appears as the inherent philosophical pattern in neurological approaches to the human brain. It leads us to believe, that language processing is (1) founded on "the way humans use words to communicate ideas and feelings", and as a consequence (2) on "how such communications are processed and understood". Both (1) as well as (2) embrace the particle story and its foundational discourse, as Chap. 3 illustrated. In this context the "use" theory of language is recovered and given a foundational function in understanding the brain as separated from the complexity of its B_0M^{br}. That partitioning is important, especially in the context of meaning, because it supports a particle-devised pattern, which ultimately serves for a mapping of the brain. Kaku reminded us that in the history of brain research, "trying to map the brain has often been called 'cartography for fools'".[6] That reference to a so-called 'foolish cartography' is made all the more understandable by the dominance of the particle story.

[5] S. Freud: *Der Mann Moses und die Monotheistische Religion,* 1939, Gesammelte Weerke Vol. XVI: Imago Publ. Co. London/ S. Fischer Verlag, Frankfurt/M. [Moses and Monotheism], New York 1939 (Katherine Jones, Transl.) p. 162.

[6] M. Kaku: *The Future of the Mind*, Op. Cit., p. 18.

If a neurologist claims: “this is how the brain creates and understands language”, then the meaning of the word ‘brain’ differs decidedly from the ‘brain’-concept in the B_0M^{br}. But also ‘language’ is involved in that differentiation of meaning. Language *separated from* the B_0M^{br} meaning-field is understood as the outcome of brain-activity on its own, but *within* the meaning-field of B_0M^{br} language has others sources, as the wealth of the sign pools of everyday life illustrate. This might be a motive for neurologists to claim that cortical areas create symbolic representation, which is more socialized than what comes from an individualized brain concept. But they still consider those forms of representation too often as occurrences at a one-to-one scale with particles and not as an all-embracing process. The brain-language relation differs along the layer of attitude in which meanings in language are conceived. One could propose the idea that in a word-to-word conception of language the brain is understood at a naïve-natural level, whereas there are other, non-naïve levels with other meanings of understanding the brain differently, as the B_0M^{br} illustrates. Neither Body nor Mind can form a unity and be one with the Brain at a naïve-natural level—integration and growth towards unity only takes place at intertwining naïve-natural *and* non-naïve natural levels. Integration, in itself a riddle despite all the neurological information, unfolds at the level of language. What does this imply? Human growth, as Haeckel suggested, seems to be a multiplying change of ‘life in language layers’.

2.2 *Brain Development and Narrativity*

That question focuses our attention on an interesting observation: differences in evolutionary developments seem to be more important than brain size or other criteria we can think of. This is most clearly expressed in the growth phenomenon, since growth and evolution are more often observed than the creation of new structures in brain areas. Changes in existing neural networks are recorded; they determine brain components, which reign language acquisition.

Mapping those areas provided insight in series of phenomena, which are altogether categorized as ‘language’. They reach from (a) ‘separate word’ to (b) ‘spoken words considered as language’[7] to (c) more integrated forms of spoken language called ‘speech’. In other words: the brain-language maps illustrate an exponential complexity of linguistic phenomena that reaches from a single awareness of a separate word towards speech. All regard language as a major instrument of articulation, unique to the presence of humans in the cosmos. But the idea that understanding the brain is a matter of understanding an individual entity, a wonderful and admirable power source, an engine *in* the human body remains persistent in the background. There is no awareness of a need to consider those wonders as belonging to a form of integration and evolution, which is for instance indicated as the B_0M^{br}. The latter

[7] The latter go back perhaps 2 million years, with changes that enabled the brain to process that language more and more effectively.

form of understanding requires a basic, integrated plurality of time consciousness, brain-related articulation abilities specified in language, social relations, and an awareness of spatial orientation pertaining to human activity. The most general expression we use for that basic and integrated feature (missing in brain research) is *narrativity*.

Neurologists consider that "written language goes back … scarcely 4000 years, in contrast to spoken language, i.e. words."[8] In this light we can conclude that narrativity (an integration of spoken and written language) could be dated according to neurological and brain-research time indications: a difference between millions of years for the merely spoken word and four thousand for the written is a clear enough challenge. A narration is a sequence and an integration of written or spoken words plus still or moving images: this form of articulation transcends all other forms located on the brain-language map from simple word to speech. The narration clarifies the fact that our meaning-creating brain is not merely the organ as a specified entity in the human body, but needs to be correctly understood at another attitude level, a level of a non-naïve natural character, a level of integration and development rather than a one-to-one functionality, for short: a level of the B_0M^{br}. A moment of actuality, a moment of here and now comes into the totality of linguistically articulated meaning along with narration. That actuality is above all a moment of plurality. To ask about "the most basic material" or the "kind of materials, such as neurons, etc." of the human brain is an issue in the particle story, and that will not bring an answer at the level of meaning that plays a role in any human articulation's awareness concerning the universe. Haeckel's slogan is up to date: neither Creation nor the Universe is understood by means of analyzing their materiality. Their involvement in the process of meaning, Haeckel suggested, seems to deliver us the appropriate material for understanding.

The series of language components related to brain functions based on giving names to brain areas cannot deliver appropriate insight into the emergence of meaning at a cosmic level or pertaining to the concept of the universe(s). A narration does not become meaningful solely through simple words—a word is hardly an element of a narration. Narrativity is based on expressive coherence, on a unity of words, acts, visions, images, time slots and many more elements in order to advance a meaning to live with in the sign pools of life. All components of a narration are presented in order to confer an integrated meaning so that social, psychological, ethical or political and other consequences can play their roles and exercise their duties.

When brain researchers date the origin of speech to approximately 4000 years ago, they did not mention the necessary ingredient of speech in human relations: the narration. The latter seems, however, to be adequately dated by means of that number. A not yet established 'socio-neurology of language' would confirm that adequacy. The B_0M^{br} enhances a culture's stories as a form of late development. An infant who is learning to speak, to write and to listen is preparing himself to become able to follow the ground lines of stories it will be told. Those stories awaken the

[8] http://www.thebrain.mcgill.ca/flash/d/d_07/d_07_s/d_07_s_tra/d_07_s_tra.html

completion of its innermost B_oM^{br} on the basis of this late phenomenon in the evolution of humankind, which is yet a crucial component of man's storytelling attitude towards the universe: altruism.

2.3 Preliminary Conclusions

A short list of conclusions leads to a number of challenging insights.

1. Language is a particular phenomenon of extreme importance in human cultures and the variety of linguistic articulations reaches from a simple registration to the reading, the writing and the speaking of words. In that evolution, the tendency in the heart of language is to multiply and complicate all that is related to the word: its autonomous existence diminishes with an intensification of social functions, but that intensification does not culminate in speech but in a far less researched form of articulation called *narration*. The latter, however, plays a major role in the development of the concept of meaning.
2. Brain–language relations, in particular those revealed by our surprising and most challenging neuro-sciences, are developing a great importance for meaning. Their unfolding finds a culmination point in the recently investigated brain neocortical brain areas. Modern technology, for instance MRI, EEG Scans, PET Scans, Deep Brain Stimulation techniques, has extended our insight and knowledge in this field. However, the philosophical foundations for those neuro-scientific techniques and their results are based on *more geometrico* thought patterns, the particle story and its foundational discourse. As a result, the 'word' is neurologically evaluated as in twentieth century linguistics: as the basic unit of language. In terms of the ongoing mapping of the brain, the phenomenon of language is millions of years old in contrast to speech, which is estimated to be around four thousand years of age.
3. Where speech comes to the fore, the individualization and the solo roles of the word no longer hold. The step from speech to narration, as we signaled, is important in view of the *attitude change* as basic for meaning.[9] The latter concept appears to be evolutionary in each detail of its function and at every moment in the sign pool of life. In daily life we are not fully aware of the fact that our ideas and judgments are an outcome of *a continuously changing brain*: the immense surface and its folds that characterize the neocortical brain never rest in evolution. They thus play a dominant role in the forthcoming and historical functions of our foundational narrations. The latter are never historical facts; they belong to the material amidst which our infants (and all infants in all cultures and languages) grow and become educated.

[9] The steps are, as mentioned in this book on every page, from the naïve-natural to the non-naïve natural levels and culminate in the experience of their unification in the B^oMB^r.

4. Narrations are of utmost importance when human beings orientate themselves on their existence in the universe. Cosmic questions are often too complicated and too large to be directly articulated—narrations often fulfill this task. When in the evolution of the brain around four thousand years ago speech unfolded, narrations began to grow and become important. It is fascinating that the brain-age of narrations is the same as the age of the first narratives of Creation. That seems foundational for understanding meaning; it is the trace we follow to finalize our research.

3 Approaching Creation

No wonder that the consideration of 'meaning' does indeed approach the concept of Creation. Approaching the latter is approaching foundational narrations, as we have repeatedly stressed. 'Creation' as a brute fact did not take place at some unknown moment in the past and is not a dissipating phenomenon somewhere behind a horizon. Creation evolves at every moment of life's unfolding, physical as well as psychological or social. All of our lives, every second of our time, pursues Creation in all possible regards. The Creation is a particular and the most significant story in all cultures. It is mostly guided by the same trends and loaded with the same mixtures of respect for the many marvels narrated along with their consequences to be lived in various contexts, rites and attitudes. Meaning appears out of its silent shadows and emerges from circumstances paradisiacal in which meaninglessness appears. It all unfolds through what is articulated in the Creation narratives in which a human being gradually comes to fulfill the role of signifier. The latter role determines the narration and the opinions as well as the prejudices of the narrators. The famous Rashi elucidations in and about the Torah stressed the political power inherent in the proclaiming of the Jewish Creation story, which became dominant in Occidental cultures.[10] If the existence of a nation among other nations can be justified by the unfolding of that nation's being identical with the Creation *qua talis*, then no further arguments are needed, one could argue.[11]

Narrations do not *cause* meaning to function logically and rationally, in context, but rather *invite* meanings to unfold and deliver clarity and understanding. *Meanings need their narrations*, and vice versa. This elucidates again in what regard an attitude determines the specificity of a language pattern, its structure and possibility of articulation. It also makes clear that meaning is a process, an activity far beyond the "X means Z" slogan: meaning profiles the core essence of speech while the latter confirms human existence in the sign pool of life.

[10] Rashi is an acronym for the medieval French rabbi Shlomo Yitzchaki (1040–1105): his Torah commentaries have been honored worldwide since the mid 1500s.

[11] Rabbi Yisrael Isser Zvi Herczeg: The Torah: *with Rashi's Commentary Translated, Annotated and Elucidated.* The Art-Scroll Series/The Sapirstein Edition, Vol. I, New York 1997, p. 2.

3.1 Silence

In order to understand and to be understood, meaning reaches deep into its proper pre-history to the regions where meaning meets *silence* and thus experiences a confrontation with its narrative origin. That silence was described in the first chapter of this book as a "cosmic silence", also characterized as a "silence *before* breach", such as for instance the philosopher Charles S. Peirce experienced. It has already been stressed more than once that this '*silence before*'- differs from any '*silence after-*'. The first is *created*, whereas the latter seems a matter of unpredictable and never-determined *consequences* on the basis of this creation. We should, however, be aware of a fundamental question: in view of what purpose is the '*silence before–*' narrated?

In the Torah, probably the first narration in history told to justify man's position in the cosmos some 3300–4000 years ago, there is mention of the creation of the earth and no word about a cosmos, a universe or universes created. And the Creation of the Earth occurred through partitioning.[12] First, there is the description of the silence in which that partition took place: "when the earth was bewilderment and void, with darkness over the surface of the deep, and the breath of God was hovering upon the surface of the waters".[13] The silence in which the partition took place was a cosmic silence represented/symbolized by a narrated description of the '*silence before–*', which appears as an origin of meaning. Also here, as in philosophies millennia later, a breach of silence dominates—the most important breach being the disposal of words to *narrate* meaning and purpose under the heading of Creation: "God's creating the heavens and the earth".[14] With it, meaning steps out of silence. The Creation story destroys each one-to-one determination. Meaning is here, as always, creatively present in chains of signifiers with multiple layers of other meanings, and never fills out one particular sign. A sign has no meaning, or it has access to and is supported by many meanings. Even the narrator cannot and should not decide. The narrator did not in this case and never did: "the heavens and the earth" were a sign of multiplicity and of multilayered articulations. Meaning is always process and awareness of otherness, always something else and thus (at least in part) silence. Meaning is always its own suspension that creates more meanings: more, and so we live in our sign pool. In the form of a word, meaning is always incidental and presenting its proper pre-history: silence while in search of origin.

---

[12] Numbers pertaining to the age of Creation stories or the age of mankind are related to the great diversity of culture(s). David A Leening: *Creation Myths of he World,* ABC-CLIO, LLC, 2010, (www.abc-clio.com) distinguishes 5 *Types of Creation Myths* and some 220 *Creation Myths.* Concrete dates vary immensely: Zoroastrianism has a number of 12,000 year in its cosmogony, Egyptian Culture mentions around 250,000 years, Chinese sources 30,000 years BC. The parallel between the developing of the neocortical brain area and the Torah's Creation narration is remarkable.

[13] Meaning also: "astonishment and bafflement"; "baffled over the void within".

[14] Rabbi Yisrael Isser Zvi Herczeg: The Torah: *with Rashi's Commentary Translated, Annotated and Elucidated.* Op. Cit.,, p. 5.

One of the paradoxes of understanding silence is that it violently urges us to return to its proper liquidation. A cosmic silence is there to remain and to ascend into articulation at the same moment. This brings us to an important component in our understanding of the Creation-narrative that the Torah presented us. The Creation has never been understood as a one-time Event but embraces all structures of the narration: its dynamics are at work through (1) partition, (2) name-giving, and (3) confirmation. Partitioning concerns light, water, time, earth, vegetation, animals and Man; they are all given a name, and all are confirmed, receiving an ontological status and thus become fixated. The fruits of breaching silence emerge by partitioning receive a name, and are thus fixated.

It should be noticed how tensions inherent in this triad focus in the first place on meaning: its implied 'pre-history' requires a partitioning *act*, its identification, a *name* and its permanence: a *fixation*. Those steps of meaning are, bewilderingly enough, steps to self-destruction. It is an astonishing insight, that if those dynamics of self-destruction were not inherent in meaning, the latter could not be articulated or narrated. Only deferrals can be narrated; in the narration of Creation, as a narration of happiness and acquisition, its narrated final state destroys and liquidates itself in its own words. Creation meant confusion, error, instability in unison with closure, full and final meaning. A narrative "… is a distortion of what will be made straight; a holding in suspense or a putting into question of what will be resolved or answered."[15] In short: each narrative returns to silence. To bring a narrative towards its state of fulfillment, one could argue, is to end it. That is the most powerful force to cope with in our awareness of the narrative character of each concept of the Creation.

3.2 *Language*

Before dealing with some of the semiotic or sign-related issues implied in the above lines, attention should be given to a generally well-considered issue: the changes of language in the first lines of the Torah's Creation narrative. When the cosmic silence breaks open and allows the first articulations (see the comparable observations in Chap. 1), the latter want to create the impression of being the language of a Maker, the language of command—rather than the language of conversation. The only

[15] D.A. Miller: *Narrative and its Discontents*. Princeton UP, 1981 p. 3 ff. One could furthermore, on the basis of these observations, draw an extremely speculative conclusion. The unfolding of the neocortex in the human brain, which became manifest in forms of linguistic articulation some 4000 years ago, would sustain the often mentioned master—master discourse and its particle story since those days, as the Torah's Creation narrative seems to illustrate. It would furthermore be one step to declare the very same discourse as belonging to human nature—a formulation based on cortical brain research. That conclusion would destroy the thesis on meaning defended in this book: meaning relates to the various levels of layered language structures and is never a one-to-one relationship, not even if our neocortical brain area as a physical entity is involved, because that area is in terms of meaning not solely and uniquely physical.

conversation in the beginning of the Creation narrative is internal, a language directed by God with a Godly Self as a Companion. We refer again to the words: "God's creating the heavens and the earth". This terminology mentions: "God's creating" and not "Hashem's creating", because at first, *it rose in thought,* Rashi suggested. God considered, so to speak, an attitude the narrators called 'the attribute of Strict Judgment'. But "He saw that the world could not last if He did". So He integrated both the Mercy and the Strict Judgment Attributes. That integration is a "psychological" moment within the Deity. A use of both Names indicates that God created the world with a synthesis of two of His attributes. The need for that synthesis is reflected in the notion of language, as suggested in the lines above: Command and Conversation, Strict Judgment and Mercy, have to join, yes to integrate, in order to accomplish the Creation.

An "internal dialogue", a partitioning, seems to lie at the origin: remember how this linguistic feature is in the center of the dynamic moves from 'partitioning' towards 'name-giving' and from there to 'ontological fixation'. The 'name-giving' at issue is not a description; it is a speech act of the highest importance with an ontological statement accompanied by fixative dimensions in its innermost dynamics. The latter are for the concept of meaning most challenging and risky. From a wealth of possible meanings there are, among others: water, earth, light and darkness selected to serve its purpose—the Creation as an effect of partitioning. The Naming bears the same feature of necessity; meaning can turn into anti-meaning at every moment: after all, partitions endanger. A history reverberates in names. Silence has been forced into articulation, positions of sign-functions change from the very first moments on; elements left after partitioning are on their way to be named 'particles' and to become positivisms despite Mercy being their source.

Those are inherent risks of any narrative. They are not risks of the Creation-in-the-Beginning only, unless one forgets, leaves out, neglects or denies the *narrative* character of a Creation concept. Those risks are a sign, in any case. Names, words, are signs from their very beginning, that is: from their initial breach with silence. It can and should be read in the linguistic features, which the narrative ascribes to the Creator. *These signs are also signs of what threatens Meaning.* The threat brings meaning back to its pre-history, to the breach, to the name giving, to the Creation. Threat shimmers in the word: what is it's meaning?

3.3 Articulation

Is a spoken or written word ever safe and reliable? Are only thoughts in words 'sound and safe'? What is safe, what is reliable?—It seems that all words are endangered because of the multilayered features they share with other forms of articulation. The story of Creation is made safe as a mono-linguistic story and a monotheistic occurrence. Meanings are ordained. Words spoken in the Creation narrative appear for that powerful reason to be safe. A master—master discourse seems to be initiated with them. Partitioning dominates; conversational words stay far away—threat keeps its distance. At issue is not the individual word, but its context, the power that initiated it—a power exercised as *signature*, as an all-embracing *discourse*. Not the words as such but what governs them, forms a threat. Foucault once remarked eye to eye with the master—master discourse: "It is a question of what *governs* statements, and the way in which they *govern* each other so as to constitute a set of propositions that are scientifically acceptable and, hence, capable of being verified or falsified by scientific procedures. … At this level, it's not so much a matter of knowing what external power imposes itself on science as of what effects of power circulate among scientific statements, what constitutes, as it were, their internal regime of power…"[16]

The regime of articulation, in which linguistic articulation plays a major role, threatens the Creation narrative from two sides: from the side of being necessarily acknowledged as a narration (often called a 'myth') with all the features of its distortion and hermeneutic failures, and from the other, through emerging from cosmic silence, and thus having no other point of return than silence. All articulation, all words in the Creation narrative are necessarily looking in one direction: forward. Languages evolve only later, plurals will only then become installed, only then will layers grow, and the unison will finally be orchestral.

The difference between the Creation- and the Paradise narration is important. The first could be characterized as *the realm of the singular*, preparing for the second, which is *the realm of the plural* that brings differentiation and decision-making. A word is engraved in silence, and only a change of the character of that silence can bring articulation. Later, in the realm of the plural, a word is an articulation under the spell of magic. We may have to distinguish between two types of 'Word of God': one is inherent in the Creation narrative, and seems decisive even in the fulfillment of its Naming tasks. The other is in the Paradise narrative where Naming opens up to multiplicity and layered language. Those observations for Meaning are mirrored in the status of Names.

The Creation story narrates Names, which become immediately after the partitioning process ontologically anchored as God-given: day and night, sea and land. The Paradise story introduces the first Man as Name-giver after the Fall. In Walter Benjamin's considerations on language, the "Word of God" stood out but Benjamin did not distinguish between those two dimensions.[17] When the two are mixed up, then the emergence of meaning and shadows of its essence remain in the dark. The Names in the Creation narrative were ordained so that meanings were monolinguistic, single-leveled articulations in-between the phase of partition from cosmic silence and focusing on ontological determination and fixation. Those

[16] M. Foucault: "Truth and Power", in: *Power: Essential Works of Foucault 1954–1984*. J.D. Faubion (Ed.) New York 2000, Vol. 3, p. 114. See also: Giorgio Agamben: *Signatura Rerum: Sul Metodo* [The Signature of All Things], New York 2009. p. 81 ff.

[17] W. Benjamin: "Uber Sprache überhaupt und über Sprache des Menschen", in: *Gesammelte Schriften,* (GS) Band II, 1. Suhrkamp Frankfurt/M 1977; Engl. Ed.: *Selected Writings,* (SW) Vol. 1, Bullock & Jennings, (Eds) Harvard 1996. p. 63 ff.

mono-linguistic Words are eventually the only words, which are not limited by the plural character of linguistic articulation.

Of them, one can conclude what was already mentioned in the third chapter when dealing with Benjamin's philosophy of language: That Word Is. Only this expression stands, and in that standing it reaches beyond meaning: 'That Word Is'. It is Prominence in the form of a word and Benjamin as well as Rosenzweig reflected upon the word because they understood that extreme prominence. The being of that word is a key for a philosophical approach to language; it is religiously unbounded and experiential on a level of language that includes indeterminable spheres of articulation. It is given, naïve and non-naïve, grammarless and not in need of any syntax at the same time.[18] All other words, one should say, can only be treated *within* the boundaries of language. What role does meaning play in view of this contrast? It illustrates forcefully that any cluster of meaning relates to and depends for its understanding and application upon the relevant layer of linguistic articulation.

Articulation has in these perspectives two layers of meaning. There is, firstly, the articulation that leaves cosmic silence behind—in the words of Chap. 1: "during a transition from A to B". This articulation remains no more than a beginning, an opening, an initial unfolding, and a linguistic exploring of social dimensions. In that perspective, articulation embraces language as a possible means to come. There is, secondly, articulation already accomplished and functioning as a social medium, at its innermost connected with the self-understood essence of a human being. Benjamin would classify the latter as taking place *after* the Creation, i.e. for him more precisely: *after* the Fall. *Only then, and thus after an exodus from meaninglessness, can the word/the name become a prevailing component and a layer of meaning.*[19]

Yet, the concept of articulation will achieve those two connotations even in the world of today: it has creative power and leads our meanings away from fixation by its original cosmic silence, particularly as linguistic articulation, and shares the intricacies and enjoyments of communication via human language. Articulation is therefore not a 'human-subject-bound' process but it has cosmological implications in which a human subject seems destined to live as one of a plurality of signifiers. Here we meet again the consideration that the great partition is not only in effect at

[18] See Chap. 3: *Word – Benjamin's Word (The Word of God).*

[19] Philip T. Grier observed (personal communication): "The significance of naming as a fundamental act has been more clearly exemplified in the recent explorations of the solar system than at any time perhaps since the Age of Exploration in the early modern period. Whenever close-up imagery of rocky planets or moons with solid surfaces has become available for the first time, *naming* of the fixed, visible features is one of the first activities to be carried out. The recent acquisition of imagery of Pluto from the New Horizons mission is the latest, and a particularly spectacular example. Its scientists have been preoccupied with giving preliminary names to each of the features of the dwarf planet as they came into view. The care and deliberation with which the naming has been carried out is indicative of many things: first of all, it illustrates that merely *seeing* a new feature is insufficient to incorporate it fully into the human cosmos. For that to occur, each has first to be *named.* Only then does each become a "known" aspect of the existing cosmos. (In the case of extra-terrestrial bodies, of course, the act of naming can be finalized only by action of the International Astronomical Union). See the August 3, 2015 announcement by the New Horizons team for the complete map of *preliminary names* for Pluto and its moon Charon."

the level of an individualized ontogeny: the partition creates us individually as it created human reality in its entirety.

This insight is decidedly against for instance Nietzsche's view that all philosophy results from and depends upon a human subject and its potentialities—a view already corrected by Husserl and his phenomenological approach. The continuous remembrance of the breach with cosmic silence is an enduring mark of articulation; as a tool in a human hand, it forges meaning and 'post-meaning' into one position. That thought should ground man's self-understanding in its transcendence of subjectivity. But it does not secure the idea that a 'post-meaning' like Nietzsche's 'beyond good and evil' is ever possible in the realm of human articulation. The latter is by no means solely incorporated in a story of human morality; it rather finds a place in articulations of reality as cosmologically relevant. To repeat this view in other words: *a de-centering of the human subject is the major condition for understanding the unfolding of meaning from its cosmic origin towards human freedom.* The meaninglessness of meaning was meaningful, we concluded. A future 'post-meaning' concept is like a master—master discourse without a master and yet away from ordinary nihilism; a philosophy of meaning could then welcome that concept as an ultimo of articulating freedom.

4 Force Lines of a Great Partition: Fall and Articulation

The concept of meaning is not an issue of the Creation narrative but rather of the Paradise story. That is visible in the language shifts and the multiple changes of linguistic articulation in the stories. The Paradise story ends in a bewildering contrast with the mono-level of articulation that reigns in the Creation story. That is perhaps the most important observation to be offered. Meaning seems to have an origin in this contrast. *Has meaning an origin?* If one would indeed like to speak in terms of 'origin' (a requirement of our narrative structures), then that origin is not a factual issue reported or narrated in a story, but in a change of language level *in* the narration before any notion of a difference between spoken or written language can seize a grip on narration or communication.

We thus encountered two narratives. Our knowledge ignited by them must follow their laws of narration; it is these laws that decide about our insight in meaning—they are literary insights, which supposedly came into a first activation some four thousand years ago. So we are not confronted with brute facts, but experience how in that period humans were able to construct narrations about questions we share intensely with them, and what that means for us. Reading the stories is for that reason a hermeneutic activity that fits approaches pertaining to the concept of meaning. They play an important role in Occidental culture; comparison with other cultural stories is difficult because of their variety in images, signs, symbols etc.[20]

[20] See for example the Chinese Creation myths at: http://www.crystalinks.com/chinacreation.html or the website of the Wikipedia https://en.wikipedia.org/wiki/Chinese_creation_myth; the latter mentions *six* important cosmogonic mythologies and *two* Creation mythologies.

4.1 *The Paradise Story*

The Paradise story expresses a growing complexity pertaining to levels of linguistic articulation in the narration. The meaning concept is involved in all of them. Various components developing from the *location* of the Paradise called 'The Garden of Eden' to the *exodus* of man and his wife, called Adam and Eve, display differentiated language levels that are relevant for the evolution of the meaning concept.

4.1.1 Location

First, there is the *location* where man's narrated history unfolds. Its determination has political implications. That location is introduced as a Supreme Garden (the Garden of Eden), which seems the maximum of what the imagination of a human being that lives in natural circumstances can achieve. The Garden has two groups of markings, which are meaningful in their relation to language. Both are articulated by means of Names. The *first* mark is by four rivers demarcating the territory and named with the precision of an environmentalist.[21] The region they frame has rich resources—perfect onyx and crystals are mentioned, and "the gold of that land is good". Beauty or wealth of the rivers is not mentioned, but the quality of the gold is: a sense of economic value already seems to be a motive for the narrator. The *second* marks the narrated wealth of the Garden: in its center is a *Tree of Life* and a *Tree of Knowledge*—Knowledge of Good and Evil. Notice, that these names are in the narration said to exist *before* Man is created—the character of those names should yet be understood as ordained names.

As a consequence, the Paradise narration embraces in its beginning the same level of language articulation as the Creation narrative. A localization of the Paradise characterizes 'meaning' in its pre-historical sense—it is with given names and void of conversational language; even its major signs (rivers, trees, stones, gold) are introduced at the level of *command*. The interpretant, to quote Ch. S. Peirce, is in this linguistic articulation identical with the creator of the signs. The location's name–assignments are mono-linguistic and confirm a monotheistic attitude, which is reinforced by the language level of the narration in which the 'command' plays a major role. It seems that the narrative, which must first of all introduce the location, can only later unfold meaning in freedom and multiplicity. Even the partitions, on which the narrated location is based, will not change or energize this structure.

[21] See Genesis 2:11.

4.1.2 Language

Narrations are integrated in articulation; it is important in what language the authors expose them. Even after thousands of years, the stories have the then-unfolding forms of articulation in common with our life in the sign pool today. *All creativity is in essence articulation*. Articulations seem to be pillars of creativity from long before any neocortical brain was in operation until the days in which speech and narration became an issue, and from there until today's flirtations between naïve-natural and non-natural, mainly electronic, means of communication.

The Paradise narration has one path: the path to the Fall, which is also in essence a matter of articulation and with it of meaning. Profiled attitude-changes lead to an understanding that connects an early concept of meaning with the story of the Tree of Knowledge. There is in the first place a conversion from a mono- to a multi-purpose articulation, which is a great change in language structure as compared with the Creation story. The antagonist/serpent pervades the mono-articulations in the Garden—his language places Hashem God the Creator in a position *outside* the mono-level and treats the One Who has been speaking until now as *a Third*: "Did, perhaps, God say: You …".

4.1.3 Identity

We, readers of the story thousands of years later, know its purpose. Identity is at issue—that is the second link with the symbol called the Tree of Knowledge. A breach with the Solo-positioning of the sole Speaker in Paradise is necessary to broaden the potentials of knowledge. Multiple views unfold. Meanings originate. A multiple-layered name giving is initiated: there is no indication of Adam's name being ordained; narrators of the story just wrote his name as if it were incidental. An explicit mention by Adam naming his wife 'Eve' is "because she had become the mother of all the living"—new naming powers and identities unfold.

The Creation story was completed only at the end of the Paradise narration, one must conclude. The importance and function of differences in articulation can only be estimated by means of separating and comparing the two stories. Did the particle story prevail here? Identities were established and requirements were met to have a narration followed up. Man cannot live in mono-linguistic structures: multiplicity, in which meaning plays the major role in his life is his life in the sign pool of the everyday, as we formulated. To read the story is to read about a knowledge that only exists when a breach, called 'The Fall', symbolized by focus on the Tree of Knowledge, is performed: a newly-born multiplicity is its sign; identity: its result. This is what the separation of the two stories elucidates: there is no meaning without multiplicity. Multiplicity symbolized by the Tree of Knowledge is itself a plurality of symbols: Good and Evil. Those symbols are not a matter of ethics; epistemology reaches with them cosmological relevance.

4.1.4 Adamic Articulation

Before the narrators provided a name for what they called "the man", and before any other human being was created, this man was assigned to "call to a living soul its name".[22] His associating signs with objects occurred all over the Creation environment—an articulation activity that is fundamentally the process of name giving. It took place *before* the creation of "the woman" who came to life in *an already named* world—notice: *he was not* explicitly named! So: was she of any good to cope with loneliness? A named world is empty and the silence of meaninglessness reigns in it. No wonder that she later, after having listened to the antagonist/serpent, saw the Tree of Knowledge as "desirable for comprehension".[23] A desire for meaning thus unfolded in Eve's mind and this desire implied breaching the silence of meaninglessness. A double motive is at stake: day and night, sea and land, animals and a man were already created—and now "the man" had to name them *again*. Repetition is appropriation. The walk in Paradise stood before him; his involvement in what in Occidental culture would be called "the Fall" would lead him to an outer world. The location of Paradise is the location of the birthplace of Meaning—by breaching silence, finding new identity and changing the level/attitude of articulation: components of the Name altogether. Silence dominated because all names were already given and all words spoken at the linguistic level of a Divine Naturalness; His Being; His Naïvité *par excellence*. Only an attitude-change leaving that level behind and effective in articulation, makes history alive through awakening meaning. This change is the challenge of Adam's paradisiacal articulation.

4.2 Names to Language

What's in a name! that which we call a rose
by any other name would smell as sweet;

W. Shakespeare: *Romeo and Juliet, II, 1.*

Who considers meaning, considers language. Language is a multi-level phenomenon and meaning shares that quality. All language implies a variety of layers as soon as meaning unfolds and is directed by the wealth of attitudes that are possible in life. Names are signs of such an unfolding. They have to be given, created, ordained, or mastered to remain linguistic articulations within language. Philosophers who do not take these features seriously miss the point and will not achieve a relevant insight. They will support the linguists for whom, as we explained in Chap. 3, the word is the basic unit of language. This is at issue in this story: its names and words mirror those of the Creation. Language mimes the Divine language; names show their meaninglessness and its silence prevailing in language: a Divine language has only one meaning, and thus no meaning other than the fixated silence of obedience.

[22] Gen. 2: 19–21.

[23] Gen. 3: 6.

Acquiring knowledge in the context of Life remains the major risk implemented in human language—not, as we often think: communication. Can that language thus go on mirroring *and* be meaningful in the human sign pool of life?

Philosophers have been wrestling with that question. Walter Benjamin formulated straightforwardly: Names are at essence in any philosophical consideration. Not Plato but Adam was the supreme philosopher who provided Names, he concludes in the early years of his literary and philosophical activity.[24] Idea and name should acquire their long-neglected identity. Words, not as single units of language but in the context of their encompassing articulation, are the sole medium for knowledge and the sciences. A larger distance to any (neo-)positivistic viewpoint seems untenable. The arts, and in particular literature, would bridge the abyss between idea and name. They were driven apart millennia ago as this book's Chap. 4 suggested.

The Paradise story tells us that immediately after the Fall scene "the man and his wife" were hiding from Hashem God, so that He called out to them and said: "Where are you?" Theologians and philosophers have been contemplating this fragment of the story, but did not highlight its close relation to the character of language displayed in those words: mainly the implied shift of linguistic level-attitude. Its importance for the concept of meaning is immense. The words "Where are you?" are the first to display a conversational attitude: the latter was a result of establishing a level of language in which the silence of the word being spoken solo has disappeared. Those words are the first in the two stories, which are not a mime of any word already uttered in the Creation. Social philosophers did not notice to what extent this expression, which articulates the beginning of recognition of an O/other, not only accesses another person but also creates meaning to play its role.

The Fall, the finale of the Paradise story, exhibited the multiplicity of language levels and thus established different identities coming to an understanding based on meaning as a plurality. The Gap created by the disobedience in Paradise is bridged by a shift of language attitude: from the mono-linguistic to the pluriform in which a place is provided for another speaking identity. At the moment of the question "Where are you?" the Creation was accomplished and naming activity became meaningful.[25] "Where are you?"—the narrator of the Creation story needs the Paradise location to narrate the creation of language. The riddle of meaning is encountered again.

[24] W. Benjamin: *Selected Writings,* (SW) Op. Cit., Vol. 1, Bullock & Jennings, (Eds) Harvard 1996.

[25] This change ignites various questions at the level of facts. (See Gen. 3: 7, 21) It appears that after the act of disobedience, a new self-awareness was awakened. How did this awareness emerge? After that same act, words hitherto not spoken were articulated. Who taught that new idiom? Whence did it emerge? In the new dialogic mood, signs and symbols were included (for instance nakedness), which were actively answered (the leaves, later the garments of skin). How did the new language bring those acts to the fore?

4.3 Attitude Change

How can it be? How can the narrator of the Paradise story suggest with the sentence "Where are you?"—spoken in all languages at every moment of the day—that these words create(d) language? The answer, provided in various sections of this book, concentrates on the concept of *attitude* and *attitude-change* that plays two roles: (a) the role of articulation determinant and (b) the role of ultimate meaning-making force. As was mentioned before, these words were spoken from a hitherto not articulated attitude in the two stories. That attitude was no longer mono-linguistic but conversational, and thus recognized the identity of the receiver while opening itself for an answer—opening a totally different layer of language.

Husserl already introduced the attitude/Einstellung concept based on his Gymnasium education and his reading of crucial texts of Von Schiller. Husserl's view on reality and language guided many of our observations. They give a clear description of the fact, that *there is no linguistic articulation* (including meanings performed by speech acts) *that does not emerge from a specifiable attitude*. His unfolding of the concept had an important impact on the paradigmatic character of the sciences and philosophy. Peirce made the same discovery in parallel to Husserl; the two indicated each step in the hierarchically ordered attitudes as a *breach* with a prior attitude from which all insight emerged. Husserl's favored foundational attitude was called the naïve-natural, and from there others could be exploited. Kant alluded already some centuries earlier to such experiences; they were appreciated as most relevant for knowledge-formation (the real *vs.* the transcendental) as well as for ethics or in a terminology only introduced later, for human rights. No wonder that there was for some time a world-wide interest in Kuhn's discussions on paradigm changes that had an impact on thinking and experiencing themes of Occidental culture. Foucault reinforced that idea and focused on the specificity of a paradigm's discourse. His focus had semiotic relevance. The recognition of a sign presupposes a knowledge that has a paradigmatic character, because it has to occur within the boundaries of codes, habits, languages and the like. But the meaning of a sign is rather an issue of a hermeneutic character—the two do not fully complement each other. The basic thesis of this book illustrates the many ways in which an *attitude,* and above all an *attitude-change,* shapes our life in the various sign pools.

Meaning was the major issue in various contexts. It was formulated more than once that, as Walter Benjamin once suggested, we could treat of language only within language. While perhaps silently thinking, while talking about language, or while performing arts or writing poetry, we never take a position *outside* of language. The linguistic features of attitude-change are not a privilege of a being that exists beyond language; those features are, on the contrary, fully engaged within language. In other words: there is no meaning possible beyond a linguistically articulated totality. Ontological perspectives seem to be subordinated to linguistic articulation; philosophical considerations of 'idealist' signature ultimately fail to sustain the meaning concept; the latter transcends any subject-object relation as soon as it exercises its power of articulation. Each meaning-maker experiences what in philosophical thought appears as evident: each meaning created by a subject determines that subject as 'only' a maker of meaning, and therewith transcends it. The meaning of a 'self', in whatever context it appears, disqualifies that 'self' if it is not understood by itself as a component of a cosmological reality, which puts all partitioning in perspective.

Our narratives seem to unfold that once, millions of years ago, there was The Great Partition, which justified the Particle story and functioned as the First source of Meaning. This book has stressed the importance of that narrative, and the ontological consequences of the fact that it is indeed a narrative humans need. The question remains therefore, whether there does exist *one single* partition, being *one single* event that eventually could be described as the cause of meaning or of meaning's engenderment? But on the basis of all the above considerations this would be a misconception. The great partition is always an action *and* a result, a partition *and* a partitioning, a narrative event *and* its history, and a partitioning that does not *alter* the whole it partitions. It is inherently a process that even challenges the space-time dimensions of the multiple sign pools of life. Those features accord with to the complex structure of partitioning as a single result *as well as* a recurring event. They are linked with a continuous mirroring, whereby pre-existing features of the partitioned whole are re-presented in the process of mirroring. What we think or say about 'Reality' is laid down and even governed by the rules and meanings of their narrations. Even a breach between word and reality is a matter of the word, and thus of meanings embedded in encompassing articulation processes. Any 'Realty as such' (not unlike the Kantian 'Ding an Sich') is a narration to be coped with in sciences, philosophy and culture. The latter task should unfold philosophically beyond classical asymptotes such as idealism or realism.

5 Mirroring Partitions

An example pertaining to the importance of the dynamics of mirroring was given when we mentioned that a word on its own is not a word, or a sign on its own not a sign, because the presence of other words and other signs is needed for it to become word or sign. Narrations demonstrate the impact and the truth of this observation. Recall how the Creation story and the Paradise story were based on a carefully staged mirroring. The two let us see the mirroring of a word (the Word of God) or of a sign (The Tree of Knowledge) by a human being. The Paradise story illustrates the mono-lingualism of the Divine Language Level (Command) as it is mirrored in the pluri-lingualism of another Divine Language Level directed towards Adam (Question/Conversation). But that is not all; it is not the final fact to be mentioned: the story offers furthermore a narration concerning the *Fall* (Disobedience/Good and Evil) and its mirror (Cain's *murder* of Abel). The Creation story narrates in parallel how a cosmic silence arrived at a *breach* when the creative Word of God was mirrored. Those mirroring powers make clear that if events are narrated (and do not remain a factual and fixated particular), then *meaning* becomes possible thanks to its dynamics. Without the latter any occurrence seems meaningless; events that are isolated from the dynamics of mirroring are incomprehensible.

So, *a narration is never without its specific mirroring activity*. At the end, this observation will pertain to ontological foundations: that which is, needs to be *said to be*—and: that which is said to be, *is*. A distinctive element of meaning is that each partitioning, each separation, each differentiation is a mirrored double: a *here* and a *there*. The Great Partition is thus a sign of life's character in the context of life itself: the *here* and the *there* are embedded contextually. All reaches back towards the cosmic dimensions of life's elusive past as well as its unknown futures. Partitioning is the master of our life, the dynamics of our knowledge, the backbone of our continuously recited particle story. Any partition is only a division, a fence, or a particle if it maintains the closest relation with its process character. Narrations represent (or more precise: *mirror*) the multiple phases of the process. The earth and the sea, one is attempted to say, as well as the lights of day and night or the power of gravity, not to forget Newtonian physics or Bohmian wholeness—all are covered by the blanket of human narratives. Without that blanket there is no meaning; even a fundamental ontology has no other place. The Great Partition and its inherent partitioning power are a fact, but as a fact they are primarily a topic to be narrated, to be discussed, to enable attitude-changes and thus to make meaning.

The riddle of meaning becomes perceivable where a particle story unfolds and takes us in its grip. The above pages guided us through various philosophical, physical and artistic approaches, which altogether form a story about how the world is put on stage for us as a comprehensible whole of parts and particles. That story will, however, seldom tell us how and in what ways it creates us, the narrators, who are completely immersed in and emerge from that story-telling activity. The particles and the narrators are always an element of a cosmic transition into forms of articulation no narrator will ever master, so that silence, as we emphasized in the first chapter of this book, appears as their origin.

Meanings are coins of the human mind spent in the sign pools of everyday life. Their uses unfold in articulations, which reach towards supreme non-naïve natural language levels. A mind's travel through those spheres is often like a science fiction experience and sometimes a moment of supreme human rationality. Meaning can become apparent in fixation and formalization, but must awaken in layers of human language as preferred forms of nearly cosmic articulation. Our verbs are signs, our words indicators of multiplicity; they are not what they are and never merely what they seem to be—the Lord Chandos' letter that we read in the first chapter of this book was not written in vain.

5.1 Roadblocks

The path to understanding meaning has roadblocks to be cleared out; some are clearly visible, others are mainly in the mind of a traveler on that path. We mention three such roadblocks, which were also analyzed in the preceding pages.

THE FIRST IS "the word" , as argued in Chap. 3. It is perhaps one of the most important roadblocks: a turn towards "name-language" is not only a turn towards *names* but also towards the *word,* without which a language seems inconceivable. The block makes it impossible for us to proceed with our walk on the path to meaning, unless we acquire full awareness of that path's existence, its content and meaning. The concept of a word in its singularity was cultivated in the particle story, where it acquired a standardized meaning called "the basic unit of language" which sustains the 'master—master discourse' that governs our observations. The road to understanding 'meaning' is powerfully blocked by the latter, and a clearance of that road is nearly impossible. One component of the block was disturbing to encounter. It pertains to the discovery of how deeply neurologists and brain researchers are engaged in the 'basic unit' ideas pertaining to language. Brain research appears, entirely against our expectations, to be embedded in a theory of language and meaning we evaluated critically and judged as incorrect from the beginning of our research. In the light of that criticism, initiated in Chaps. 2 and 3, the brain investigations seem completely enslaved by the master—master discourse. This is particularly visible where they defined 'language' as 'producing or articulating words', and thus understood words as the basis of linguistic activities effectuated by specific brain areas or/and nerve networks. Notice that this roadblock to meaning cannot be lifted or be replaced from its location. It should be dealt with through an intensified awareness of its function and engenderment, as well as our own attitude in confrontation with that block. We stumble, for instance, as long as we have not taken care to ask whether, on the path to meaning, we are speaking of the *body*, the *body's mind* or the *minds' body*, of an *I* or a *You* or an *IYou* or a *YouI,* as mentioned in the foregoing pages. Walking the path to meaning obliges us to achieve a higher awareness of the wealth of layers an everyday language can provide us. Roadblocks appear to be signs amidst an often-startling and busy traffic of articulation fragments. They are signs of the specific features involved in perceiving meaning while underway.

THE SECOND IS attitude. Attitudes accompany each step on the path towards meaning. They require a deepened awareness of multiplicity and changeability when linguistic expressions become articulated. A human being is always under the spell of the serious necessity to appeal to language and to linguistic attitude when dealing with meaning. That is never a mono-linguistic or solitary activity of a single human mind, we concluded. Each meaning manifests itself in an interpretation sustained by the interpretant, Peirce suggested famously. But a "sign user" is because of that dependency a "sign-subordinate" at the very same moment in which he is a "sign supporter". Benjamin also noticed this partition, when he stressed that to name things (which are originally in a "nameless language of things") our power of articulation must change into the "name-language of man" without which knowledge is not possible. Attitude-change is the perhaps most important feature for meaning and is exemplary throughout. Each articulated word faces, as the articulating subject-in-action experiences, the necessity of turning back on itself in a movement of completion. The latter is essentially a matter of delimitation, and thus expands the authenticity of its proper subjectivity. The partition, which accompanies this authenticity, will be completely internalized in this development towards meaning. 'Self-reflection' seems an old-fashioned expression in this context. The roadblock concerned will not let a voyager go free to walk the path unless he or she is prepared to accept such a change. Hence the many times a philosopher like Kant, Hegel, Nietzsche or Husserl stressed the view that subject and reflection go together as a key for any creative articulation.

THE THIRD IS articulation. In particular, the quality of articulation has strong bonds with meaning. Articulation supports the two other roadblocks; they possess common interests. It is extremely important to see that our entire linguistic articulation shows a tendency to suppress or to leave out an awareness of the fact that the unfolding of language depends upon the positioning of the speaker by means of considering his or her actual attitude. A deficient awareness of the always-involved attitude leading to articulation blocks the path from all sides. Aiming at understanding meaning requires therefore a careful and attentive consideration of this type of (self-)awareness. That is not a matter of a simple psychological issue or of a change of one articulation or habit for another—it is rather a matter of completing an articulation as a creative process in its own right, as we mentioned already in the third chapter. This makes the close proximity to the (self-)reflection of the subject clear, which is packed in the second roadblock and which we encounter here again.

At issue is a broader insight necessary in order to walk the path towards understanding meaning. It is a path at great distance from decisions about the existence of Reality as such—if that exists! As already explained, each human being who is able to articulate any language within a cultural setting is equipped with a variety of attitudes that determine the meaning of what is articulated. Our lives in the sign pool of the everyday unfold normally at a distance from any awareness of the attitude we assume while living this life. This neglect of that awareness contributes to a formidable lack of well-understood meaning in social life as well as in the conduct of individual life.[26] Even contemporary theories of meaning do not point to the fact that there is no meaning nor any articulation without a specific linguistic attitude—always one out of a rich composite of language layers. The latter have to become specified along either a naïve-natural or a non-naïve natural level of language. One can employ further differentiations originating in the latter. Neither meaning in general nor meaning in a particular context is feasible without acknowledging such an attitude as the source of articulation.

The three blockages display a peculiar structure: they block *and* make the path free at the same time! Blocking happens when the traveler does not consider their true nature, which is to provoke change. The roadblocks intensify our experience of

[26] Its political implications are manifold. See: The Invisible Committee: *To Our Friends*, Semiotext(e), Intervention Series No. 18, 2014, Engl. Ed.: MIT Press, Cambridge/London 2015, p. 46: "For moderns, there is the World on one side, themselves on the other, and language to bridge the gulf. A truth, we are taught, is a solid point above the abyss—a statement that adequately *describes* the World. We've conveniently forgotten the slow apprenticeship during which we acquired, together with language, a relationship with the world. Far from serving to describe the world, language helps us rather to *construct* a world. Ethical truths are thus not truths *about* the world, but truths on the basis of which we dwell therein."

meaning at every step of that road and its trajectory, not only at the horizon of our path through the sign pool in life. They can hardly be removed; the weight of their effect, especially their anchors in human history, overwhelm. But we cannot walk along our way without paying attention to them or trying to move them; passing them without notice or simply overlooking their sign character is destructive. There is for that reason no way to keep up with the simple use of an "X means Y" formula, because there is no way for the concept of meaning to be treated as an issue belonging to a world apart from us, from our perception, our knowledge, our habits and traditions of coping with life.

5.2 *The Great Partition*

The Great Partition is not a brute fact, not a point of logic to find an explanation of meaning, not a basic history to explore the ground lines of human reasoning, we can conclude. As mentioned from the very first pages of this book on, mysterious beaches in the cosmic silence gave birth to further developments of a power of articulation, which the human mind could share. Depth structures of articulation, anchored in silence, reached out towards surface structures. These dynamics made them approach the boundaries of articulation structures. A motive from the Torah's Creation story claimed: the earth was void but the breath of God hovered over the waters. Were they named? Was cosmic silence named? No, no language was possible in the context of that silence-driven absence of articulation. The pre-historic cosmic silence was marked by a lack of articulation, and meaning could thus not exist. What should occur?

It is of great interest that any awareness of the Great Partition seems to result from narrations, which use a specific linguistic expressivity. These have, however, a tendency to limit any understanding of reality by means of selecting explanatory expressions that master their references. Partitions depend upon and aim at a purposeful partitioning: the selection of expressivity by means of mirroring is, as we explained, an important tool. Narrations mostly offer generally accepted surface-structures (Peirce called them 'habits' and appreciated their semantic power) and leave their depth structures out. Even the occurrence of language was not enough for the emergence of meaning: the concept of a 'great partition' depended upon the occurrence of a breach of surfaces and an orientation towards the *inner* structure of language, indicated by what we called a 'change of attitude'. That could be narrated only recently, some 4000–3500 years ago, for instance most famously in the Torah. The latter embraces the Great Partition in the form of a transition from the command- to the conversational level, taking place in the heart of disobedience in Paradise. It encountered mirroring and many replications, and is still repeated in our lives in the sign pools of today. No, the Great Partition is not a brute event in nature but a narration for which a layered language concept seems necessary. Meaning is not a cosmic occurrence but a cultural datum.

We repeat: the Great Partition is generated out of a cosmic silence and escapes articulation from its earliest stages of clarity on. A striving to embrace more and more phenomena that could in any cultural context be attributed to powers pushing toward articulation is noticeable despite those escapes, which pertain to our conceptualization powers rather than Reality itself. The Great Partition as a concept creates fragments of meaning only through human intuition: including artistic scenery, scientific research or philosophical reflection. It follows that thoughts concerning the function of theory share their fate with experiences of the meaningful. The qualification of meaninglessness is in that context no longer a nihilistic reproach but rather a challenging aspect of the partition scene in its entirety. That scene is a most remarkable setting among the many experiences to be had in the human sign pool. Partition scenes never change Reality. They cannot be touched by narrated conceptions of Reality; attitude-changes make our conceptions and articulations grow, but human beings can for instance not change the stars although they observe their lights and measure their distances.

An absolutely predominant mark of the Great Partition remains its close tie with *articulation*. The latter is a cosmic process with larger dimensions than language and not a matter of logics or causality. A Great Partition is not at an end of the road to meaning, a result, or a destination to be finally reached—because that road has no end. A Great Partition cannot be the source of meaning nor its first cause, because that partitioning transcends dimensions of meaning and its forces of articulation. Does it suffice to notice that the Great Partition took place *in* cosmic silence, as mentioned in the first chapter, so that there is a silence *before-* and a silence *after* that phenomenon? Most probably not, because the consideration that a 'silence after-' cannot be identical to 'silence before-' makes it clear that the role of linguistic expressivity is important but seldom definitive on the path to understanding meaning. That lack of definitiveness is characteristic for meaning in its entirety. Hence the danger of meaning-fixation, as has been asserted throughout this text.

That is indeed at issue: meaning is put forth as soon as articulation is active and unfolding in human lives, long before their neocortical brain richly folds. The suggestion of an originating Great Partition is mirrored in the multiple changes of attitude and the all-empowering articulation process in which humans are caught up.

Their first attitude change is captured in narrations: for example, the Paradisiacal change from a command- level into a conversational level was expressed in the form of the iconic question: "Where are you"? That inherent partitioning diversifies language layers (also called attitudes). Meaning became a specific form of articulation with this partitioning—all roadblocks included. The latter inspire us to grasp the multitude of meaning, a grasping rather cosmological and fundamental than personal, psychological or political decision-making.

An unfolding of the meaning concept from its drive from depth structures in cosmic silence towards surfaces in articulation—the key story called "The Great Partition" included—will never lead to a "post-meaning concept". The birth of meaning does not know a death scene. That is perhaps the greatest riddle of meaning. As long as either a cosmos or a universe exists, meaning as a consequence of the continuous presence of a Great Partition will stand.

References

Agamben, Giorgio. 2009. *Signatura Rerum: Sul Metodo* [The Signature of All Things]. New York: Zone Books.

Benjamin, Walter. 1977. Uber Sprache überhaupt und über Sprache des Menschen. In: *Gesammelte Schriften,* (GS) Band II, 1. Suhrkamp Frankfurt/M [Engl. Ed.: *Selected Writings,* (SW) Vol. 1, Bullock & Jennings, (Eds) Harvard 1996].

Foucault, Michel. 2000. Truth and Power. In: *Power: Essential Works of Foucault 1954–1984*, vol. 3, ed. J.D. Faubion. New York: The New Press.

Freud, Sigmund. 1939. *Der Mann Moses und die Monotheistische Religion*, [Moses and Monotheism. Trans. Katherine Jones. New York, 1939].

Haeckel, Ernst. 1866. *Generelle Morphologie der Organismen* [General Morphology of the Organisms]. Berlin: Reimer.

Haeckel, Ernst. 1876. *Die Perigenesis der Plastidule* [The Generation of Waves in the Small Vital Particles]. Berlin: Reimer.

Haeckel, Ernst. 2008. *Art Forms in Nature*, Engl. Ed. Munich: Prestel.

Herczeg, Yisrael Isser Zvi. 1995. The Torah: *with Rashi's Commentary Translated, Annotated and Elucidated,* ed. Sapirstein. New York: Mesorah Publ. Ltd.

Husserl, Edmund. 1913. *Ideen zu einer reinen Phänomenologie und phänomenologischen Philosophie* [Ideas pertaining to a Pure Phenomenology and to a Phenomenological Philosophy – First Book: General Introduction to a Pure Phenomenology. Trans. F. Kersten. The Hague: M. Nijhoff, 1982].

Husserl, Edmund. 1929. *Formale und transzendentale Logik—Versuch einer Kritik der Logischen Vernunft* [Formal and transcendental Logic—A Critique of logical Reason]. Halle: Niemeyer

Invisible Committee. 2014. The: *To Our Friends*, Semiotext(e), Intervention Series No. 18, Paris [Engl. Ed.: MIT Press, Cambridge/London 2015].

Kaku, Michio. 2014. *The future of the mind.* New York: Doubleday.

Leening, David A. 2010. *Creation myths of the World.* Santa Barbara: ABC-CLIO.

Miller, D.A. 1981. *Narrative and its discontents*. Princeton: Princeton University Press.

Author Index

J.M. Broekman, *Meaning, Narrativity, and the Real*,
DOI 10.1007/978-3-319-28175-9

Subject Index

J.M. Broekman, *Meaning, Narrativity, and the Real*,
DOI 10.1007/978-3-319-28175-9

MIX
Papier aus verantwortungsvollen Quellen
Paper from responsible sources
FSC® C105338

If you have any concerns about our products,
you can contact us on
ProductSafety@springernature.com

In case Publisher is established outside the EU,
the EU authorized representative is:
Springer Nature Customer Service Center GmbH
Europaplatz 3, 69115 Heidelberg, Germany

Printed by Libri Plureos GmbH
in Hamburg, Germany